Police Socialisation, Identi

Sarah Charman

# Police Socialisation, Identity and Culture

## Becoming Blue

Sarah Charman
University of Portsmouth
Portsmouth, United Kingdom

ISBN 978-3-319-87467-8      ISBN 978-3-319-63070-0    (eBook)
DOI 10.1007/978-3-319-63070-0

Printed on acid-free paper

This Palgrave Macmillan imprint is published by Springer Nature
The registered company is Springer International Publishing AG
The registered company address is: Gewerbestrasse 11, 6330 Cham, Switzerland

*To my mother, Liz Charman*

# Acknowledgements

This book and the research contained within it were inspired by a conversation with Superintendent RJ in what I have called 'Evermord Constabulary', who was intrigued by the changes which took place in new recruits to the police service within the first few years of their policing careers. Thanks are due to him for planting that seed of a question which inspired the next four years of my academic research and for his continued support throughout that process. Thanks must clearly also go to the new recruits of Evermord Constabulary for putting up with four years of endless questions and getting very little chocolate by way of compensation. I promise to leave you in peace for at least a few years before I start knocking on the windows of your stations again. Also extending my gratefulness to Abi Stark (now at the University of Sheffield) and Dr Stephanie Bennett (University of Portsmouth) for their invaluable help with the quantitative data analysis—I may now be a convert!

Many thanks to Steve for reading through all of the drafts of the manuscript, often at very short notice, and for wisely only making polite suggestions. Many thanks too to the grammar queen that is my mother for reading the manuscript aloud to check for mistakes and for letting me know that I have more work to do on my prepositions! Thanks to Jo for the name of the force and, importantly, for the therapeutic games of squash. 'Thanks' might be the wrong word for the contribution of Dan and Jacob because, as teenagers, their job description states that they must do nothing at all to help and simply be an enormous source of distraction! Nonetheless, they remain the most joyous and the most inspiring part of my life, so for that, yes, thanks.

# Contents

# List of Figures

# List of Tables

# 1

# Introduction

In a BBC radio interview on 'crony capitalism', the discussion between Conservative MP (Member of Parliament) Matthew Hancock and Labour MP Mike O'Brien turned to the issue of organisational culture. When prompted by interviewer Evan Davies about the possible solutions to crony capitalism, Hancock replied, "the most important thing to do is change culture and that means lots of different rule changes" (2012). It was not clear which organisations needed to change their culture and which rules would have to be enforced to achieve this, but what was more remarkable was the notion that 'culture' could simply be manipulated by organisations and that workplace rules could effect that change. The potential for the senior members of an organisation to change or indeed even to affect the culture of an organisation is the subject of some debate.

In a similar vein, then Home Secretary Theresa May showed the same desire to change an organisation's culture, that of the police service. Following the publication of a critical Her Majesty's Inspectorate of Constabulary (HMIC) report on the police response to domestic violence and abuse, she commented that "[t]he police now must take urgent action. The HMIC report shows that there needs to be a fundamental change in police culture" (May 2014).

© The Author(s) 2017
S. Charman, *Police Socialisation, Identity and Culture*,
DOI 10.1007/978-3-319-63070-0_1

There have been frequent calls from both within and outside of the policing organisation for cultural change which regularly bring the issue of policing cultures and the apparent problems surrounding policing cultures to the forefront of the policing agenda. It is therefore also of regular interest on the criminological agenda. The publication of the Macpherson Report in 1999, following the death of Stephen Lawrence, questioned the presence of a negative police culture and suggested that improvements within the police service necessitated cultural change (Macpherson 1999). This built upon the recommendations of the Scarman Report, published after the Brixton disorders in 1981, which argued for changes to the structure of the police, *coupled* with cultural change (Scarman 1981). Macpherson's conclusions were in turn echoed by senior police officers within the police service, who came out strongly in favour of the report, arguing that "a fundamental overhaul of the entire working culture of the police is needed" (Travis 1999). As more and more pressure is felt by an organisation, it is often far simpler to suggest cultural changes than structural changes. Whereas structural changes have been attempted and failed, an alternative strategy is often to attempt cultural change. This is not necessarily an easy option, if indeed it is possible at all. Benedict (1967; cited in Young 1991) noted that once a process of reflexivity begins within a persistent and resilient culture, there is a danger that any organisational cohesion will simply fall apart.

Police cultures are then the subject of some criticism, but is that criticism justified? What in fact constitutes police culture? Is the culture of the police alluded to persistently throughout the academic literature (if in fact we can refer to it in such homogeneous and singular terms) still reflected in the same attitudes, behaviours and values that we witness in the police service of the twenty-first century? The social context of policing has fundamentally changed since the early academic writings on policing cultures in the 1960s. How far therefore have the 'working personalities' (Skolnick 1966) of police officers doggedly persisted despite this radical change in their working environment? Has the strength of policing cultures managed to supersede all of the structural and environmental changes to policing; the structural, political, social and economic changes to society; and the rapidly changing profile of the new recruits to the police service? Or as Sklansky argues, are we instead too influenced by the traditional conceptions of policing cultures and is our understanding of these cultures a "story of cognitive burn-in" (2007, p. 20)? Much like old television screens that used to leave image burn-in when a static image was shown for too long, Sklansky argues that the same can be true of ideas, and particularly those concerning policing cultures.

More recent work in the UK by Loftus (2008) and in the US by Skolnick (2008), who use the phrases 'classic themes' and 'enduring issues' in their article titles, would suggest that there is still a firm belief in the persistent and recalcitrant nature of policing cultures. If, therefore, there is an assumption that these persistent cultures remain, despite all of the changes outlined above to the policing organisation and to the world inhabited both by the police and the policed, then how and to what extent are these values, attitudes and beliefs transmitted and understood by new recruits? The academic literature on policing cultures has tended to consider a more static analysis of lower-ranking police officers and, through interview and observational methods, has recorded and analysed officers' working practices, their perceptions of their role and their attitudes towards the policing world they inhabit and the world which they police. What these accounts cannot tell us however is how far these values, attitudes and beliefs have *changed* over the course of those new recruits' early development as police officers. They also cannot tell us what these important and changing influences are upon those new recruits in the early days of their policing careers. If there are persistent and recalcitrant policing cultures which persist through generations of police officers, who are those responsible for their reproduction? It is therefore in an analysis of the socialisation of police officers that we can discover more about these issues, a topic which has often been neglected in favour of a more static cultural analysis.

Longitudinal research in this area of policing cultures has also been a rarity. Two pieces of research however stand out as having achieved this. Nigel Fielding wrote 'Joining Forces: Police Training, Socialisation and Occupational Competence', published in 1988. In this research, a sample of 125 English police recruits were chosen, and over the course of their first two years as police officers, a subsample were interviewed at various stages of training and service. Fielding considered the changing nature of police recruits during the influential stages of both formal and informal socialisation into the police service. Janet Chan wrote 'Fair Cop: Learning the Art of Policing', published in 2003, research in which she followed 150 Australian police recruits over their first two years, again interviewing approximately a third of these officers at regular interviews. Chan's aim was to confront the "pessimistic view of police socialization" (2003, p. 4) by challenging the perception of an all-powerful homogeneous police culture that was apparently readily accepted by new police recruits. The publication dates of these two pieces of work however indicate that a contemporary longitudinal analysis of the socialisation of new police recruits is long overdue, which this book aims to address. Both the structural conditions in which policing operates and the social environment in which police officers operate have changed immeasurably, ever since the turn of the century. This research aims to consider the impact of those changes on the formation and development of policing cultures in the lives of new recruits to the police service and also how new recruits learn to become police officers.

This book is structured into two parts. Part I attempts a full analysis of the literature that is relevant to a consideration of learning to be a part of an organisation, both formally and informally. Research focusing upon police cultures regularly considers the cultural literature in that specific area but without also appreciating the wider sociological, educational and psychological literature which analyses how and why people learn and how and why identity is shaped. Policing cultures are influenced not only by the members of that organisational group but also by the wider structural context in which those members operate. In Bourdieu's (1984) terms then, it is important to analyse both the 'field' (or setting) and the 'habitus' (cultural knowledge or 'dispositions') of new police recruits. Part I therefore considers the development of both organisational and social identity, analyses the formal and informal mechanisms of police training, and offers a broad analysis of the police socialisation and policing cultures literature.

Part II analyses the longitudinal research upon which this book is based. This research seeks to consider the influences upon, and the changing attitudes of, a sample of new police recruits over the course of the first four years of their careers as police constables. It therefore intends to follow these new recruits for *twice* as long as previous studies.

This will enable a fuller understanding of the developing cultural characteristics amongst current police officers. It is not enough to acknowledge that a culture exists, nor to be able to describe its characteristics. It is important to be able to go beyond these descriptions and to understand what shapes and influences those cultural attitudes, values and beliefs about the nature of the job. Paoline (2003) has argued that any future accounts of policing cultures should not rest at providing descriptions of cultural variations within policing services, but must instead seek to explain the factors which are relevant in the shaping of those variations. He suggests that longitudinal research may be able to provide this richer and deeper understanding of cultural dynamics, particularly during the socialisation stages.

This research project thus has two specific aims:

- To assess the presenting and changing attitudes, values and beliefs of new recruits to the police service in the early stages of their police career.
- To evaluate the key influences upon the formation and development of those attitudes, values and beliefs of new police recruits.

# Part I

Chapter 2 seeks to understand the literature surrounding organisational culture and organisational identification. In doing so, an analysis of the organisational identity of the British police will therefore be possible, an identity which can be understood in both its tacit and its explicit forms. In doing this, it will consider the symbolic significance of policing within British culture through an analysis of the imagery of the 'bobby on the beat' against the more formal organisational role of the police officer. The power of the police to symbolise the contrasting and conflicting roles of legal actor, law enforcer, state representative and community leaders, for example, will also be explored. The chapter therefore seeks to contextualise the changing organisational identity of British policing in order to later more fully understand how new recruits to the police service adapt to their position within the organisation.

Whilst policing is very often characterised in terms of its legal roles and functions, Chap. 3 seeks to provide a more sociological account of policing as a 'cultural institution' which has changed fundamentally since its inception. The chapter builds upon the theme of identity by moving from the organisational to the cultural. As individuals, we construct our identities in relation to the groups with which we interact. This chapter seeks to explore the issues of social and personal identity and the formation of the self. This will be done through an analysis of the social identity and intergroup relations literature. Understanding organisations is as much about understanding the individuals who work within those organisations as anything else, and this can be more fully understood through an understanding of cultural attitudes, values and beliefs. Appreciating how these attitudes, values and beliefs are formed within the organisational environment is essential to a fuller understanding of the development of policing cultures, which this research aims to examine.

In Chap. 4, the focus will move from identity to learning and, in keeping with the structure of the book, will, first, consider this from an organisational perspective. Training and education within the British police has changed on numerous occasions throughout history. This chapter will seek to chart these changes by exploring the changing nature of entry-level police education and training. It will do this by, first, more fully analysing the difference between education and training, and then by considering the changing focus of this within the policing environment. The policing organisation has moved from a time where all training and some education took place 'on the job' to the current situation of recruitment, often solely coming from the wider police family and recruits funding aspects of their training through pre-join qualifications.

Again, the book moves from the organisational to the cultural and, in Chap. 5, examines how recruits 'learn' to become police officers. Although a significant section of the literature on learning focuses on formal learning, in the context of policing, it is as important to consider the growing interest in 'informal learning' within the workplace as a key, if not the key, influence on the behaviour and performance of workers. 'Situated learning' (referred to within policing circles as learning 'on the job') and the impact of social interaction on learning will therefore be the focus of this chapter. An analysis of the 'communities of practice' literature will also seek to position police learning as a more dynamic style of learning which does not all flow from 'master' to 'student', but is instead based on an exchange of information and the social interaction of the actors involved.

The book moves in Chap. 6 from a focus on 'learning' to a cultural analysis of 'being' a police officer. Policing cultures remain an enduring area of enquiry, a situation which has remained unaltered since Skolnick, Westley, Cain and Banton were writing in the 1960s and 1970s. What also, in many cases, remains unaltered is the almost universal condemnation of the cultures of the police as a site of masculine hegemony, racism, prejudice, discrimination and sexism. This narrative is rarely challenged. The chapter seeks to acknowledge these debates, but also to attempt to explore and perhaps even to appreciate the role of policing cultures and how it is and could potentially be utilised.

## Part II

Chapter 7 sets out the aims and objectives of the four-year longitudinal research project and identifies the nature of the research process. After a consideration of the distinct methodological challenges of both longitudinal cultural research and research within the police service, the chapter considers both the quantitative and qualitative elements of the research. It outlines the research themes to be explored and the manner in which the interviews were conducted.

The main focus of the interviews is in the format of a semi-structured discussion of the experiences of learning to be, becoming and being a new police officer. However, one quantitative element is also part of the research process. This involved asking respondents to 'rank order' influences upon police officers, plus their characteristics and priorities. It also involved asking respondents to assess the strength of their beliefs towards a whole range of issues about the nature of policing and on being a police officer. This has been done for two specific reasons. First, in order to precisely *measure* and *compare* the opinions of the new recruits across a wide range of issues. In doing this, a clearer sense of the proportionality of opinion can be gauged. Second, a quantitative element has been added in order to be able to measure the potential for a change in those opinions over time. It is therefore the *movement* that may be captured between one set of opinions and another that is of interest. The aim of this research was to better appreciate the changing nature of the new recruits to the police service, and one of the ways to achieve this was via an element of quantitative data. Chapter 8 will focus therefore upon the results of that quantitative element. The first section of the chapter considers the three questions that respondents answered to rank order certain issues relating to policing. These were the most important priorities of a police officer, the most important characteristics of a police officer and, finally, the people who had influenced the new recruits' development as officers. The second section of this chapter then goes on to consider a set of statements relating to both policing itself and being a police officer where respondents are measured upon the extent of their agreement or disagreement.

A full analysis of the qualitative aspect of the research interviews with the sample of new recruits to the police service over a period of four years is carried out in the following three chapters. Chapter 9 focuses on the area of *learning*, whilst Chap. 10 focuses upon *becoming* and *being*. Chapter 11 then focuses upon policing challenges. When discussing their *learning*, the new recruits answer questions about how they can best 'learn' to become a police officer and be a part of the policing organisation. They also consider the role and impact of each of the important players in the training process. On *becoming* a police officer, the new recruits are asked about the characteristics of a 'good' police officer, their motivations for joining the service and whether, and at what stage, they identify themselves as a police officer. Discussions of *being* a police officer focus upon both the external behavioural adaptations to their new role and their internal adaptations to their sense of 'self' through their potentially altered identities. Further questions consider the various areas of satisfaction and dissatisfaction in their new jobs. Many of these questions are designed to not only provide a fuller picture of the changing behaviours, attitudes and beliefs of the new recruits to the police service, but also to appreciate more about the working cultures of the policing organisation, particularly at the lower ranks. In addition to this being surmised through the areas mentioned already, the new recruits are also explicitly asked about what they feel are the characteristics of the policing culture as they understand it. This will provide an interesting analysis of what they feel policing cultures were and are, and what the impact of a heavily value-laden term such as 'police culture' might have upon them.

The empirical data upon which this book is based is further analysed in Chap. 11. One of the areas of questioning in all of the interviews with new police officers was related to what they felt were the major challenges facing modern policing. It was also a question asked of other participants in the research project who acted as tutors or Student Development Recruitment Officers (SDROs). These questions were asked over a four-year period of quite considerable political, social and economic change. The results of this analysis will therefore achieve two things. First, it will provide a valuable insight into the views of current serving officers (with varying years of experience) as to what they feel are the challenges facing police officers in a rapidly changing policing environment. Second, it will also provide some insight into the changing nature of the priorities of new police officers as they slowly become more integrated within policing cultures. The new recruits' views on what the challenges are which are facing police officers are not only changed by their level of experience as officers and by the changing circumstances in which they are policing, but also by their changing attitudes to the role and purpose of the police, which fundamentally alter as they become more culturally embedded within the organisation.

Chapter 12 concludes the book and seeks to bring together the cultural and organisational strands of the early parts of the book together with the empirical longitudinal research in order to further develop the literature about what it means to learn to become a police officer. The areas of police socialisation, identity and culture will all be reviewed in order to establish whether the traditional conceptions and frameworks can still be applied to the modern police officer. The chapter will also seek to offer some further analysis about where the sources of influence upon new recruits are situated and whether the current framework of police education and training is the most effective method of equipping young recruits for a career in the police service.

The book ends on a light-hearted note, with a consideration of some of the realities of social science research in Appendix 1. In a series of 'dos and don'ts', I paint a picture of some of the highlights and lowlights of this four-year longitudinal research and provide what may be some amusing, if not useful, tales of life in the field.

# References

Bourdieu, P. (1984). *Distinction: A Social Critique of the Judgement of Taste.* London: Routledge.

Chan, J. (2003). *Fair Cop: Learning the Art of Policing.* Toronto: University of Toronto Press.

Hancock, M. (2012, January 7). *Today.* London: BBC Radio 4.

Loftus, B. (2008). Dominant Culture Interrupted: Recognition, Resentment and the Politics of Change in an English Police Force. *British Journal of Criminology, 48*(6), 756–777.

Macpherson, W. (1999). *The Stephen Lawrence Inquiry Report.* London: HMSO.

May, T. (2014). HMIC's Inspection of Police Handling of Domestic Violence and Abuse. *Written Statement to Parliament.* Retrieved from https://www.gov.uk/government/speeches/hmics-inspection-of-police-handling-of-domestic-violence-and-abuse

Paoline, E. (2003). Taking Stock: Toward a Richer Understanding of Police Culture. *Journal of Criminal Justice, 31*(3), 199–214.

Scarman. (1981). *The Brixton Disorders 10–12 April 1981: Report of an Inquiry by the Rt. Hon. The Lord Scarman (Cmnd 8427).* London: HMSO.

Sklansky, D. (2007). Seeing Blue: Police Reform, Occupational Culture, and Cognitive Burn-In. In M. O'Neill, M. Marks, & A. Singh (Eds.), *Police Occupational Culture: New Debates and Directions* (pp. 19–46). Oxford: Elsevier JAI.

Skolnick, J. (1966). *Justice Without Trial: Law Enforcement in Democratic Society.* New York: Wiley and Sons.

Skolnick, J. (2008). Enduring Issues of Police Culture and Demographics. *Policing and Society, 18*(1), 35–45.

Travis, A. (1999, February 19). Police Chief: This Can't Go On. *The Guardian.* Retrieved from https://www.theguardian.com/uk/1999/feb/19/lawrence.ukcrime

Young, M. (1991). *An Inside Job.* Oxford: Oxford University Press.

# Part I

## Interpreting Police Socialisation, Identity and Culture

# 2

# Organisational Culture and the Policing Organisation

The study of culture has traditionally been the bedrock of anthropologists and has been of intermittent and periodic interest to other parts of the social sciences. However, over the past few decades, culture has staged something of a comeback and is being considered not only as an academic tool of discovery but also as a tool of organisational reform. But what is the culture of an organisation, and is it worth discovering? Or is culture, in the words of Hofstede and colleagues, "a fad … Fads pass, and this one is no exception" (Hofstede et al. 1990, p. 286)? This chapter will consider the literature on organisational culture, identification and commitment before going on to analyse this in relation to the policing organisation. The identity of the British police will be examined in both its explicit and its more tacit, symbolic terms. An appreciation and contextualisation of the changing organisational identity of British policing will enable a later appreciation of how new recruits to the police service adapt to their evolving positions within the organisation.

© The Author(s) 2017
S. Charman, *Police Socialisation, Identity and Culture*,
DOI 10.1007/978-3-319-63070-0_2

# Organisational Culture

The more recent phenomena of the study of culture within the organisational and management disciplines emerged initially in the 1950s and then moved on apace during the 1960s and 1970s. The publication of *Corporate Cultures* (Deal and Kennedy 1982), followed by *In Search of Excellence* (Peters and Waterman 1982), firmly cemented the concept into management discourse. What appealed to the corporate world about the concept of culture was that there was a sense in which culture could not only be created within an organisation but could then be moulded and strengthened in order to boost productivity, alleviate workplace tension and assist with strategic change. Marvin Bower, in *The Will to Manage*, argued that it was the responsibility of the manager of an organisation to dictate and communicate the culture of the organisation to the employees, as without that, they would have no understanding of the expected ways of working in the organisation (1966). Culture was seen as something that was very much an aspect of an organisation which could be adapted and moulded in the same way as a marketing strategy. That is not to say that cultural change was attempted lightly. Johnson et al. (2008) argue that almost all other forms of organisational change will be attempted prior to cultural change, even when culture is highlighted as the dominant issue. The complexity (and perhaps futility) of embarking upon cultural change renders it an unpopular strategic move.

Organisational culture was also felt to be a positive contributor to other facets of organisational life such as providing a sense of identity to workers and enhancing organisational commitment (Alvesson 2013). Research on the integration of mental health services in Somerset found that managers were of the belief that they only had to 'create' a shared culture amongst staff from the different organisations in order to achieve a new and effective organisation (Peck et al. 2001). However, organisational culture is not only considered for its potential positive impact upon the workplace. It is also viewed by organisational research as a negative force, one to be identified and understood not in order to utilise its power but in order to 'outmanoeuvre' its grasping reach. Culture is seen instead to be an obstacle to reform, commitment and productivity (Alvesson 2013). These approaches towards organisational cultures as something malleable and manipulable sit firmly within the notion that culture is something which an organisation *has* (Smircich 1983). This is the favoured approach of corporate analysts. However, residing mostly within academia is the notion that culture is what an organisation *is* (referred to by Smircich as "culture as root metaphor" (1983, p. 347)), and with it, the belief therefore that culture is not so easily changed (Lynn-Meek 1994, p. 274). It is to this more academic notion of organisational culture, rather than the corporate world of management consultancy, that this chapter now turns.

Unsurprisingly, there is little agreement from the disparate disciplines which embrace analyses of culture, about its form and function. Yet despite this, there is broad agreement that its centrality within organisations renders its concept worthy of deeper analysis. Understanding the culture of an organisation is a way of making sense of an organisation (Peck et al. 2001). It is argued that human programming takes on three levels: the *universal* (or biological) level, shared by all; the *collective* level, shared by some but not all; and the *unique* characteristics, exclusive to each person (Hofstede 2001). Culture embraces that second, collective level of mental programming. Societies, organisations and, most relevant to this book, occupational groups have ways of successfully reproducing these cultural schemas over time. Culture embraces all that is generally known but mostly unseen within an organisation. Indeed, the culture of an organisation is not a concrete, tangible entity, framed in organisational documentation. It is rather a socially constructed reality. Its features include the shared values and assumptions of the organisation plus the more symbolic aspects such as its myths, its stories and its rituals. These values and beliefs (which are deemed to remain constant over time) manifest themselves, to an extent, in the behaviours of the group.

It is this deeper level of understanding of an organisation, through an appreciation of the symbolism of the organisation (and of the meaning of that symbolism), which is so important. Analysis of organisational culture has the potential to provide a link between macro-level understandings of organisations and micro-level appreciations of the everyday lived experiences of the employees. In policing terms, these micro-level lived experiences of police officers manifest themselves regularly in police–public encounters. These encounters are what the majority of the public base their assessments of 'good policing' upon. Additionally, much power and discretion reside with the lower ranks of the police service, where many of those encounters take place. It is therefore of vital importance that these encounters are more fully understood. Whereas corporate analysis focuses more upon organisational strategy and direction, organisational culture considers the more holistic macro- and micro-level aspects of an organisation and thus provides a deeper and more complete understanding of an organisation. The importance of this deeper level of understanding, however, does not hide its complexity. Organisational cultures are a complex phenomenon, as difficult to define and understand as they are to research.

Organisational culture tends to be portrayed pictorially as an onion with varying layers (see Hofstede et al. 1990; Johnson et al. 2008 or Spencer-Oatey 2000 for examples). Although not universally consistent in their choice of layers, what are most often described by writers are those unseen characteristics of an organisation which, as you journey through the layers, become increasingly less conscious, tangible and observable but are nonetheless key characteristics of the culture. These include rituals, stories, routines, behaviours, symbols, values, beliefs and paradigms. These cultural artefacts make up what has been referred to as the 'cultural web' (Johnson and Scholes 1992). Whilst different theorists place different elements at the core of the model of organisational culture (for Hofstede et al. (1990), it is 'values'; for Johnson et al. (2008), it is 'paradigms'; for Trompenaars and Hampden-Turner (1997), it is 'basic assumptions'; and for Schein (1991), it is 'underlying assumptions'), there is general agreement that organisational culture is both learned and shared. According to Schein, therefore, culture is

> [a] pattern of shared basic assumptions, invented, discovered, or developed by a given group, as it learns to cope with its problems of external adaptation and internal integration, that has worked well enough to be considered valid, and, therefore, is to be taught to new members of the group as the correct way to perceive, think, and feel in relation to those problems. (1984, p. 3)

Schein argues that these assumptions are the result of the beliefs and values of early organisational members becoming accepted and validated by newer members and, by being based upon experience, are now no longer required to be tested (1992). As time passes, these assumptions become less tangible, more tacit and therefore more ingrained within the organisational culture. Organisational culture is therefore learned by its members through a process of socialisation (Van Maanen and Schein 1979). Cultural learning will be the focus of Chap. 5 of this book. This learning works to both integrate and assimilate the newcomers into their role but also functions as a positive reinforcement of effective working practices and a method of avoiding less effective measures. Groups will adopt behaviours which preserve or enhance a positive group identity (Tajfel 1982).

In order to continue and maintain an organisation's activities, there must be a sense of shared meanings and understandings and taken-for-granted assumptions. That is not to say that individual and personal symbols, meanings and interpretations are not apparent in organisations; these are, however, of less interest in a cultural understanding of an organisation. In adapting to a role, the values of an organisation's member become validated and, as such, form into assumptions (Schein 1991). This notion of the creation of culture fits much more with the "culture as root metaphor" (Smircich 1983, p. 347) referred to earlier. Rather than reflect the views and interests of the management of the organisation or be imposed by the management, the symbols and meanings of organisational culture tend to be more broadly shared values. Shared understandings and shared meanings (how something is interpreted) are what makes occupational cultures both interesting and important. These are not necessarily apparent to members themselves but are tacit, generally unspoken, taken-for-granted ideas and beliefs (Van Maanen and Schein 1979; Alvesson 2002). The capacity of occupational cultures to have a "cultural memory" (Assmann and Czaplicka 1995, p. 126), to reproduce themselves over time, is almost a test of their strength and their validity. Culture can therefore be seen to act as the *glue* which holds an organisation together (Alvesson 2002, p. 7).

However, there is a 'new' kid on the block when it comes to organisational research. Where once there was a burgeoning literature on 'organisational culture' and 'corporate culture', we now see similar levels of enthusiasm for the concept of 'organisational identity'. One of the first works considering the concept was from Albert and Whetten (1985), although more recently, Whetton has suggested that the notion is suffering from an "identity crisis" (2006, p. 220). The question we must ask is whether this is a semantic change or whether there are indeed fundamental differences between these two concepts. I would argue that the latter holds more weight, that there are indeed some important differences between these two concepts, which I shall now seek to explain.

Whereas the focus of organisational culture is on the often tacit symbols, meanings and shared understandings between members of an organisation, the focus of organisational identity is much more outward facing. It is concerned with how rhetoric is used to construct an image of an organisation for public consumption and how this might best be moulded (potentially manipulated) in order to refine this image. Organisational identity represents what an organisation stands for and what it might be able to achieve in the future. This is unlikely to be driven by its members, but rather by its managers, and so is a much more top-down, externally focused approach to organisational analysis, rather than the more inward-looking bottom-up approach of organisational culture. As such, the concept of organisational identity fits more with the notion described earlier of culture as something which an organisation *has* (Smircich 1983) and can potentially change. Organisational identity can therefore be seen as an aspect of organisational culture but one which has a narrower concern and focus. This explanation should not suggest that an organisational identity is easily constructed, homogeneous and manipulable. Research indicates that organisations have multiple identities, often with conflicting features (Sillince and Brown 2009). Organisational identity, however, should not be confused with social identity or self-identity (how individuals define themselves), which will be the focus of Chap. 3. These concerns are however not entirely mutually exclusive. Whilst how individuals identify with an employing organisation will have an impact upon how individuals define themselves, it is not perhaps the case that it is the official discourse of the organisation or indeed the entire organisation that employees most relate to.

He and Brown (2013) have suggested that there are four different perspectives relating to organisational identity. The *functional perspectives* are identities which are very much organisationally driven and will feature the heavy hand of marketing teams. These identities are not the tacit, invisible, difficult-to-capture meanings associated with organisational culture, but are instead the physical and more concrete features of an organisation such as logos, organisational speeches and official documentation. The *social constructionist perspectives* relate more to understandings about what is unique or distinctive about an organisation based upon its own members' understandings. These understandings evolve not from the more tangible detritus of organisational marketing but lie more in the complex interactions between workers. The *psychodynamic perspectives*, according to He and Brown (2013), attempt to harness organisational identity and identity work to counter the psychological threats faced by employees as a result of conflicting personal and individual aims. Organisations can thus play a role in enhancing the "collective self-esteem" of their workers (He and Brown 2013, p. 9). Finally, there are the *postmodern and non-standard perspectives*, which, whilst clearly not offering a collective view on organisational identity, do stress the importance of dialogue and narratives in both the creation and the adaption of organisational identity. This is a continual process and, as would be expected in a postmodernist approach, is negotiated by all participants.

Caution must be taken, however, with the often confused and conflicting accounts of organisational culture as opposed to organisational identity. Some authors use the terms interchangeably and some see little difference between the two concepts (Alvesson 2013). Where corporate analysts and change management consultants stumbled in their attempts to mould organisational culture, their work appears to be revitalised in the less abstract and more superficial concerns of organisational identity.

## Organisational Commitment and Identification

The debate surrounding organisational *identity* has inevitably led to a debate in another area which is relevant to cooperation in groups and that is organisational *identification*. This is sometimes referred to as organisational *commitment*. This will not be discussed in depth here because, as it has already been stated, the focus of organisational identity is in the narrower domain of the outward-facing image of an organisation, what it stands for and what it might achieve in the future. It is driven more by its managers than by its members and does not encompass the broader, more sociological and cultural phenomena relating to organisational culture, such as rituals, stories, routines, behaviours, symbols, values, beliefs and assumptions, which this book is interested in. However, a brief consideration of what organisational identification is and what factors can lead to its emergence is important in order to understand, albeit tangentially, the areas relating to employee satisfaction.

Ashforth and Mael (1989) argue that organisational identification occurs when employees feel at one and a sense of belonging with an organisation. This is likely to be enhanced by strong leadership, social exchange factors and the perceived attractiveness of the organisation (He and Brown 2013). The social exchange factors are important here. Social exchange theory argues that when individual 'A' acts in such a way as to favour individual 'B', then individual 'B' would be right to expect a return of that favour from individual 'A'. Although this can be framed in economic terms, *social* exchange theory focuses upon socio-emotional aspects of exchange (Blau 1964). In organisational terms, therefore, individuals who perceive an organisation to be supportive of them and their goals will enter into a reciprocal relationship with the employer by showing higher levels of organisational commitment (Rhoades et al. 2001). This affirmative relationship not only works to conform with commonly held views of social exchange behaviour and reciprocity but also helps the individual to maintain a positive self-image and enhance his or her sense of self (Marique et al. 2013).

Organisational identification is closely related to the concept of *affective organisational commitment*, which encompasses both identification and emotional attachment (Meyer and Allen 1991). Whilst organisational identification provides the *cognitive* impetus for performance, affective organisational commitment provides the *motivation* to drive that performance (Bergami and Bagozzi 2000). Research has indicated that affective organisational commitment is a stronger determinant of employee performance than organisational identification alone (Marique et al. 2013).

A number of research studies concerning organisational identification with police officers in Australia (although referred to as organisational commitment) conducted some interesting analysis (Savery et al. 1991; Wilson 1991; Wilson and Beck 1995; Beck and Wilson 2000). Contrary to research within other organisations, commitment did not increase with the length of service within the organisation, but actually decreased. Longitudinal research into non-police organisations has consistently found that although levels of commitment drop in the very early days of employment (most commonly attributed to shock, negative experiences and frustrated expectations), this tended to increase shortly afterwards, as employees started to feel a growing loyalty and sense of belonging with their organisation (Beck and Wilson 2000). However, with research within policing organisations, it was found that the longer an employee was working within the police, the lower the levels of organisational commitment were. On entry into the organisation, commitment was high, but this decreased dramatically later (Beck and Wilson 1997). The authors comment that the implications of this are very important, yet its causes remain unknown. The longitudinal research reported on within this book seeks to answer some of these questions about organisational commitment. Organisational commitment in the study by Beck and Wilson (2000) was described as an acceptance of, and a belief in, the organisational goals, a desire to undertake work for the organisation and an appetite to remain within the organisation. What is of concern to policing organisations is not only that commitment is linked with performance but, most pertinently in relation to this book, that low levels of commitment and negative attitudes towards an organisation are passed on to new recruits and shape their identity as police officers. As we shall discuss in Chaps. 9 and 10, the strong and pervasive "high octane" (Owers 2012, p. 5) cultures of the police, combined with the manner in which new recruits are trained and developed within the police, mean that the attitudes and beliefs of longer-serving police officers have the potential to be highly influential in a new recruit's socialisation. Van Maanen's longitudinal study on the socialisation of new police recruits found that changes to organisational commitment were closely aligned with elements of police socialisation (1975). Police socialisation will be the focus of Chap. 5.

# The Policing Organisation

The focus of this book is on the more sociological, more holistic concept of organisational culture and, in particular, on the assimilation and learning of shared meanings and cultural artefacts by an organisation's new members. The policing organisation in the UK has a long and both chequered and illustrious history. It is rooted in British history and has a cultural symbolism which stretches far beyond its organisational structure. Its significance is felt in both its fictitious and non-fictitious forms, and it has the dubious honour of being one of a select group of merchandising options (along with red buses and the London Underground) which is regularly featured in British tourist shops.

From a relatively straightforward legal and organisational perspective, the police are tasked with the maintenance of law and order, the protection of the public and their property, and the detection, investigation and prevention of crime. But we also know that the realities of policing involve a very much less clearly defined role, indeed a very much less crime-focused role which concentrates upon dispute management, order maintenance and welfare concerns. Bittner's often quoted account of what the police do is as relevant today as when it was first written. Police officers find themselves responding to and intervening regularly in situations. This is a reactive response to events and represents "something-that-ought-not-be-to-happening-and-about-which-somone-had-better-do-something-now" (Bittner 1990, p. 249). Marenin's interpretation of the role of police officers as engaged with "parking tickets and class repression", perhaps more than most, sums up the enormous variety inherent in the policing role (1982, p. 241).

The public sector cuts that were felt from 2010 onwards in the fields of health and social care and mental health services brought into sharp focus the enormous range of non-crime-related activity which the police are associated with. Brodeur (1983) has distinguished between two policing tasks—'high policing' and 'low policing'. 'High policing' is perhaps more readily associated with the role of the police that is often portrayed in fictional crime dramas and indeed by the police themselves when engaged in the cultural storytelling that is often a feature of their profession. This involves intelligence-related policing activities which utilise both human and technological intelligence apparatus. 'Low policing' refers to the more mundane day-to-day reality of much of the policing role which focuses upon responding to criminal or potentially criminal incidents, order maintenance, reassurance and community engagement.

Millie (2013) has conceptualised this further by dividing 'low policing' into 'wide policing' and 'narrow policing'. He argues that historically, but most notably since the early 1990s, the role of the police has become wider and wider and now encompasses the diverse and multifaceted demands of anti-terrorism, reassurance, fear of crime, catching criminals, crime prevention and crime reduction. Neighbourhood policing, reassurance policing, problem-oriented policing, zero tolerance policing and intelligence-led policing are just a few examples of the many styles of policing which the police are required to adopt depending on the political context of the time. Millie (2013) calls for a more 'narrow' definition of policing. He notes Reiner's (2000) distinction between *preserving* social order and *producing* social order and maintains that the latter could well be passed on to other agencies. Millie stops well short of Theresa May's version of 'narrow policing' (when in the role of Home Secretary), with her demands for the police to be "tough, no-nonsense crime-fighters" (May 2011), but argues that by considering the police as one of a group of agencies associated with social control, rather than the only group responsible for social control, there is the potential for less conflict and potential role confusion (Millie 2013).

If there is confusion about the extent and limits of the policing role, there is confusion too over who are the officers to perform those roles. A House of Commons Home Affairs Committee report indicated that Government pledges to protect 'front-line policing' were hampered by poor and unsatisfactory definitions from Her Majesty's Inspectorate of Constabulary (HMIC) of what the 'front-line' actually constituted (HASC 2011). A subsequent report from HMIC (2011) outlined its interpretation of 'front-line' policing (which included visible and non-visible, available and non-available staff), but the term appears to be loosely interpreted and poorly understood.

# Narratives and Symbolism in British Policing

This discussion about 'front-line' policing should not, however, be misinterpreted as a purely organisational and structural issue. The reason for the myriad of opinion, disquiet and debate over what is 'front-line' and what is 'back-office' in policing terms is far more to do with the unique status of the police as the carriers of not only legal power but also symbolic power. The British police (whether fairly or unfairly, whether negatively or positively) are, without doubt, a dominant symbolic and cultural icon in the UK, and that status has not diminished despite vast social, cultural and political changes. In a similar vein to the Royal Family, both newspaper editors and TV programme commissioners know that policing in its factual and fictitious forms fascinates and excites the public. The public hold a firm belief in *their* ownership of the British police and in their desire to maintain the latter's supposed historic status as the guardians of public order—the 'thin blue line'. An example of that presumed ownership can be seen in the public's attitudes towards police patrol. The public's demand for 'bobbies on the beat' has so far continued unabated and also continues to be a staple of the political lexicon, despite all evidence to the contrary over their effectiveness in any other regard but the luxury of reassurance (Quinton and Morris 2008).

The police, however, have been adept at using their status as defenders of the 'thin blue line' to their best advantage. The Police Federation (representing officers from police constables to chief inspectors) campaigns are notorious for using the symbolic imagery of the 'bobby on the beat' to mobilise public support in the face of internally opposed change (e.g. 'Say Hello to Dave. Wave Goodbye to Your Police Service' (2012); 'Cuts Have Consequences' (2015)). Gagliardi (1986) argues that all organisations have both a primary and a secondary strategy. The latter is generally explicitly linked to specific and stated aims and objectives, yet the former is perhaps more interesting. It is here that the symbolic power of the organisation takes precedence, as it is in this primary strategy that the sacred values of the organisation reside. These are the values which are an essential component of the image and identity of an organisation, and which generally portray an organisation in its most positive light. Universities as 'seats of learning', doctors as heroes, members of Parliament (MPs) as representatives of their public, hospitals as staffed by a multitude of Florence Nightingales are perhaps all examples where the reality may not live up to the imagery. The 'sacred cow' of policing lies in its 'defenders of the peace' image, and it is this image which the police work hard to maintain. Loader (1999), however, has warned that the increasing 'commodification of policing' (through such developments as managerialism, consumerism and promotionalism) risks eroding the public's levels of satisfaction in policing, as the reality of their interventions inevitably fails to match the public's expectations.

The police will also act to *reframe* the narratives around policing in order that they contribute to, rather than conflict with, the overriding and positive identity of the policing role that they wish to adhere to. In seeking to conceptualise community policing within the more legitimate notions of 'real policing', Davies and Thomas (2008) found that regardless of rank, officers sought to promote the 'thief-taking', 'agents of social change' discourse of community policing, which tied in more fully with the accepted narratives of policing. The police are not unique in this regard. Ashforth and Kreiner (1999) identify three techniques that workers use to protect their positive identities and indeed to strengthen them. *Reframing* seeks to alter the meanings attached to specific jobs, *recalibrating* attempts to recategorise more unacceptable tasks and *refocusing* attempts to draw attention away from these unacceptable tasks and onto more savoury aspects of the job. Although the police are no longer the only gatekeepers of information and cannot fully control the flow of information in a way that they once could, they are nonetheless still in a relatively strong position to at least manage their identity and maintain their imagery in ways that they choose.

Loader (1997) is one of a handful of policing scholars who have attempted to reinvigorate the *sociology* of policing and have in particular focused upon the strong position held by the police with regard to their symbolic power. Drawing upon the French sociologist Pierre Bourdieu's work on symbolic power, Loader has sought to evaluate the significance of policing as a cultural category. Bourdieu's analysis of symbolic power is that, whilst it is invisible, it is nonetheless an active agent in the relationships between those who exercise power and those who submit to that power (Bourdieu 1991). This is not necessarily a harmonious relationship, but a continual struggle whereby different groups are attempting to impose their definitions of the social world upon the social order. This struggle is based not only on words but also upon the power of symbolism. Manning (2010) has argued that the police are able to convey strong messages about order, censure and trust in ways that affirm their position as the 'guardians' of society. The police ('defenders of freedom', 'force for good', etc.) are in a constant struggle with those who seek to undermine this order and stability through engaging in criminal and disorderly behaviour. Importantly for this book, and the research contained within it, is that what creates and maintains this symbolic power is a belief in the *legitimacy* of those who exercise it (Bourdieu 1991). The legitimacy of policing will be discussed later in this chapter.

Symbolism and symbolic power, as just mentioned, are an active, and not a static, process and play a role in the maintenance of social order. According to Durkheim, what is essential to the building of solidarity amongst groups is the sharing of this symbolic system (1893/1984). Symbolism therefore has a social function in addition to a dividing function. Where there is an 'out-group' (in the case of the symbolic power of the police, this would be those who seek to undermine the consensus and order established by the police), there is also an 'in-group' (in this case, the police acting to protect the public from harm). Bourdieu believes that once the dominant culture has established its ideologies and beliefs, then all other subcultures are defined by their distance from the beliefs of the dominant culture (1991). When that dominant culture, in the form of the police, has the symbolic power associated with order, stability and morality, then all other subcultures will struggle for acceptance. The police do not have to coerce and manipulate the public into an acceptance of their position as the moral guardians of social order. Whilst attempts are made by policing bodies to portray and promote policing in a positive light, they are assisted by strong historical, cultural and fictional icons and artefacts, all of which contribute to the strength of the symbolic power of British policing.

It should not be forgotten, however, that within this seemingly benign symbolic status of the police lie other voices that are therefore not heard or are ignored. Where the police voice is deemed legitimate, other voices will be deemed illegitimate. Where the police claim to offer an inclusionary vision for all citizens, there must also be those who are excluded. As Loader has argued:

> Every stop, every search, every arrest, every group of youths moved on, every abuse of due process, every failure to respond to call or complaint, every racist snub, every sexist remark, every homophobic joke, every diagnosis of the crime problem, every depiction of criminals – all these send small, routine, authoritative signals about society's conflicts, cleavages, and hierarchies, about whose claims are considered legitimate within it, about whose status identity is to be affirmed or denied as part of it. (2006, p. 211)

It is for this reason that an analysis of the rituals, stories, routines, behaviours, symbols, values, beliefs and assumptions of police officers, those working on a day-to-day basis with members of the public, is so vitally important, not only to understand their attitudes to their own work but also to interpret the potential effects of these attitudes upon the symbolic status of policing. Manning has argued vociferously that policing studies has become too preoccupied with 'fixing' policing, too close to the police themselves and too willing to research whatever is recently fashionable in policing circles (2010). The result of this has been "too much [focus] on the police and too little on the context or culture of policing" (Manning 2010, p. 100). This book seeks to further address some of those concerns.

Loader (1997) has suggested that the effects of a strong public attachment to policing are not necessarily all in the best interests of the police. Whilst they can more easily invoke the language required to support the imposition of more widespread police powers (the now defunct Association of Chief Police Officers was highly successful in this regard in the 1990s—see Savage et al. 2000), they also suffer from the public's belief in the ability of the police to solve all of society's ills (Loader 1997). Additionally, the discourse of 'fighting crime' and 'defending social order' also contributes to the relatively oversimplified portrayal of police officers as daily crime-fighters. As mentioned previously, research by Davies and Thomas (2008) indicated that the police had to reframe the policing narratives of their community policing endeavours in order for both internal and external acceptance of the 'soft' side of policing. This is all part of what Manning would refer to as the "drama of control" of the police (2003, p. 16). The actions of the police are not just actions but representative of what the police stand for and symbolise. This misinformed belief in the fundamental role of the police to engage in the 'fight against crime' impacts negatively in two different ways. First, it impacts upon the public when that fight is never won, both in terms of their levels of satisfaction in the police and their rational and irrational levels of fear of crime. Second, it impacts upon the police themselves, who struggle to embrace the more routine aspects of the police role, who attempt to deny the important social function of policing, and who act to reframe their identity with more crime-fighting narratives.

There is therefore some confusion here. On the one hand lies the cultural symbolism of the police, which is influenced by a number of sources. It is held in the abstract beliefs of the public. It is found in the media representations of policing, both fictional and non-fictional. It is encouraged by various governments (Loader refers to the UK Coalition Government of 2010–2015 seeing itself as "releasing the police's inner crime-fighter" (2014, p. 43)). It is also found in the physical icons of policing. On the other hand, there is the reality of the policing role. How the identities of an organisation are constructed and developed is in an interpretation of these meanings, which, we can see, are attributed to policing from a large variety of sources. The interpretation of these meanings is part of the sense-making of the police occupational culture (Rantatalo 2016). The confusion illustrated, however, has the potential to create a vacuum in the understandings of new recruits to the police service, which police cultural characteristics are waiting to fill. If there is a gap between the perceived and actual realities of the role of the police, and there is a gap in the prescribed police training and the necessary skills, then the normative and cultural practices which are passed down from one generation of the police to another will, in the absence of anything more useful and relevant, be allowed to flourish.

These arguments bring us to the understanding that what the police symbolise is as important as what the police do. The power of the police to use force against citizens places them in a unique and highly responsible position. Weber argued that this power requires that the police use both their head and their soul (1919/1977). How the police are perceived by victims, by offenders, by others in the general public are affected not just by how the police act and behave but by how the police are perceived by others and how the police perceive themselves. According to Tyler et al. (2014, p. 752), every interaction between the police and the public is a "teachable moment" in which something is communicated and learned by both parties. All of these encounters then become assimilated into the working practices (the "recipe knowledge" (Sackmann 1992, p. 21)) of the police and the public's attitude towards them. What the police perceive to be their role and their status within the functioning and order of society will play a large part in how those encounters are performed and in their impact on levels of trust and cooperation from the public. The field of *procedural justice* has much to say on these processes, and it is to this issue that we now turn.

## Procedural Justice

Analysis of procedural justice within the field of policing has flourished in recent years. Whilst issues of legitimacy and consent were very much part of the policing literature landscape in the 1970s and 1980s, they were temporarily replaced by a much more managerial focus, for example, on performance, which is more recently being challenged again by the issues of trust, legitimacy and cooperation (Jackson et al. 2012). In policing terms, procedural justice focuses upon the extent to which people believe that they have been treated with fairness and dignity during encounters with the police, both in terms of the encounter itself and in terms of the outcome of the encounter. Much of the work on procedural justice stems from the work of the American psychologist Tom Tyler, and the numerous studies which have emanated from this have mostly taken a quantitative, survey-based approach to test their hypotheses. Tyler (1990) suggests that compliance with the police rests with two contrasting judgements. On the one hand are the instrumental or coercive factors associated with a legal obligation to obey the police. This model of instrumental compliance is supplemented by a range of sanctions for non-compliers which work both to punish those who do not comply and to deter those who are tempted to not comply. More interesting, however, is normative compliance from the public, which is the belief that the police are a legitimate holder of state power, which then fuels an internal motivation to comply. People believe, quite simply, that compliance with the police is the right thing to do. This is arguably a much more effective way of maintaining social order than coercion. Tyler and Huo (2002) refer to this as 'process-based regulation' where the relationship between the police and the policed is one of self-regulation, which flows from the belief in a set of shared values, combined with a sense of obligation and responsibility to their community. Normative compliance increases with stronger beliefs in the legitimacy of the police. Whilst normative compliance is a more effective means of maintaining social order than coercion, Brodeur claims that, in effect, the police are *unable* to operate without the existence of order (2010). They only function within an established system of social order, rather than by way of contributing to the creation of social order.

Legitimacy has been conceptualised in two different ways. First, there is empirical legitimacy (or social legitimacy), which can be traced back conceptually to Weber (1919/1977) and maintains that an obligation to obey follows from an acceptance by the public of the belief in legality and the legitimacy of doing so, irrespective of the principles contained within the rules to obey. Second, there is normative legitimacy, which requires that the individual shares the moral or ethical position of the institution (Jackson and Bradford 2010). Beetham (1991) has added to this a third layer of legitimacy, which is that the institution is itself a legitimate authority which has confidence in its legality. Legitimacy is a complex subject which has been necessarily abridged here. Although this conception of legitimacy is generally accepted in the majority of the procedural justice literature, there are some who would question the benign belief in the validity of authority and of the lack of analysis of an institution's role in cultivating or manipulating this belief (Lukes 2005; Harkin 2015).

Police legitimacy can be considered through a macro-level analysis of corruption, relationships with Black and Minority Ethnic (BME) communities and public order, or can be considered through a micro-level analysis of the day-to-day encounters between the police and the public (Bradford et al. 2014). The attitudes, behaviours and beliefs of the officers involved in these day-to-day encounters have the potential to either enhance or threaten that legitimacy. Police cultures, and their various characteristics, have the potential to play an important role in shaping these encounters. In order to more fully understand this, an analysis of the developing attitudes of new recruits to the police service is very important. The results of this longitudinal analysis will form the basis of later chapters in this book.

Enhancing police legitimacy is no easy task. Cooper has stated that the mandate for policing in no way contributes towards the establishment of legitimacy (2014). The police are being asked to wage an unwinnable war ('fighting crime') with unworkable tools ('the power to arrest'). The legitimacy of the police is influenced not only by the *outcomes* of police actions, but, crucially in relation to procedural justice theories, also by the *processes* that lead to those outcomes (i.e. the behaviour of the police). Where citizens are treated with respect, are reassured, are given a voice, and their status is not demeaned, they will feel that the processes involved are fair and legitimate. This is irrespective of the outcome of the encounter and further informs future compliance with the police. The focus lies therefore not in the effectiveness of the outcome but in the perceived fairness of the process (Sunshine and Tyler 2003). This then shifts the focus strongly from a more quantifiable measure of policing effectiveness to an emphasis much more on the social and cultural aspects of legitimacy in policing. This is not necessarily something that is supported or encouraged either externally from those controlling the police or internally from those managing the police.

How the police treat the public therefore is crucial in terms of compliance, cooperation, satisfaction and, ultimately, perceptions of legitimacy. It is in these day-to-day mundane encounters with the public that this legitimacy can flourish or flounder. Australian research has indicated that it is precisely in these localised encounters with the police that judgements about trust and efficacy may lie (Sargeant 2015). Seeking to understand what might best predict collective efficacy in the police, Sargeant's research indicated that trust in procedural justice and police effectiveness were far more relevant and significant than the obligation to obey the police (2015). She explains this, in part, by arguing that effectiveness and procedural justice are much more likely to be apparent in a neighbourhood context, which is where most police–public encounters take place, rather than the more abstract notions of obedience and obligations to obey, which can be understood as more abstract.

We have so far considered situations where policing behaviours result in judgements of fairness and legitimacy. Conversely, when police processes, actions and behaviours are deemed to be unfair, unjust and, perhaps, excessive, the police will have to rely more upon their coercive powers in order to perform their job. This will also affect future cooperation, behaviour and compliance. Whereas Reiner (2000) would argue that the 'sacred cow' status of the police has been in steep decline, the public's level of confidence in the police is still relatively high in comparison with many other public bodies (Ipsos MORI 2016). However, where once this legitimacy of the police would have been taken for granted, assumed and habitual, it is now a much more contested and continually negotiated arena (Jackson and Bradford 2010).

This chapter has argued that procedural justice is vitally important in the relationship between the police and the public and is a contributor to the public's perceptions of the police as a legitimate or an illegitimate source of authority. We have also seen the importance of analysing police behaviour and police attitudes in order to more fully appreciate the influences upon that behaviour and those attitudes. Procedural justice is therefore an important element in a fuller understanding of policing cultures and their impact upon the public. However, procedural justice is not only relevant and interesting from an outward-looking perspective in the consideration of police encounters with the public. It is also worthy of analysis from a more inward-looking organisational perspective. This is will be undertaken in Chap. 3, when a more micro-level interpretation of social identity and the social identity of the police will be considered.

Chapter 3 seeks to explore the issues of social and personal identity and the formation of the self. This will be done through an analysis of the social identity and intergroup relations literature. Understanding organisations is as much about understanding the individuals who work within those organisations as anything else, and this can be more fully understood through an understanding of cultural attitudes, values and beliefs. Appreciating how these attitudes, values and beliefs are formed within the organisational environment will be essential to a fuller understanding of the development of policing cultures, which this research aims to examine.

The procedural justice literature reveals that public confidence in the police impacts upon both compliance with the law and future cooperation with the law. The legitimacy of the police rests with the public's judgements about the way in which police officers conduct their business. If the public view the police as legitimate, then compliance with the law and, going one step further, self-regulation will mean that the police can focus more upon other concerns (Sunshine and Tyler 2003). What we have long known is that the police can, at best, have only a marginal impact upon crime rates. However, where they do hold all of the influence is over their own behaviour, which according to procedural justice theorists has the potential to have a much greater impact upon crime. The police and the public are bound together in an ecology (Cooper 2014), with each influencing the other in terms of behaviours and attitudes. In relation to this book, therefore, analysis of the rituals, stories, routines, behaviours, symbols, values, beliefs and underlying assumptions of police officers is crucial in this regard.

## References

Albert, S., & Whetten, D. A. (1985). Organizational Identity. In L. Cummings & M. Staw (Eds.), *Research in Organizational Behaviour Volume 7* (pp. 263–295). Greenwich: JAI.

Alvesson, M. (2002). *Understanding Organizational Culture*. London: Sage.

Alvesson, M. (2013). *Understanding Organizational Culture* (2nd ed.). London: Sage.

Ashforth, B., & Kreiner, G. (1999). "How Can You Do It?" Dirty Work and the Challenge of Constructing a Positive Identity. *The Academy of Management Review, 24*(3), 413–434.

Ashforth, B., & Mael, F. (1989). Social Identity Theory and the Organisation. *Academy of Management Review, 14*, 20–39.

Assmann, J., & Czaplicka, J. (1995). Collective Memory and Cultural Identity. *New German Critique, 65*, 125–133.

Beck, K., & Wilson, C. (1997). Police Officers' Views on Cultivating Organizational Commitment: Implications for Police Managers. *Policing: An International Journal of Police Strategies and Management, 20*, 175–195.

Beck, K., & Wilson, C. (2000). Development of Affective Organizational Commitment: A Cross-Sequential Examination of Change with Tenure. *Journal of Vocational Behaviour, 56*, 114–136.

Beetham, D. (1991). *The Legitimation of Power*. London: Macmillan.

Bergami, M., & Bagozzi, R. (2000). Self-Categorization, Affective Commitment and Group Self-Esteem as Distinct Aspects of Social Identity in the Organization. *British Journal of Social Psychology, 39*, 555–577.

Bittner, E. (1990). *Aspects of Police Work*. Boston: Northeastern University Press.

Blau, P. (1964). *Exchange and Power in Social Life*. New York: John Wiley.

Bourdieu, P. (1991). *Language and Symbolic Power*. Cambridge: Polity Press.

Bower, M. (1966). *The Will to Manage*. London: McGraw-Hill.

Bradford, B., Jackson, J., & Hough, M. (2014). Police Futures and Legitimacy: Redefining 'Good Policing'. In J. Brown (Ed.), *The Future of Policing* (pp. 79–99). London: Routledge.

Brodeur, J. P. (1983). High Policing and Low Policing: Remarks About the Policing of Political Activities. *Social Problems, 30*(5), 507–520.

Brodeur, J. P. (2010). *The Policing Web*. Oxford: Oxford University Press.

Cooper, J. (2014). *In Search of Police Legitimacy: Territoriality, Isomorphism and Changes in Policing Practices*. Texas: LFB Scholarly Publishing.

Davies, A., & Thomas, R. (2008). Dixon of Dock Green Got Shot! Policing Identity Work and Organizational Change. *Public Administration, 86*(3), 627–642.

Deal, T., & Kennedy, A. (1982). *Corporate Cultures: The Rites and Rituals of Corporate Life*. Reading, MA: Addison-Wesley.

Durkheim, E. (1984). *The Division of Labour in Society*. Basingstoke: Macmillan. (Original work published 1893).

Gagliardi, P. (1986). The Creation and Change of Organizational Cultures: A Conceptual Framework. *Organization Studies, 7*(2), 117–134.

Harkin, D. (2015). Police Legitimacy, Ideology and Qualitative Methods: A Critique of Procedural Justice Theory. *Criminology and Criminal Justice, 15*(5), 594–612.

HASC. (2011). *The New Landscape of Policing*. London: The Stationery Office.

He, H., & Brown, A. (2013). Organizational Identity and Organizational Identification – A Review of the Literature and Suggestions for Future Research. *Group and Organization Management, 38*(1), 3–35.

HMIC. (2011). *Demanding Times*. London: The Stationery Office.

Hofstede, G. (2001). *Culture's Consequences: International Differences in Work-Related Values* (2nd ed.). London: Sage.

Hofstede, G., Neuijen, B., Daval Ohayv, D., & Sanders, G. (1990). Measuring Organizational Cultures: A Qualitative and Quantitative Study Across Twenty Cases. *Administrative Science Quarterly, 35*, 286–316.

Ipsos MORI. (2016). *Trust in Professions.* Retrieved from https://www.ipsos-mori.com/researchpublications/researcharchive/3685/Politicians-are-still-trusted-less-than-estate-agents-journalists-and-bankers.aspx#gallery[m]/1/

Jackson, J., & Bradford, B. (2010). Police Legitimacy: A Conceptual Review. *National Policing Improvement Agency Wiki.* Retrieved from http://papers.ssrn.com/sol3/papers.cfm?abstract_id=1684507

Jackson, J., Bradford, B., Hough, M., & Murray, K. (2012). Compliance with the Law and Policing by Consent. In A. Crawford & A. Hucklesby (Eds.), *Legitimacy and Compliance in Criminal Justice* (pp. 29–49). London: Routledge.

Johnson, G., & Scholes, K. (1992). *Exploring Corporate Strategy.* Harlow: Pearson Education.

Johnson, G., Scholes, K., & Whittington, R. (2008). *Exploring Corporate Strategy* (8th ed.). Harlow: Pearson Education.

Loader, I. (1997). Policing and the Social: Questions of Symbolic Power. *British Journal of Sociology, 48*(1), 1–18.

Loader, I. (1999). Consumer Culture and the Commodifcation of Policing and Security. *Sociology, 33*(2), 373–392.

Loader, I. (2006). Policing, Recognition, and Belonging. *The Annals of the American Academy of Political and Social Science, 605*(May), 202–221.

Loader, I. (2014). Why Do the Police Matter? Beyond the Myth of Crime-Fighting. In J. Brown (Ed.), *The Future of Policing* (pp. 40–51). London: Routledge.

Lukes, S. (2005). *Power:Aa Radical View.* London: Palgrave.

Lynn-Meek, V. (1994). Organisational Culture: Origins and Weaknesses. In D. McKevitt & A. Lawton (Eds.), *Public Sector Management* (pp. 265–280). London: Sage Publications.

Manning, P. (2003). *Policing Contingencies.* Chicago: University of Chicago Press.

Manning, P. (2010). *Democratic Policing in a Changing World.* Boulder: Paradigm Publishers.

Marenin, O. (1982). Parking Tickets and Class Repression: The Concept of Policing in Critical Theories of Criminal Justice. *Contemporary Crises, 6*(3), 241–266.

Marique, G., Stinglhamber, F., Desmette, D., Caesens, G., & de Zanet, F. (2013). The Relationship Between Perceived Organizational Support and Affective Commitment: A Social Identity Perspective. *Group and Organization Management, 38*(1), 68–100.

May, T. (2011). *Speech to the Conservative Party Conference.* Retrieved from http://www.politics.co.uk/comment-analysis/2011/10/04/theresa-may-speech-in-full

Meyer, J., & Allen, N. (1991). A Three-Component Conceptualization of Organizational Commitment. *Human Resource Management Review, 1,* 61–89.

Millie, A. (2013). The Policing Task and the Expansion (and Contraction) of British Policing. *Criminology and Criminal Justice, 13*(2), 143–160.

Owers, A. (2012). *Independent Oversight of Police Complaints: The IPCC Eight Years On.* Retrieved from https://www.ipcc.gov.uk/sites/default/files/Documents/speeches/speech_dame_anne_owers_john_harris_memorial_lecture.pdf

Peck, E., Towell, D., & Gulliver, P. (2001). The Meanings of 'Culture' in Health and Social Care: A Case Study of the Combined Trust in Somerset. *Journal of Interprofessional Care, 15*(4), 319–327.

Peters, T., & Waterman, R. (1982). *In Search of Excellence.* New York: Harper and Row.

Quinton, P., & Morris, J. (2008). *Neighbourhood Policing: The Impact of Piloting and Early National Implementation, Home Office Online Report 01/08.* Retrieved from https://www.bl.uk/britishlibrary/~/media/bl/global/social%20welfare/pdfs/non-secure/n/e/i/neighbourhood-policingthe-impact-of-piloting-and-early-national-implementation.pdf

Rantatalo, O. (2016). Media Representations and Police Officers' Identity Work in a Specialised Police Tactical Unit. *Policing and Society, 26*(1), 97–113.

Reiner, R. (2000). *The Politics of the Police* (3rd ed.). Oxford: Oxford University Press.

Rhoades, L., Eisenberger, R., & Armeli, S. (2001). Affective Commitment to the Organization: The Contribution of Perceived Organizational Support. *Journal of Applied Psychology, 86,* 825–836.

Sackmann, S. (1992). Culture and Subcultures: An Analysis of Organizational Knowledge. *Administrative Science Quarterly, 37,* 140–161.

Sargeant, E. (2015). Policing and Collective Efficacy: The Relative Importance of Police Effectiveness, Procedural Justice and the Obligation to Obey Police. *Policing and Society.* Advance online publication. http://dx.doi.org/10.1080/10439463.2015.1122008

Savage, S., Charman, S., & Cope, S. (2000). *Policing and the Power of Persuasion*. London: Blackstone Press.

Savery, L., Soutar, G., & Weaver, J. (1991). Organizational Commitment and the West Australian Police Force. *The Police Journal, 64*, 168–177.

Schein, E. (1984). Coming to a New Awareness of Organizational Culture. *Sloan Management Review, 25*(2), 3.

Schein, E. (1991). What Is Culture? In P. Frost, L. Noore, M. Louis, C. Lundberg, & J. Martin (Eds.), *Reframing Organizational Culture* (pp. 243–253). London: Sage Publications.

Schein, E. (1992). *Organisational Culture and Leadership* (2nd ed.). San Francisco: Jossey-Bass.

Sillince, J., & Brown, A. (2009). Multiple Organizational Identities and Legitimacy: The Rhetoric of Police Websites. *Human Relations, 62*(12), 1829–1856.

Smircich, L. (1983). Concepts of Culture and Organisational Analysis. *Administrative Science Quarterly, 28*, 339–358.

Spencer-Oatey, H. (2000). *Culturally Speaking: Managing Rapport Through Talk Across Cultures*. London: Continuum.

Sunshine, J., & Tyler, T. (2003). The Role of Procedural Justice and Legitimacy in Shaping Public Support for Policing. *Law and Society Review, 37*(3), 513–548.

Tajfel, H. (1982). Social Psychology of Intergroup Relations. *Annual Review of Psychology, 33*, 1–39.

Trompenaars, F., & Hampden-Turner, C. (1997). *Riding the Waves of Culture: Understanding Cultural Diversity in Business*. London: Nicholas Brearley.

Tyler, T. (1990). *Why People Obey the Law*. New Haven: Yale University Press.

Tyler, T., & Huo, Y. (2002). *Trust in the Law: Encouraging Public Co-operation with the Police and Courts*. New York: Russell-Sage.

Tyler, T., Fagan, J., & Geller, A. (2014). Street Stops and Police Legitimacy: Teachable Moments in Young Urban Men's Legal Socialization. *Journal of Empirical Legal Studies, 11*(4), 751–785.

Van Maanen, J. (1975). Police Socialization: A Longitudinal Examination of Job Attitudes in an Urban Police Department. *Administrative Science Quarterly, 20*(2), 207–228.

Van Maanen, J., & Schein, E. (1979). Toward a Theory of Organizational Socialization. In B. Staw (Ed.), *Research in Organizational Behaviour* (Vol. 1, pp. 209–264). Greenwich: JAI.

Weber, M. (1977). *Politik Aals Beruf*. Berlin: Duncker and Humblot. (Original work published 1919).

Whetten, D. A. (2006). Albert and Whetten Revisited, Strengthening the Concept of Organizational Identity. *Journal of Management Inquiry, 15,* 119–234.

Wilson, C. (1991). *The Influence of Police Specialisation on Job Satisfaction: A Comparison of General Duties Officers and Detectives, Report No. 109.* Adelaide: National Police Research Unit.

Wilson, C., & Beck, K. (1995). *The Impact of the Redesign of the Job of General Duties Patrol on the Motivation, Job Satisfaction and Organizational Commitment of Patrol Officers, Report No. 109.1.* Adelaide: National Police Research Unit.

# 3

# Social, Personal and Group Identity

The theme of identity will now be built upon by moving from the organisational to the cultural. As individuals, we construct our identities in relation to the groups with which we interact. This chapter seeks to explore the issues of social, personal and group identity and the formation of the self. This will be done through an analysis of the social identity and intergroup relations literature. Understanding organisations is as much about understanding the individuals who work within those organisations as anything else, and this can be more fully understood through an understanding of cultural attitudes, values and beliefs. Appreciating how these attitudes, values and beliefs are formed within the organisational environment is essential to a fuller understanding of the development of policing cultures, which this research aims to examine.

Chapter 2 sought to tease out the differences between the more traditional literature on 'organisational culture' and 'corporate culture', and the more recent and currently favoured focus upon 'organisational identity'. Whilst some, it was argued, use the terms interchangeably, the terms appear to have fundamental conceptual differences between them which require more than a semantic separation. The focus of organisational identity is outward looking, management focused and driven by a belief

© The Author(s) 2017
S. Charman, *Police Socialisation, Identity and Culture*,
DOI 10.1007/978-3-319-63070-0_3

in the tangible and discoverable nature of the identity of an organisation. This is crucial in terms of its use in the corporate world as a measure of the standing of an organisation and its future potential. Organisational culture is a broader concept which embraces the less tangible, tacit and symbolic symbols of an organisation, which include its shared values, beliefs, assumptions, myths, stories and rituals. These cultural artefacts make up what has been referred to as the 'cultural web' (Johnson and Scholes 1992). This debate has been briefly restated here in order that the following discussion of social, personal and group identity is not confused with organisational identity, which is a much more corporate and organisationally driven concept.

## Social Identity Theory

Social identity theories have emerged within the field of social psychology relatively recently and were first developed by Henri Tajfel in the 1970s in the UK. They now form a significant part of the social psychological literature and the area continues to grow and expand. It is not the intention of this book to focus extensively on these issues, as there are analyses and reviews of this concept elsewhere (Tajfel 1978; Moscovici 1972). This book seeks to explore the sociological and cultural phenomena of the development of policing cultures and the important influences upon the early stages of a police career. An extensive focus upon social psychological phenomena is therefore not necessary. However, an understanding, however limited, of the psychological interpretations of group behaviour should help us to appreciate more about the changing nature of new recruits to the police service.

Fundamentally, social identity theories are concerned with the relationship between the individual, the self and the group. An individual's social identity is the "knowledge of his membership of a social group (or groups) together with the value and emotional significance attached to that membership" (Tajfel 1978, p. 63). The interests of social identity theories lie in all aspects of group life and, in particular, in the notion that collective action can better be explained through group activity and intergroup relations than through individual action or interpersonal interaction. Indeed, Tajfel is highly critical of the discipline of social psychology, which he believed had failed to adequately address the importance of collective behaviour in social life in its pursuance of a greater appreciation of individuals and their interactions (1981). Whilst it is important to acknowledge that social behaviour does originate within individuals, it is nonetheless apparent, according to Tajfel, that the social context of this behaviour has been neglected. Additionally, it is not enough to merely attempt to understand group behaviour as individual behaviour in groups. Social identity is not individualistic but concerned with "socially-shared patterns of individual behaviour" (Tajfel 1981, p. 49). Social identity is therefore distinct from personal identity, where the latter focuses more upon the third level of human programming referred to in Chap. 2—the *unique* characteristics which are exclusive to each individual (Hofstede 2001). Personal identity is that sense of self which is built up over time. Whilst personal identity focuses on the differences, on the idiosyncrasies of a person, social identity conversely looks to the shared aspects of individual interaction and collective behaviour.

The applicability of social identity theories goes far and wide, and it is no surprise that the literature in the area is prolific. The approach is used in analyses of

> prejudice, discrimination, ethnocentrism, stereotyping, intergroup conflict, conformity, normative behaviour, group polarization, crowd behaviour, organizational behaviour, leadership, deviance, and group cohesiveness. (Hogg 2006, p. 111)

Social identity is therefore a mainstay of social psychology in explaining many social and group phenomena. As this chapter will later illuminate, it has also more recently been "rediscovered" by criminology (Bradford et al. 2014, p. 527).

Although there are clearly variations in approach and terminology from the large number of social psychologists who have an interest in this field, there is enough general agreement to be able to report upon some recognisable stages and consequences of identity formation. The two which will be considered here are, first, categorisation and, second, comparison. Identity is formed through a process of self- or social cate-gorisation. People are motivated towards self-categorisation with the group when they adhere to the values of the group, are given a voice within the group, support the group's leaders and identify with the role that has been assigned to them (Bradford et al. 2014, p. 529). Throughout their lives, people will belong to a number of groups (or categories). These social categories are already formed within our structured society (albeit in their socially constructed state) and therefore individuals 'join' or 'adopt' these categories already in place (Hogg and Abrams 1988). A person's identity can therefore be seen as a sum of the multiple social categories that they have adopted. What makes a person unique is the combination of social categories that have been adopted (Stets and Burke 2000).

One of the consequences of self- or social categorisation is that mem-bers will emphasise those behaviours, attitudes and beliefs of theirs which are *perceived* to be fundamental to the essence of the group and in tune with the other group members. Additionally, 'new' members will high-light and accentuate the differences between themselves and out-group members (Stets and Burke 2000). Members will remain within the group so long as that membership contributes in a positive way to the self-image of the member (Tajfel 1981).

Whilst this notion of self- or social categorisation tells us much about the human capacity to organise and categorise the environment in which they live, it tells us nothing about the impact of that categorisation or how those categorisations are used and understood by those at the cen-tre of them. Therefore, the second stage of identity formation that will be considered here is comparison. No group survives in isolation, and as has already been seen, much of this group formation and self- or social categorisation emerges as a result of selectively choosing categories or groups based upon the *perceived* similarities of the individuals with the group and, therefore logically, the *perceived* differences between other groups or categories. This very political idea of exclusion and of 'other-ness' has a long history in both sociology and criminology. Within social identity theory too, 'comparison' appears to be its lifeblood. Humans evaluate their opinions, their successes, their abilities and more through a comparison with others (Festinger 1954). This was first referred to by Sumner as 'ethnocentrism' (1906; cited in Tajfel 1982), which aimed to encapsulate both the hostility to out-groups and the referencing to all other values in terms of their similarity or difference to those of the in-group. This comparison with others is done not only with those individuals and groups who are perceived to be similar but with those individuals and groups who are perceived to be different. The purpose of this differentiation is not only to sustain the group itself but also, on a more individual level, to contribute to the self-image and to enhance the self-image of the group member. As Tajfel has stated, "we are what we are because *they* are not what we are" (1981, p. 323, original emphasis). This works to more clearly define the boundaries of the group and to emphasise the group's shared meanings. The outcome of this categorisation then is that the differences between in-group members become minimised and the differences between out-group members become more sharply exaggerated (Tajfel 1982).

We can see here how the impact of storytelling, a cultural artefact much associated with police officers (and discussed in later chapters), will play a part in the maintenance and reinforcement of these boundaries. Through constructing these boundaries, group members are setting the limits on what is 'in' and what is 'out' in a manner that Nietzsche referred to as the 'constitution of horizons' (1874/1997). In doing this, group members are also establishing a cultural memory, which is the holder of shared knowledge with which a group can not only identify but also guide future behaviour (Assmann and Czaplicka 1995).

This boundary-setting demarcation activity within groups based upon perceived similarities and differences with other groups has an impact on members within the group and those outside of it. Hacking (2011) discusses the 'looping effect' of classifying human beings in this manner. People, once classified, may well alter their behaviour based upon common preconceptions of what it is to be classified as such. For example, when a person becomes a police officer, they may change their behaviour based upon their or other people's perceptions of what it is to be a police officer. Continuing my exemplar of a police officer, Hacking's 'looping effect' cycle has a second stage, which is that people may have to then change their perceptions of what it is to be a police officer because those who are newly classified do not quite fit the notions of what they felt being a police officer was about (2011). This then may subsequently affect the people who are classified. This looping effect therefore perpetuates. These ideas share much with the labelling perspectives of criminology and clearly highlight the very fluid and dynamic nature of social identity. This idea of social identity as relational and contextual fits much more with the social constructionist (rather than the more psychological) approach to identity, which means that identity can be reformulated and reshaped in the context of the groups with which the individual is interacting (Dick 2005).

As has hopefully been illuminated in this brief discussion of social identity and its formation, the focus lies within the group and the individual's perception of their position within that group. However, identity, as opposed to social identity, has a slightly different focus (Stets and Burke 2000). Whereas the focus of social identity theory lies in the group and the people within the group, the focus of identity theory is on the *role* of the person within the group. This role-based analysis still values the importance of self-categorisation (although referred to as identification), but is related to categorisation within a role rather than within the membership of a group. Whereas acquiring a social identity entails finding similarities with others in a group or groups, acquiring an identity requires the fulfilment of the expectations of the role (Stets and Burke 2000). This is a fundamental difference therefore between support for the notion of *the group* being the underlying basis for the formation of identity (social identity theory) and support for the notion of *the* role that someone performs being the basis for the formation of identity. However, the dynamic nature of groups and identity should also be acknowledged (Oberweis and Musheno 1999). Stets and Burke (2000) would argue that actually both the group and the role need to be fully understood and appreciated because "being and doing are both central features of one's identity" (p. 234). Subsequent chapters in this book will focus upon the development of policing cultures within the lower ranks of the police service and the acquisition of occupational identity in very similar terms—learning, becoming and being.

# The Self

Although this chapter has so far concentrated on the development of social identity, particularly in relation to group activity, that is not to say that some analysis of the development of personal identity, or the self, is not relevant here. The development of social identity and the development of the self, plus the interaction between the two within the groups of which we are a part, are not clear linear developments but rather more unaligned and contradictory. Understanding the group also requires an understanding of the individual. An important element of our sense of self relates to how we believe other people perceive us and particularly how that manifests itself in our shared groupings. Taken that way then, an understanding of the self is important for an understanding of the group, and an understanding of the group is important for an understanding of the self.

Social scientists have long been interested in both the self and the socialisation of the self. Cooley's famous 'looking glass self' considered these perceptions on three different levels—how we feel others perceive us, how we imagine others judge us and, finally, our self-image (1902). George Herbert Mead's analysis of the self also incorporated a more outward-looking focus (1934). He believed the 'self' was an inherently social concept. Some of his most influential work focused on the conceptual differences between an analysis of the 'I' (an individual's sense of themselves) and that of the 'me' (the sense of self that we create having reacted and responded to the feedback of others). It is the interaction between the 'I' and the 'me' which creates our sense of 'self'. Mead also considered how our self-image develops through different stages, particularly during childhood (1934). However, adopting the social constructionist approach to identity, as mentioned earlier, our sense of self is not a static, fixed entity, and the movement through to adulthood does not imply that the construction of the self is a mission accomplished. Significant life developments and changes will undoubtedly have an impact on the sense of self due to the interaction with, and reactions from, others. This is likely to be particularly the case when it involves the transition into new occupational groups.

Goffman's ground-breaking dramaturgical model of social life and the presentation of the self remind us that we are playing a number of different and often contradictory roles (1959). Additionally, other people's interactions with us as we play those roles will have an impact on the 'performance'. From a cultural perspective, and in terms of our interest in the development of culture, this is extremely interesting, as Goffman refers not just to the social and verbal interactions between people but also to the more tacit cultural phenomena such as rituals, body language, gestures and even silences. Goffman distinguishes between 'front-stage' and 'back-stage' performances (1959). These front-stage performances, as in everyday life, are well-rehearsed scripts which conform to set conventions and are generally known and understood by both actors and audience. In policing terms, these front-stage activities would refer to police–public interactions plus police interactions with more senior officers. Back-stage activities however are different from front-stage activities and are those activities which are more hidden from public view. In Goffman's original work based upon his fieldwork on the Shetland Isles, his back-stage analogy was used to describe the waitress at home or with friends rather than serving tables (1959). However, we should not assume, as many do, that back-stage activities are where the 'real' self emerges. Goffman focuses clearly on *roles*, and the self is constituted of a variety of these roles, each fundamentally contributing to the overall self. In policing terms, back-stage performances would be located in patrol cars, in police canteens and restrooms, and in non-public-facing areas.

It would be naïve however to imagine that the development and crafting of the self takes place in a world devoid of power, politics and history. Goffman distinguishes between the more conscious communicative signs which are displayed during interactions and the less conscious and more unintended signs, which can play their role in undermining the management of impressions (1959). Hallett (2003) relates these unintended signs of Goffman to the work of Bourdieu and his concept of habitus. Bourdieu views society as being influenced by the social, cultural and economic capital of its inhabitants (1990). It is not a fixed entity and is constantly renegotiated and relegitimised, guided by what he refers to as the 'habitus'. Bourdieu defines habitus as "a structuring structure, which organises practices and the perception of practices" (1984, p. 170). A person's habitus is therefore unique and is guided and influenced by the way an individual has developed within their social space. It is not however an individual process, as that individual will have developed their habitus within a social context. How an individual acts (their 'practice') is therefore the external manifestation of their habitus. This in turn will reflect their experiences of their position within the social order. This is where the conditions of power are therefore apparent.

Power was an essential feature of the work of the French philosopher Michel Foucault, whose academic career was built upon an analysis of the relationship between power and knowledge. In his later work, he added a consideration of the development of the self. In addition to his work on ethics, which was concerned with the relationship that an individual has with themselves, Foucault also considered the position of the 'subjective individual' (1980). Individuals are not influenced merely by the structures surrounding them but by what he refers to as 'power-knowledge'—a pervasive and dispersed power which is spread throughout modern life and involves control over what is defined as knowledge (Foucault 1972). Therefore, the self, according to Foucault, is influenced strongly by how that individual appears to other social actors, rather than how the individual experiences themselves through self-reflection. Much like Goffman and Mead then (although admittedly from different standpoints), Foucault argues that the 'self' does not emerge from within, but rather in interaction with others and in response to others. Social identity is therefore connected to the more 'social self', which provides a link between individuals and groups. An analysis of the development of policing cultures amongst new recruits to the police service therefore needs to take account of this. Officers' views of themselves with their new identity as police officers (and as such, holders of coercive powers) are shaped by their interactions with others and the reactions of others to their new identity. This comes in the form of all of the many groups to which new officers belong and all of the many new interactions they have with other groups—family, friends, old colleagues, new colleagues, tutors, managers, members of the public and so on. An analysis, from the perspective of new recruits, of who they feel plays the most important role in shaping their new identities will be a feature of Part II of this book.

# Collectivism and Collective Memory

The recognisable stages and consequences of identity formation, and in particular a consideration of, first, categorisation and, second, comparison, were discussed earlier in this chapter. One of the logical consequences of identity with a group is a sense of obligation to act in the best interests of the group, to adhere to the values and norms of the group and to cooperate in a collective manner with the group's activities. Collectivism can be said to occur within groups when "the demands and interests of groups take precedence over the demands and needs of individuals" (Wagner 1995, p. 153). The study of cooperation and collectivism has a long history. Tönnies wrote of the differentiation between *gemeinschaft* and *gesellschaft* (1887/1957), along with Durkheim's *mechanical* and *organic* solidarity (1893/1984), Weber's *social relationships* (1922/1978) and Parsons' self-orientation and collectivity orientation (1951). Although these accounts are not bound by similarities in their stance on the *development* of the more collective nature of group rather than on individual activity, all share an appreciation of the *nature* of collective orientations being shaped by shared obligations, affective bonds and the desire to pursue group interests, at the expense of individual interests. Collectivists favour the quest of group interests and are likely to pursue opportunities, where possible, for collaborative activity, irrespective of any personal ramifications of so doing (Wagner 1995).

Stephenson and Stewart (2001), in their typology of collectivism, identify three stages of occupational collectivism, which it will be useful to consider in the context of the development of policing cultures. The first stage is trade union collectivism, where activity and a collective 'voice' are led by one group, most often a trade union. The second stage is referred to as workplace collectivism, which is defined by a willingness of colleagues to support each other, irrespective of whether it is a work or non-work issue. The third stage of occupational collectivism, as defined by Stephenson and Stewart (2001, p. 3.2), is referred to as the "social collectivism of everyday life". These networks of support are characterised by their extension outside the workplace and incorporate friends, family and work colleagues but may impact on both home life and work life. The stronger the levels of collectivism, illustrated in this typology by a move-ment from the trade union model of collectivism to the collectivism of everyday life, the greater the levels of cooperation amongst group mem-bers. This therefore goes beyond collectivism being described as merely a "passive social-coping mechanism" (McBride and Martinez-Lucio 2011, p. 801), which indeed is an explanation of police behaviour seen regularly in the policing cultures literature. Collectivism and collective behaviour are instead connected in a much more integrated way to one's personal, social and occupational identity.

The collective memory also plays a role in the development of collec-tivism (Assmann and Czaplicka 1995; McBride and Martinez-Lucio 2011). Human beings possess a collective memory which is constituted of two parts (Assmann and Czaplicka 1995). The 'communicative mem-ory' is based upon everyday communication and relates to membership of the various groups that an individual belongs to. The 'cultural mem-ory', on the other hand, is fixed in time and relates more to the organisa-tional symbols which, over time, become culturally understood as relating to that organisation. Assmann and Czaplicka (1995, p. 130) refer to this as the "store of knowledge" of an organisation. This might be in the form of historical events, texts, rites and so on—the recollection of past experi-ences and past support work to reinforce the shared positions that groups adopt. In policing terms, this operates as much with negative past experi-ences as it does with positive past experiences. Reference to the past con-tributes to the shared identity of officers but also guides future behaviour in indicating what 'works' and what 'fails' in terms of policing responses. This links closely with the literature on organisational culture. Schein (1985) has argued that culture is transmitted in two different ways, either through 'problem-solving'/'positive reinforcement' or through 'anxiety avoidance'/'trauma'. The former refers to a policy of repeating successful work strategies, the latter to a policy of avoiding unpleasant situations by basing thought and action on previous negative experiences. Whether the police use their organisational memory to good effect by reflecting upon and learning from their organisational history is up for question (Savage 2007), but what is important in this context is the power of occupational memories to cement and bolster occupational identities. The strong sym-bolic power of the police, as discussed in Chap. 2, coupled with a strong collective memory, plays a significant role in the development of new recruits' identities as police officers, which will be examined closely in Part II.

## Cooperation in Groups

Social identity theory is therefore a useful framework through which to analyse an individual's engagement with their group or groups. The group engagement model attempts to appreciate why people engage in their groups and considers the influence that the group has on a person's sense of self (Tyler and Blader 2003; Blader and Tyler 2009). The authors argue that it is particularly important to understand group behaviour in order to more fully appreciate the antecedents of attitudes, values and cooperative behaviour. Therefore, in terms of an analysis of the development of policing cultures amongst new recruits to the police, an understanding of where their attitudes and values emerge from and what they are influenced by is especially important. It is the *discretionary* cooperation which is built upon values and attitudes, rather than *mandatory* cooperation, which is based upon sanctions for non-compliance, which is of more relevance here. Clearly, a group will be stronger and more cohesive if it relies upon the former, rather than the latter, model of cooperation.

Cooperation with the group and effort on behalf of the group are determined both by how strong that identification is with the group and how much being part of the group features in a person's definition of their social identity. A stronger identification will, in part, be connected with how the group treats the individual (Bradford 2014; this relates to procedural justice evaluations, which will be examined shortly). However, there should be no collective pressure felt by the group to persuade or cajole individuals to cooperate. Members are essentially motivated to meet the needs of the group and to foster the success of the group because of the strong overlap between the group and the self (Blader and Tyler 2009). Members are motivated to cooperate in order to maintain and to promote a positive identity. As was previously discussed, group members reinforce and accentuate those positive elements of the group which coalesce with their interpretations of themselves, and therefore, this overlap, whether objectively or otherwise, will always be present.

Where a strong social identity is present within an organisation, research has identified that there is an increase in motivation, work effort, loyalty and collective action (Blader and Tyler 2009). Indeed, these authors also found that social identity is a stronger determinant of the extent to which employees will go beyond what is expected in terms of fulfilling their role than economic outcomes. The study concluded therefore that social identity can be considered to be the "primary basis of people's engagement in their groups" (Blader and Tyler 2009, p. 457).

## Policing and Social Identity

With social identity being so fundamental to not only the formation of an individual's sense of self and identity but also to the manner in which individuals engage with others, both personally and professionally, it is no surprise that the academic literature on policing and social identity has begun to grow. Chapter 2 considered some of the narratives of policing which are closely connected with the strong symbolic power which the police hold, for example, police officers as 'defenders of the peace'. This is a strong cultural message about the function of the police and is an image which is not discouraged from within the organisation. Chapter 2 however focused more upon the identity of the police as seen from outside the organisation. Representations and commonly held understandings of policing come from a wide variety of areas of social life, from politics, from the public and from the media, for example. These understandings (and sometimes misunderstandings) about the identity and role of the police work in ways that both eulogise and demonise the police. The police are held up to be potential crime fighters in a fight against crime that is without structure or meaning. What is of interest in this chapter is not those externally held interpretations of the identity of the police but the social identity of police officers as seen from the inside. It would be impossible to be able to demonstrate a homogeneous identity of police officers. As this chapter has illustrated, individuals are members of multiple groups and a person's identity can therefore be seen as a sum of the multiple social categories they have adopted. Being a police officer is one part of that sum. Research has indicated that it is an extremely significant part but nonetheless not on its own (Oberweis and Musheno 1999; Ashforth and Kreiner 1999). What makes a person unique is the combination of social categories that have been adopted (Stets and Burke 2000). However, an attempt to appreciate how the police perceive their identity plays an important role in how they enact their duties in relation to the public and is therefore worthy of further investigation here.

One interesting framework which has been invoked to better understand the occupational ideologies of police officers is that of 'dirty work'. Dirty work was a phrase first used by Everett Hughes and referred to occupations which might be perceived by others to be degrading, disgusting or requiring regular contact with 'undesirable' people (1951). Hughes later defined this more clearly as occupations (or indeed tasks) which involve a moral, social or physical taint (1958). Subsequent work has focused upon policing as being a part of the 'dirty work' arena due to the 'social taint' of coming into regular contact with events and people who are viewed to be 'undesirable' and who themselves are stigmatised (Dick 2005). The interest, from a social identity perspective, is in how police officers, despite this stigma, manage to portray their identities in a positive light, given that occupational identities form a major part of the overall sum of identity-making material.

Ashforth and Kreiner (1999) argue that in order to convey a positive social identity and to therefore enhance self-esteem, 'dirty workers' will use a variety of techniques to neutralise the more negative aspects of the job and to promote the more positive ones. This is extremely relevant in terms of the police use of storytelling and other cultural techniques in order to construct a favourable social and cultural identity, which will be examined in later chapters. The three techniques that Ashforth and Kreiner (1999) outline are reframing, recalibrating and refocusing. Reframing seeks to provide an alternative meaning to the stigmatised work, so in policing terms, the 'no day is ever the same' narrative is an alternative portrayal of the often unpleasant and difficult situations that police officers come across. Recalibrating involves accentuating those elements of the job which are conducive to the self-identified image of the work. In policing terms, this might involve a focus upon the 'crime-fighting' aspects of the work, rather than on the 'peace-keeping' elements. Finally, refocusing involves an entire movement of focus away from the more stigmatised elements of the job and onto the positive features. From a policing perspective, this would involve invoking the narratives of the 'thin blue line' and 'protection of victims', for example, rather than alternative versions of coercive control. All of these techniques are important to the new recruit. A newcomer to an organisation is engaged in the challenging role of sense-making and identity formation. An important element of our sense of self relates to how we believe other people perceive us. These techniques therefore not only contribute to the social identity of the individual within the group but also work towards enhancing the occupational identity of the group, as will now be seen.

The results from this 'dirty work' research are very interesting from a social identity perspective. Rather than the stigma of dirty work *threatening* the identity of occupational groups, research in this area has indicated that the nature of the work actually serves to *enhance* the occupational identity of 'dirty workers' (Ashforth and Kreiner 1999; Dick 2005). The predicted threat to the occupational identity is manipulated and reversed so that, rather than the threat be internalised, it is instead turned outwards and attributed to the public. It is the public and their perceived views of dirty workers that becomes the threat. The outcome of that threat is an enhanced interpretation of 'us' versus 'them' and the construction of sharp psychological boundaries around the dirty workers as a group (Ashforth and Kreiner 1999).

The strategies to counter what are then considered to be potential threats from the outside are not only to differentiate your group from those outsiders but also (as seen earlier in the general discussion of social identity theories) to enact "downward social comparisons" (Gibbons and Gerrard 1991, p. 319). An upward social comparison is associated more with motivational or aspirational purposes, whereas downward social comparisons are a more defensive mechanism, often associated with inherent vulnerabilities within the occupational group. Interestingly, these comparisons are not exclusively focused outside of the occupational group or groups. These comparisons can be used between and even within occupational groups (Ashforth and Kreiner 1999). In policing terms, this downward comparison has been seen between police officers and fire officers (Charman 2013), and is also a feature within police departments, such as the attitudes of firearms officers towards other policing colleagues (Cain 2012).

Ashforth and Kreiner's work (1999) was not focused upon policing but upon the more general principles of 'dirty work' and on the consequences of this for identity formation and occupational ideologies. What is interesting however is that the authors go on to list certain conditions of occupational groups which are likely to lead to an enhanced sense of identity and cohesion, all of which are relevant to policing. These conditions, which promote the development of subcultures, include collective socialisation, isolation, group longevity, inherent danger, and unconventional working hours and habits (Ashforth and Kreiner 1999). This research on 'dirty work' and its application to policing highlights the importance of the social identity of the police in terms of enhancing cohesion and maintaining self-legitimacy. How police officers see themselves and legitimise their role and their actions is fundamental to a better understanding of their behaviour. This relates to another area that was first discussed in Chap. 2, of procedural justice.

## Policing, Social Identity and Procedural Justice

Chapter 2 considered some of the general principles of procedural justice in relation to policing. When the principles of procedural justice are transferred to the workplace, rather than to police–public encounters, which were discussed in Chap. 2, we can see that when an organisation employs the principles of fairness, equity, transparency and dialogue, this will enhance the legitimacy of the organisation in the eyes of the employees. In policing terms, this is also likely to enhance and encourage a more service-oriented approach towards policing activities (Bradford et al. 2014). Argentinian research has particularly highlighted the importance of open communication and dialogue between police managers and police officers as a key feature in enhancing internal legitimacy (Haas et al. 2015).

The legitimacy of the police in the eyes of its members is therefore of critical importance. It relates not only to officers' attitudes towards the organisation itself but also plays an important role in shaping their self-legitimacy and, relating to that, their sense of group identity. This legitimacy is formed through interpersonal interaction. Research has found that officers who are confident with the sense of their own legitimacy are more likely to positively identify with their organisation and are more likely to utilise the principles of procedural justice in their encounters with the public (Bradford and Quinton 2014). This self-legitimacy is important in enabling officers to conduct themselves in acceptable ways and is based upon both their identification as police officers (thus marking themselves out as different from ordinary citizens) and their identification as power-holders (Bradford and Quinton 2014). A more cynical cultural adaptation to policing is negatively linked with levels of self-legitimacy. Bradford and Quinton conclude however by saying, "Perhaps, it is simply 'being' a police officer … that makes people feel they are legitimate power-holders" (2014, p. 1040). It is 'being' a police officer that is a focus of the research upon which this book is based and will be one of the themes in Part II of this book.

How and to what extent police officers identify themselves as such is thus very important as a part of this debate. The ways in which policing cultures will impact upon police officers and the ways in which they adapt and adopt aspects of the policing cultures will have an impact both upon their sense of legitimacy and the behaviours that flow from that. Social identity then is clearly an important discussion not only in terms of the internal cultures of the police but in the very essence of the way in which citizens are policed.

As discussed in Chap. 2, a citizen–police encounter will be aided by the presence of a shared acceptance of the values of the police. Compliance is based not only upon the threat of sanctions but upon a belief in the right of the police to hold authoritative power. Likewise, if police officers align themselves with the shared values and beliefs of their group, then they are more likely to act in ways which support that group and will seek to identify with that group. Members will emphasise those behaviours and attitudes they hold which are *perceived* to be fundamental to the essence of the group and in tune with the other group members. Using the word 'group' here, rather than 'organisation', is deliberate.

Police officers may well build their identities with reference to occupational groups whose values and attitudes they adhere to and perhaps aspire to. Those occupational groupings which may relate to training colleagues, shift members, line managers and so on do not necessarily represent the policing organisation. This is where the fundamental difference between organisational identity and organisational culture is perhaps most apparent.

If we accept that organisational identity refers to the more outward-looking, management-focused aspects of an organisation, and organisational culture is a broader concept which embraces the less tangible, tacit and symbolic symbols of an organisation, then this argument becomes clearer. Whilst organisational identity is important from a strategic and management perspective, what cannot be ignored is organisational culture, because this is where the stronger influences may lie. This is where the influences of policing cultures play their very important role. Adherence with the 'group' and that group's values and beliefs in whatever form that takes within policing may not necessarily mean that the group will share the values and beliefs of the organisation as a whole. Understanding the influences upon new police recruits is essential then in hoping to form a better understanding of the formation of social identities within policing. Compliance, based upon the principles of procedural justice, combined with an enhanced sense of social identity, is more likely to be achieved if members share the values and beliefs of a given group. The consequences of this are cooperation, satisfaction, high levels of trust and commitment.

Blader and Tyler (2009) therefore link procedural justice, social identity and behaviour together. Behaviour is linked with treatment by the group. If a positive judgement is made about the group's treatment of an individual, then according to the principles of social exchange theory discussed in Chap. 2, reciprocal cooperative behaviour is likely to result. This has the potential to enhance the identification with the group, which then increases the commitment to the group. Social identity therefore provides a clear link between fair treatment and cooperation. As Blader and Tyler (2009) have argued in relation to their group engagement model described earlier:

(a) procedural justice impacts behaviour, (b) procedural justice impacts social identity, and (c) social identity impacts behaviour, and ... social identity accounts for at least part of the reason that procedural justice impacts behaviour. (2009, p. 447)

This clearly has an enormous impact upon police–citizen encounters. However, in terms of the relevance for this book, it also has an important impact upon how and why officers may act in the ways that they do. How they identify with their occupational group and how they are treated by that group will not only impact upon their behaviour with their colleagues, but also has the potential to impact upon their behaviour with the public. This could potentially move the focus of police legitimacy away from the macro-level concerns of corruption, public order and politics, and more towards the micro-level story of the low-level, often-overlooked everyday encounters between the police and the public (Bradford et al. 2014; Bradford 2014). It is important therefore that we understand more about these "identity-relevant aspects of officer behaviour" (Bradford et al. 2014, p. 544). Sociologists have long argued that police actions shape people's social identities (Becker 1963; Ericson 1975). What a consideration of procedural justice can help us to do when considered from within the organisation is identify how and to what extent the social identities of the police can shape not only their own actions and behaviours but also those of the public.

This is not to say that organisational goals too cannot be influenced by procedural justice. Research within the policing field has indicated that managers' use of procedural justice in their encounters with staff not only positively impacts upon levels of trust within the organisation but also shows the potential for officers themselves to be more likely to adopt the principles of procedural justice in their encounters with the public (Bradford et al. 2014). There are calls therefore for police recruitment policies to take more account of a proclivity towards the principles of procedural justice within the screening and selection process (Bond et al. 2015). In addition, Argentinian research inside a police organisation found links between trust in supervisors, internal procedural justice and increased compliance when clear decision-making and communication were apparent (Haas et al. 2015). If, through its actions, communications, policies and behaviours, an organisation is able to provide its individual members with a positive sense of self and a favourable social identity, then cooperation is likely to ensue and the motivation to perform (seen in Chap. 2 in relation to affective organisational commitment) is likely to flourish (Bradford et al. 2014).

This chapter has sought to make sense of the literature relating to social identity. This is important in the context of the research considered within this book, which attempts to understand how cultures are formed and learned by new recruits to the police. New recruits are not acting within a vacuum, and therefore, collective action can better be explained through group activity and intergroup relations than through individual action or interpersonal interaction. Social identity theories focus upon those patterns of individual behaviour which are socially shared. The joining of these occupational groupings brings with it the processes of self- or social categorization, meaning that members will emphasise those behaviours, attitudes and beliefs of theirs which are *perceived* to be fundamental to the essence of the group and in tune with the other group members. Additionally, 'new' members will highlight and accentuate the differences between themselves and out-group members. This self-categorisation, in addition to the social comparison with other groups, plays an important role in how police officers acclimatise to their new role, how they justify their actions and how they interact with members of the public.

# References

Ashforth, B., & Kreiner, G. (1999). "How Can You Do It?" Dirty Work and the Challenge of Constructing a Positive Identity. *The Academy of Management Review, 24*(3), 413–434.

Assmann, J., & Czaplicka, J. (1995). Collective Memory and Cultural Identity. *New German Critique, 65*, 125–133.

Becker, H. (1963). *Outsiders: Studies in the Sociology of Deviance*. New York: Free Press.

Blader, S., & Tyler, T. (2009). Testing and Extending the Group Engagement Model: Linkages Between Social Identity Theory, Procedural Justice, Economic Outcomes and Extra Role Behaviour. *Journal of Applied Psychology, 94*(2), 445–464.

Bond, C., Murphy, K., & Porter, L. (2015). Procedural Justice in Policing: The First Phase of an Australian Longitudinal Study of Officer Attitudes and Intentions. *Crime, Law and Social Change, 64*, 229–245.

Bourdieu, P. (1984). *Distinction: A Social Critique of the Judgement of Taste.* London: Routledge.

Bourdieu, P. (1990). *The Logic of Practice.* Cambridge: Polity Press.

Bradford, B. (2014). Policing and Social Identity: Procedural Justice, Inclusion and Co-operation Between Police and Public. *Policing and Society, 24*(1), 22–43.

Bradford, B., & Quinton, P. (2014). Self-Legitimacy, Police Culture and Support for Democratic Policing in an English Constabulary. *British Journal of Criminology, 54*(6), 1023–1046.

Bradford, B., Jackson, J., & Hough, M. (2014). Police Futures and Legitimacy: Redefining 'Good Policing'. In J. Brown (Ed.), *The Future of Policing* (pp. 79–99). London: Routledge.

Bradford, B., Murphy, K., & Jackson, J. (2014). Officers as Mirrors: Policing, Procedural Justice and the (Re) Production of Social Identity. *British Journal of Criminology, 54*(4), 527–550.

Bradford, B., Quinton, P., Myhill, A., & Porter, G. (2014). Why Do 'the Law' Comply? Procedural Justice, Group Identification and Officer Motivation in Police Organizations. *European Journal of Criminology, 11*(1), 110–131.

Cain, D. (2012). *Gender Within a Specialised Police Department: An Examination of the Cultural Dynamics of a Police Firearms Unit, Unpublished Professional Doctorate.* Portsmouth: University of Portsmouth.

Charman, S. (2013). Sharing a Laugh: The Role of Humour in Relationships Between Police Officers and Ambulance Staff. *International Journal of Sociology and Social Policy, 33*(3–4), 152–166.

Cooley, C. (1902). *Human Nature and the Social Order.* London: Transaction Publishers.

Dick, P. (2005). Dirty Work Designations: How Police Officers Account for Their Use of Coercive Force. *Human Relations, 58*(11), 1363–1390.

Durkheim, E. (1984). *The Division of Labour in Society.* Basingstoke: Macmillan. (Original work published 1893).

Ericson, R. (1975). *Criminal Reactions: The Labelling Perspective.* Farnborough: Ashgate.

Festinger, L. (1954). A Theory of Social Comparison Processes. *Human Relations, 7*, 117–140.

Foucault, M. (1972). *The Archaeology of Knowledge and the Discourse on Language.* London: Tavistock.

Foucault, M. (1980). *Power/Knowledge: Selected Interviews and Other Writings*. London: Harvester Wheatsheaf.

Gibbons, F., & Gerrard, M. (1991). Downward Comparison and Coping with Threat. In J. Suls & T. Wills (Eds.), *Social Comparison: Contemporary Theory and Research* (pp. 317–345). Hillslade: Lawrence Erlbaum Associates.

Goffman, E. (1959). *The Presentation of Self in Everyday Life*. New York: Doubleday Anchor.

Haas, N., van Craen, M., Skogan, W., & Leitas, D. (2015). Explaining Officer Compliance: The Importance of Procedural Justice and Trust Inside a Police Organization. *Criminology and Criminal Justice, 15*(4), 442–463.

Hacking, I. (2011). Between Michel Foucault and Erving Goffman: Between Discourse in the Abstract and Face-to-Face Interaction. *Economy and Society, 33*(3), 277–302.

Hallett, T. (2003). Symbolic Power and Organizational Culture. *Sociological Theory, 21*(2), 128–149.

Hofstede, G. (2001). *Culture's Consequences: International Differences in Work-Related Values* (2nd ed.). London: Sage.

Hogg, M. (2006). Social Identity Theory. In P. J. Burke (Ed.), *Contemporary Social Psychological Theories* (pp. 111–136). California: Stanford University Press.

Hogg, M., & Abrams, D. (1988). *Social Identifications: A Social Psychology of Intergroup Relations and Group Processes*. London: Routledge.

Hughes, E. (1951). Work and the Self. In J. Rohrer & M. Sherif (Eds.), *Social Psychology at the Crossroads* (pp. 313–323). New York: Harper and Brothers.

Hughes, E. (1958). *Men and Their Work*. Glencoe: Free Press.

Johnson, G., & Scholes, K. (1992). *Exploring Corporate Strategy*. Harlow: Pearson Education.

McBride, J., & Martinez-Lucio, M. (2011). Dimensions of Collectivism: Occupation, Community and the Increasing Role of Memory and Personal Dynamics in the Debate. *Work, Employment and Society, 25*(4), 794–805.

Mead, G. (1934). *Mind, Self and Society*. Chicago: University of Chicago Press.

Moscovici, S. (1972). Society and Theory in Social Psychology. In J. Israel & H. Tajfel (Eds.), *The Context of Social Psychology: A Critical Assessment* (pp. 17–68). London: Academic Press.

Nietzsche, F. (1997). *Untimely Meditations*. In D. Breazeale (Ed.), *Cambridge Texts in the History of Philosophy*. Cambridge: Cambridge University Press. (Original work published 1874).

Oberweis, T., & Musheno, M. (1999). Policing Identities: Cop Decision Making and the Constitution of Citizens. *Law and Social Inquiry, 24*(4), 897–923.

Parsons, T. (1951). *The Social System.* London: Routledge and Kegan Paul.

Savage, S. (2007). *Police Reform: Forces for Change.* Oxford: Oxford University Press.

Schein, E. (1985). *Organisational Culture and Leadership: A Dynamic View.* San Francisco: Jossey-Bass.

Stephenson, C., & Stewart, P. (2001). The Whispering Shadow: Collectivism and Individualism at Ikeda-Hoover and Nissan UK. *Sociological Research Online, 6*(3), 1–15.

Stets, J., & Burke, P. (2000). Identity Theory and Social Identity Theory. *Social Psychology Quarterly, 63*(3), 224–237.

Tajfel, H. (1978). Interindividual Behaviour and Intergroup Behaviour. In H. Tajfel (Ed.), *Differentiation Between Social Groups: Studies in the Social Psychology of Intergroup Relations* (pp. 27–60). London: Academic Press.

Tajfel, H. (1981). *Human Groups and Social Categories.* Cambridge: Cambridge University Press.

Tajfel, H. (1982). Social Psychology of Intergroup Relations. *Annual Review of Psychology, 33*, 1–39.

Tönnies, F. (1887). *Gemeinschaft und Gesellschaft.* Leipzig: Fues's Verlag. (Translated, 1957 by Charles Price Loomis as *Community and Society.* East Lansing: Michigan State University Press.)

Tyler, T., & Blader, S. (2003). The Group Engagement Model: Procedural Justice, Social Identity and Co-operative Behaviour. *Personality and Social Psychology Review, 7*(4), 349–361.

Wagner, J. (1995). Studies of Individualism-Collectivism: Effects on Co-operation in Groups. *The Academy of Management Journal, 38*(1), 152–172.

Weber, M. (1978). *Economy and Society.* California: University of California Press. (Original work published 1922).

# 4

# Training and Education in Policing

In this chapter, the focus will move from identity to learning and, in keeping with the structure of the book, will first consider this from an organisational perspective. Training and education within the British police has changed on numerous occasions throughout history. This chapter will seek to chart these changes by exploring the changing nature of entry-level police education and initial training. It will do this by, first, more fully analysing the difference between education and training, and then by considering the changing focus of this within the policing environment. The policing organisation has moved from a time where all training and some education took place 'on the job' to the current situation of recruitment, often solely coming from the wider police family and recruits funding aspects of their training through pre-join qualifications.

## Training or Education?

Historically, there has always been a rather uneasy relationship between the policing and education sectors. This has been characterised by distrust on both sides, trepidation and suspicion of the others' activities and a reluctance to engage in more meaningful collaborations. That is not to

S. Charman, *Police Socialisation, Identity and Culture,*
DOI 10.1007/978-3-319-63070-0_4

say that there were not pockets of innovation and collaboration between the two sectors, but it is to say that a more national picture of partnership was not apparent. There is no doubt that the current situation with regard to the relationship between the police service in England and Wales, and the higher education sector is markedly different. However, it is also clear that not all of the questions have been answered, not all of the suspicions have been allayed and not all of the potential has been unleashed.

But why the interest in the relationship between these two sectors anyway? Surely, it is the responsibility of the police service to train their new recruits to be competent police officers and the responsibility of universities to educate their students to be critical thinking graduates. This is where the interesting dichotomy between training and education comes into play. As the police service seeks to professionalise the occupation and move from being considered a 'trade' or 'craft' with its associated 'artisan status' to being considered a 'profession', so too do the requirements to more broadly invest in the *education* of its recruits, instead of thinking only in *training* terms. Although some authors have suggested that the differences between education and training are overstated (Wood and Tong 2009), there is more broad agreement that whilst training involves the acquisition of specific skills which are essential to perform a series of tasks, education is focused upon the development of critical thinking skills through embracing more conceptual and theoretical analyses (Jones 2016; Kratcoski 2004). Lee and Punch (2006, p. 81) have referred to these questioning, analytical, written and verbal skills as "social capital". What marks out the difference between a curriculum which is education focused and a curriculum which is training focused is the philosophy of the aims and objectives, the delivery methods and the assessment methods. The physical location of the delivery is not related to the pedagogical philosophy of the teaching and learning. White and Heslop (2012) propose that education is classroom based and training is street based, but as the following discussions will hopefully illuminate, the situation is far more complex than that.

The discussion about the inherent differences between training and education is relevant here only insofar as there might be a debate about what the role and functions of our police officers are. What do we want them to be? What do we want them to know? Are we content with officers having acquired the legal, technological and administrative skills associated with some aspects of police work? Or are we expecting police officers to also have a broad philosophical understanding of their own social history and that of the communities which they serve? Collier (2001, p. 451) refers to this distinction as the difference between "intellectual capital" (a stock of knowledge) and "intellectual capacity" (a flow of knowledge). That debate has unsurprisingly been apparent within policing organisations and the police studies literature in the UK and around the world for decades. The debate between education and training is therefore very important. The purpose of this chapter is to explore some of the historical approaches towards police training and the underlying ethos of what it sought to achieve. Learning to become a part of an organisation involves both formal and informal processes, and a more complete picture of this socialisation can only be drawn once all aspects of these processes are considered.

One of the mountains which policing organisations need to attempt to scale is that whilst education, as has been previously stated, has been viewed with suspicion and trepidation, training too has struggled to achieve high status (Oakley 1994). It is viewed as inferior to 'real' police work by many within the ranks and deemed to be not as effective as 'learning on the job' (Bayley and Bittner 1984). This is despite the fact that training is often cited as both the problem of, and the solution to, a variety of policing crises. The Scarman Report into the Brixton disorders in the early 1980s, the Macpherson Report into the death of Stephen Lawrence (published in 1999), the screening of the BBC *Secret Policeman* documentary in 2003 and the Commission for Racial Equality report in 2005 have all questioned the role that poor and/or inadequate training has had in the negative events which have unfolded (Scarman 1981; Macpherson 1999; Ford 2003; Commission for Racial Equality 2005). In a Home Affairs Committee debate on police reform, the importance of initial police training was made explicitly clear by Hazel Blears MP:

> [U]nless we get the probationer training right the culture change that I talked about in terms of police reforms … is not going to happen … it is when people first come into the service that you are setting their standards, their ethos, their skills and the nature of the encounter that they have with the public. (2004, Q320)

# Initial Police Training

Police training in England and Wales has historically favoured a militaristic and behaviourist approach. Behaviourism incorporates many individual theories of learning but broadly operates under the assumption of the learner as a machine that is 'fed' information or stimuli. The methods by which that input is controlled results in an outcome which can be predetermined (Birzer 2003). Learning outcomes are central to a behaviourist approach and can be objectively measured through observable changes in student behaviour. This style of learning is particularly suited to the acquisition of knowledge and skills, and to a more military style training. However, the net result of this is an officer who is a "quasi-military warrior" (McNeill 1982, p. viii) and a teaching style which has not allowed for the acquisition of less technical qualities such as problem-solving, leadership and judgement (Birzer 2003, pp. 30–31). A policing ethic, it is argued, cannot be either 'imposed' or 'taught' (White 2006). For an organisation where the largest amount of discretion lies with the most junior of its ranks, it is anomalous that the history of police training has focused upon this more rigid behaviourist stance.

This strong, militaristic style approach was very much a feature of police training for new recruits throughout much of the twentieth century. It was even delivered in establishments which had previously been armed services training facilities such as Ryton in the Midlands and Hendon in London. Various reports and committees attempted to tinker with aspects of the curriculum and delivery. Various organisations were established and then disbanded to oversee such changes: the Central Planning Unit, National Police Training, Centrex, the National Policing Improvement Agency and now the College of Policing. However, despite attempts to modify the classroom-based curriculum over the years to respond to these criticisms, it was the remainder of the police probationer training which took place on the streets in individual forces which was to remain the more significant site of the development of cultural attitudes (White and Heslop 2012).

A 1973 Home Office Working Party recommended a stronger focus on community relations rather than upon drill, first aid and law. This review also saw the introduction of the Central Planning Unit to better oversee and coordinate police training nationally. The University of East Anglia (UEA) review of training (commissioned by the Home Office) followed in 1986, which recommended a modular approach to police training, regular attachments to workplace environments and a more structured tutor constable scheme (MacDonald et al. 1986). This was in part due to the criticism of police training voiced by the Scarman Report regarding inner-city disorder in the early 1980s. This modular approach saw a number of stages that a new recruit passed through, including a mixture of residential training centre and force deployments.

Police training also saw change resulting from the Home Office Review of National Police Training (1998), Managing Learning from HMIC (1999a) and recommendations from the Stephen Lawrence Inquiry Report (Macpherson 1999), which encouraged police training to consider the 'why' of policing in addition to the 'how' (Clements and Jones 2009, p. 204). However, despite these reports and enquiries, police training continued to be delivered in this militaristic, behaviourist manner which focused upon the acquisition of knowledge, assessed by regular tests. Indeed, one of the conclusions of the UEA review was that the Central Planning Unit focused upon these test scores alone as the measure of success of the training, rather than any more evaluative judgement about the nature of the recruits (MacDonald et al. 1986). Initial police training was, during the majority of this period of time, conducted over a two-year period. Recruits were trained in one of eight regional training centres, where they were residential for a number of weeks (regularly changed but mostly approximately 12–15 weeks) and taught by police trainers (seconded serving police officers, generally of long service). What was evident was that there was a huge variety of teaching styles and competencies of police trainers, resulting in some variations in police training approaches (Constable and Smith 2015). Mathias (1988) described this training approach as

> training for the masses, mass produced, teacher centred, knowledge based, done in a traditional classroom setting and completely from the point of view of the police officer. (1988, p. 101)

The impetus for more substantial change had been building for many years, and the regular criticism and reviews of police training briefly mentioned here signalled a broader and more fundamental shift. However, the two 'touch papers' which signalled the end to the then methods of delivering police probationer training came in the rather different forms of an HMIC inspection report and a BBC documentary.

The HMIC published its 'Training Matters' thematic inspection of police probationer training, which included 59 recommendations for change in 2002. It was a powerful and comprehensive review of the system which concluded that police probationer training was not fit for purpose. Criticism revolved around six aspects of the training programmes: the management structure, the learning requirement, inconsistency of delivery and lack of quality assurance, the fragility of the tutor constable scheme, ineffective and inadequate supervision, and insufficient community involvement (HMIC 2002). The curriculum had changed little in the previous 20 years and still retained the teaching of physical education and drill without any justification for so doing. The report indicated that the emphasis on the acquisition of legal knowledge came at the expense of skills such as communication, problem-solving, teamwork and techniques of reducing crime, which were considered to be much more appropriate and relevant for officers' policing in the twenty-first century (HMIC 2002).

However, what is particularly of interest within the context of the longitudinal research examined later in this book is the identification by the HMIC that police probationer training also needed to consider and explore the issue of attitudes and behaviours. The report identified that although the Police Training Council strategy for probationary training focused upon the importance of incorporating all aspects of the KUSAB (Knowledge, Understanding, Skills, Attitudes and Behaviours) model into training, there was a definite imbalance in which aspects of this model took precedence (HMIC 2002). Although not explicitly mentioned in this report or in many other reports and enquiries of this nature, what is being sometimes only alluded to and sometimes more openly stated is that there are issues around the culture of the police, which is seen to have been allowed to flourish at police training centres, which then have a long-lasting and fundamental impact upon the new police recruits as they entered their police career. As we shall see throughout this book, changing or challenging the cultures of the police is a statement seen regularly throughout the policing literature from both academic and government sources. What is lacking is an indication of what police cultures actually are, how they are formed and whether indeed they can be changed. The difficulty for governments and policing organisations is that although reform through organisational and procedural change can be challenging, it is not insurmountable. Changing a 'culture' which is neither properly examined nor identified remains a very different proposition.

The issue of the problematic nature of police probationer training which focused more upon knowledge acquisition than it did upon developing the attitudes and behaviours of its recruits came sharply into focus with the screening of the BBC documentary *The Secret Policeman* in 2003 (Ford 2003). Mark Daly, an undercover BBC journalist, joined Greater Manchester Police as a new police recruit and began secret filming of his fellow recruits as they were undergoing their probationary training at Bruche regional training centre in Cheshire. Whilst the manner of obtaining comments and opinions of his fellow recruits can be questioned, what is incontrovertible is that the levels of racism displayed by a number of fellow recruits shocked viewers and generated a large amount of negative publicity. Criticism was levelled not only at the behaviours of eight of the most notably racist recruits within Daly's cohort but also at the poor levels of training seen by the police trainers. Trainers were seen to 'list' words which were deemed to be racist, but recruits were provided with no historical, social or political context of why that might be the case. What was particularly of concern about the programme was the portrayal of not only racist attitudes but racist behaviours in the discretionary treatment of black and minority ethnic community members who were stopped by some of these police officers. The response from the Labour Government and from the Association of Chief Police Officers (ACPO) was fairly immediate; change had to happen. Foster summed up many of these concerns:

> Training school therefore provides a rehearsal of how occupational culture can nurture and protect its members, where cultural values emanate from the couching of ideas, the examples given and the style of filling-in talk, back chat and corridor conversation as much as from the formal teaching and curriculum. (2003, p. 203)

What the HMIC report 'Training Matters' (2002) and the 2003 screening of the BBC documentary *The Secret Policeman* revealed was that both the formal and informal training of new police recruits needed a radical overhaul. The overhaul of the formal learning was not long in the making.

# The Initial Police Learning and Development Programme

Police training in England and Wales has undergone many changes and modification over the years, but one of the most significant of these was the introduction of the Initial Police Learning and Development Programme (IPLDP). After first being piloted with five police forces in 2005, the scheme was implemented nationally from April 2006. From April 2010, a new Level 3 competency-based qualification was added, the Diploma in Policing, which new recruits must work towards during their initial training and complete within their two-year probationary period. The IPLDP intended to offer a more locally based training experience which would be more relevant to local officers and one that would be better tailored to the context within which officers were working (Constable and Smith 2015). This new approach to police training was intended to not only professionalise the police service but also to "deliver cultural change" (Heslop 2011, p. 299). Gone were the regional training centres and the residential training that went with it, and ushered in was the advent of training delivered by individual forces, sometimes in part-nership with further or higher education institutions (HEIs).

It is important at this juncture to consider the IPLDP in depth, as this is the route that was taken by the new recruits who feature as part of the longitudinal research within this book. The IPLDP consists of three sepa-rate strands of training. First, there is the classroom-based training deliv-ered either by the force themselves or in conjunction with educational establishments. Second, there is on-the-job training delivered via phases with a tutor constable, placements and external input. This phase is left deliberately less prescriptive in order for individual forces to be able to respond appropriately to the demands of police training in their area. Third, and in direct response to the recommendations of the Macpherson Inquiry into the death of Stephen Lawrence (although first mooted by the Scarman Report in 1981), there is a community element to the training, where new recruits spend time on a community placement. The intention of this is to provide officers with a greater awareness and appreciation of the cultures of the neighbourhoods in which they are working (Peace 2006).

The programme attempted to redress some of the criticisms of previous police training being too focused upon the acquisition of legal knowledge by instead seeking to offer more by way of the context in which policing operates (Alcott 2012). This was also seen as a response to the ongoing criticisms of the cultures of the police service, which displayed elements of racism, sexism and a limited understanding of different cultures and communities (Scarman 1981). This was not the first time that education or training was seen to be the 'solution' to the 'problem' of policing cultures. From the 1970s and for over 30 years, Essex Police was one of a number of forces that sponsored a small number of police officers each year to go to university full time in what was believed by one of those taking part in an attempt to "overcome that dear old police culture" (Lee and Punch 2006, p. 27).

The IPLDP attempted to do this by adopting a Learning Requirement which was recommended by the UEA group that had previously reviewed training during the late 1980s (Elliott et al. 2003). This Learning Requirement consisted of seven parts: understanding and engaging with the community, enforcing the law and following police procedures, responding to human and social diversity, positioning oneself in the role of a police officer inside the police organisation, professional standards and ethical conduct, learning to learn and creating a base for career-long learning, and qualities of professional judgement and decision-making. Elliott et al. (2003) specifically argued that the Learning Requirement should be seen as the ethos and guiding principles of the curriculum, rather than directly related to any competencies which recruits must be assessed against. However, as White has noted (2006) and as will be discussed later in this chapter, this was not done. The Home Office then went on to directly map the Learning Requirement to the 22 National

Occupational Standards (NOS) against which officers would be assessed. Despite the introduction of a more local flavour to probationer police training and despite the addition of an element of community place-ment, new recruits to the police service were to be assessed against 22 NOS. This number has since been reduced by the College of Policing in 2013a to ten key areas. The NOS were developed by a number of govern-ment skills organisations. This was a competency-based approach, and evidence of having achieved the required levels of competency was to be recorded in a recruit's Student Officer Learning and Assessment Portfolio (SOLAP). A conference of police professionals was told in 2002 by the Police Skills Standards Organisation (now Skills for Justice) that "[a] police officer needs to know nothing more and nothing less than what is contained in a National Occupational Standard" (Jackson 2002; cited in White 2006, p. 388). The impact of this competency-based approach to the assessment of new recruits will be examined shortly.

## The Tutor Constable

One aspect of probationer police training that survived the radical over-haul was the input from the tutor constable. What was a ten-week period of patrolling under the tutelage of a tutor constable under the old train-ing regime continued to be a ten-week period of patrolling under the tutelage of a tutor constable within the IPLDP. Despite criticisms from the HMIC inspection about the selection and training of tutor constables and of the quality assurance and resilience measures in place (HMIC 2002), the basic principle of spending ten weeks with a more experienced officer in force was deemed to be fundamental to the success of police training (HMIC 2002). The report went on to recommend national selection criteria for tutor constables, formal recognition and more regu-lar training (HMIC 2002). This recommendation to focus upon tutor constables in the training process came despite criticisms in the early 1980s about their role from a force review, which the then Director of Training for the Metropolitan Police Service described as making "hor-rific reading" (Stradling and Harper 1988, p. 200). This also came despite an HMIC report which found fundamental differences between the ideas and views expressed to new recruits during training and the ideas and views expressed to new recruits by tutor constables (HMIC 1999b).

Since the introduction of the IPLDP, new recruits have had to successfully perform all of the tasks which are described in the Police Action Checklist whilst they are in the tutor phase of their training and before they will be signed off as 'independent'. These will include situations which student officers have to successfully navigate (e.g. statement-taking, making an arrest). Evidence is also collected in relation to the completion of the 22 (now 10) NOS. This replaces the previous objectives of the tutor constable attachment, which included such activities as developing good police–public relationships, conducting vehicle checks, becoming proficient in the use of the radio and, interestingly, recognising well-known active criminals (Stradling and Harper 1988). However, as we shall see later, when the qualitative research upon which this book is based is examined in depth, the tutor phase of police probationer training remains perhaps the most significant but least well-evaluated aspect of police training. When inspectors and traffic officers were asked how the skilful use of discretion is acquired by police officers, both placed tutor constables at the top of a list of eight choices, which included divisional training, experience and supervisors (Stradling and Harper 1988). What is very clear but which requires much further examination (see Chap. 8) is the role of tutor constables in imparting both the formal and informal guidelines, both the official and the unofficial policy upon which new police recruits build their careers. It is this transmission of occupational norms to new police recruits which remains a central interest of this book.

## The Impact of the IPLDP

The introduction of the IPLDP was heralded as a radical reform of the training of police probationers in England and Wales. However, a much closer examination of this is required to see whether genuine change was achieved. The 'classroom' element of the training changed insofar as the curriculum was enhanced to take account of the context in which officers would be working. However, the delivery methods remained the same, with these elements being taught by a police trainer in a local, rather than a regional, training school. Although the introduction of the IPLDP and the Police Reform Act 2002 encouraged local forces to work in partnership with local colleges and universities to jointly deliver some of this training, partnerships of this sort were certainly not the norm (Wood and Tong 2009). New recruits continued to progress to the next stage of the training programme by working in force, first under the supervision of a tutor constable and then independently. The addition of a community placement programme was a significant development in the training of new police officers, but the reality was 3–5 days in one or a number of local community groups, with the possibility of being asked to present findings or complete a report or a questionnaire, which were all unassessed. Comments on police recruitment blogs, such as "it isn't assessed or marked … no biggy" and "Don't worry about your placements, even if they're crap, it's only for a few days", reveal that the importance of this element of the training programme was perhaps not well communicated or understood (UKPoliceOnline 2008). The question must be asked therefore as to whether the radical overhaul of police training which was introduced in 2006 was actually that radical at all or whether we were witnessing "more of the same" (White 2006, p. 391)? The main criticisms of the IPLDP from policing commentators appear to come from two broad backgrounds—the delivery methods and the assessment methods. It is to these areas that we now turn.

## IPLDP Delivery

Andragogy was a term first used by Malcolm Knowles to describe what he felt was a neglected aspect of the literature surrounding learning, that of the adult learner (Knowles 1990). According to Knowles (who builds upon the work of Kolb 1984, amongst others), we can assume that adult learners use experience as one of the sources of their learning. They learn more effectively when they understand the real-life connection with what they are learning and are self-directed, and they prefer to be able to understand the justification for the content of their learning (Peace 2006). The central argument is that adults learn very differently from children, and as such, the teaching methods employed should reflect those differences. Teaching should be less directive and more facilitative, and should utilise shared experiences and knowledge. Those delivering adult learning can employ role plays, interaction between tutors and students, simulations, problem-solving activities and, importantly, critical discussion (Birzer 2003; White and Escobar 2008). Although role plays and simulations are used in new recruits' training, these are often poorly managed and assessed (Birzer 2003). As we shall see in Chap. 8, it is these specific aspects of formal learning that are most welcomed by new recruits to the police service.

Earlier in this chapter, we considered the methods of teaching displayed by the police trainers in the BBC *Secret Policeman* documentary which exemplify the problems of adult learning techniques. New recruits were informed of words they were not permitted to use without any critical discussion of the context in which they might have been used in the past and the impact of the use of such words in contemporary society. Marenin, in an analysis of United Nations human rights training for police officers, also found an excessive focus on what 'not' to do (2004). An andragogical approach to learning would approach this particular element of the syllabus in a very different way. As we know, the IPLDP is delivered locally by forces with or without partnerships with local colleges and universities. Clearly then, there will be a variety of delivery methods utilised throughout the country. However, both the syllabus and the Learning Requirement are such that there is insufficient scope and indeed space within the syllabus to be less directive and more critical and engaging. It is indeed desirable to have a curriculum which offers a broad, inclusive and critically reflective philosophy, but if the syllabus that flows from this is narrow and restrictive, then the aims of that curriculum will not be realised. The intent of the programme however is not of concern here—the specified methods of delivery are. Constable and Smith's (2015) empirical study of student officers going through their initial training found that opportunities were missed in the early stages of training to examine and discuss those broad philosophical underpinnings of the training that considered the wider role of policing in particular. In not taking advantage of this opportunity, the ethos of the programme returns to a more task-oriented position.

## IPLDP Assessment

It is the assessment methods of the IPLDP which also contribute to this delivery method stalemate. Critical discussion, problem-solving activities and interaction between students and tutors (all features of the andragogical approach to adult learning) are only ever going to be supplementary to the requirement to fulfil the NOS (which, as we learned earlier, was all a police officer needed to know, "nothing more and nothing less" (Jackson 2002; cited in White 2006, p. 388)). The Flanagan Review of Policing criticised the NOS for requiring a duplication of evidence and unnecessary amounts of supervisory testimony, and, importantly, for 'borrowing' the standards from other public sector bodies without assessing their relevance to policing (Flanagan 2008). A competency-based approach to assessment sidelines critical reflection and rules out other alternative perspectives (Constable and Smith 2015). Values, attitudes, beliefs and, ultimately, potentially behaviours are unlikely to be able to be assessed within a competency-based framework. The achievement of these competencies becomes the only desirable outcome of the learning process; the *ends* are therefore all important, the *means* becoming largely irrelevant. White argues that the result of this is that "[h]uman social relations are mapped like machine systems, with objective inputs/outputs connected by casual laws" (2006, p. 390).

The result of this is a 'hidden curriculum' which continues to show a greater appreciation of practice over theory and fact over value (White 2006). The compliance-based hidden curriculum implies that going through the motions is all that is necessary in order to complete the required competencies (reinforced by trainers and tutor constables) in order to move onto the stage of the 'real learning' which happens on the streets. Additionally, there is the question of *what* is actually being measured and what is deemed to be valuable within the assessment procedures (Burkhart 1980). The focus upon 'crime fighting' is apparent. Constable and Smith (2015) found that the assessment aspects of initial police training were accorded very low status. The SOLAP (now eSOLAP) is a good example of this.

The SOLAP replaced the Probationer Development Portfolio (PDP), which had been criticised for being overly bureaucratic and taking unnecessarily large amounts of the time of both recruits and their supervisors (an average of 11.5 hours per week for supervisors alone (Flanagan 2008)). The SOLAP which followed (and subsequently eSOLAP) was then estimated to take an average of 35.2 hours per student and was described as a "bureaucratic nightmare … self imposed" (Flanagan 2008, p. 46). Despite a streamlining of the SOLAP by the National Policing Improvement Agency in 2009, recent research indicates that student officers and their tutor constables are both still openly hostile to this method of assessment, referring to it as the "e-So crap" (Constable and Smith 2015, p. 54). This issue will be returned to when aspects of the longitudinal research upon which this book is based are examined in Part II. New recruits are therefore encouraged to conform to the assessment requirements by ticking the required boxes. Cultures are then engendered within new police recruits that 'lip service' can be paid to these and other policing initiatives, whilst in reality, policing is and continues to be intuitive, instinctive and learned 'on the job'. As White has argued, "we get exactly the police officers we ask for, and they behave in just the way they have been trained" (2006, p. 397).

The opportunities therefore for an analysis of the wider context of policing through critical discussion and analysis, features which are closely aligned with education rather than with training, are subsequently lost. White uses the analogy provided by Stenhouse in 1983 of Mr Toad in *The Wind of the Willows*. Mr Toad knows technically how to both row a boat and drive a car. He however knows nothing of their value or of the social responsibility which this knowledge entails (White 2006).

So, could a more andragogical approach to learning which focused upon the experience of the adult learners and utilised their more inherent self-direction through less prescription and more facilitation become a feature of police training? This could be unlikely. For Heslop, there are three important reasons why this is unlikely (2006). First, the police service remains a very hierarchical organisation that promotes a rigid curriculum with competencies based upon the NOS. The needs of the organisation are therefore more likely to take precedence over the needs of the individual learners, and there is a mismatch between the mission, the organisation and the training (Birzer 2003). Second, whilst trainers are themselves trained to consider the different characteristics of adult learners, this in itself is taught in a prescriptive manner which is often scantily understood or applied (Heslop 2006). This can, in part, be attributed to the relatively limited training that police trainers themselves receive (Peace 2006). Third, the current competency-based assessment methods do not comply with an andragogical approach to learning but more with the behaviourist principles which were discussed earlier in the chapter and again by White in relation to the 'machinery' approach to learning (2006). The learner is akin to a machine that is 'fed' information or stimuli. The methods by which that input is controlled result in an outcome which can be predetermined (Birzer 2003).

Upon a closer analysis of the approaches utilised in police training, it would appear that whilst a broader, more critical reflection on the wider role of policing is espoused, the reality of the training syllabus does not match these goals. Peace (2006) considered Rachal's (2002) criteria for a true andragogical approach to learning. Six criteria were analysed by Peace (2006): voluntary participation, the adult status of learners, collaboratively determined objectives, performance-based assessments, the measure of satisfaction and an environment conducive to learning. With the exception of the adult status (mostly, but not always, met if age is not the only indicator of adult status) and a conducive environment in which to learn (possibly met but very dependent on the individual trainers), then police training did not meet the criteria to be considered an andragogical approach to learning.

Teaching police officers about discretion, communication and the wider social issues of policing in a democratic society is a far more challenging task than teaching them how to use the radio or complete a statement. Likewise, changing the culture of an organisation (if even possible) is a far more challenging task than adjusting the policies and procedures within that organisation. It is of no surprise therefore that policing organisations, like many other organisations in the public and private spheres, have focused upon attempting to achieve what is more easily achievable rather than facing the uphill task of attempting the more challenging discussions around task, culture, attitudes and behaviours. However, there needs to be a better match between what new recruits are learning in their formal learning environment and what they are being required to do in their subsequent role as police officers. The paradox of police training as it is currently formulated is that new recruits are learning in a rigid, inflexible and behaviourist environment but are actually required to understand how to police in a democratic society (Birzer 2003). This involves such complex tasks as neighbourhood disputes, community engagement, the modern threats of terrorism and cyber-enabled crime. A concentration on the more technical aspects of the law and its procedures at the expense of the 'softer' skills of conflict resolution and problem-solving may result in gaps in the required skills of a police officer (Peace 2006).

## The Role of Higher Education in Police Training

As was noted at the outset of this chapter, relationships between policing organisations and universities have not always been convivial and have regularly been characterised by distrust, suspicion and detachment. One graduate police officer recalls the reaction of his colleagues upon discovering he had a degree, "Bloody hell, so you're the clever bastard with the ten O' levels; we'll soon knock that out of you" (Lee and Punch 2006, p. 8).

Whilst some sections of the police would consider higher education to be instructional and measurable through performance- and competency-based indicators, higher education would prefer to see itself through the prism of reflexivity, measurable through critical thinking and innovation (Jones 2016). This has been compounded by an additional complication, which is that the police service has historically been highly suspicious of research, and particularly academic research. The understandable scenario of 'little to gain and much to lose' had guided the police in their traditional reluctance to accept outside researchers. It is this same suspicion which hindered good relations between the police and the media in previous years. Suspiciousness is perhaps a cultural characteristic that transcends all police work. This reluctance to accept outside researchers, coupled with some first-hand experience of accepting researchers only to be heavily criticised by them (Smith and Gray 1983), had led to a closed-door policy throughout much of the latter part of the last century. However, change was evident. The combination of the development of the Home Office Research and Planning Unit (subsequently the Policing and Reducing Crime Unit), the changing nature of police research (which moved from work which was highly critical of police practices to research that was more interested in providing 'solutions') (Reiner 2000) and the thawing of relations between the police and academia, all aided the development of police research. This thaw could also be attributed to the changing cultures of senior police officers themselves (Savage et al. 2000). Senior police officers were becoming much more open to research, in part due to their own academic interests and research, furthered through their espousal of higher education on a personal basis.

So whilst there was a thawing of relations between the police and the university sector in terms of research access and dissemination, there also appeared to be a willingness to work more closely with the higher education sector in contributing to the delivery of police training. As has previously been discussed, the introduction of the IPLDP heralded a new role for higher education in forming partnerships with local police forces for the purpose of delivering police training. This however did not become a widespread practice, and in the majority of forces, training continued to be delivered by police trainers on police property. Still, although the opportunity was not widely embraced, it did still represent a sea change in thinking of governments and senior police officers that there was potentially a role to play for higher education in supporting the development of new police recruits. This was seen very clearly in the Flanagan Review of Policing commissioned by the Labour Government and published in 2008, and the Neyroud Review of Police Leadership and Training commissioned by the Coalition Government and published in 2011. Both called for closer relationships between the police and HEIs (Flanagan 2008; Neyroud 2011). The basis for this argument appears to come from two strands.

First, it is argued that the type of learning which police officers require to operate in the modern world is one most closely associated with the learning that takes place within a university setting. Second, it is argued that 'similar' professions such as nursing and education not only require its new recruits to have a university degree but to have financed this degree themselves before application and selection (Flanagan 2008).

Neyroud specifically recommended a pre-entry national qualification, with delivery being split between HEIs, which would focus upon the wider context of policing in society, and police training centres, which would focus on more practical policing skills (2011). Comparison with the nursing and teaching sectors is an interesting analogy in a number of ways, but particularly because students in these two professions are assessed through their involvement with higher education, whereas police officers are deemed competent through the completion of the practical, rather than the more theoretical, elements of the initial training programme (White and Heslop 2012).

There have been numerous initiatives, programmes, degree courses and pathways which have been coordinated between local police forces and HEIs over the past 20 years. That is not to say that this venture into higher education was a new one for the police service. Over the course of the last century, the police service has, amongst other local initiatives, seen the Trenchard scheme, the Special Course and the Bramshill Scholarship, which have all involved the sponsorship of police officers through university, often being given a free rein over the choice of their subject of study. It is not the intention of this chapter to consider any of these in detail, as the scope of interest for this book is on the broader socialisation aspects of police training, rather than on the intricacies of particular programmes. However, broadly, these more recent collaborations (focusing upon the lower ranks of the police service) have been pre-service qualifications, initial service qualifications or in-service qualifications.

The format with the longest history is that of *in-service* undergraduate and postgraduate qualifications in the field of Policing Studies, which were firstly offered to serving police officers in the early 1990s by the University of Portsmouth and the University of Leicester. These were largely individually sponsored by forces or were self-funded and followed a broad social science curriculum. *Initial service* programmes were enabled through the passing of the Police Reform Act 2002 and were linked with the IPLDP. These most often took the form of a Foundation degree in Policing, a new qualification which was established by the Labour Government in 2001. They were mostly designed in collaboration with local forces, delivered in HEIs (often by retired police officers) and generally took two years to complete. Finally, there are *pre-service* qualifications, a new but growing area of training delivery. Collaboration between the University of Portsmouth and Surrey Police in 2008 resulted in the establishment of a Certificate in Police, Law and Community (PLC), the knowledge- and legal-based elements of initial police training which became a pre-requisite for joining Surrey Police. This idea grew and the College of Policing (the professional body for policing established in 2013a after recommendation from the Neyroud review (2011)) established a more national Certificate of Knowledge of Policing. The College accredits providers (HEIs, further education institutions and private companies), and successful completion of this programme allows potential recruits to apply to their chosen police force. Many, but not all, police forces adopted this approach. It is no guarantee of recruitment and the costs are borne by the individual. All of the new recruits who are the focus of this research study took this Certificate of Knowledge in Policing.

There has been much discussion in this chapter considering the narrow initial police training syllabus which focuses upon knowledge acquisition and the passing of competencies at the expense of a broader more theoretically underpinned analysis of the social context within which policing operates. The involvement of HEIs in the delivery of aspects of the initial police training curriculum should therefore surely be welcomed as a step in the right direction in addressing some of those concerns. There are clearly many advantages of involving HEIs in this delivery. It responds to the police professionalisation agenda, it responds to the suggestion that a far more diverse crime threat requires a better-educated police officer and it satisfies political demands for a more sensitive service (Wood and Tong 2009). It also, as mentioned earlier in this chapter, potentially moves police officers from possessing "intellectual capital" to possessing "intellectual capacity" (Collier 2001, p. 451). Survey research by Jones (2016) found that officers who had completed a policing studies degree considered there to be four main benefits of a university education. These were feeling more connected to the policing organisation, understanding the 'why' in addition to the 'how', an ability to be more reflexive in their practice and the development of wider transferable skills (Jones 2016). The broader knowledge base of university-attending police officers and the ability to be a more reflective practitioner were also noted by research conducted in Wales (Blakemore and Simpson 2010). The development of critical thinking skills, higher levels of communication and enhanced writing skills are all attributes which should be associated with a university graduate. One of the Essex Police officers sponsored to complete a degree during the 1970s stated that he was

> more insightful and self-reflective, and less likely to accept an argument, however initially persuasive it might seem, without first putting it under a magnifying glass just to see exactly what the strength of its appeal was. (Lee and Punch 2006, p. 74)

However, whilst the sponsorship of police officers to complete degrees either full time or in the own time (in-service qualifications) has largely been a positive move for both the police service and the HEIs involved, the initial service qualifications have had a rather more problematic existence. Macvean and Cox (2012) have argued that assumptions were made by the HMIC (2002) in its *Training Matters* inspection report that the involvement of HEIs would inevitably bring with it a more critical thinking police officer who would have been exposed to a variety of different teaching styles in an environment conducive to challenge and debate. The reality however was not so close to those assumptions. Christopher (2015) found that the design of the foundation degree programmes, in consultation with local forces, left little time and space for students to become critical and reflective thinkers because of the programmes' very intensive nature. Whilst Jones (2016) found that one of the motivations for experienced police officers wanting to return to formal education was to address their regrets at not engaging with education at an earlier stage in their lives, those taking initial service qualifications had only recently become police officers. Christopher (2015), Heslop (2011), White and Heslop (2012) and Macvean and Cox (2012) all reported a negative approach from officers towards the learning at university, their lecturers and a disengagement from the syllabus which they were studying. White and Heslop (2012, p. 344) describe this as "learner-hostility". This hostility appeared to stem from levels of discontent at their isolation (physical and psychological) from other students on campus and their inability to identify themselves as either students or professionals (Heslop 2011).

A further difficulty lies with the lecturers delivering the learning. There is no doubt that HEIs eagerly heralded the announcements from the HMIC and the Labour Government for universities to work in collaboration with local police forces in delivering aspects of the initial police training curricula. What many of these HEIs quickly established was that they did not have the personnel in place in order for this collaboration to be realised. Police studies is a relatively new field of academic enquiry and only very few HEIs had a significant number of academic staff working in this area. The solution was seen to be the employment of retired police officers and retired police trainers to fulfil these roles. As White and Heslop (2012) have noted, the field of expertise for many of these officers was either in practical policing or, in the case of the trainers, in the field of adult education. Neither of these groups were police studies academics who were able to introduce and analyse the wider issues of the social context of policing, which was the original intention of this collaboration. In fact, Macvean (2010) found that there were divisions between the academic staff and the retired or seconded police officers. The latter group favoured the 'war stories' approach to teaching and valued 'practical knowledge' more highly than 'academic knowledge'. The result of some of these collaborations between local police forces and HEIs was that the ethos, teaching and curriculum of police training were simply moved from the local training schools to a university setting, with little by way of any further meaningful change (Cox 2016). Heslop argues:

> Making remedial changes to the training so that the police recruits spend time at a university campus rather than at a police academy seems merely to have swapped one cultural socialisation for another. (2011, pp. 309–310)

## The Future Direction of Initial Police Training

Initial police training is undergoing significant change. Winsor's recommendation of a minimum of three A levels for new recruits was taken further by the College of Policing, which, in a desire for increasing professionalisation of the police service and in line with similar professions such as nursing, social work and probation, began work on proposals to make policing a graduate-only profession (Winsor 2012; College of Policing 2016). This has seen the development of the Policing Education Qualifications Framework, with, at entry level, all new recruits expected to complete a police constable degree apprenticeship, a specific pre-join professional policing degree or, for existing graduates, a graduate conversion programme. The potential ramifications of these proposals are significant and cannot be speculated upon here. There are however concerns around reducing the diversity and accessibility of the police service, including from minority ethnic communities, older applicants and those with caring responsibilities. At the time of writing, there are still considerable ongoing negotiations between the College of Policing and the higher education sector, but these changes seem almost certain to go ahead in some form. The implications of these changes will be seen in the future, but as we shall see throughout this book, the impact of learning on the future attitudes, values and behaviours comes from a variety of sources and not just from 'training'. It also comes from learning at a variety of levels and directions—the formal, the informal, the horizontal and the vertical.

This chapter has provided a brief chronology of police training in England and Wales in recent years, most particularly since the introduction of the IPLDP in 2006. However, despite the changes in training programmes and delivery methods, what remains apparent is that police training is still regarded as low status within the policing organisation, and classroom-based training in particular is perceived to be inferior to on-the-job training. If we disregard the arguments in favour of the educational environment for a moment and accept this line of thought, then what can we seek to understand from the experiences of officers that can be used systematically in the training of future officers? Bayley and Bittner (1984) argue that experience does teach police officers many things, and that understanding the value of this experience can provide a structure for future learning. First, experience has taught officers about *goals* and how to manage many of them at once, which are of a very different nature (Bayley and Bittner 1984). Second, experience has taught officers about *tactics* and *tactical decision-making*. Despite officers claiming that every incident is different, Bayley and Bittner (1984) estimate that there are approximately seven variables. Third, they argue that experience teaches officers about *presence*, and that being an effective police officer is as much about 'being' as it is about 'doing' (1984). Experience of the 'craft' of policing can therefore be utilised within the 'science' of police training.

Bayley and Bittner (1984) go on to examine how these three aspects of experience can be better used within the learning process. First, the complex nature of patrol work could be taught through debate, case study and simulation. As this chapter has regularly revealed, the more complex issues of policing and of policing change are often relegated to the background in favour of the more straightforward solutions. Likewise, the instruction of radio use is far simpler to teach, assess and map to learning outcomes than a debate about the role and behaviours of a patrol officer in a variety of different scenarios. Palmiotto et al. (2000) argue that if we want our police officers to be proficient in community (or neighbourhood) policing, then the training of new police recruits should point to social history, social indicators of crime and the philosophies of community policing. White has rejected the notion that this has been apparent in police training in England and Wales, arguing that "[t]he philosophy underpinning the current approach to police training has developed in an intellectual vacuum, oblivious to the history of ideas" (2006, p. 388).

Second, Bayley and Bittner argue in favour of "master craftsmen" (1984, p. 54) to assist new recruits. They highlight a long-held view that tutor constables, as they are referred to in England and Wales, are often cajoled into the role for a myriad of other reasons than for their skills in mentoring. This will be discussed in more detail in Chap. 9. The College of Policing policy documentation about police trainers (2013a) indicates the lower levels of competency required to be a tutor constable than to be a police trainer. A Level 3 standard for tutor constables, rather than a Level 4 standard for police trainers, is required. Level 3 incorporates the skills of assessing others' performance but mentions nothing about mentoring or, indeed, tutoring. The difficulty of a competency-based assessment framework is again exposed. New police recruits have to pass competency-based tests in order to be able to progress through their probationary period. Tutor constables have to be proficient in assessing these competencies. However, the most influential aspect about the role of the tutor constable (that of mentoring, tutoring or guiding the new recruit) does not have to be of a required standard to be fulfilled. Third, Bayley and Bittner argue that learning must be viewed as a cumulative process and not something to be completed in the early stages of a police career—"Officers must be helped to learn from one another less haphazardly then they do in the front seats of patrol cars" (1984, p. 55).

By understanding what police experience can teach other officers and building this experience more scientifically into the training curriculum, Bayley and Bittner argue that police morale will be boosted, the service will have to develop techniques for measuring effective levels of skill and, resultantly, it will become a more reflective, more self-conscious institution (1984). They conclude:

> If police improved performance by testing the 'lessons of experience' for efficacy, both through controlled observation and the sharing of collective police experience, and then imparted those lessons more systematically to police officers, the public might have more confidence in the police as moral arbiters. (1984, p. 58)

It is to these 'lessons of experience' that this book now turns. This chapter has examined the *formal* training that is in place for new recruits to the police service. However, much of the discussion about the formation and development of policing cultures within the policing organisation has focused on the *informal* learning that is established in the very early stages of a policing career and continues throughout that career. Before we seek to examine the impact of both formal and informal learning on the sample of new recruits, which forms the basis of this longitudinal research, it is important to analyse the concept of informal learning and socialisation, especially within the policing context, in more depth.

# References

Alcott, C. (2012). Reforming the Force: An Examination of the Impact of the Operational Sub-culture on Reform and Modernisation Within the Police Service. *British Journal of Community Justice, 10*(1), 5–14.

Bayley, D., & Bittner, E. (1984). Learning the Skills of Policing. *Law and Contemporary Problems, 47*(4), 35–59.

Birzer, M. (2003). The Theory of Andragogy Applied to Police Training. *Journal of Police Strategies and Management, 26*(1), 29–42.

Blakemore, B., & Simpson, K. (2010). A Comparison of the Effectiveness of Pre- and Post-employment Modes of Higher Education for Student Police Officers. *The Police Journal, 83*, 29–41.

Blears, H. (2004). *Home Affairs Select Committee Proceedings on Police Reform, Q320*. Retrieved from http://www.publications.parliament.uk/pa/cm200304/cmselect/cmhaff/c1038-iv/uc103802.htm

Burkhart, B. (1980, February). Conceptual Issues in the Development of Police Selection Procedures. *Professional Psychology*, pp. 121–129.

Christopher, S. (2015). The Quantum Leap: Police Recruit Training and the Case for Mandating Higher Education for Pre-entry Schemes. *Policing, 9*(4), 388–404.

Clements, P., & Jones, J. (2009). Police Training and the Impact of Lawrence. In N. Hall, J. Grieve, & S. Savage (Eds.), *Policing and the Legacy of Lawrence* (pp. 193–213). Cullompton: Willan.

College of Policing. (2013a). *Police Sector Standards for the Training of Trainers*, Version 2. Retrieved from http://www.college.police.uk/What-we-do/Standards/Pages/Training-Roles.aspx

College of Policing. (2016). *Proposals for Qualifications in Policing*. Retrieved from http://www.college.police.uk/News/College-news/Pages/peqf_consultation.aspx

Collier, P. (2001). Valuing Intellectual Capacity in the Police. *Accounting, Auditing and Accountability Journal, 14*(4), 437–455.

Commission for Racial Equality. (2005). *The Police Service in England and Wales*. London: CRE. Retrieved from http://news.bbc.co.uk/1/shared/bsp/hi/pdfs/08_03_05_cre.pdf.

Constable, J., & Smith, J. (2015). Initial Police Training and the Development of Police Occupational Culture. In P. Wankhade & D. Weir (Eds.), *Police Services: Leadership and Management Perspectives* (pp. 45–60). New York: Springer International Publishing.

Cox, C. (2016). *Police Culture and Socialisation Within a UK University, Unpublished Doctoral Thesis*. Preston: University of Central Lancashire.

Elliott, J., Kushner, S., Alexandrou, A., Dwyfor-Davies, J., Wilkinson, S., & Zamorski, B. (2003). *Independent Review of the Learning Requirement for Police Probationer Training in England and Wales*. Bristol/Norwich: University of the West of England/University of East Anglia.

Flanagan, R. (2008). *Review of Policing: Final Report*. London: HMSO.

Ford, R. (2003). Saying One Thing, Meaning Another: The Role of Parables in Police Training. *Police Quarterly, 6*(1), 84–110.

Foster, J. (2003). Police Cultures. In T. Newburn (Ed.), *The Handbook of Policing* (pp. 196–227). Cullompton: Willan.

Heslop, R. (2006). 'Doing a Maslow': Humanistic Education and Diversity in Police Training. *The Police Journal, 79*, 331–341.

Heslop, R. (2011). Reproducing Police Culture in a British University: Findings from an Exploratory Case Study of Police Foundation Degrees. *Police Practice and Research, 12*(4), 298–312.

HMIC. (1999a). *Managing Learning: A Study of Police Training*. London: HMSO.

HMIC. (1999b). *Police Integrity: Securing and Maintaining Public Confidence*. London: HMIC.

HMIC. (2002). *Training Matters*. London: Home Office.

Home Office. (1998). *Review of National Police Training: Draft Report*. London: Home Office.

Jones, M. (2016). Creating the 'Thinking Police Officer': Exploring Motivations and Professional Impact of Part-Time Higher Education. *Policing, 10*(3), 232–240.

Knowles, M. (1990). *The Adult Learner: A Neglected Species* (4th ed.). Houston: Gulf Publishing Company.

Kolb, D. (1984). *Experiential Learning: Experience as the Source of Learning and Development*. Englewood Cliffs: Prentice-Hall.

Kratcoski, P. (2004). Police Education and Training in a Global Society: Guest Editor's Introduction. *Police Practice and Research, 5*(2), 103–105.

Lee, M., & Punch, M. (2006). *Policing by Degrees*. Groningen: de Hondsrug Pers.

MacDonald, B., Argent, M., Elliott, J., May, N., Miller, P., Naylor, J., & Norris, N. (1986). *Police Probationer Training: The Final Report of the Stage II Review*. London: HMSO/University of East Anglia.

Macpherson, W. (1999). *The Stephen Lawrence Inquiry Report*. London: HMSO.

Macvean, A. (2010). *A Clash of Cultures: Policing the Academics*. Chester: University of Chester.

Macvean, A., & Cox, C. (2012). Police Education in a University Setting: Emerging Cultures and Attitudes. *Policing, 6*(1), 16–25.

Marenin, O. (2004). Police Training for Democracy. *Police Practice and Research, 5*(2), 107–123.

Mathias, P. (1988). Paving the Way for Philosophy and Practice at Peel Centre. In P. Southgate (Ed.), *New Directions in Police Training* (pp. 100–111). London: HMSO.

McNeill, W. (1982). *The Pursuit of Power: Technology, Armed Forces and Society Since AD1000*. Chicago: University of Chicago Press.

Neyroud, P. (2011). *Review of Police Leadership and Training*. London: Home Office.

Oakley, R. (1994). The Police and Black People: The Training Response. In M. Stephens & S. Becker (Eds.), *Police Force, Police Service; Care and Control in Britain* (pp. 85–106). Basingstoke: Macmillan.

Palmiotto, M., Birzer, M., & Unnithan, P. (2000). Training in Community Policing. *Policing: An International Journal of Police Strategies and Management, 23*(1), 8–21.

Peace, R. (2006). Probationer Training for Neighbourhood Policing in England and Wales: Fit for Purpose? *Policing: An International Journal of Police Strategies and Management, 29*(2), 335–346.

Rachal, J. (2002). Andragogy's Detectives: A Critique of the Present and a Proposal for the Future. *Adult Education Quarterly, 52*(3), 210–227.

Reiner, R. (2000). *The Politics of the Police* (3rd ed.). Oxford: Oxford University Press.

Savage, S., Charman, S., & Cope, S. (2000). *Policing and the Power of Persuasion.* London: Blackstone Press.

Scarman. (1981). *The Brixton Disorders 10–12 April 1981: Report of an Inquiry by the Rt. Hon. The Lord Scarman (Cmnd 8427).* London: HMSO.

Smith, D., & Gray, J. (1983). *Police and People in London IV: The Police in Action.* London: PSI.

Stradling, S., & Harper, K. (1988). The Tutor Constable Attachment, the Management of Encounters and the Development of Discretionary Judgement. In P. Southgate (Ed.), *New Directions in Police Training* (pp. 199–218). London: HMSO.

UKPoliceOnline. (2008). *Thames Valley Community Placement.* Retrieved from http://www.ukpoliceonline.co.uk/index.php?/topic/29094-thames-valley-community-placement/#comment-306626

White, D. (2006). A Conceptual Analysis of the Hidden Curriculum of Police Training in England and Wales. *Policing and Society, 16*(4), 386–404.

White, M., & Escobar, G. (2008). Making Good Cops in the Twenty-First Century: Emerging Issues for the Effective Recruitment, Selection and Training of Police in the United States and Abroad. *International Review of Law Computers and Technology, 22*(1–2), 119–134.

White, D., & Heslop, R. (2012). Educating, Legitimising or Accessorising? Alternative Conceptions of Professional Training in UK Higher Education: A Comparative Study of Teacher, Nurse and Police Officer Educators. *Police Practice and Research, 13*(4), 342–356.

Winsor, T. (2012). *Independent Review of Police Officer and Staff Renumeration and Conditions, Final Report* (Vol. 1). London: The Stationery Office.

Wood, D., & Tong, S. (2009). The Future of Initial Police Training. *International Journal of Police Science and Management, 11*(3), 294–305.

# 5

# Learning to Become a Police Officer: Police Socialisation

The focus of this book moves again from the organisational to the cultural and, through an analysis of the literature, seeks in this chapter to examine how recruits 'learn' to become police officers. A significant section of the literature on learning focuses on formal learning. However, in the context of policing, it is vitally important to consider the growing interest in informal learning within the workplace as a key, if not the key, influence on the behaviour and performance of workers. Heslop has argued that the processes involved in learning to be a police officer have rarely been explored (2011). This will be done here through an analysis of some of the 'classic' works on police socialisation, a consideration of the literature focusing upon 'situated learning' (referred to within policing circles as learning 'on the job') and the impact of social interaction on learning. An analysis of the 'communities of practice' (CoP) literature will also seek to position police learning as a more dynamic style of learning which does not all flow from 'master' to 'student', but is based on an exchange of information and the social interaction of the range of actors involved.

© The Author(s) 2017
S. Charman, *Police Socialisation, Identity and Culture*,
DOI 10.1007/978-3-319-63070-0_5

## Organisational Socialisation

Organisational socialisation refers to the processes by which organisational members either accept or learn the different behaviours and attitudes which are necessary in order to participate as a member of the organisation (Van Maanen 1975). There are opportunities for organisational socialisation at all stages of an employee's career. Those belonging to an organisation are continually reshaping the lived realities of their membership through negotiation, validation or challenge (Daymon 2000). However, it is generally acknowledged that this learning takes place predominantly in the early stages of entry into an organisation. The newcomer must therefore make the necessary adjustments to attitudes, values, beliefs and, possibly, identity in order to successfully navigate a position within the new organisation. This is particularly the case in a rank-centred and experience-focused organisation such as the police. In order for the culture of the organisation to survive, new members must appreciate their organisational world and their organisational reality in much the same way as their more experienced colleagues (Van Maanen and Schein 1979). It is a case of the newcomer conforming to the existing norms, rather than the organisation being shaped by the newcomer (Campbell 2009).

Socialisation involves both formal and informal stages of learning. It also involves a process of social assimilation (Morrison 1993). Taken together, these experiences combine to produce a means of adaptation to a new group and survival therein (Bourdieu 1977). New members must be equipped with the correct information and knowledge about the processes and procedures of the organisation in order to be able to perform their new roles. They must also be familiar with the 'language' of the organisation and the normative practices which shape police action. However, Fielding (1984) takes this one step further and argues that unless the new recruit knows how to routinely use this language and how to routinely interpret policing situations so that its use is unproblematic and unnoticed, they are not quite at the stage of assimilation. This collective sense-making involves the interplay between formal and informal elements of learning and comes to represent a guide to the organisational reality of policing. Van Maanen (1976) argues therefore that the purpose of socialisation is to provide the new member with the knowledge, the ability and the motivation to be able to perform their role. It ensures continuity of normative values and practices (whether desirable or otherwise) and provides a framework for new members to make sense of the minefield that a new organisational encounter can bring (Cable and Parsons 2001). Where levels of discretion and autonomy are high and where informal adaptations to formal rules are an occupational characteristic (both seen particularly within policing), the influence of that socialisation can be even more apparent. Its study is therefore imperative.

The previous chapter considered the structure and organisation of the formal stages of learning that new and old police recruits have faced upon entry to the police organisation. This chapter considers this more informal, tacit learning that takes place in contacts with existing members and in the early stages of a police recruit's career. The combination then of formal and informal learning results in what Schein has referred to as a "psychological contract" (1971, p. 38), which links both the individual and the organisation. It is the results (positive or otherwise) of the socialisation process which will actually inform the nature of that contract.

It should not be assumed, as is often the case, that learning and working are two entirely different activities that rarely overlap (Eraut 2004). In policing terms, this is all too often the case with learning being considered to be the mainstay of the police training environment, whereas the 'real work' takes place when recruits are assigned to patrol. This is closely related to the assumption that only formal learning takes place within police training and only informal learning takes place 'on the streets'. There are opportunities for both informal learning within the training environment (through the use of trainers' war stories, through role-play scenarios, through the socialising of new recruits, etc.) and formal learning within the attachments to local forces (through the competency based e-SOLAP assessments). Indeed, it is in the very nature of the policing function, the uncertainty and sometimes the unpredictability, which contributes to the proliferation of informal learning at *all* stages of the process.

Alongside this assumption about where formal and informal learning takes place, there is also the linked assumption that socialisation therefore follows a clear linear pattern, with a convenient end-state (Fielding 1988a, b; Fielding and Fielding 1991; Van Maanen 1975). This argument suggests that new recruits are subject to influential formal socialisation via training centres, whose influence is then diminished when the more powerful informal socialisation takes effect when new recruits are situated within the working policing environment. Whilst this is and can be the case, the issue is not a simple uncontested process which progresses regularly in one direction, but is instead affected by individual identity adaptation, directional change, the role of the tutors within police forces and indeed the location of the first posting. Chan has suggested that learning is affected by both where and with whom the initial training takes place (2004).

The literature refers to both organisational socialisation and occupational socialisation. Like Van Maanen (1976), it is clear that the direct setting in which the informal socialisation takes place has a significant impact upon the nature and outcomes of that socialisation. Although the occupational attributes of policing are key to the development of values, attitudes and belief amongst officers (and will be a key feature of the following chapter on policing cultures), the term organisational socialisation is generally preferred, with its emphasis on place and setting, which, as will be seen, is a major influence on the socialisation process.

## Learning at Work

Traditional learning theories have associated learning with the transmission of static knowledge to passive learners within an often unknown setting. Little attention has been paid to the context within which this learning takes place and the context within which the practice will subsequently take place. These theories largely ignore both the nature of human interaction and the notion of learning being an inherently social process (Campbell 2009). However, more recently, a significant section of the literature on learning now focuses on the importance of informal learning within the workplace as a key (if not *the* key) influence on the behaviour and performance of workers. By using the term 'informal learning', greater flexibility and agency are accorded to the learner and the importance of learning from others is recognised (Eraut 2004). Rules and routines are learned, memorised and repeated, all the whilst shaped by the cultures and norms of the organisation (Kerosuo and Engeström 2003). The learner is not alone, and is not impotent but active within the learning process. Heslop asks us to consider the metaphor of learning as participation (2011). It is impossible to consider learning without an awareness of both the social being and the social setting in which the learning takes place (Hodkinson and Hodkinson 2004). This is important, as criticism has been directed towards models of socialisation which have neglected the issue of context and setting, as we shall see later in this chapter.

'Situated learning' and the impact of social interaction on learning therefore draw our attention away from more formal settings and instead consider the learning which takes place every day in all walks of life, most especially, in the context of this book, in the workplace. Workplace functioning is thus influenced not only by the cultures and norms of the organisation but also crucially by learning from and with others. Policing is an inherently 'social' occupation, whether in relation to interaction with fellow officers, other public sector agencies or, indeed, the public. Learning takes place within a social context and is also then developed and adapted within a social context. Fellow recruits, supervisors, colleagues, the public and others, all operate within a shared social space which enables them to have an impact upon the learning of each new recruit. However, these relationships at work and the more emotional dynamic of the professional culture of an organisation are areas which are felt to have been less than well recognised (Eraut 2004). One framework which analyses cultural learning and techniques of socialisation effectively is the 'communities of practice' (CoP) model.

# Communities of Practice

The CoP framework was introduced by Lave and Wenger (1991) and later refined by Wenger (1998). It is a regularly cited (and regularly criticised) situated learning theory which proposes that people learn by coming together in the pursuit of shared goals and by mutually engaging in the processes of social interaction and activity with one another. This could be in the form of a youth gang or a charity ball event, but finds its more natural home in the descriptions of workers who share expertise, goals and, very often, location. A CoP can be a formal group or an informal group. The essence of the framework lies in learning and, in particular, in the *triadic* relationships between 'masters', 'young masters' and 'apprentices' (Lave and Wenger 1991, p. 56). The relationship varies enormously from the traditional teacher–student dynamic in that learning does not flow in only one direction. Newcomers are not merely the recipients of information but must also make their contribution (Fox 2000). In doing so, the move from novice to expert is eventually completed (Fuller and Unwin 2003). Within policing terms, there is not only the more traditionally vertical learning from trainers and tutors to new recruits but also the more horizontal learning from one other. Becoming a member of a CoP therefore involves a process of acclimatisation, of learning the cultural norms and values of the community (Holmes and Marra 2002).

The CoP framework shares some features of social identity theories, which were discussed in Chap. 3 (Tajfel 1978; Tajfel and Turner 1986). These theories stress that behaviour is closely governed by membership of groups and relationships with other groups. Social network theories also share some features of the CoP framework, with a focus on people or groups of people and their relationships or ties with other people or groups of people. However, with social identity theories, even weak ties or relationships are an important part of the mapping process. In CoP, however, the focus rests on the quality, rather than on the quantity, of the interactions (Holmes and Meyerhoff 1999).

An attraction of the CoP framework is that it is largely 'intuitive' (Lave and Wenger 1991, p. 42) and not encumbered by overly complicated typologies which attempt to 'measure' or 'categorise' unquantifiable social interactions and communications. The very essence of social interactions with work colleagues or across occupational boundaries is about the subconscious exchange of tacit knowledge, which is therefore unlikely to be recognised by participants or indeed measurable. Membership of a CoP may not even be recognised by its very members (Roberts 2006). This *implicit learning* is defined as:

[T]he acquisition of knowledge independently of conscious attempts to learn and in the absence of explicit knowledge about what was learned. (Reber 1993, p. 115)

What the CoP framework offers is a way of understanding and conceptualising social interactions and communications.

Wenger (1998) identified three crucial dimensions of a community of practice. *Mutual engagement* described the regular interactions between community members. *Joint enterprise* is a characteristic of CoP which focuses on the negotiated and shared goals which members define, which operate in spite of more official influences. The 'looseness' of this particular aspect of CoP has been the subject of some criticism (Holmes and Meyerhoff 1999). The final characteristic of CoP is *a shared repertoire of communal resources*, which include the linguistic resources of humour, storytelling and other cultural artefacts. Wenger (1998) went on to be more specific about some of the features of CoP. Those identified as most relevant in this regard are shared ways of doing things; the lack of necessity for introductory discussions or problem set-up; overlap in discourse of 'who belongs'; shared humour, stories and perspective on the world; and shared notions of appropriate actions and behaviour.

Learning theorists have attempted over the years to develop the framework further. One example of the development of the CoP framework has been in its appreciation of not only the learning which takes place within the CoP, but also the potential for learning across multiple CoP (Österland 1996; cited in Fuller 2007). Traditional theories of learning often place the emphasis on the imparting of knowledge vertically within an organisation, from an expert to a novice. However, the imposition of regulation from above does little to increase social integration below (6 et al. 2006). Where collaboration based upon the exchange of interactions on a repeated basis, rather than on instruction from above, is utilised and results in positive gain, collaboration will be repeated. The CoP framework pays heed to the role of horizontal influences both within a community and via other communities.

However, despite its more obvious limitations, including the focus on stability and harmony and the lack of attention to issues of inequality, what the CoP framework does achieve is to act as a tool with which to more fully explore the ways in which learning takes place within organisations. It does this via its focus not on the individual worker but on the social, emotional, relational, collective and often tacit features of workplace learning. How this tacit knowledge is transferred and reproduced is fundamental to this concept:

> Lave and Wenger's primary aim was not to construct a treatise on how learning *ought to be* but, rather, to develop an approach which could help reveal learning as it *actually is*. (Hughes 2007, p. 32)

Tacit knowledge is thought to be utilised far more regularly by those who work in naturalistic settings (such as medical diagnosis or policing), as they consider informal workable solutions or adaptations to formal rules (Eraut 2004).

Amin and Roberts (2008) analysed over 300 publications on CoP in order to develop a typology of 'knowing in action' in order to better understand informal learning, innovation and how knowledge is created. Their work results in four distinct groupings, named as task/craft-based, professional, epistemic/highly creative and virtual. The characteristics of the first and most relevant of these, the task/craft-based groups, appear to be very closely related to the learning environment of police officers. First, workers use a combination of formal codified knowledge and informal knowledge learned through participation and practice in order to guide their action. Second, workers have a language which is specific to their community and which uses stories and strong ties of trust and dependence in order to function. Knowledge of this type is transmitted verbally and physically. Third, there is an emphasis on the preservation of existing knowledge and the transmission of this knowledge to those new to the community. This does not imply a static set of cultural characteristics, as evolution comes through the changing social context of the job, but does appear to preclude more radical innovation. Finally, learning within task/craft-based communities often occurs within organisations which are hierarchical and rank focused. An understanding of Amin and Roberts' (2008) typology and of the potential for how knowledge is transmitted is essential if we are to appreciate and contextualise the new recruits' interpretation of their learning in subsequent chapters of this book.

# The Stages of Socialisation

The police socialisation literature has focused upon both the 'stages' that police officers can potentially go through in the process of moving from an 'outsider' to an 'insider' and the impact and influence of differing socialisation tactics on that process. Areas of most interest are role, motivation, commitment and satisfaction (Oberfield 2012; Van Maanen 1975). Although refined and 'tested' by subsequent authors, there is still an emphasis on the work of Van Maanen (1973, 1975, 1976, 1978a, b; Van Maanen and Schein 1979), who pioneered the analysis of organisational socialisation (particularly in the field of policing) or, as he often termed it, 'people processing' (1978a). The difficulties inherent in both analysing the tacit, often unseen and unconscious strategies and processes of organisational socialisation and conducting longitudinal research to examine the impact of socialisation mean that although the 1970s and 1980s saw an initial interest in the area of police socialisation, this has not attracted a focused interest in more recent years. The notable exceptions to this are Fielding's (1988a) longitudinal study of 125 police recruits over two years in England and Chan's (2003) longitudinal study of 150 police recruits over two years in Australia. These will be discussed in this and subsequent chapters.

Whilst much of the remainder of this book will be devoted to the words and individual adaptations of the police recruits themselves, who were interviewed at various stages of their first four years as police officers, there is value too in considering some of the many models of socialisation which have been developed elsewhere. Although no model or framework is going to tell the story of each and every individual and their adaptation to their new role, there are patterns and trends in these models which appear to transcend both occupation and location. Some concentrate on the time served and the changes that occur at different time periods during the socialisation process. Others instead focus upon the description of how socialisation occurs and the potential variations in its impact depending on the socialisation tactics used. Clearly, the individual themselves, their sense of self and identity, and their pre-socialisation experiences will also have an impact. Finally, what is of particular interest with regard to this longitudinal research is the impact and influence of reference groups outside of the individual recruits themselves and the effects of these at different time periods during the socialisation process.

Although Van Maanen slightly amended and refined these categories over time, the stages of socialisation which are most often referred to are anticipatory, encounter (or change) and metamorphosis (1976). These three stages will be explained over the course of this chapter. It is to the stage of anticipatory socialisation that this chapter now turns, and with it, a consideration of motivations for joining the police and whether the idea of a 'police personality' has any supporting evidence.

## Anticipatory Socialisation

Anticipatory socialisation refers to the extent to which the soon-to-be employee of an organisation is prepared to and willing to adopt the occupational position that has been assigned to them (Van Maanen 1976). This therefore refers not only to the formal acceptance of the position via contracts and attendance at training and induction events, but also to the more informal cultural perspective in terms of the extent to which the new recruit is willing and prepared to accept and adapt to the dominant values, attitudes and beliefs that are part of those occupational cultures. Conti (2006) uses Goffman's work on the mortification of the self to analyse the pre-entry stage of police recruits. He argues that there are three stages of pre-entry into the police: civilian, contestant and anticipatory recruit. At each stage of the process to be accepted as a police recruit, there is the potential for elevation through acceptance and progression, plus the potential for degradation through failure and rejection. In order to maximise the potential for success, it would not be surprising were recruits to actively seek to conform to the accepted policing norms.

Anticipatory socialisation has the potential to have been occurring at all stages of the new recruit's life and is affected by a number of factors. This would include the influence of family and friends with experience of a police career, the influence of family and friends who have had experiences of dealing with the police (professionally or personally, positively or negatively) and the influence of the media, in both fictional and non-fictional ways, in its portrayal of policing and police officers. Bennett (1984) argues that two factors will influence the outcome of this anticipatory stage of police socialisation. First is the amount of time the potential recruit spends at this stage, and second is the accuracy of the information received during this stage from those influences. However, it is difficult to assess what is 'accurate' information and what is 'inaccurate' information. Negative or positive experiences of policing, whether experienced from within or outside of that organisation, are valid individual emotions and, as such, can have an influence on others, irrespective of whether those emotions have a valid basis in reality or not.

Fielding (1988a) is however keen to stress that although anticipatory socialisation may tell part of the story of how police officers are socialised into the organisational cultures of the police service, its significance should not be overstated. As the further stages of socialisation will reveal, there are more powerful influences to come. This reasoning would coalesce with research by Fekjær (2014) which considered the different social backgrounds of all Norwegian and Swedish police recruits during one calendar year and considered the impact of this upon their early attitudes to their jobs. The results indicated that although there was considerable variety in the social background of the recruits, this was not reflected in the differences in their attitudes shortly after training began. The impact of anticipatory socialisation is referred to by Fekjær (2014), who surmises that the myths, stories and common ideas regarding what 'real' policing is all about have already caused an adjustment in the recruits' habitus before they begin the formal entry process. Bourdieu refers to this adjustment as being one that is "capable of being converted into the required habitus" (2000; cited by Chan 2003), which, as Chan considers, suggests a willingness to change and a softening of attitudes, rather than a wholesale and dramatic shift in perspective (2003).

The potential recruits' perception of what the job of policing will entail is very likely to be related to the positive features of employment that they are seeking. Potential recruits are seeking entry into an organisation that they hope will be able to fulfil those expectations. It is very likely therefore that for the majority of recruits, their pre-joining perceptions of the policing organisation are positive and correlate closely with what they are seeking in terms of employment characteristics, opportunities and prospects. Research evidence on what motivates a potential recruit to apply to join the police service would appear to support this idea.

## Motivations for Joining the Police

It is important to have a better understanding of the reasons why policing might be attractive as a career choice. A person's expectations of what this choice entails will play a significant part in their style of working (depending on what they believe is the fundamental role of the police officer) and their levels of job satisfaction (how far the reality of the job is different from their expectations). Both of these aspects are crucial determinants of the way in which police officers carry out their function.

Despite differences of time and place, there is a remarkable similarity in the reasons given by police officers as to their motivations for joining the service. This will also be analysed in Chap. 10 in terms of the recruits who were part of the longitudinal research that forms the basis of this book. Being outdoors, excitement, helping others, job security and the opportunity to be doing something different every day were all reasons cited in Hopper's (1977) research conducted in the US. Many of these themes were also cited by Van Maanen (1973), who was considering this issue in a similar time and space as Hopper—he refers to his research subjects wanting to be involved in meaningful work, wanting to be involved in work that had the potential to help society, plus the advantages of being outside (and with 'outside' comes connotations of adventure). Van Maanen (1973) also found evidence of people wanting to join what was felt to be an elite organisation, a factor emphasised by the long recruiting process and the formality of early entry into the organisation. Research published in the US and Canada some decades later (the first of which compared two cohorts of data from the 1980s and from the 2000s) found strong similarities with much of this previous data (Foley et al. 2008; Ellis 1991). Helping people, job security, excitement, prestige and the potential to fight crime were all raised by new recruits. Foley et al.'s (2008) conclusions were that motivations for joining the police remained very stable over time. In the UK, Fielding (1988a) analysed 80 essays written by new recruits about why they wanted to join the police service, which again revealed variety, excitement, being outdoors and the potential to help people and serve the community highlighted as the most important motivations for applying. Fielding (1988a) found few explicit references to 'crime fighting' and the focus of the essays was couched much more in the language of community service. In Australia too, Chan (2003) found that the most often cited reasons for wanting to join the police service were related to these community policing principles of working with people and serving the community, plus an emphasis on variety and security. The new recruits also (and not surprisingly) rated the police very highly in terms of honesty, professionalism and prestige (Chan 2003).

What all of this research suggests is that either potential police officers have a clear and accurate perception of what the job of policing will entail or the narratives and symbolism surrounding policing, which were explored in Chap. 2, have also had an impact on the beliefs of those who are seeking to join the organisation. These expectations are important, as they have the potential to shape police officers' subsequent adaptations to the realities of the job in the next phase of socialisation. Research from Norway concluded that officers who were motivated to join the police because of the potential for 'thrill-seeking' were more likely to become frustrated, cynical and fatigued than officers who joined with more community service–oriented motivations, or as he termed them, 'social workers' (Sollund 2008). Much of the research indicates that the decision to apply to join the police is not one that is taken casually. Additionally, the process of joining the police is in many parts of the world a fairly lengthy and arduous process. With the combination of these two factors therefore comes high levels of expectations and, generally, highly motivated candidates (Hazer and Alvares 1981; Van Maanen 1973, 1975; Fielding 1988a; Alain and Baril 2005).

However, does this research showing high levels of similarity in terms of motivations to join the police service amongst new recruits simply indicates that policing attracts a certain type of person? A person who is perhaps motivated by the images and narratives of policing seen in popular culture? This is an area which has divided mainly psychologists and sociologists for many years and one to which this chapter shall briefly turn.

## Importation Versus Socialisation Hypothesis

Similarities in terms of motivations prior to joining and then similarities of cultural adaptations to the job post joining have led some researchers (mainly from a psychological standpoint) to suggest that there is such a thing as a 'police personality'. This is a person who possesses certain personality characteristics (most notably mentioned are authoritarianism, conformity and extroversion (Bardi et al. 2014; Gudjonsson and Adlam 1983; Brown and Willis 1985)) prior to joining the police and who is attracted to the job on the basis that these qualities are associated with the role, are rewarded and will be found in the majority of policing colleagues. This is known as value-fit (Bardi et al. 2014) and potential employees will seek out organisations which fit them in the same way that organisations will seek out employees which fit them (Schneider 1987).

However, the evidence is this regard is far from compelling, and alternative explanations which focus upon the impact of organisational socialisation and the absence of personality characteristics which differ from those of the general population (particularly the working-class population) suggest that the importation hypothesis may be overstated (Van Maanen 1973; Burbeck and Furnham 1985). Indeed, Van Maanen (1976) is reluctant to presume that human beings have fixed personality characteristics, arguing instead that we are "always in the process of 'becoming'" (1976, p. 68). Research using fire officers as a control group found no evidence of the importation hypothesis but much support for the impact of socialisation through an analysis of authoritarian attitudes post training (Brown and Willis 1985).

Even within those research studies which found some evidence for the attractiveness of certain personality 'types' to the police, there was also acknowledgement that the process of police socialisation also played a very prominent part in developing normative attitudes and values, particularly with regard to reduced levels of empathy (Gudjonsson and Adlam 1983). Those who argue against the police personality thesis and instead favour the influence of occupational socialisation (mainly from a sociological standpoint) focus strongly on the nature of the policing role and its unique demands. The argument is that the occupational culture is so salient and strong, and the socialisation process (both formal and informal) so intense as to negate the influence and importance of pre-employment characteristics (Skolnick 1966; Britz 1997; Fekjær 2014; Paoline 2001; Bennett 1984).

The influence therefore appears to lie in the structural aspects of the job, which then affect the cognition (Bennett 1984); it is the field (or the 'setting') affecting the habitus (Bourdieu 1977), rather than pre-entry perceptions of the job affecting the development of the police officer. Anticipatory socialisation may already have played its role. Indeed, if the police service attracted a certain 'type' who was motivated by their perceived notions of what policing entailed, what would happen to these officers when their expectations met with the reality of policing? Whether there is a difference between these expectations and realities will be explored shortly. Despite Fielding's hope that this debate between personality and socialisation "may properly be consigned to sideshow status" (1988a, p. 5), it continues to rumble on, although with seemingly much more support for the influence of socialisation. Having discussed the potential impact of anticipatory socialisation which related to the police officer's motivations for joining the job, this chapter now turns to Van Maanen's (1976) second stage of the socialisation process—encounter (or change).

## Encounter

The new recruit to the police service has often been through a lengthy application and interview process before being accepted into the role. Delays between being accepted and commencing training are also a common feature of the beginning of many police careers. The influence of anticipatory socialisation has been considered, and the impact of that socialisation then plays a role in the early stages of a police career. The expectations of the job of a police officer when compared with the realities of the job can have an important influence in the adjustments or maladjustments to the role. It is no surprise that the effects of anticipatory socialisation are to personally identify with the more positive aspects of the job, the more idealised version of policing, and to contain the more negative aspects (Van Maanen 1976; Chan 2003).

However, in order to begin the identification with the new role, there must first involve a 'de-socialisation' process with the old role, that of civilian. In the case of the recruits who took part in this longitudinal research, for many, it was also the role of voluntary Special Constable or Police Community Support Officer (PCSO) that needed 'de-socialisation'. This is not only an individual adaptation to the demands of the new role (both formally and informally) but also encouraged at an organisational level by trainers who persist in the narrative of the police being the 'new family', with the old family now being superseded in importance (Chappell and Lanza-Kaduce 2009; Conti 2011). Using Braithwaite's model of 'reintegrative shaming', Conti (2009) describes the process of early socialisation into the police as one of shaming the new recruit's previous civilian status and embracing the new police status. This is particularly evident in the informal socialisation that takes place in training via the utilisation of 'war stories', which will be discussed in more detail later in this chapter (Conti 2011). This process of 'de-socialisation', of the stripping of the old self in Goffman's (1959) terms, is referred to in different ways throughout the literature, as a "destructive phase" (Van Maanen 1976, p. 84), "unfreezing" (Lewin 1952; cited in Van Maanen 1976) or "neutralizing" (Ford 2003). Gallo's police memoir refers to these very notions of birth and death in this account:

> However quirky Chicago cops seem, they begin their career just like law-enforcement officers everywhere – with a gruelling, intensive program at the Training Academy. It's a place designed to turn reasonably normal young men and women into cops, a place where dreams die and are born again, where illusions are trashed and replaced with a tenuous hold on reality, or what's real in the eyes of the Police Department. (2001; cited by Conti 2009, p. 415)

What is continually stressed in these and other accounts is socialisation through conformity. Conformity to the organisational requirements, to the organisational norms and to a shared ideology and culture.

Although there are many characteristics of the early socialisation of the new police recruit, what is most often described is "reality shock" (Hughes 1958; cited in Van Maanen 1976). This shock stems from the disconnect between the expectations of the job (linked to both anticipatory socialisation and the reasons for joining—excitement, being outdoors, community service principles) and the reality of the job. This can take effect from the very early stages of the socialisation process, even before the new recruit has experienced the realities of the job for themselves. It comes from both the formal and informal instruction of trainers within the training academy or centre (Fielding 1988a). In the vast majority of cases, this conflict between the expectations and the reality of policing is the major cause of self-initiated resignation from the police service (Haarr 2005). There are, according to Alain and Grégoire (2008), two levels of disappointment. The first is endogenous disappointment (which stems from the gap between the individual's expectations and the reality), and the second is exogenous disappointment (which stems from observations of the words, attitudes and behaviours of more experienced colleagues in their descriptions of the nature of the job). Results from this Canadian study of new police recruits suggest that both are present, with a much quicker onset of exogenous disappointment from the influence of more experienced colleagues (Alain and Grégoire 2008).

The 'reality shock' described above manifests itself in a variety of ways and relates, in part, to the misguided or misinformed impression of the role of policing. In terms of the organisation itself, recruits cited boredom, paperwork, shift work and responsibility without power as some of the prominent features of the gap between expectation and reality (Chan 2003; Ellis 1991). These new recruits also no longer valued the job security elements of a police career, as there was a drop in the numbers of those new recruits anticipating a long career in the police service (Ellis 1991).

In terms of the nature of the policing task, research also found a decreasing emphasis on, and disillusionment with, community service principles, plus feelings of alienation from the public (Ellis 1991; Chan 2003; Alain and Baril 2005; Alain and Grégoire 2008). There was also an increasing appreciation of the limits of the criminal justice system and an inability to have much influence over crime (Tuohy et al. 1993; Garner 2005; Chan 2003). Both of these points are illustrated in research from the US, which suggested an increase in perceptions of the necessity for force from new recruits in the early stages of organisational socialisation, yet increasingly as time progressed, an appreciation of the ineffectiveness of this course of action (Oberfield 2012). Recruits in both Chan's (2003) and Ellis' (1991) research felt that they had become more cynical and more suspicious.

The realisation from many new recruits that there are limits to the power of the criminal justice system to have much by way of impact on either the lives and future behaviours of offenders or the rate of offending itself relates to the parallel realisation of the limitations of the law and of formal police policy. New recruits quickly begin to appreciate that the law which governs their practice must be constantly negotiated, adapted and interpreted. It is this creative assigning of meanings to actions which then produces a patterned, informal understanding of how to respond to policing events, which forms the basis of organisational cultures—the focus of Chap. 6. Part of the 'reality shock' of the early stages of a police career therefore involves the negotiating of this vacuum between police law and police practice (Fielding 1984, 1988b). Where such a vacuum exists, the potential for attitude change is considerably stronger. Attitude change is more likely when there are discrepancies present, when attitudes have not been formed through direct experience and when prior attitudes are weak (Garner 2005). The on-street experience of new recruits provides the actual behavioural experience which police training lacks, plus involves the recruits' desire to be accepted and assimilated into the organisational cultures. This combination of factors can have an important impact upon the socialisation of the new recruit and provides the potential for attitude change (Garner 2005).

The strength and lofty idealism of the new recruits' expectations means that in many ways the fall to reality is that much further and difficult to cushion. If a newcomer to an organisation focuses more upon the extrinsic value of their new role, that is, salary and social status, those expectations are in a sense more of a known quantity and have therefore been more likely to have been established, in fact, prior to employment. Where a newcomer is focused more upon the intrinsic values of the job, that is, pride in the work, involvement or, in the case of the police, community service and helping society, then it may only be upon commencement of the role that the realisation about the nature of the job becomes much clearer. In research from the US about new police recruits, Hazer and Alvares (1981) found that it was these very intrinsic values, rather than extrinsic values, which were most prominent amongst new recruits at the time of entry into the organisation.

Research has also noted differences in the expressed attitudes and values of new recruits at different *times* during the socialisation process. These are seen in the relative swiftness of the effects of socialisation upon the attitudes of new recruits (Fielding 1986; Tuohy et al. 1993). However, these are most frequently seen in the temporary liberalising effects of the training school or academy, followed by a return to more authoritarian attitudes after the impact of street experiences (Colman and Gorman 1982). Indeed, longitudinal research from Stradling et al. (1993) found that it was possible to predict, with 90% accuracy, as to at which stage of a two-year probationary period police officers were, based upon their responses to questions about their self-image. Levels of isolation and apprehension increased and levels of self-worth decreased during training, but were then restored by the end of the probationary period. Levels of commitment and empathy, which were high upon entry into the organisation, fell during training and did not recover. The authors attribute this latter observation to the coping mechanisms of new police officers, which will be examined in the next section of this chapter.

Although, in many ways, some of this research is most likely influenced by time and place, research from Colman and Gorman (1982) in the UK and from Wortley and Homel (1995) and Christie et al. (1996) in Australia confirmed the existence of this temporary liberalising effect of police training. They found significantly more conservative attitudes (at best) and intolerant attitudes (at worst) amongst police officers with around two years' service than they did amongst new recruits. Brown and Willis (1985), whose research confirms the findings above, attribute this to, amongst other factors, the realities of the job. Undertaking hypothetical scenarios and artificially staged events in training school can afford the new recruit the opportunity to be less than authoritarian and more liberal, but the demands of operational policing suggest that this 'luxury' is subsequently more difficult to maintain (Brown and Willis 1985). Research which highlights the different effects of socialisation in recruits who are initially based in urban, rather than rural, settings would appear to confirm the veracity of this argument. Those beginning their police careers in an urban environment display much higher levels of authoritarianism in their subsequent police careers than do those socialised into a rural setting, suggesting a rural posting first could well have an important impact on future police behaviour (Brown and Willis 1985; Sato 2003).

Much of this research would confirm Chan's (2003) and Ellis' belief (1991) that the influence of the training school or academy in inculcating negative dispositions amongst new police recruits is overstated. The impact of attitude change may be swift, but research also appears to indicate that parts of it may be temporary. Chan's (2003) longitudinal research pointed instead to recruits who were far more influenced by the more powerfully socialising elements of their street experiences than by their short-lived initial training experiences.

## Metamorphosis

This chapter has provided evidence of a gap, which emerges relatively quickly after the new recruit becomes a police officer, between the expectations of the job (influenced by anticipatory socialisation) and the realities of the job as experienced within training and early field experiences. What is important to consider now is the impact of that reality shock. Van Maanen (1976) calls this stage 'metamorphosis', and it relates to the coping mechanisms and strategies which the new recruit adopts in order to be able to continue with the job, to assimilate and function as a member of the organisational culture and, importantly, to be perceived to be functioning according to the normative beliefs and attitudes of the group.

Hopper (1977) suggests that for the new recruit to the police service, there are effectively three lines of adaptation. She stresses that the presence of different lines of adaptation confirms the lack of homogeneity amongst new recruits to the police service, a point that Chan (2003) has always been very keen to emphasise. This is attributed to the differences in background knowledge of the policing world and is compared with Becker's (1961; cited in Hopper 1977) medical students, who through their pre-employment education would have more consistency of perspectives. Hopper (1977) labelled the different lines of adaptation as idealistic, practical and realistic. The first of these relates closely with some of the characteristics of anticipatory socialisation, with its emphasis on public service. The practical line of adaptation reflected a more pragmatic, open-minded, almost blank-slate approach to the job. Finally, there were the realists, who had already had experience of law enforcement. In the later analysis of the data for this research project, we shall examine whether the new recruits' previous experience of serving as a Special Constable or as a PCSO impacted upon their perceptions of what the job might entail. Hopper's research indicated that new recruits moved between groups during the early stages of their police careers. Idealists who remained in the job (as this was the group most likely to resign) moved more towards the practical group and those associated with the practical group moved more towards the realists.

Schein (1968) suggests that the options for the organisational newcomer are rebellion, creative individualism or conformity. In this analysis, Schein draws heavily from Merton's (1957) strain theory, with his individual adaptations to cultural goals. Van Maanen extends this and develops what he refers to as a 'partial' typology (1976, p. 113), which attempts to explain different methods of adaptation. What is of interest here is that Van Maanen separates these adaptations into those which are organisationally acceptable and those which are acceptable to the group (1976). The beginning of a police career will always be a negotiation as to which of these has the most impact. Whilst not completely contradictory by any means, there are clearly aspects of police behaviour that will be acceptable to one side and not to the other. Van Maanen (1976) identifies the 'team player' and the 'warrior', both of which are acceptable to the group, but only the former to the organisation. Whilst the team player seeks to conform to both organisational and cultural expectations, the warrior is more likely to be at odds or even at loggerheads with the organisation. On the other hand, Van Maanen (1976) identifies the 'isolate' and the 'outsider', both of which are unacceptable to the group, but the former acceptable to the organisation. In later work with Schein, Van Maanen simplifies these adaptations to either custodian or innovator—those who maintain the status quo or those who attempt to be more creative in their role, either through role innovation or content innovation (Van Maanen and Schein 1979). In order to adopt the custodian approach,

[o]ne simply learns the substantive requirements of the job and the customary strategies that have been developed to meet these requirements (and the norms of use that surround them) and the successful accomplishment of the mission is assured. (Van Maanen and Schein 1979, p. 31)

The custodianship approach to socialisation is frequently referred to in the police socialisation literature and evidenced through longitudinal research in the area.

As part of the strategy of maintaining the status quo, there appear to be three informal rules which become important to new recruits to the police service—to 'lay low', to 'value the team' and to 'make the law work'. These will now be considered in turn.

### (a) 'Lay Low'

As we have seen during the course of this chapter, police officers are characterised by their high levels of expectation, idealism and motivation at the start of their police careers. That idealism, in many circumstances, comes to be replaced with a more instrumental approach to the job. Chan's (2004) cohort of new recruits became progressively more cynical, suspicious, liable to stereotype and negative over the period of their 18-month training. Fielding (1988a) posed questions relevant to instrumentalism to his cohort of 125 new police recruits and found that, over time, those instrumental views increased considerably. Van Maanen (1975) considers this to be a fairly natural response to the nature of the job. Within policing, there are many potential pitfalls. Waddington refers to policing being a "punishment-centred bureaucracy" whose officers face "draconian penalties" for improper behaviour (1999, p. 301). By seeking out work and adopting a more proactive approach to the job of policing, a police officer increases not only their own personal vulnerability but that of the team, as policing very much identifies with a team ethos. Van Maanen's research astonishingly found a positive correlation between low levels of motivation and supervisors' positive ratings of new recruits (1975). The same effect was not however found when considering commitment. It was the officers' displaying higher levels of commitment who were given the most positive ratings by supervisors. This contrasts interestingly with another finding which suggests that high performance within training schools is inversely related to supervisors' positive ratings of new recruits (Van Maanen 1975). What is valued in the job is not academic success nor seeking out potentially risky work, and therefore potentially causing difficulties for the team as a whole, but to 'lay low'. In order to cope with this realisation, new recruits must adopt the "learning of complacency" (Van Maanen 1973, p. 415). This emphasises the development of "an 'in the same boat' collective consciousness stressing a 'don't make waves' occupational philosophy" (Van Maanen 1975, p. 220).

Organisational cultures are maintained and strengthened by their members choosing to adopt strategies that work and discarding strategies that fail. When choosing which cultural tools will best assist new recruits in an almost unnoticed assimilation into the group, the line of least resistance will always be to adopt the characteristics of the group—to maintain the status quo. Innovators, whether of role or content, will face a more precarious period of socialisation and innovation is therefore a less likely choice of strategy. This low-profile strategy links closely with a second informal rule for the new recruit—the important value placed on the team and the cohesiveness of the group.

### (b) 'Value the Team'

The emphasis placed by trainers upon the notion of the new police family raised earlier becomes more prominent to the police recruits as they begin their experiences within their force post training. Its importance is highlighted as being an essential component of teamwork and reliance on colleagues, which is a necessary aspect of the job of policing (Bahn 1984). Research from Obst and Davey (2003) found that the most enjoyable factors associated with police training were all associated with elements of being part of a team, which included camaraderie, bonding, the social life and teamwork being cited as the most important. When asked to rate the factors most likely to be associated with acceptance by fellow officers, new recruits rated being a team player in the top position, whilst being hard-working was down in the seventh position (Ellis 1991). The importance of camaraderie and of the beginnings of 'us versus them' in new recruits can be evidenced in Alain and Baril's (2005) research, which suggests that new recruits favoured standing with the group rather than the potential dangers in standing alone. The power of the group can then affect how a police officer approaches the difficult navigation of the gap between police law and police practice.

(c) 'Make the Law Work'

The high levels of idealism which have been discussed in relation to new recruits to the police service relates to the recruits' views and understandings about the nature of the job and their potential impact and influence on those who come into contact with the police, both offenders and victims. Those high levels of idealism are also affected therefore by the realities of the job in terms of the inability of the legal process to have any considerable impact on the myriad of social problems that the police come into contact with on a daily basis. Any account of organisational socialisation must acknowledge the interaction between the process and the structure of socialisation within a real-life context (Fielding 1984). The importance of 'situated learning', as discussed earlier in this chapter, can be seen in this context of police officer socialisation. It is both context and content dependent (Oberfield 2012). The reality for police officers is that they find a gap between 'law in books' and 'law in action' (McBarnet 1981). For new recruits, this is most often characterised by a softening or decline in the ethical standpoint that is stated before joining or during initial police training (Alain and Grégoire 2008; Garner 2005) and is expressed as a strategy of reduced compliance.

This softening of what are often fairly absolutist principles in favour of a more relativist approach is seen to reflect a combination of the presence of the organisational culture and a better understanding of the complex nature of police decision-making. A police officer's exercise of discretion can feature in more than just their actions with the public (Catlin and Maupin 2004). Evidence for this can be seen in a willingness to enforce the law differently for fellow officers (Tuohy et al. 1993), an acceptance that they may break orders to do what they feel is necessary to complete work effectively (Ellis 1991) and a preparedness to act resourcefully and creatively in responding to a perceived lack of legal powers (Alain and Baril 2005). These three informal rules of 'lay low', 'value the team' and 'make the law work' become part of Van Maanen's metamorphosis stage of police socialisation, where police officers start to create the working conditions and internalise the normative values that become associated with their workplace functioning.

This chapter has considered the influence of different stages of socialisation upon the new police recruit's attitudes to the policing organisation, their role and their colleagues. This is part of a process of identity building and change which is at its most transformative during these early stages of police socialisation. However, the new recruit is not just affected by the timing of the stages of socialisation but also by the nature of that socialisation process. This and the preceding chapter have considered the impact of both formal and informal socialisation methods on the development of their working personality (Skolnick 1966). Within those formal and informal methods however lie other models of socialisation that have the potential to affect the levels of performance, satisfaction and commitment of the new recruit.

## Models of Socialisation

Van Maanen (1978a) describes six strategies utilised by organisations to socialise their new members. These strategies have been chosen by organisations (whether by design or by accident), and that choice can have a long-lasting impact on every aspect of the recruit's attitudes towards the organisation and the inward- and outward-facing roles that the work involves. Each of Van Maanen's six strategies comes with its polar opposite and is presented on a continuum.

*Formal (*versus *informal) socialisation* refers to the extent to which newcomers are segregated from existing members during the initial training programme. Formal socialisation would involve the newcomer being treated differently from existing members and generally defines the first stages of entry into an organisation. *Individual (*versus *collective) socialisation* refers to the extent to which newcomers are 'batched' together to go through initial training together or whether newcomers embark on the process alone. *Sequential (*versus *non-sequential) socialisation* refers to the extent to which a newcomer must pass through a set of clearly defined stages or processes before they move onto the next stage of the training or initiation process. *Fixed (*versus *variable) socialisation* refers to the extent to which the newcomer is aware of a timetable of progression through the initial training before the transition to organisational member. *Serial* *(versus disjunctive) socialisation* refers to the extent to which newcomers to an organisation are coached and trained by experienced members. Disjunctive socialisation techniques would not utilise a role model approach to initial training. Finally, there is the *investiture (versus divestiture) socialisation techniques*, which refer to the extent to which the planned socialisation process is intended to build upon the newcomer's existing talents, skills and characteristics (investiture) or whether it intends to treat the candidate as a clean slate upon which to build a 'desirable' organisational member.

The socialisation of new police recruits to the policing organisation currently adopts both a formal and an informal programme of socialisation which utilises the collective, sequential, fixed, serial and divestiture tactics. New police recruits are initially trained together and are aware both of the stages that they must pass and of the programme and timetable that they are following during the training process. As has already been discussed within this and the previous chapter, newcomers to the police service are provided with more experienced members to guide them through their first experiences of policing on the streets in the form of a tutor constable and are encouraged through the narratives of the training process to join the 'police family', which is likened to starting a new life.

Van Maanen (1978a) believes that a more formal process of socialisation is linked with an organisational desire to influence the newcomer's attitudes and values. Newcomers are exposed to everything that is deemed relevant to them, and their inexperience means that they are not generally in a position to understand or appreciate which of those aspects of the formal training process will be most relevant to them. This has the potential for subsequent frustration when the reality of the role requires far fewer skills (Van Maanen 1978a). An organisation can choose to attempt to influence the newcomer not only through the formal process of socialisation but also through collective processes. Collective socialisation has the potential for building shared understandings and shared solutions amongst the members of that socialisation process and the development of an 'in the same boat' ethos (Van Maanen 1978a). Finally, both the serial and the divestiture processes are almost the embodiment of approaches to police training. Divestiture processes relate to identity, and once the new recruit has embarked upon the not-insignificant task of building a new identity, they are motivated to promote the new self-image that is associated with that identity (Van Maanen and Schein 1979). Not to do so would nullify the difficulties inherent in that identity building. Indeed, the self-narratives surrounding these new identities appear to extend to a misremembering of previous attitudes and values. Despite evidence of considerable attitude change with regard to police role and conduct, over 95% of a sample of US police recruits felt that their attitudes had remained stable (Garner 2005). Likewise, new police recruits who had previously praised the value of a community placement during initial training then denied its usefulness when interviewed after further police training and on-the-street experiences (Heslop 2011).

As discussed in this and the previous chapter, social and situated learning, learning 'on-the-job', is highly valued by both police organisational members and police recruits. Research suggests that the more participatory and situated learning in force is considered by new police officers to be the most important phase of new recruit learning (Heslop 2011). Encouraging the new recruit to embark upon a new life as a police officer has the potential to contribute to higher levels of loyalty, solidarity and commitment to the new family (colleagues, if not the organisation itself) and widen the gap between members and non-members. Divestiture and serial processes of socialisation are the clearest method of maintaining and cementing the working practices of an organisation through the use of narratives and stories which serve to inculcate the new recruit into the organisational realities of the policing role. Research from Cable and Parsons (2001) suggested that newcomers to an organisation would experience greater person–organisation fit when they learn from existing organisational members. What is neglected in this research is whether that 'fit' is with the informal culture or with the organisation itself, which may not have compatible aims. The concern of the newcomer may be more with a person–colleagues fit than with a person–organisation fit. This is exemplified in the use of stories.

Narratives and stories are used by existing organisational members to encourage the new recruit into an awareness of the working practices and the patterned responses which are appropriate to the lived reality of police officers. These stories can assist in the 'sense-making' process of assimilation into the new organisational cultures. They require only 'plausibility', rather than 'accuracy' (Weick 1995). Often referred to as 'war stories', these narratives are used to generate common-sense knowledge amongst new recruits. It is this common-sense knowledge emanating from existing or former police officers that is most highly valued by new recruits (Karp and Stenmark 2011). These methods are deemed to be an appropriate way to assist in cementing that gap between police law and policy, and police practice and to enable the new recruit to differentiate between the 'usual' and the 'unusual' (McNulty 1994). As such, war stories can contribute significantly to the patterned responses that new recruits develop in order to cope with the challenges presented in the early years of their policing careers. They provide a "partial organizational history" (Van Maanen 1973, p. 410).

These 'war stories' were delivered by those people whom new recruits found to be the most relevant and compelling in their early socialisation. The content of those stories is then important to appreciate, for it is within those stories that the meanings regarding what policing is about and what are standards of 'good' and 'bad' policing will be conveyed. Ford (2003) identified 269 separate stories during interviews with 89 US police recruits. These were in the main associated with teaching street skills and coping with the dangers and uncertainties of the job. War stories are unsurprisingly focused upon the physical, crime-fighting, rather than community-based, order maintenance aspects of the role (Chappell and Lanza-Kaduce 2009). Ford (2003) identified that 83% of these stories supported the informal subculture. This lends weight to the previous criticism of seeing 'organisational fit' as being related to the formal, rather than the informal, aims of an organisation. A person may 'fit' with the informal cultures of an organisation which may be at total odds with the expressed aims of an organisation.

The impact of the use of collective, formal, sequential, fixed, serial and divestiture socialisation tactics by the policing organisation is more likely to lead to a 'custodial' (Van Maanen and Schein 1979) or 'institutionalised' response (Jones 1986) from the newcomer, which, as discussed earlier, focuses largely upon the maintenance of the status quo. Ashforth and Saks (1996) and Jones (1986) tested these theories and argued that, with the exception of divestiture tactics, the more 'institutionalised' organisational approach to socialisation would lead to person change, job satisfaction, organisational commitment and organisational identification. This had the effect of increasing attachment and loyalty, stimulating attitude change and ensuring conformity. This solidarity is enhanced through the narratives and storytelling associated with the informal teaching methods used by both tutors and trainers within the police service (Chappell and Lannza-Kaduce 2009). The importance of these different and often unobserved areas of influence on the early socialisation of new police recruits has been observed by policing commentators in discussions about 'police reference groups'.

Reference groups provide a frame of reference, or a filter, within which meanings can be understood and explained (Bennett 1984). According to Harris (1973; cited in Fielding 1988a), there are three reasons that new police recruits turn to police reference groups as a source of support in the early stages of their socialisation into the organisation. They do so for guidance and support, they do so in the face of ambiguity and uncertainty emanating from the organisation about the policing role, and they do so to counteract the isolation and anxiety associated with the public-facing nature of policing. The extent to which the new recruit is influenced by and affiliated with these reference groups will affect the extent to which they abide by the norms of the group (Bennett 1984). Morrison (1993) suggests that organisational newcomers are in search of information about their role, the organisation and how to adapt to both. They can find this information either through a process of monitoring (observing others) or through enquiry (requesting the information). Survey results indicated that newcomers are much more likely to engage in monitoring which gives more prominence to the stated attitudes and displayed behaviours of both tutor constables and shift colleagues (Morrison 1993).

Within UK policing, once the new recruit has moved to an individual police station, it is the tutor constable and the colleagues in the shift to which that recruit is assigned who will have the closest daily contact with the recruit. The formal role of the tutor constable was assessed in the previous chapter. What is perhaps more important and worth pursuing is the informal status of mentor, guide, role model and paragon that the tutor constable and shift colleagues are accorded by new recruits. Evidence suggests that the values of new recruits change during training in the direction of these more experienced officers (Bennett 1984). It is a classic example of the *triadic* relationships between 'masters', 'young masters' and 'apprentices' (Lave and Wenger 1991, p. 56) that was discussed earlier in this chapter in relation to the CoP model of learning. Research by Paoline and Terrill (2014) found that the vast majority of their sample of US officers believed that most of the learning took place 'on the job' and with the guidance of other officers. This aspect of both the formal and informal training of police officers is one of the least understood aspects of police training and socialisation. This will be analysed in depth via an analysis of the interviews with new recruits as part of this research study in Part II.

This chapter has attempted to analyse the ways in which new recruits learn how to be police officers through the process of socialisation. In the process of 'becoming' a police officer, new recruits are acquiring the necessary skills and adapting their 'habitus' in appropriate ways in order to 'fit' with the organisational and cultural demands of membership (Heslop 2011). Organisations make choices about aspects of this socialisation which consequently have an impact on the nature of the process and its results. Organisational behaviour is also influenced by the more informal socialisation processes that are member driven and aim to fill the gap between policy and practice. This is part of a process of identity building amongst new police recruits which is particularly evident during these early stages of police socialisation. This gap between policy and practice is reflected in the gap between training school learning and on-the-street learning. By bridging the gap between learning on the streets and learning in training schools, there is the potential for less recourse to informal, culturally accepted methods of action and more recourse to research-evidenced, organisationally driven objectives. Police training should aim to reduce levels of uncertainty amongst new recruits and build confidence in a supported environment (Eraut 2004; Jones 1986).

Understanding these processes and the influences upon new recruits provides a far better appreciation of the nature of police behaviour. There is no doubt that although there is the potential for change throughout a police career, the most fundamental aspects of attitude change and the absorption or rejection of the organisational cultures will be at an advanced stage by the end of the probationary period of a police constable. Research analysed in this chapter has suggested that these new recruits, upon joining the organisation, are generally highly idealised and highly motivated with a strong public service ethos. Participation in both the formal and informal training, plus experience of policing on the streets, results in, for many officers, two levels of disappointment—endogenous (which stems from the gap between the individual's expectations and the reality) and exogenous (which stems from observations of the words, attitudes and behaviours of more experienced colleagues in their descriptions of the nature of the job). The potential result of this disappointment is a more cynical, suspicious, alienated officer who displays lower levels of empathy and higher levels of authoritarianism. The informal rules of 'lay low', 'value the team' and 'make the law work' appear to be strong guiding principles. These are clearly not strategies adopted by all officers, as there is much evidence to suggest that officers are discerning self-selectors of the most appropriate elements of the informal cultural characteristics (Chan 2003). However, police officers also display strong characteristics of conformity and of compliance in terms of their desire for acceptance and to benefit from organisational solidarity. These cultural characteristics will be explored further in future chapters.

# References

6, P., Bellamy, C., Raab, C., Warren, A., & Heeney, C. (2006). Institutional Shaping of Interagency Working: Managing Tensions Between Collaborative Working and Client Confidentiality. *Journal of Public Administration Research and Theory, 17*, 405–434.

Alain, M., & Baril, C. (2005). Crime Prevention, Crime Repression, and Policing: Attitudes of Police Recruits Towards Their Role in Crime Control. *International Journal of Comparative and Applied Criminal Justice, 29*(2), 123–148.

Alain, M., & Grégoire, M. (2008). Can Ethics Survive the Shock of the Job? Quebec's Police Recruits Confront Reality. *Policing and Society, 18*(2), 169–189.

Amin, A., & Roberts, J. (2008). Knowing in Action: Beyond Communities of Practice. *Research Policy, 37*, 353–369.

Ashforth, B., & Saks, A. (1996). Socialization Tactics: Longitudinal Effects on Newcomer Adjustments. *The Academy of Management Journal, 39*(1), 149–178.

Bahn, C. (1984). Police Socialization in the Eighties: Strains in the Forging of an Occupational Identity. *Journal of Police Science and Administration, 12*(4), 390–394.

Bardi, A., Buchanan, K., Goodwin, R., Slabu, L., & Robinson, M. (2014). Value Stability and Change During Self-Chosen Life Transitions: Self-Selection Versus Socialization Effects. *Journal of Personality and Social Psychology, 106*(1), 131–147.

Bennett, R. (1984). Becoming Blue: A Longitudinal Study of Police Recruit Occupational Socialization. *Journal of Police Science and Administration, 12*(1), 47–58.

Bourdieu, P. (1977). *Outline of a Theory of Practice.* Cambridge: Cambridge University Press.

Britz, M. (1997). The Police Subculture and Occupational Socialization: Exploring Individual and Demographic Characteristics. *American Journal of Criminal Justice, 21*(2), 127–146.

Brown, L., & Willis, A. (1985). Authoritarianism in British Police Recruits: Importation, Socialization or Myth? *Journal of Occupational Psychology, 58*, 97–108.

Burbeck, E., & Furnham, A. (1985). Police Officer Selection: A Critical Review of the Literature. *Journal of Police Science and Administration, 13*(1), 58–69.

Cable, D., & Parsons, C. (2001). Socialization Tactics and Person-Organization Fit. *Personnel Psychology, 54*(1), 1–23.

Campbell, M. (2009). Learning in Early-Career Police: Coming into the Workplace. *Asia-Pacific Journal of Cooperative Education, 10*(1), 19–28.

Catlin, D., & Maupin, J. (2004). A Two Cohort Study of the Ethical Orientations of State Police Officers. *Policing: An International Journal of Police Strategies and Management, 27*(3), 289–301.

Chan, J. (2003). *Fair Cop: Learning the Art of Policing.* Toronto: University of Toronto Press.

Chan, J. (2004). Using Pierre Bourdieu's Framework for Understanding Police Culture. *Droit et Société, 56–57*, 327–347.

Chappell, A., & Lanza-Kaduce, L. (2009). Police Academy Socialization: Understanding the Lessons Learned in a Paramilitary-Bureaucratic Organization. *Journal of Contemporary Ethnography, 39*(2), 187–214.

Christie, G., Petrie, S., & Timmins, P. (1996). The Effect of Police Education, Training and Socialisation on Conservative Attitudes. *The Australian and New Zealand Journal of Criminology, 29*(3), 299–314.

Colman, A., & Gorman, L. (1982). Conservatism, Dogmatism, and Authoritarianism in British Police Officers. *Sociology, 16*(1), 1–11.

Conti, N. (2006). Role Call: Preprofessional Socialization into Police Culture. *Policing and Society, 16*(3), 221–242.

Conti, N. (2009). A Visigoth System: Shame, Honour, and Police Socialization. *Journal of Contemporary Ethnography, 38*(3), 409–432.

Conti, N. (2011). Weak Links and Warrior Hearts: A Framework for Judging Self and *Others* in Police Training. *Police Practice and Research, 12*(5), 410–423.

Daymon, C. (2000). Culture Formation in a New Television Station: A Multi-Perspective Analysis. *British Journal of Management, 11*(2), 121–135.

Ellis, R. (1991). Perceptions, Attitudes and Beliefs of Police Recruits. *Canadian Police College Journal, 15*(2), 95–117.

Eraut, M. (2004). Informal Learning in the Workplace. *Studies in Continuing Education, 26*(2), 247–273.

Fekjær, S. (2014). Police Students' Social Background, Attitudes and Career Plans. *Policing: An International Journal of Police Strategies and Management, 37*(3), 467–483.

Fielding, N. (1984). Police Socialization and Police Competence. *The British Journal of Sociology, 35*(4), 568–590.

Fielding, N. (1986). Evaluating the Role of Training in Police Socialization: A British Example. *Journal of Community Psychology, 14*(3), 319–330.

Fielding, N. (1988a). *Joining Forces: Police Training, Socialization, and Occupational Competence.* London: Routledge.

Fielding, N. (1988b). *Joining Forces: Police Training, Socialization, and Occupational Competence.* London: Routledge.

Fielding, N., & Fielding, J. (1991). Police Attitudes to Crime and Punishment. *British Journal of Criminology, 31*(1), 39–53.

Foley, P., Guarneri, C., & Kelly, M. (2008). Reasons for Choosing a Police Career: Changes over Two Decades. *International Journal of Police Science and Management, 10*(1), 2–8.

Ford, R. (2003). Saying One Thing, Meaning Another: The Role of Parables in Police Training. *Police Quarterly, 6*(1), 84–110.

Fox, S. (2000). Communities of Practice, Foucault and Actor-Network Theory. *Journal of Management Studies, 37*(6), 853–868.

Fuller, A. (2007). Critiquing Theories of Learning and Communities of Practice. In J. Hughes, N. Hewson, & L. Unwin (Eds.), *Communities of Practice: Critical Perspectives* (pp. 17–29). London: Routledge.

Fuller, A., & Unwin, L. (2003). Learning as Apprentices in the Contemporary UK Workplace: Creating and Managing Expansive and Restrictive Participation. *Journal of Education and Work, 16*(4), 407–426.

Garner, R. (2005). Police Attitudes: The Impact of Experience After Training. *Applied Psychology in Criminal Justice, 1*(1), 56–70.

Goffman, E. (1959). *The Presentation of Self in Everyday Life.* New York: Doubleday Anchor.

Gudjonsson, G., & Adlam, K. (1983). Personality Patterns of British Police Officers. *Personality and Individual Differences, 4*(5), 507–512.

Haarr, R. (2005). Factors Affecting the Decision of Police Recruits to "Drop Out" of Police Work. *Police Quarterly, 8*(4), 431–453.

Hazer, J., & Alvares, K. (1981). Police Work Values During Organizational Entry and Assimilation. *Journal of Applied Psychology, 66*(1), 12–18.

Heslop, R. (2011). Community Engagement and Learning as 'Becoming': Findings from a Study of British Police Recruit Training. *Policing and Society, 21*(3), 327–342.

Hodkinson, P., & Hodkinson, H. (2004). *A Constructive Critique of Communities of Practice: Moving Beyond Lave and Wenger.* Seminar paper presented at 'Integrating Work and Learning – Contemporary Issues' seminar series. Retrieved from http://hdl.voced.edu.au/10707/18014

Holmes, J., & Marra, M. (2002). Having a Laugh at Work: How Humour Contributes to Workplace Culture. *Journal of Pragmatics, 34,* 1683–1710.

Holmes, J., & Meyerhoff, M. (1999). The Community of Practice: Theories and Methodologies in Language and Gender Research. *Language in Society, 28,* 173–183.

Hopper, M. (1977). Becoming a Policeman: Socialization of Cadets in a Police Academy. *Urban Life, 6*(2), 149–170.

Hughes, E. (1958). *Men and Their Work.* Glencoe: Free Press.

Hughes, J. (2007). Lost in Translation: Communities of Practice. In J. Hughes, N. Hewson, & L. Unwin (Eds.), *Communities of Practice: Critical Perspectives* (pp. 30–40). London: Routledge.

Jones, G. (1986). Socialization Tactics, Self-Efficacy, and Newcomers' Adjustments to Organizations. *The Academy of Management Journal, 29*(2), 262–279.

Karp, S., & Stenmark, H. (2011). Learning to Be a Police Officer. Tradition and Change in the Training and Professional Lives of Police Officers. *Police Practice and Research, 12*(1), 4–15.

Kerosuo, H., & Engeström, Y. (2003). Boundary Crossing and Learning in Creation of New Work Practice. *Journal of Workplace Learning, 15*(7–8), 345–351.

Lave, J., & Wenger, E. (1991). *Situated Learning*. Cambridge: Cambridge University Press.

McBarnet, D. (1981). *Conviction: Law, the State and the Construction of Justice*. London: Routledge.

McNulty, E. (1994). Generating Common Sense Knowledge Among Police Officers. *Symbolic Interaction, 17*(3), 281–294.

Merton, R. (1957). *Social Theory and Social Structure*. New York: Free Press.

Morrison, E. (1993). Newcomer Information Seeking: Exploring Types, Modes, Sources, and Outcomes. *The Academy of Management Journal, 36*(3), 557–589.

Oberfield, Z. (2012). Socialization and Self-Selection: How Police Officers Develop Their Views About Using Force. *Administration and Society, 44*(6), 702–730.

Obst, P., & Davey, J. (2003). Does the Police Academy Change Your Life? A Longitudinal Study of Changes in Socialising Behaviour of Police Recruits. *International Journal of Police Science and Management, 5*(1), 31–40.

Paoline, E. (2001). *Rethinking Police Culture: Officers' Occupational Attitudes*. New York: LFB Scholarly Publishing.

Paoline, E., & Terrill, W. (2014). *Police Culture: Adapting to the Strains of the Job*. Durham: Carolina Academic Press.

Reber, A. (1993). *Implicit Learning and Tacit Knowledge: An Essay on the Cognitive Unconscious*. Oxford: Oxford University Press.

Roberts, J. (2006). Limits to Communities of Practice. *Journal of Management Studies, 43*(3), 623–639.

Sato, M. (2003). Police Recruits' Training and the Socialisation Process: From the Network Perspective. *The Police Journal, 76*, 289–303.

Schein, E. (1968). Organisational Socialization and the Profession of Management. *Industrial Management Review, 9*, 1–16.

Schein, E. (1971). Organizational Socialization and the Profession of Management. *Industrial Management Review, 2*, 37–45.

Schneider, B. (1987). The People Make the Place. *Personnel Psychology, 40*(3), 437–453.

Skolnick, J. (1966). *Justice Without Trial: Law Enforcement in Democratic Society*. New York: Wiley and Sons.

Sollund, R. (2008). Tough Cop-Soft Cop? The Impact of Motivations and Experiences on Police Officers' Approaches to the Public. *Journal of Scandinavian Studies in Criminology and Crime Prevention, 9*(2), 119–140.

Stradling, S., Crowe, G., & Tuohy, A. (1993). Changes in Self-Concept During Occupational Socialization of New Recruits to the Police. *Journal of Community and Applied Social Psychology, 3*(2), 131–147.

Tajfel, H. (1978). Interindividual Behaviour and Intergroup Behaviour. In H. Tajfel (Ed.), *Differentiation Between Social Groups: Studies in the Social Psychology of Intergroup Relations* (pp. 27–60). London: Academic Press.

Tajfel, H., & Turner, J. (1986). The Social Identity Theory of Intergroup Behaviour. In W. Austin & S. Worchel (Eds.), *Psychology of Intergroup Relations* (pp. 7–24). Chicago: Nelson Hall.

Tuohy, A., Wrenall, M., McQueen, R., & Stradling, S. (1993). Effect of Socialization Factors on Decisions to Prosecute: The Organizational Adaptation of Scottish Police Recruits. *Law and Human Behaviour, 17*(2), 167–181.

Van Maanen, J. (1973). Observations on the Making of Policemen. *Human Organization, 32*(4), 407–418.

Van Maanen, J. (1975). Police Socialization: A Longitudinal Examination of Job Attitudes in an Urban Police Department. *Administrative Science Quarterly, 20*(2), 207–228.

Van Maanen, J. (1976). Breaking In: Socialization to Work. In R. Dubin (Ed.), *Handbook of Work, Organization and Society* (pp. 67–130). Chicago: Rand McNally College Publishing Company.

Van Maanen, J. (1978a). People Processing: Strategies of Organizational Socialization. *Organizational Dynamics*, Summer, 19–36.

Van Maanen, J. (1978b). Kinsmen in Repose: Occupational Perspectives of Patrolmen. In P. Manning & J. Van Maanen (Eds.), *Police: A View from the Street* (pp. 115–127). Santa Monica: Goodyear Publishing Company.

Van Maanen, J., & Schein, E. (1979). Toward a Theory of Organizational Socialization. In B. Staw (Ed.), *Research in Organizational Behaviour* (Vol. 1, pp. 209–264). Greenwich: JAI.

Waddington, P. (1999). Police (Canteen) Culture: An Appreciation. *British Journal of Criminology, 39*(2), 287–309.

Weick, K. (1995). *Sensemaking in Organizations*. Thousand Oaks: Jossey-Bass.

Wenger, E. (1998). *Communities of Practice: Learning, Meaning, Identity*. Cambridge: Cambridge University Press.

Wortley, R., & Homel, R. (1995). Police Prejudice as a Function of Training and Outgroup Contact: A Longitudinal Investigation. *Law and Human Behaviour, 19*(3), 305–317.

# 6

# Being a Police Officer: Policing Cultures

A central concern of this book is on 'learning' and on 'becoming'. As previously discussed, debates about the formal and informal processes of socialisation into a new institution, with the adoption of a potentially altered social and personal identity, are too often overlooked at the expense of description of apparently homogeneous cultural characteristics of police officers. The adoption of these characteristics is often presented as a *fait accompli*. This book has attempted to address these shortcomings through a close analysis of the socialisation and identity literature, and will continue to do this in Part II through an analysis of the qualitative interviews with new recruits in the first stages of their police careers. However, we must also seek to examine what it is that these new recruits are being socialised into, and what it is they are learning to 'become'. In doing so, it is important to unravel many decades of policing research which has sought to identify what is meant by 'policing cultures'.

Policing cultures remain an enduring field of enquiry, a situation which has remained unaltered since Skolnick (1966), Westley (1970), Cain (1973) and Banton (1964) were writing in the 1960s and 1970s. Although their work was not specifically concerned with policing cultures, but rather a sociological analysis of the police officer and police work, it

© The Author(s) 2017
S. Charman, *Police Socialisation, Identity and Culture*,
DOI 10.1007/978-3-319-63070-0_6

provided a wealth of material through observation and analysis that was later to be used to formulate theories of policing cultures. What also, in many cases, remains unaltered is the almost universal condemnation of the cultures of the police as sites of masculine hegemony, racism, prejudice, discrimination and exclusion. Further research suggested that police officers exhibited the characteristics of secrecy (Goldsmith 1990; Punch 1983), cynicism (De Lint 1998; Scripture 1997), authoritarianism (Waddington 1999a), aggression (Reiner 1992; Fielding 1994; Christensen and Crank 2001), hostility (Reiner 1992; Scripture 1997), suspicion (Skolnick 1966) and prejudice (Drummond 1976). More recent research has maintained the enduring continuity of some of these characteristics (Loftus 2009), despite considerable change both externally, in the social, political and cultural climate in which police officers work, and internally, through demographic and organisational change. A handful of authors have challenged this orthodoxy and pointed to the necessity of a re-evaluation of this conception (Chan 1997; Waddington 1999a; Sklansky 2006), yet the original narrative persists. Policing cultures are repeatedly referred to as being rigid, immutable and "deeply entrenched and pervasive" (Davies and Thomas 2003, p. 682). This chapter seeks to acknowledge but also advance these debates by exploring and appreciating the role of policing cultures and how they are utilised by members.

Any academic enquiry considering the thorny subject of policing cultures raises almost as many questions as it can provide answers. Ignoring the issue of whether we can state with any confidence that an organisational or occupational culture even exists, we are then confronted with a range of complex issues. As we discovered in Chap. 2, culture embraces all that is generally known but mostly unseen within an organisation. The culture or cultures of an organisation are not concrete, tangible entities, framed in organisational documentation, but rather socially constructed realities. This point raises the first of these complex issues. Should we continue to discuss police culture as a homogeneous set of values, attitudes and behaviours which transcend time, location, role and rank, or should we instead allow for the incorporation of multiple conceptions of culture into our understanding of policing (Chan 1997)? Relatedly, to what extent are the characteristics of policing cultures (if it is possible to identify such traits) shared across different organisations and in different jurisdictions? Second, to what extent are the characteristics of policing cultures identified during the 1960s and 1970s still relevant today once these are considered alongside the rapidly changing policing landscape across the world? Third, what role do police officers themselves play in the adoption and/or rejection of the cultural norms associated with policing? Are they the passive recipients of aggressive organisational cultures or are they active cultural agents who shape and mould those cultural norms to suit their working practices? Fourth, what impact do the attitudes and values associated with policing cultures have on the behaviours of officers when understanding their work (Waddington 1999a)? What is the relationship (if indeed there is one) between 'talk' and 'action'? This is by no means an exhaustive list of the questions and challenges which the scholars of policing cultures face. It is however the basis upon which this chapter will be structured.

It will begin with an analysis of what policing cultures 'were' or at least what they were purported to be by some of the early writers in this field. This will be considered from the standpoint of those who wrote about the universal themes of police culture and those who instead favoured, and still favour, the production of cultural typologies to examine the different 'types' of police officer. This will be followed by an analysis of the 'challengers' to these traditional notions of policing cultures who have raised some of the questions which have just been referred to. This will be a consideration of what policing cultures 'are' or purport to be. However, there is also another school of thought that argues that although the descriptions of policing cultures can be expanded upon, policing is still very much influenced by the enduring characteristics of a recalcitrant police culture which is dominant despite the fundamental changes to the policing environment. This standpoint will also therefore be analysed. Finally, the chapter will examine the issue of what policing cultures 'do'. It will do this not necessarily from the standpoint of cultures as an impediment to policing practice but from the standpoint of cultures as a resource, or as a tool, with which to navigate the difficult terrain of policing citizens.

There are however two points of note. First, although acknowledging the potential for there being multiple police cultures within policing environments, the terminology used in this chapter will follow tradition and refer to police culture in the singular. This is not to deny the existence of multiple cultures but for ease of reading and understanding the arguments put forward. Second, when police culture is being discussed, it is within the two contexts in which police officers operate—the occupational setting and the organisational setting (Paoline 2003). The occupational setting refers to officers' connections and interactions with the public, and the organisational setting refers to officers' connections and interactions with colleagues and managers. Any analysis of police culture must accommodate the potential for alternative cultural characteristics emerging in those two very different 'front-stage' and 'back-stage' arenas (Goffman 1959).

## What Police Culture 'Was': Part I—The Traditional and Universal Themes of Police Culture

Van Maanen (1978) has suggested that the police are strongly influenced in their beliefs and attitudes by two distinct occupational perspectives. Taken together, they form the basis for a police officer's understanding of their position and their subsequent behaviour. The first of these perspectives is the unique position that the police officer occupies in society and, in particular, as an outsider in that society. The second relates to the nature of the work that police officers are involved with and, importantly, how to cope with performing that role.

One of the earliest works concerning police culture was undertaken in the US by Skolnick. His analysis of police culture has been cited in work conducted in this area ever since. His argument was that certain characteristics of policing or "distinctive cognitive tendencies" (1966, p. 42) emerged, in part, due to certain aspects of the police task. The combination of danger (through exposure to the public), authority (through being the custodian of law) and pressure (through the need to achieve results), and a preoccupation with these factors, places the police officer in a unique position. This combination of working attributes, which are felt individually by other professions but not in their entirety, leads the police officer to display signs of suspiciousness, isolation and, through that, solidarity. Solidarity is considered to be a powerful bond which unites police officers in their work, both in terms of the public and from external oversight via the 'blue code of silence' (Westmarland 2005; Westmarland and Rowe 2016; Chan 2003; Goldsmith 1990). Westley (1970), in an analysis of the functions and activities of the police, also considered the prevalence of secrecy and self-protection amongst police officers. These characteristics emerge because of the working environment of the police officer. These important themes of suspiciousness and isolation, of there being a distinctive 'us versus them' mindset amongst police officers which sets them apart from the public, have been more widely pursued (Holdaway 1983; Van Maanen 1973; Young 1991). These notions play to the ideology of the unique status of policing and of police officers.

Much of the early research on police culture referred to it as all-encompassing. Skolnick has argued that "being a police officer is a defining identity" (2008, p. 35). In much the same vein as some of the early positivistic accounts of criminality depicted incontrovertible differences between offenders and non-offenders, likewise the early police culture literature characterised the features of police culture as all-consuming and therefore potentially isolating. The military-style rank structure, the promotion of discipline and obedience, the uniform and the 24-hour nature of the job, all fed into an institutionalised ideology of a unique organisation set apart from the public. The inevitable impact of isolating those outside of the organisation was a promotion of the imagery of solidarity and communality amongst its members and an expectation of remaining a member of that organisation for life (Soeters 2000). A result of this investment in the group is the gaining of what Bourdieu refers to as 'social capital', which enhances levels of solidarity through the affirming and reaffirming of shared values (1986). Organisations such as these have been referred to as "greedy institutions" (Coser 1974). Ahern (former New Haven, Connecticut police chief) perhaps aptly suggests:

> The day the new recruit walks through the door of the police academy, he leaves society behind to enter a profession that does more than give him a job, it defines who he is. He will always be a cop. (1972, cited in Skolnick 2008)

The identification of police culture as an academic line of enquiry, which began in the 1960s, started to become more prominent in subsequent decades. Psychological research, in particular, began to attempt to measure the extent to which these characteristics were consistently found in police officers. Research by Butler and Cochrane (1977) attempted to empirically test the personality of the English police officer through questionnaires. Results indicated that as police officers progressed through their careers, they displayed higher levels of both autonomy and aggression. Personality measures were also used to assess levels of punitiveness amongst US police officers, which were found to be higher than amongst the general population (Carlson and Sutton 1975).

Others have questioned the extent to which these apparent characteristics of police culture are unique to police officers or whether they are indeed more reflective of the characteristics of the broader, mainly working-class populations that police officers are drawn from (Waddington 1999a). In a survey of officers about a range of social and political issues such as the right to strike and capital punishment, there was no evidence of a difference in views held between police officers and the general public (Scripture 1997). Although there will inevitably be a reshaping of personal identity on entering a new occupational and/or organisational culture, it is unlikely that all previous identities would be eradicated. Chan (2004) argues that on entering a new organisation, new recruits bring with them the 'habitus' from the previously inhabited 'field'. Both Waddington (1999a) and Crank (1998) argue strongly that the cultural characteristics of the police are a reflection of broader societal values:

> It is far from the case that the police are a repository for authoritarianism, racism and conservatism within a liberal population brimming over with the milk of human kindness. (Waddington 1999a, p. 292)

Given the plethora of individual characteristics that are used to describe police officers (sometimes just listed and sometimes 'tested'), it is hardly surprising that Reiner's 6 (1978) and subsequently 11 (2010) of the most widely cited such characteristics are oft quoted. These are as follows: a sense of mission, the focus on action (referred to elsewhere as a preoccupation with the 'crime-fighting image'), cynicism, pessimism, suspicion, isolation, solidarity, conservatism, machismo, racial prejudice and pragmatism. Crank (1998), in his analysis of police culture in the US, suggests that there are 18 such characteristics which, he argues, are common to all police officers. He incorporates many from Reiner's list but additional themes of guns and force perhaps reflect the different nature of policing in the US. There is potentially a danger therefore in adhering to the portability of these characteristics across continents and jurisdictions.

The descriptions of police culture from the early studies both in the UK and in the US strongly featured these themes of solidarity, crime-fighting, masculinity and suspicion. Most were written to encompass all police officers, as research was very much concentrated on officers engaged in street patrol work. However, whilst these more universal descriptions of police culture continued to be worked upon and added to, an alternative approach to police culture was also being considered by another group of academics who preferred to categorise police culture into typologies or ideal types.

## What Police Culture 'Was': Part II—Typologies of Police Culture

Whilst the universal descriptions of the characteristics of police culture explained above focus upon the similarities within police culture, a further strand of police research aimed to highlight the variations inherent in individual policing styles. Wilson's three departmental styles (watchman style, legalistic style and service style) were the first of these typologies (1968). However, the characteristics described in the universal descriptions of police culture are still present in at least one of the categories of all of these typologies. Paoline (2004) has noted that Broderick's (1977) 'Enforcer', Brown's (1988) 'Old- Style Crime Fighter', Muir's (1977) 'Enforcer', Reiner's (1978) 'New Centurion', Walsh's (1977) 'Action Seeker' and White's (1972) 'Tough Cop', all encapsulate the action-oriented, crime-fighting, authoritarian officer who is described in the more homogeneous descriptions. To this, we could also add Paoline's

(2004) 'Traditionalist', Cochran and Bromley's (2003) 'Subcultural Adherent' and Mastrofski et al. (2002) 'Tough Cops'.

However, these typologies of police officer characteristics go further and allow for the possibility of there being different styles of policing behaviour which are influenced by different conceptions of the role of the police officer. This can be seen in the number of additional police officer 'types' (generally, although not always, between three and six 'types') identified in the research mentioned above. It would be neither feasible nor desirable to outline all of the typologies of police 'types' in this chapter but merit perhaps in selecting a handful of these typologies for further consideration. Four of these stand out from the others for varying reasons. The four chosen incorporate both the US and Europe, cover a wide span of history and have used contrasting methods in reaching their conclusions. Reiner (1978) and Muir (1977) present two of the classic police typologies which consider both the UK and the US and utilise observational and interview research. The typologies of Paoline (2004) and Hendriks and van Hulst (2016) can provide a more contemporary consideration of the US and the Netherlands using survey and interview data and 'grid-group cultural theory' (GGCT).

Reiner's (1978) original conception of six types was subsequently (1985) honed to four, with the loss of the 'social worker' and the 'Federation activist'. This potentially also provides us with an insight into the changing sensibilities of not only police officers but wider British culture. However, the four remaining 'types' were first the 'Bobby', who was characterised as being an 'ordinary copper' who remained committed to the traditional culture of policing and was generally favourable towards his job (gender is not referred to in these early typologies). Similarly, but potentially more pronounced in his views was the 'New Centurion', an officer who had high opinions of the role of police officers as being a virtue of good fighting evil, with the 'fighting' of crime very much being the metaphor. The contrast to this type is Reiner's (1978) 'Uniform Carrier', an officer who favoured the 'lay low' approach referred to by Van Maanen (1975) in Chap. 5 of this book and displays the characteristics of cynicism and disillusionment. A further contrast is found in the 'Professional', a much more liberally minded officer who adheres more to the formal, rather than the informal, organisational goals and has high ambitions for his career.

William Muir (1977) aptly subtitled his account of police culture 'Streetcorner Politicians' and his in-depth ethnography of 28 police officers in one North American city revealed four 'types' of police officer. Whilst Muir identified one type he deemed to be (and named them) 'Professionals' (in a similar vein to Reiner's 'Bobby'), he determined that this was accompanied by three further types, whom he referred to as 'non-professionals'. These were:

> (1) enforcers – police who had passion, but lacked perspective; (2) reciprocators – police who had perspective, but lacked passion; and (3) avoiders – police who lacked both passion and perspective. (Muir 1977, p. 55)

Whilst portrayed in a more negative light than Reiner's typology of officer 'types', there are certainly similarities and the two accounts were published at a similar time. Reiner (2010) himself sees parity between the 'New Centurion' and the 'Enforcer', the 'Uniform Carrier' and the 'Avoider', and his 'Professional' against Muir's 'Reciprocator'.

Almost 30 years on, research in the US by Paoline (2004) reinforced many of the previous conceptions of policing 'types', but also supplemented this with two new categories. Importantly, Paoline argued that demographic changes to policing personnel, combined with changes within policing philosophies (e.g. the introduction of community policing), necessitated a reconsideration and an addition to the previous categories of police officer found in the original typologies of the 1970s. His 'Lay Low', 'Old Pro', 'Traditionalist', 'Peacekeeper' and 'Law Enforcer' were all still present, but to this Paoline added the 'Anti-Organisational Street Cop' and the 'Dirty Harry Enforcer' (2004). Whilst the 'Anti-Organisational Street Cop' shared much in common with the 'Lay Lows' and the 'Traditionalists', they also exhibited strongly negative attitudes towards their supervisors and strongly positive attitudes towards citizens. They highly valued their ability to use discretion in their role. The second of the new categories, the 'Dirty Harry Enforcer', stands in stark contrast to this. These officers strongly support more aggressive tactics of patrol and hold more negative attitudes towards citizens than the 'Anti-Organisational Street Cops'. They would also support the infringement of the rights of citizens and the non-enforcement of the law should they feel that the need arises (Paoline 2004).

Hendriks and van Hulst's (2016) application of the GGCT to the study of policing culture moves the debates around typologies of police culture one step further. Instead of manipulating officers into 'types' who will respond to each and every policing event with manifestly similar attitudes and behaviours, the GGCT presupposes that organisations function through the interplay between multiple value and belief systems (Thompson et al. 1990). This has been likened to 'step-dancing' (Hood 1998) or 'tap dancing' (Hendriks and van Hulst 2016) in that organisational practices need to adapt to changing environments.

In the policing world, there is much to commend this approach. Writers have long argued that in the multiplicity of roles and positions that police officers hold (see Chap. 2), there are tensions that emerge from working within the policing organisation and tensions inherent in managing citizens outside of the organisation (Van Maanen 1978; Paoline 2003). In working with the public, police officers are highly visible, are required to be immediately responsive and, in doing so, are able to draw upon the use of coercion. In working with their supervisors and managers, police officers are mostly invisible, work within a rigid hierarchal structure, are required to be less immediately responsive and need to account for their activities. The possibility therefore that these different scenarios would elicit different attitudes and behaviours must be accounted for.

Hendriks and van Hulst (2016) adopt the GGCT for police culture which takes the form of a grid encompassing four modes of organisational participation delineated across two lines—the group dimension ('me culture' or 'we culture') and the grid dimension (roles ascribed or roles achieved). Hendriks and van Hulst (2016) still utilise the styles first depicted in the 1970s, but also highlight the police officer's movement between these types as they utilise the appropriate cultural tools which are available to them. 'Atomism in policing' ('me culture', roles ascribed) is associated with laying low and staying out of trouble, which is likened to Muir's (1977) 'Avoider'. 'Individualism in policing' ('me culture', roles achieved) depicts the competent, problem-solving police officer, similar to Muir's 'Professional'. 'Hierarchy in policing' ('we culture', roles ascribed) is closely related to Muir's 'Enforcer' and stresses law enforcement and rank structure. Finally, 'enclavism in policing' ('we culture', roles achieved) focuses upon the characteristic of solidarity both with colleagues and with the public through community policing, likened to Muir's 'Reciprocator'.

Hendriks and van Hulst (2016, pp. 12–13) call for 'cultural versatility' in the approach towards police culture, to see new characteristics of that culture as not replacing the old but simply adding to the 'sedimentation' of policing practices. This reflects Bourdieu's conception of the cultural knowledge (habitus) of an organisation's members as a layering or sedimentation of social history (Bourdieu 1986). Whilst the language and classifications of these police cultural typologies may be different, and whilst it may only be more recently that we have seen calls for a more fluid approach to understanding them, similar underlying characteristics emerge—the cynic, the professional, the law enforcer and the peacekeeper (Reiner 2010), which vary little from Wilson's first analysis of departmental styles (1968). Where we must turn now is to those who sought to challenge these frameworks.

# What Police Culture 'Is': Part I—The Challengers

The literature on police culture remained fairly uncontentious for many years. Ethnographic studies had, through careful observation, highlighted some of the features and characteristics of police officers and police work. The results however were rarely challenged, and it was only after many years of police culture research that we began to see a body of work that questioned these 'core assumptions' (Chan 1997) about policing.

## Criticism 1: Universal Police Culture

The first fixed belief in the policing literature according to Chan (1997) is that there is a unitary police culture. As Fielding has noted:

> [I]f occupational culture is to serve as an empirically satisfactory concept as well as a theoretically necessary one, the sense of its internal variations and textures must be brought out in the same fashion as have conceptions of culture in relation to delinquency. (1988, p. 185)

This does not just mean rank differentials. More recently, this has been addressed with a much greater consideration of the many different types of police culture. Some authors have acknowledged the existence of multiple cultures between different policing tasks, between rural and urban police, between special forces, between genders, between ethnic backgrounds, and between uniform and non-uniform officers (Fielding 1989, 1994; Cain 1973; Waddington 1999a; Reiner 2010; Chan 1997; Glomseth and Gottschalk 2009). However, we should caution against an assumption that previous scholars of police culture were blind to the notion of multiple cultures. The early cultural analyses of police work began the discussions by highlighting some similarities in characteristics, but some, including Skolnick (2011), were aware that although police work may be viewed through a typically collective lens, the strength of that lens would vary according to the different circumstances of policing. Holdaway (1989) importantly highlighted the existence of both core and peripheral features of police culture. It will be useful to outline some of these themes of difference based upon rank, role and location.

(a) Cultural Differences Through Rank

Throughout the studies of culture within the police and throughout the work reviewed above, there is a reference to only one police culture, that is, the culture of the lower ranks, 'street police culture'. Organisational cultures are, according to some, rank specific (Fielding 1989). Within the organisational literature, a main focus is on the differences between managers and workers; however, these definitions are rarely discussed within police culture. There could be various explanations for this rather obvious omission. First, there are the numbers involved within policing, with only 0.2% of police officers in England and Wales occupying senior management positions (although more are clearly part of middle management). Another reason is historical. With few exceptions, almost all of the policing literature and all the research conducted about policing have been concerned with the lower ranks. Policing literature has burgeoned within the last few decades, but rarely within the senior ranks of the police (see Reiner 1991 and Savage et al. 2000 for exceptions). The police service themselves were historically slow to accept the onslaught of social scientific research. Where they have been almost at a standstill is in the secret domain of police management. Academics have been hampered in their pursuit of understanding senior police culture without the traditional research tools of access, interviews and observation. Some attempts have been made to draw distinctions between two types of police culture but these have tended to be 'street cops' and middle management, rather than those at very senior rank (Reuss-Ianni and Ianni 1983; McManus 1997).

What studies of 'management' culture within the police service reveal is how very different that culture is from the street police culture, and indeed the work on more senior culture is usually conducted for that very comparison. This work frequently considers the attitudes of the culture of the lower ranks towards the higher ranks and vice versa. Punch, considering corruption in the Amsterdam Police Department, found that officers felt that their police management were "incompetent, careerist, mercenary, slippery, cowardly and lazy" (1983, p. 240). Reuss-Ianni and Ianni (1983), on work conducted in the US, found total juxtaposition between the two cultures. The difficulty with this research (also felt with Punch's Dutch research, although not to the same extent) is the very different policing environments within which the research took place. Reuss-Ianni and Ianni discussed the problems with police managers coming to the police from different employment backgrounds, the problems arising due to the inability to comprehend each other's work experiences and the different class backgrounds between management and workers (1983). The difference between the situation in the US and the situation in England and Wales is that, in the case of the latter, senior police officers have served in all ranks (with few exceptions) up to their current position, they have personal experience of the nature of policing and chief officers are mostly drawn from the working and middle classes. The transference of ideas about junior level street police culture between different societies is generally more successful than at senior level. Differences in both police structure and different entry points at senior levels makes international comparisons more challenging.

## (b) Cultural Differences Through Role

A further challenge to the more monolithic conceptualisation of policing cultures comes in the form of differentials between the different roles that police officers occupy. Carlson and Sutton (1975) found in their survey that levels of authoritarianism and punitiveness varied depending on the different roles that police officers occupy. Patrol officers were the most authoritarian, followed by new recruits and, finally, detectives.

Anecdotally, this cultural role differential became clear during police station visits as part of a previous research project when I was informed that, in one police kitchen area, it was necessary to have two fridges, one for traffic officers and one for firearms officers. This was seen to be necessary, as there were 'issues of trust' concerning milk consumption. Firearms officers were also the focus of Cain's (2012) doctoral research. The original proposition had been to consider the cultural barriers that were deterring more female officers from joining a firearms unit in an English police force. The results however showed that rather than a deeply entrenched macho attitude from existing officers which sought to exclude female officers, there was the discovery of something rather different. There was indeed evidence of a strong 'us versus them' mentality; however, this was not along gender lines but was much more associated with the 'us' being firearms officers and the 'them' being any other type of police officer. Admission to the firearms unit required hard-fought and highly prized physical and mental strength, and in passing those 'tests', the officers gained not only organisational entry to the firearms team but occupational acceptance.

Further research highlights similar cultural disparities between other roles within the police service. Much of this research has been on the role of investigation work. Young (1991) found divisions between uniform police officers and their detective colleagues, which was also supported by Hobbs (1988) in his work on East End detectives. Filstad and Gottschalk (2010) found in their study in Norway that detectives were less motivated by collectivism and were more individualist in their approach than counterterrorist officers. This finding highlights the nature of the role, which encompasses less emphasis on teamwork, reliance on colleagues and a fast time response than would be found amongst counterterrorism or, indeed, many other policing roles. More recently, Loftus et al. (2016) found a distinct organisational culture amongst covert police officers, with a focus on deception, identification and secrecy. These aspects became prominent due to the unique and sometimes frustrating dimensions of the role of the covert police officer.

There is clearly much more work that could be undertaken in this area, but the limited analyses so far point in the direction of requiring a more nuanced appreciation of policing cultures, rather than resorting to the more traditional and monolithic descriptions that are regularly witnessed within the policing literature.

(c)  Cultural Differences Through Location

The focus upon differences between urban and rural (mostly referred to as non-urban in US literature) policing began to surface as one of the earliest acknowledgements of differences and variations in the supposed monolithic police culture. Cain (1973) found that officers in rural forces were more aligned and integrated with their community than those in urban forces. Banton (1964) highlighted differences between rural and urban police officers in terms of their preferences of law enforcement. Where there is a belief that coercive authority is required to maintain the 'thin blue line' in more urban areas (much more aligned with the 'us versus them' mentality), greater formal enforcement measures are utilised. However, where there is a belief that officers require the local community's support to maintain order in more rural environments, there is less use of formal enforcement measures. Therefore, when the police feel that they have a more reciprocal relationship with the public, which is more common in rural areas (reliant upon them and supported by them), they are less likely to adopt crime-fighting ideologies and behaviours associated with a strong in-group identity (Dick 2005). In a similar vein to an earlier observation that any analysis of police culture must accommodate the potential for alternative cultural characteristics emerging in 'front-stage' and 'back-stage' arenas, so it is also crucial that any analysis of police culture must accommodate the potential for alternative cultural characteristics emerging in parallel but different arenas. There is not one but multiple policing 'fields' or stages upon which police officers 'perform'.

Other research has been less than definite however about the potential for marked differences between policing cultures based upon their location. Nickels and Verma (2007) found some level of similarity in the characteristics of police culture in their survey of police officers in Canada, India and Japan. These similarities were centred around conceptions of routine police work involving patrol, investigation and emergency assistance. There were also similar patterns of understandings of community policing. However, where these similarities diverged was in the much broader question of the appropriate means by which those policing activities are undertaken.

Christensen and Crank (2001) began from the more unusual standpoint of suggesting that police culture in the US was fundamentally similar across the country, as police officers were recruited from the same backgrounds, adapting to the same demands and developing similar mindsets. Their research however in a non-urban setting revealed a more complex story. Whilst there were indeed thematic similarities with a focus on increasing crime rates, a focus on juvenile crime and a connection with 'traditional' police practices, there were also more nuanced differences in comparison with officers from urban settings. These were in relation to the meanings associated with policing activities. Being 'on patrol' and 'public order' did not resonate with the same sense of potential danger in non-urban settings and officers were not routinely concerned about their own personal safety. In a similar vein, public relations were seen as an opportunity for positive reflection rather than an attempt to negate hostility (Christensen and Crank 2001). These differences in the meanings attached to activities provide a different conceptual framework within which police officers view their work and their role. If police culture is about providing a patterned response or a "vocabulary of precedents" (Ericson et al. 1987, p. 348) which guides the action that officers take, then the differing structural conditions in which police officers operate will inevitably impact upon that response.

## Criticism 2: Passivity of Police Officers

The second assumption about police culture is that police officers passively, and to the same extent, absorb police culture (Chan 1997). The suggestion, although not explicit in the literature, is that police officers are all subconsciously exposed to the cultural aspects of police life, which are then subconsciously accepted and then subconsciously become a part of their *modus operandi*. This assumes more than a little passivity on the part of police officers. Chan has drawn our attention to this by arguing that "while the culture may be powerful, it is nevertheless up to individuals to accommodate or resist its influence" (1996, p. 111).

As police officers adapt themselves to the work involved within policing, they also adapt themselves to the policing cultures (Fielding 1989). Police officers use aspects of the culture to make sense of what they are doing or, as Reiner has said, because of its "psychological fit" (1992, p. 109). It is not passive, it works. Shearing and Ericson believe that police officers are active in the creation of 'their' culture and are not "cultural dopes" (1991, p. 500; term borrowed from Garfinkel 1967). The officers select instead from a cultural tool-kit (Shearing and Ericson 1991). However, at the same time, the authors argue that police officers are unaware of the informal rules that they inherit from more experienced officers and cannot recognise the learning experience. If all officers passively absorbed aspects of the street police culture, then we would surely see all officers displaying all of the attributes of that culture. Police culture is not deterministic (Fielding 1989) but a process of personal construction and interpretation. In the same way, our social identities do not determine action but instead can be understood as a framework of appraisal (Reicher et al. 2010) which is both contextual and situational.

The presumed passivity of police officers is also highlighted by other writers who question the relationship between 'talk' and 'action' (Waddington 1999a; Fielding 1994). Should we assume that there is a relationship between the cultural talk and stories used to invoke a particular narrative about policing and the exhibition of particular behaviours and actions which reflect that talk? This discussion has not been resolved and is highly complex. As Reiner notes, it is difficult to argue that "people's *perspectives* ... bear *no* relation to their practices" (2010, p. 115). However, it is also difficult to conceptualise how a policing culture which is diverse and multifaceted, rather than monolithic and static, could influence the behaviours of a significant proportion of passively obedient police officers.

Waddington (1999a) suggests that it is the context in which police officers operate that has far more impact upon variable police behaviours than expressed opinions (which may be subject to exaggeration (Holdaway 1983)). We do not always act in ways which are compatible with our values (Campeau 2015). Action on the streets is characterised as being instrumental, with talk in the 'canteen' or 'backstage' as being more expressive (Waddington 1999b). According to Waddington (1999a), the prime motivating factor of police officers when undertaking their duties on the street is not the enactment of the more expressive 'back-stage' talk but more concerned with 'staying out of trouble'. The direction of influence runs from the front stage (street) to the back stage (canteen) rather than the other way around.

This is however a disputed area in discussions of policing cultures. In his analysis of the occupational responses to amendments to 'stop and search' legislation in England and Wales, Shiner (2010) argues that our sense of self and identity is shaped by our social interactions with others, and that these self-narratives *do* have an impact in guiding future behaviour and actions. It is suggested that it might be naïve to consider that those who engage in 'talk' and 'stories' in the back-stage arena of policing are doing so only to create a world of make-believe (van Hulst 2013). Shearing and Ericson stress that cultural attitudes which are formed through the telling and retelling of stories can "structure action" (1991, p. 482), which is not to suggest a deterministic linear flow from talk to action, but certainly a suggestion that culture is a resource which can actively guide action. However, officers are active, rather than passive, participants. Shearing and Ericson's (1991) analysis of the role of stories in generating cultural attitudes will be considered shortly.

## Criticism 3: Unchanging Police Culture

The criticism of the reference to only one culture relates also to the criticism that police culture is unchanging. Since the 1960s, as mentioned earlier, there have not been any distinct changes in the descriptions of police culture. Since that time, policing, police personnel and the political, economic and social world within which policing operates have all undergone significant change, yet the descriptions used about street police culture have varied little. The literature surrounding police culture neither adequately acknowledges these changes nor does it adequately account for the wider macro-level political, social and economic context within which policing operates (Chan 1997; Ganapathy and Cheong 2016). Sklansky (2006) has argued that a reorientation of policing towards community policing, with civilian oversight and delivered by a more diverse workforce, has resulted in improvements in police practice and a positive weakening of occupational solidarity and social isolation. The effects of these changes are the introduction of different voices, of both dissent and disagreement, to the policing world and therefore the possibility of competing perspectives on the role and function of police officers.

To suggest that there is continuity within policing culture not only demonstrates that there has been no change but precludes the *opportunity* for cultural change. Chan (1997) argues that any successful theory of police culture must take into account the possibility for change and not just opposition to change. Our understanding of police culture is described by Sklansky (2007, p. 20) as being "a story of cognitive burn-in". Much like old television screens can leave image burn-in when a static image is shown for too long, Sklansky argues that the same can be true of ideas, and particularly those concerning police culture.

Discussions of cultural change have considered whether (as discussed in Chap. 2) management can play a part in these changes or whether they have to be the motives of the whole organisation. This is related to the earlier argument about whether an organisation *is* a culture or whether an organisation *has* a culture. Within policing circles, discussion of reform has been concerned with either changing and tightening up the formal rules and structures of policing or attempting to change the culture (Brogden et al. 1988; Reiner 1992). The Macpherson Report (published in 1999 to examine the investigation into the murder of Stephen Lawrence in 1993) built upon the Scarman Report (published in 1981 in response to the Brixton riots earlier that year) in the sense of more and more emphasis on the importance of cultural change.

Chan (1997), in her account of police culture and, importantly, cultural change, draws upon the work of Bourdieu in order to adopt an interactive theory of police culture. By using Bourdieu's (1984) ideas of 'field' (in this case the structural conditions of policing or the 'setting') and 'habitus' (police cultural knowledge) and linking them with police practice, Chan provides an interactive model of culture which allows officers to take an active role in the part that culture plays in their work-ing environment. The complexities and uncertainties associated with the 'field' mean that the 'habitus' has to strategise reactions to the field with some level of coherence and pattern (Wacquant 1992). Importantly, police officers are not bound by a strict and implacable rulebook of potential actions, but instead presented with immeasurable options and alternatives (O'Neill 2016). That is not to say that rules are not involved but to say that spontaneity and negotiation are key features of those rules (Shammas and Sandberg 2015). Officers' actions can then be guided by, but not dictated to, these influences, what Giddens would refer to as 'practical consciousness' (1984).

The model also allows for cultural change. Adjustments in the 'field' would necessitate adjustments in the 'habitus', in order, quite simply, to navigate the new terrain (Chan 2004). Neither element in this dynamic model is superior to the other—the field does not dictate the habitus and the habitus does not dictate the field. It is not possible to journey through the field unchanged (Shammas and Sandberg 2015). However, changes to the habitus will inevitably follow changes to the field rather than vice versa (Ganapathy and Cheong 2016). Those changes are unlikely to be radical, as they are informed by a framework of existing cultural cues and the 'sedimentation' of cultural practices, but change is still possible within this analysis (Bourdieu 1990). Those changes to the field of policing are also not necessarily welcomed or accepted by police officers, as all struc-tural change will be viewed through, and made sense via, the lens of the habitus (Chan 2007a).

Evidence of these changes to the policing 'habitus' can be found in a diverse range of policing literature from around the world. Paoline and Terrill (2014) found through survey data that some less familiar charac-teristics of police culture were emerging which can, in many cases, be linked with changes to the field. Officers across seven different police agencies reported more positive attitudes towards immediate supervisors and low levels of role ambiguity, and did not reject the order maintenance role of policing. The adherence to the philosophies of community polic-ing in many parts of the world has changed the relationship between officers and their immediate supervisors, with the latter being encouraged to take a more active supervisory role (Paoline and Terrill 2014). These changes also indicate a more widespread acceptance of the order maintenance aspects or the "'soft' policing activities" of the police role (McCarthy 2013, p. 274). Cochran and Bromley's (2003) research, also in the US, found that between 25% and 30% of respondents fell into the category of more community service–oriented police officers, what the authors termed a "*nouveau* police sub-culture" (2003, p. 108), with only about a sixth of respondents fitting the crime-fighting stereotype. When police officers were asked about the 'most impressive' characteristics of their highest-performing colleagues, the interpersonal skills of eloquence, working with the community and a positive attitude were all highlighted (Willis and Mastrofski 2017).

These 'softer' policing skills are acknowledged to be a key, if not the key, function of the officers' role. This finding has spanned history. Muir (1977), in his attempted identification of what makes a 'good police officer', identified communication as a key tool in the officer's armoury, a tool used strategically to elicit information. More recently, research in Australia revealed that the ability to effectively communicate was considered by fellow officers to be the most important skill that a detective could possess (Westera et al. 2013).

Given this apparent greater appreciation of the community policing philosophies of modern policing, traditionally seen to be more associated with 'soft' policing activities, it is also noteworthy that an increasing number of researchers are moving beyond the traditional analyses of a sharp gender divide in police role and attitude characterised by the dominance of 'masculine' ideals and the suppression of female officers (Fielding 1994; McCarthy 2013). Police culture is instead considered not to have its origins in masculinity but within policing itself (Waddington 1999a). Rather than the assumption that female police officers have to either accede to the male culture or remain cocooned within certain, more 'caring' policing activities (Martin 1990; Walklate 2000), research is now developing the notion, as discussed earlier in this chapter, that policing is divided more by rank and role than by gender (Dick and Jankowicz 2001; Cain 2012). Using the repertory grid technique, Dick and Jankowicz (2001) argued that the divide between constables and supervisors was a much clearer indication of value differentials than gender. Interestingly, neuroscientific research of Mexican police officers found that police culture affects the genders equally in terms of empathy and compassion (Mercadillo et al. 2015).

In terms of changes to the 'habitus' of police officers, Paoline and Terrill (2014) also found the bonds of solidarity between police officers to have altered. Police officers were not as socially isolated as has been suggested in past cultural analyses and socialised with both police and non-police (Paoline and Terrill 2014). This is supported from Australian research indicating a decline in the social rituals associated with policing, particularly the off-duty consumption of alcohol with colleagues. This was attributed to, amongst other things, policing no longer consuming the lives of officers—"the job is not the life anymore" (Brough et al. 2016, p. 33). Paoline and Terrill (2014) also found evidence to suggest that there were limits to the loyalty that police officers would show to colleagues. This supports research in other jurisdictions which have indicated a markedly altered habitus in the face of the changing field (Ganapathy and Cheong 2016 in Singapore; Glaeser (2000) in Germany; Charman and Corcoran (2015) in Ireland). Particular interest lies in the more individualist, risk-averse and publically accountable arena of policing, where it could be argued that there is a subtle movement from the 'blue code of silence' as a dominant paradigm towards what I shall later term a 'blue code of self-protection'. Myhill and Bradford (2013) argue for a more fluid understanding of the 'code of silence', as officers are less likely to adhere to such a doctrine if they perceive their organisation to be treating them fairly and with respect. These are important and interesting changes to the perceptions of the occupational habitus of police officers and will be examined more closely when the longitudinal data collected for this research study is examined in Part II of this book.

Changes in the ways in which public services are delivered, coupled with the growth of private security networks, have also fundamentally altered the position of the public police in terms of its previously unique status as the sole agency responsible for 'fighting crime'. Multiagency working, 'joined-up' government and partnerships were all key themes underpinning the desires of the UK Labour administrations (1997–2010) for a more holistic approach to many areas of public service. Effective practice in these areas was almost exclusively seen in terms of the success of different agencies in working collaboratively. Enshrined in legislation such as the Crime and Disorder Act 1998, the police in England and

Wales have a statutory responsibility to work with other agencies on a regular and increasing basis in order to reduce crime and disorder. This has resulted in much closer collaboration with a range of other agencies. Research evidence from police and ambulance services, police and social workers, and police and private security networks have all suggested that this collaboration has shaped and altered many existing occupational cultures (Charman 2014; O'Neill and McCarthy 2014; Whelan 2017). Changes to the policing field inevitably mean that organisational members have to adapt their working practices and their "vocabulary of precedents" (Ericson et al. 1987, p. 348) in order to make sense of the new environment. Police officers are negotiating new terrain by adopting the 'tool-kit' approach of police culture. By utilising traditional policing characteristics such as pragmatism and discarding other characteristics such as suspicion, culture served as a "facilitator in partnership working, rather than a barrier" (O'Neill and McCarthy 2014, p. 156).

This section has provided a variety of evidence to support Chan's argument that many analyses of police culture fail to account for the enormous change seen within policing services and a reliance on old assumptions about the nature and role of policing and the nature of police officers themselves. Changes to both the 'field' and the 'habitus' of policing have thus been evident. However, running alongside these arguments are another group of theorists who maintain that change is not as fundamental as it may seem.

## What Police Culture 'Is': Part II—Enduring Characteristics of Police Culture

The evidence presented of both subtle and transformational shifts in some of the traditional aspects of police organisational cultures within many different policing organisations could lead one to the conclusion that the aggressive, crime-fighting ideologies and attitudes of police officers are being replaced by more progressive and open organisational cultures, wedded to the philosophies and practices of the community policing ideals. That would certainly tell part of the story of cultural change. However, it would not tell the whole story. For whilst there is certainly evidence in support of those shifts, there is also evidence of more recalcitrant elements of the policing culture which point towards this culture as an immutable and pervasive force which, despite wholesale organisational and societal change, still remains active. These two positions are not totally incompatible. Some of the research referred to in the previous section noted change but also noted continuity. Some of the research that will be referred to next noted continuity but also noted change. The picture is far from complete, in either direction.

It was the publication of Bethan Loftus' (2008, 2009, 2010) research, which involved interview and observational research in one English police force, which added weight to the argument that subtle changes in policing cultures were disguising much more persistent and steadfast elements of the occupational culture. The elements of cynicism, suspicion, bravado, 'us versus them' and a crime-fighting mindset were all tenacious features of Loftus' research which were articulated through narratives of decline (2008, 2009). Researchers, she argues, have been too concerned about searching for difference whilst at the same time ignoring the stability of cultural themes. Research evidence does point to those enduring themes (Kiely and Peek 2002; Christensen and Crank 2001). Without a fundamental overhaul of the policing role, which would be to undermine its very existence, cultural change on a significant level is unlikely. Given that much police attention is directed towards poor and marginalised communities, given that this is unlikely to change and given that "contempt towards the poor is an integral feature of the culture", change is not inevitable (Loftus 2009, p. 197).

Loftus (2008, p. 764) identifies what she calls "white space", a space where officers can be in the company of like-minded colleagues and can use the language which has now been banished from the acceptable vocabulary of police officers. Atherton (2012) too refers to the creation of alternative 'spaces' where more negative aspects of police culture can still find a voice. In an analysis of 20 police blogs operating from within the UK, Atherton found consistent elements of cynicism, isolation, solidarity and anti-bureaucracy. Interestingly, machismo was not widely expressed. This research, which considers the "virtual canteen" (2012, p. 23), also offers caution to research relying upon more formal observations and interviews of police officers. The alternative spaces of police blogs and social media are a new and potential rich source of data about policing cultures (Hesketh and Williams 2017).

The views of Loftus are shared by researchers in other jurisdictions. Steyn and Mkhize (2016) surveyed 173 South African police officers with 10, 20 and 30 years of service and found similar entrenched attitudes of solidarity, isolation and cynicism, with no apparent differences dependent upon length of service. Whilst cultural attitudes were embodied at a very early stage of socialisation into their policing careers, those attitudes were then entrenched. Steyn and Mkhize (2016) challenge the perception that community-oriented policing methods have impacted in any way upon the crime-fighting mentality of police officers.

Scerra (2011) considered the cultural knowledge that informs the investigation into serial crimes in Australia. She found that not only did the reliance of investigators upon the traditional 'scripts' and ascribed meanings of the actors involved impact upon the offenders, but it also impacted upon the victims themselves. Scerra (2011) concluded that these stereotypical assumptions about the nature of 'victims' and 'offenders' came from experience of policing on the streets, rather than from any investigative experience. Indeed, where characteristics are almost 'demanded' by "greedy institutions" (Coser 1974), it can come as no surprise when those characteristics are used to both promote and, at the same time, denigrate organisational goals. Peterson and Uhnoo (2012), in their Swedish research, found that 'loyalty' and 'tests of loyalty' amongst police officers were both used as an inclusionary and exclusionary device in relationships with other officers, particularly officers from an ethnic minority background. These 'tests' or 'rites of passage' are connected with strong occupational cultures and, although are sometimes considered to be an inevitable journey into organisational acceptance, were classified as workplace bullying (Miller and Rayner 2012).

The contradictions inherent in the policing culture literature over whether change is apparent or not, and the extent to which that change may or may not have had any impact upon policing practice, may well be explained by a reconsideration of Schein's (1984) organisational culture research, which was discussed in Chap. 2. Schein has identified three different levels at which culture operates: "artifacts", "espoused beliefs and values" and "underlying assumptions" (2004, p. 4). These move from the surface level to the conscious level and then to the unconscious level. Cockcroft (2015) has suggested that what is often seen by organisations to be evidence of cultural change is actually only change at that first 'artefact' level. Loftus (2008) could point to an absence of overt racist language in research and diversity messages printed on force mugs and mouse mats. However, the question is whether that change has moved to the more unconscious level of 'underlying assumptions'. Research endeavours will continue to grapple with this dilemma.

# What Police Culture 'Does': The Role of Police Culture

Just as Matza (1964) reached the conclusion that deviants are not in total opposition to mainstream cultural norms and values, so police officers are not totally wedded to the cultural characteristics inherent in police culture literature. What is of more interest is the commitment of police officers to these core characteristics of police culture which will inevitably "vary and waver" (Campeau 2015, p. 683). What this section of the chapter seeks to achieve is to consider, very much in the style of Janet Chan (1997), how police officers are active agents in the creation of their own cultural sensibilities. This will involve a consideration of police culture not as always an organisational impediment to be outmanoeuvred, but as a set of tools to be utilised. Campeau (2015) asks us therefore to consider police culture as a 'resource'. Foster (2003, p. 222) goes further and suggests adopting the more "appreciative inquiry" approach favoured by prisons research which seeks reform through understanding rather than through condemnation. I have sought to do this through the consideration of the role of police culture being utilised in four ways—as a tool of coping, a tool of legal vacuum-packing, a tool of reinforcement and a tool of learning.

## Culture as a Tool of Coping

Police culture can be seen as a *tool of coping* with what, at times, can be a stressful and difficult occupation:

> Any profession which is continually preoccupied with the threat of danger requires a strong sense of solidarity if it is to operate. (Janowitz 1964, quoted in Drummond 1976)

Paoline (2003) has depicted a model of police culture which considers the policing environment, the coping mechanisms and the eventual outcomes. The occupational environment is characterised by danger and coercive authority. This is coupled with the organisational environment, which features both close supervisory scrutiny and lack of clarity over the policing role. The result of working in both the occupational and the organisational environment is stress and anxiety. This then results in the emergence of the cultural characteristics of suspicion and a desire to 'maintain the edge' with the public (which emerges from the occupational pressures) and the desire to 'lay low' and promote the 'police officer as warrior' image (which emerges from the organisational pressures). This also has the potential to lower individual levels of self-esteem, as the social identity literature would suggest that self-esteem is closely linked to the fate of the group (Reicher et al. 2010). Chan refers to this adaptive response as an "emotional hardening" (2007b, p. 147). The outcomes of isolation and solidarity, it is argued, are an inevitable consequence of attempting to cope with these working conditions (Paoline 2003). A sample of officers from Chan's original new recruit research in Australia were revisited when they had between nine and ten years of service (2007b). The majority of this sample reported poor experiences of stress and pressure, with solidarity amongst colleagues being required as a support mechanism. There is also evidence to suggest that solidarity, in the form of high levels of support amongst group members, can lead to a reduction in stress and anxiety (Haslam et al. 2009).

This role confusion emerging from the sometimes conflicting demands of the occupational and organisational environments have been discussed both earlier in this chapter and in Chap. 2. Tensions emerge from handling the multitude of roles and positions whilst both working within the policing organisation and managing citizens outside of the organisation (Van Maanen 1978; Paoline 2003). Butler and Cochrane (1977) refer to the conflict between law enforcement and service, between prosecution and procedural constraints, between individuality and bureaucracy, and between the maintenance of authority and the presentation of the self. The outcome is that "all police action tends to be a compromise" (1977, p. 448) and cultural characteristics emerge as a way of coping and adapting to the dilemmas associated with policing.

Notwithstanding the potential for cultural exaggeration and glorification, to which all occupations can be prone, the job of a police officer can
be fraught with dangers. One characteristic of policing culture which is
utilised by police officers to cope with their working environment is
humour. Humour has long been seen to have the potential to help diffuse
and deflate potentially difficult circumstances and to assist in the associated relief of tension (Freud 1905; cited in Critchley 2002; Coser 1959;
Scott 2007; Meyer 1997; Roth and Vivona 2010). Joyce, at the time a
serving police officer, refers to the adage of "if you didn't laugh, you'd cry"
as having much truth to it (1989, p. 380). Whilst shouting or crying
could have similar tension-reducing effects, the use of humour by
professionals in the course of executing their duties is by far the most
socially acceptable response (Rowe and Regehr 2010).

From a psychological perspective then, humour can be considered as a
way of reducing tension and coping with the demands of the job. This is
seen by some to be an essential ingredient in allowing emergency responders to be able to continue with tasks which ordinarily might be intolera-
ble (Young 1995). The ability to both generate and appreciate humour
appears to have strong benefits in the process of coping with stress or
tension (Moran and Massam 1997). There is no evidence to suggest that
those generating humour exhibit lower levels of stress; rather, their
humour allows themselves and others around them to cope better and to
allow an element of emotional distance, or defence, between themselves
and their situation (Dixon 1980; cited in Moran and Massam 1997).

## Culture as a Tool of Legal Vacuum-Packing

A central area of discussion within policing is that of police discretion.
Much has been written on the subject (see Fielding 1991; Dixon 1997),
but in this context, it is enough to note that the manner in which policing is structured means that the police officer has a great deal of autonomy and has the ability to shape their working environment. The law is
fairly flexible, the patrol officer is of very low visibility and this leads to a
situation of high discretion for the police officer. There are clearly gaps
between 'law in books' and 'law in action' (McBarnet 1981), and Reiner

has observed that officers believe themselves to be guided by the "Ways and Means Act" (1992, p. 107). The discretion of police officers has been linked to the development and continuity of police culture, as officers adapt the law to suit their working habitat. Police officers need their own set of internalised rules to cope with situations where there are "policy vacuums" (Goldsmith 1990, p. 101). The author goes on to argue that as the lower ranks of the police rarely have an influence on police policy decisions, they are forced to make the law workable by utilising informal rules. Officers who occupy the streets as their working environment are not the 'sensegivers', to use Chan's terminology (1997), but the 'sensemakers'. Using a variety of cultural resources, they must adapt the law to suit their working practices.

The debate surrounding 'rules' and how rules direct action has been the subject of sociological discussion for some time. The rules we are presented with guide or direct our action (Shearing and Ericson 1991). In policing terms, this could be the external rules that are established within law or the internal rules that are influenced by the police culture. External rules regularly fail because, first, they do not sufficiently address the areas of police work where they are required and, second, they are in competition with strongly influential internal rules (Goldsmith 1990). Smith and Gray's (1985) distinction between working rules, inhibitory rules and presentational rules, and their acknowledgement of the influence of the former would support the primacy of the internal rules. It is suggested that police officers appear to follow the internal rules with greater consistency than the external rules, which are used as a resource (Reiner 1992; Punch 1985). The police officer is a "craftsman" rather than a "legal actor" (Skolnick 1966, p. 231). The organisational culture can also be used to avoid rules in addition to adapting rules. Indeed, Holdaway has suggested that the law is actually a constraint on the police officer and is only neutralised through the application of the policing culture (1983).

What police culture achieves is a patterned response, a 'working rule book' with an infinite number of choices and a set of values and beliefs that are shared by the organisation, and which can be utilised by officers during their working practice. In this section, culture is seen as a necessary response to the cleft between the law and the practice of policing.

## Culture as a Tool of Reinforcement

As referred to earlier, the notion of police officers faced with the daily pressure of danger is in fact not as close to the truth as policing mythologies might suggest. An oft-cited cultural characteristic of police officers is a sense of 'mission', and culture can be used as an expression of reinforcement. This can be done through the use of language and stories, which are important aspects of culture (Mukerji and Schudson 1991). There are two views on stories and storytelling in the policing literature (van Hulst 2013). The first is that stories are a crucial tool in the transmission of common-sense knowledge and practice, most especially to new recruits. The second is that storytelling is a mollifying exercise for use in the reduction of stress and tension amongst police officers.

Frewin and Tuffin (1998), in their discursive analysis of police culture, also point to the importance of language for an understanding of the police role. The police construct realities and then operate according to those realities. In their research in New Zealand, the authors found that the police, through their language, constructed images of the importance of police reputation and conformity to both formal rules and cultural norms (Frewin and Tuffin 1998).

Stories then can be used as the cultural tool of reinforcement, not untruths but often exaggerations. They require only 'plausibility', rather than 'accuracy' (Weick 1995). Stories can be used to promote the image of police officers as 'heroic' and to demonise those who are not members of the 'in-group' (Dick 2005). They can be told during action, reflecting upon action, and in whole or potted versions (Shearing and Ericson 1991). Stories can ease tensions and convince officers that their way is the best way (Holdaway 1983). Officers can talk about their activities and can be comforted by the fact that their version of reality is shared by their colleagues, "thus acquiring social anchoring in an objective truth" (Hannerz 1969, p. 111). Waddington has argued that the police canteen is the "'repair shop' of policing and jokes, banter and anecdotes the tools" (1999a, p. 295).

Narrative is thus used to reinforce the definitions of policing that are acceptable to the organisational culture (thereby legitimising their 'working rules' (Holdaway 1983)) and to dramatise the actual job of a police officer to the life of the 'TV cop'—car chasing and criminal catching. Within their organisational culture and within the context of their storytelling, there is no counterargument, there is only the strengthening of their beliefs.

## Culture as a Tool of Learning

Chapter 5 considered the role of informal socialisation practices as a device of learning for new recruits. Those arguments will not be repeated here. However, there is also a further way in which culture is transmitted as a tool of learning and that is through stories. In addition to the use of language reaffirming the role of the police officer, language and stories can also be a tool of learning. Shearing and Ericson (1991) argue that although police research has dismissed the police service for using experience to teach the young recruit, through an experienced officer taking the new recruit on patrol, it is in fact a successful method of using metaphors to create 'sensibilities' within which officers can create their own understanding. Using Sackmann's (1991, p. 21) terminology, this would constitute the acquisition of "recipe knowledge". Shearing and Ericson use the example of 'tropes', which are methods of understanding connections between things that will always be associated that way (in a sense related to axiomatic knowledge). They are the equivalent of written rules or a "library of gambits" (1991, p. 492). Although the tropes are used to set precedents for the recruit, they are not explicit and the recruits are left to make sense of the story themselves, to create their own reality. An example of this, as shown by Shearing and Ericson, might be, "taking a five foot jump over a four foot ditch" (1991, p. 493). Bearing in mind that the experienced officer would have related this in context and unless the recruit takes this as a literal solution, they may come to the conclusion that this means that you have to act with marginally more force than your opponent. Shearing and Ericson (1991) are very clear that the police officer is the active learner in creating their own set of sensibilities from which to make sense of their working environment. This is likened to a theatrical performance, where there is clearly outside direction but ultimately the actors perform independently.

At the outset of this chapter, it was stated that any analysis of the subject of policing cultures raises almost as many questions as it can provide answers. At the end of this chapter, there can be some confidence in stating the truth in this. However, that journey through the wealth of material and analysis on policing cultures is an important one. It provides us with a much deeper understanding not only of the dilemmas associated with modern policing but also of the ways in which police officers respond to those dilemmas. It is also vital that this conceptual level of analysis of police culture continues. As Cockcroft (2015) has noted, there is an increasing tendency to regard police culture as a 'technical' problem to be tackled, rather than as a 'sociological' issue to be explored and understood. The numerous examples of various different UK Government pronouncements of the requirement for a "fundamental change in police culture" (May 2014) is testament to this.

Paoline (2003) asks us to consider a new form of model of police culture which is represented as a filtering process from the occupational culture at the top of the model, through to organisations, then rank and then style. What might begin as broadly similar characteristics of police culture will be modified and adapted through the different variables of the policing role. This enables us to take account of both the enduring characteristics of policing cultures and the newer cultural descriptions which have taken into account the changing structures of policing and the differentials of rank, role and location. This also allows us to be cognisant of the idea of the 'sedimentation' of cultural characteristics. Rather than searching for new descriptions of police culture to 'replace' the traditional descriptions, a focus on "cultural pluriformity" (Hendriks and van Hulst 2016, p. 173) allows us to both appreciate the enduring role of the police in preserving and producing social order (Reiner 2000) and take account of changes to policing philosophies and practices. This reflects Bourdieu's understanding of the cultural knowledge (habitus) of an organisation's members as a layering or sedimentation of social history (Bourdieu 1986). Paoline's (2003) model then encompasses Chan's (1997) calls for a more dynamic and interactive account of police culture which presumes police officers to be active cultural agents in the creation and sustainability of their policing culture. Police culture can then be viewed as a 'resource' which police officers can utilise to guide their action and to navigate the difficult terrain of policing citizens. Rather than presuming that police officers will utilise these cultural tools in the same way and to the same extent, we should instead view these cultural tools as being positioned along a continuum, with officers adapting their policing practices according to the context of their position (Campeau 2015). As discussed earlier, this is not to say that rules are not involved but to say that spontaneity and negotiation are key features of those rules (Shammas and Sandberg 2015). By adopting these far more nuanced analyses of police culture, we can move beyond the condemnatory narratives and more towards an appreciation and understanding of the ways in which policing cultures guide the actions of police officers within a modern police setting.

# References

Atherton, S. (2012). Cops and Bloggers: Exploring the Presence of Police Culture on the Web. *Internet Journal of Criminology*. Retrieved from https://media.wix.com/ugd/b93dd4_e3fafc746b864462936d254a7c7251c9.pdf

Banton, M. (1964). *The Policeman in the Community*. London: Tavistock.

Bourdieu, P. (1984). *Distinction: A Social Critique of the Judgement of Taste*. London: Routledge.

Bourdieu, P. (1986). The Forms of Capital. In J. Richardson (Ed.), *Handbook of Theory and Research for the Sociology of Education* (pp. 241–258). New York: Greenwood.

Bourdieu, P. (1990). *The Logic of Practice*. Cambridge: Polity Press.

Broderick, J. (1977). *Police in a Time of Change*. Morristown: General Learning Press.

Brogden, M., Jefferson, T., & Walklate, S. (1988). *Introducing Policework*. London: Unwin Hyman.

Brough, P., Chataway, S., & Biggs, A. (2016). 'You Don't Want People Knowing You're a Copper!' A Contemporary Assessment of Police Organisational Culture. *International Journal of Police Science and Management, 18*(1), 28–36.

Brown, M. (1988). *Working the Street: Police Discretion and the Dilemmas of Reform* (2nd ed.). New York: Russell Sage Foundation.

Butler, A., & Cochrane, R. (1977). An Examination of Some Elements of the Personality of Police Officers and Their Implications. *Journal of Police Science and Administration, 5*(4), 441–450.

Cain, M. (1973). *Society and the Policeman's Role.* London: Routledge & Kegan Paul.

Cain, D. (2012). *Gender Within a Specialised Police Department: An Examination of the Cultural Dynamics of a Police Firearms Unit, Unpublished Professional Doctorate.* Portsmouth: University of Portsmouth.

Campeau, H. (2015). 'Police Culture' at Work: Making Sense of Police Oversight. *British Journal of Criminology, 55*(4), 669–687.

Carlson, H., & Sutton, M. (1975). The Effects of Different Police Roles on Attitude and Values. *The Journal of Psychology, 91*, 57–64.

Chan, J. (1996). Changing Police Culture. *British Journal of Criminology, 36*(1), 109–134.

Chan, J. (1997). *Changing Police Culture.* Cambridge: Cambridge University Press.

Chan, J. (2003). *Fair Cop: Learning the Art of Policing.* Toronto: University of Toronto Press.

Chan, J. (2004). Using Pierre Bourdieu's Framework for Understanding Police Culture. *Droit et Société, 56–57*, 327–347.

Chan, J. (2007a). Making Sense of Police Reforms. *Theoretical Criminology, 11*(3), 323–345.

Chan, J. (2007b). Police Stress and Occupational Culture. In M. O'Neill & A. Singh (Eds.), *Police Occupational Culture: New Debates and Directions* (pp. 129–151). Oxford: Elsevier JAI.

Charman, S. (2014). Blue Light Communities: Cultural Interoperability and Shared Learning Between Ambulance Staff and Police Officers in Emergency Response. *Policing and Society, 24*(1), 102–119.

Charman, S., & Corcoran, D. (2015). Adjusting the Police Occupational Cultural Landscape: The Case of An Garda Síochána. *Policing and Society, 25*(5), 484–503.

Christensen, W., & Crank, J. (2001). Police Work and Culture in a Nonurban Setting: An Ethnographic Analysis. *Police Quarterly, 4*(1), 69–98.

Cochran, J., & Bromley, M. (2003). The Myth (?) of the Police Sub-culture. *Policing: An International Journal of Police Strategies and Management, 26*(1), 88–117.

Cockcroft, T. (2015). Golden Ages, Red Herrings and Post Keynesian Policing: Understanding the Role of Police Culture in the Police Professionalism Debate. *Nordisk Politiforskning, 2*(2), 183–196.

Coser, R. (1959). Some Social Functions of Laughter: A Study of Humor in a Hospital Setting. *Human Relations, 12,* 171–182.

Coser, L. (1974). *Greedy Institutions: Patterns of Undivided Commitment.* New York: Free Press.

Crank, J. (1998). *Understanding Police Culture.* Cincinnati: Anderson Publishing Co.

Critchley, S. (2002). *On Humour.* London: Routledge.

Davies, A., & Thomas, R. (2003). Talking Cop: Discourses of Change and Policing Identities. *Public Administration, 81*(4), 681–699.

De Lint, W. (1998). New Managerialism and Canadian Police Training Reform. *Social and Legal Studies, 7*(2), 261–285.

Dick, P. (2005). Dirty Work Designations: How Police Officers Account for Their Use of Coercive Force. *Human Relations, 58*(11), 1363–1390.

Dick, P., & Jankowicz, D. (2001). A Social Constructionist Account of Police Culture and Its Influence on the Representation and Progression of Female Officers: A Repertory Grid Analysis in a UK Police Force. *Policing: An International Journal of Police Strategies and Management, 24*(2), 181–199.

Dixon, D. (1997). *Law in Policing.* Oxford: Oxford University Press.

Drummond, D. (1976). *Police Culture.* Beverley Hills: Sage Publications.

Ericson, R., Baranek, P., & Chan, J. (1987). *Visualizing Deviance: A Study of News Organizations.* Toronto: University of Toronto Press.

Fielding, N. (1988). *Joining Forces: Police Training, Socialization, and Occupational Competence.* London: Routledge.

Fielding, N. (1989). Police Culture and Police Practice. In M. Weatheritt (Ed.), *Police Research: Some Future Prospects* (pp. 77–87). Aldershot: Gower Publishing Company.

Fielding, N. (1991). *The Police and Social Conflict.* London: Athlone.

Fielding, N. (1994). Cop Canteen Culture. In T. Newburn & E. Stanko (Eds.), *Just Boys Doing Business* (pp. 46–63). London: Routledge.

Filstad, C., & Gottschalk, P. (2010). Collectivism Versus Individualism in Police Cultures. *International Journal of Human Resources Development and Management, 10*(2), 117–135.

Foster, J. (2003). Police Cultures. In T. Newburn (Ed.), *The Handbook of Policing* (pp. 196–227). Cullompton: Willan.

Frewin, K., & Tuffin, K. (1998). Police Status, Conformity and Internal Pressure: A Discursive Analysis of Police Culture. *Discourse and Society, 9*(2), 173–185.

Ganapathy, N., & Cheong, H. (2016). The "Thinning" Blueline: A Bourdieuian Appreciation of Police Subculture. *International Journal of Comparative and Applied Criminal Justice, 40*(4), 277–294.

Garfinkel, H. (1967). *Studies in Ethnomethodology*. Englewood Cliffs: Prentice Hall.

Giddens, A. (1984). *The Constitution of Society: Outline of the Theory of Structuration*. Cambridge: Polity Press.

Glaeser, A. (2000). *Divided in Unity: Identity, Germany and the Berlin Police*. Chicago: University of Chicago Press.

Glomseth, R., & Gottschalk, P. (2009). Police Personnel Cultures: A Comparative Study of Counter Terrorist and Criminal Investigation Units. *Criminal Justice Studies, 22*(1), 3–15.

Goffman, E. (1959). *The Presentation of Self in Everyday Life*. New York: Doubleday Anchor.

Goldsmith, A. (1990). Taking Police Culture Seriously: Police Discretion and the Limits of Law. *Policing and Society, 1*(2), 91–114.

Hannerz, U. (1969). *Soulside: Inquiries into Ghetto Culture and Community*. New York: Columbia University Press.

Haslam, S., Jetten, J., Postmes, T., & Haslam, C. (2009). Social Identity, Health and Well-Being: An Emerging Agenda for Applied Psychology. *Applied Psychology, 58*(1), 1–23.

Hendriks, F., & van Hulst, M. (2016). Shifting Repertoires: Understanding Cultural Plurality in Policing. *Innovation: The European Journal of Social Science Research, 29*(2), 161–176.

Hesketh, I., & Williams, E. (2017). A New Canteen Culture: The Potential to Use Social Media as Evidence in Policing. *Policing*. Advance online publication. http://dx.doi.org/10.1093/police/pax025

Hobbs, D. (1988). *Doing the Business: Entrepreneurship, Detectives and the Working Class in the East End of London*. Oxford: Clarendon Press.

Holdaway, S. (1983). *Inside the British Police: A Force at Work*. Oxford: Basil Blackwell Publisher Ltd.

Holdaway, S. (1989). Discovering Structure: Studies of the Police Occupational Culture. In M. Weatheritt (Ed.), *Police Research: Some Future Prospects* (pp. 55–76). Aldershot: Gower Publishing Company.

Hood, C. (1998). *The Art of the State: Culture, Rhetoric and Public Management*. Oxford: Oxford University Press.

Joyce, D. (1989). Why Do Police Officers Laugh at Death? *The Psychologist, 2*(9), 379–381.

Kiely, J., & Peek, G. (2002). The Culture of the British Police: Views of Police Officers. *The Services Industries Journal, 22*(1), 167–183.

Loftus, B. (2008). Dominant Culture Interrupted: Recognition, Resentment and the Politics of Change in an English Police Force. *British Journal of Criminology, 48*(6), 756–777.

Loftus, B. (2009). *Police Culture in a Changing World*. Oxford: Oxford University Press.

Loftus, B. (2010). Police Occupational Culture: Classic Themes, Altered Times. *Policing and Society, 20*(1), 1–20.

Loftus, B., Goold, B., & MacGiollabhui, S. (2016). From a Visible Spectacle to an Invisible Presence: The Working Culture of Covert Policing. *British Journal of Criminology, 56*(4), 629–645.

Martin, S. (1990). *On the Move: The Status of Women in Policing*. Washington, DC: Police Foundation.

Mastrofski, S., Willis, J., & Snipes, J. (2002). Styles of Patrol in a Community Policing Context. In M. Morash & J. Ford (Eds.), *The Move to Community Policing* (pp. 81–111). Thousand Oaks: Sage.

Matza, D. (1964). *Delinquency and Drift*. London: Wiley.

May, T. (2014). HMIC's Inspection of Police Handling of Domestic Violence and Abuse. *Written Statement to Parliament*. Retrieved from https://www.gov.uk/government/speeches/hmics-inspection-of-police-handling-of-domestic-violence-and-abuse

McBarnet, D. (1981). *Conviction: Law, the State and the Construction of Justice*. London: Routledge.

McCarthy, D. (2013). Gendering 'Soft' Policing: Multi-Agency Working, Female Cops, and the Fluidities of Police Culture/s. *Policing and Society, 23*(2), 261–278.

McManus, M. (1997, April). Getting Things Right for Policing: Cultural Shift or Elitist Sop? *The Police Journal, 70*(2), 99–103.

Mercadillo, R., Alcauter, S., Fernández-Ruiz, J., & Barrios, F. (2015). Police Culture Influences the Brain Function Underlying Compassion: A Gender Study. *Social Neuroscience, 10*(2), 135–152.

Meyer, J. (1997). Humor in Member Narratives: Uniting and Dividing at Work. *Western Journal of Communication, 61*(2), 188–208.

Miller, H., & Rayner, C. (2012). The Form and Function of "Bullying" Behaviors in a Strong Occupational Culture: Bullying in a UK Police Service. *Group and Organization Management, 37*(3), 347–375.

Moran, C., & Massam, M. (1997). An Evaluation of Humour in Emergency Work. *The Australasian Journal of Disaster and Trauma Studies, 3*, 1–11.

Muir, W. (1977). *Police: Streetcorner Politicians*. Chicago: University of Chicago Press.

Mukerji, C., & Schudson, M. (1991). *Rethinking Popular Culture: Contemporary Perspectives in Cultural Studies.* California: California University Press.

Myhill, A., & Bradford, B. (2013). Overcoming Cop Culture: Organizational Justice and Police Officers' Attitudes Toward the Public. *Policing: An International Journal of Police Strategies and Management, 36*(2), 338–356.

Nickels, E., & Verma, A. (2007). Dimensions of Police Culture: A Study in Canada, India and Japan. *Policing: An International Journal of Police Strategies and Management, 31*(2), 186–209.

O'Neill, M. (2016). Revisiting the Classics: Janet Chan and the Legacy of 'Changing Police Culture'. *Policing and Society, 26*(4), 475–480.

O'Neill, M., & McCarthy, D. (2014). (Re)negotiating Police Culture Through Partnership Working: Trust, Compromise and the 'New' Pragmatism. *Criminology and Criminal Justice, 14*(2), 143–159.

Paoline, E. (2003). Taking Stock: Toward a Richer Understanding of Police Culture. *Journal of Criminal Justice, 31*(3), 199–214.

Paoline, E. (2004). Shedding Light on Police Culture: An Examination of Officers' Occupational Attitudes. *Police Quarterly, 7*(2), 205–236.

Paoline, E., & Terrill, W. (2014). *Police Culture: Adapting to the Strains of the Job.* Durham: Carolina Academic Press.

Peterson, A., & Uhnoo, S. (2012). Trials of Loyalty: Ethnic Minority Police Officers as 'Outsiders' Within a Greedy Institution. *European Journal of Criminology, 9*(4), 354–369.

Punch, M. (1983). Officers and Men: Occupational Culture, Inter-Rank Antagonism, and the Investigation of Corruption. In M. Punch (Ed.), *Control in the Police Organisation* (pp. 227–250). Cambridge, MA: The MIT Press.

Punch, M. (1985). *Conduct Unbecoming.* London: Tavistock Publications Ltd.

Reicher, S., Spears, R., & Haslam, S. (2010). The Social Identity Approach in Social Psychology. In M. Wetherell & C. Mohanty (Eds.), *The SAGE Handbook of Identities* (pp. 45–63). London: Sage.

Reiner, R. (1978). *The Blue-Coated Worker.* Cambridge: Cambridge University Press.

Reiner, R. (1985). *The Politics of the Police.* Brighton: Wheatsheaf.

Reiner, R. (1991). *Chief Constables.* Oxford: Oxford University Press.

Reiner, R. (1992). *The Politics of the Police* (2nd ed.). Hemel Hempstead: Harvester Wheatsheaf.

Reiner, R. (2000). *The Politics of the Police* (3rd ed.). Oxford: Oxford University Press.

Reiner, R. (2010). *The Politics of the Police* (4th ed.). Oxford: Oxford University Press.

Reuss-Ianni, E., & Ianni, F. (1983). Street Cops and Management Cops: The Two Cultures of Policing. In M. Punch (Ed.), *Control in the Police Organisation* (pp. 251–274). Cambridge, MA: The MIT Press.

Roth, G., & Vivona, B. (2010). Mirth and Murder: Crime Scene Investigation as a Work Context for Examining Humor Applications. *Human Resource Development Review, 9*(4), 314–332.

Rowe, A., & Regehr, C. (2010). Whatever Gets You Through Today: An Examination of Cynical Humor among Emergency Service Professionals. *Journal of Loss and Trauma, 15*(5), 448–464.

Sackmann, S. (1991). *Cultural Knowledge in Organisations*. London: Sage Publications.

Savage, S., Charman, S., & Cope, S. (2000). *Policing and the Power of Persuasion*. London: Blackstone Press.

Scerra, N. (2011). Impact of Police Cultural Knowledge on Violent Serial Crime Investigation. *Policing: An International Journal of Police Strategies and Management, 34*(1), 83–96.

Schein, E. (1984). Coming to a New Awareness of Organizational Culture. *Sloan Management Review, 25*(2), 3.

Scott, T. (2007). Expression of Humour by Emergency Personnel Involved in Sudden Deathwork. *Mortality, 12*(4), 350–364.

Scripture, A. (1997). The Sources of Police Culture: Demographic or Environmental Variables? *Policing and Society, 7*(3), 163–176.

Shammas, V., & Sandberg, S. (2015). Habitus, Capital, and Conflict: Bringing Bourdieusian Field Theory to Criminology. *Criminology and Criminal Justice, 16*(2), 195–213.

Shearing, C., & Ericson, R. (1991). Culture as Figurative Action. *British Journal of Sociology, 42*(4), 481–506.

Shiner, M. (2010). Post Lawrence Policing in England and Wales: Guilt, Innocence and the Defence of Organizational Ego. *British Journal of Criminology, 50*(5), 935–953.

Sklansky, D. (2006). Not Your Father's Police Department: Making Sense of the New Demographics of Law Enforcement. *The Journal of Criminal Law and Criminology, 96*(3), 1209–1243.

Sklansky, D. (2007). Seeing Blue: Police Reform, Occupational Culture, and Cognitive Burn-In. In M. O'Neill, M. Marks, & A. Singh (Eds.), *Police Occupational Culture: New Debates and Directions* (pp. 19–46). Oxford: Elsevier JAI.

Skolnick, J. (1966). *Justice Without Trial: Law Enforcement in Democratic Society.* New York: Wiley and Sons.

Skolnick, J. (2008). Enduring Issues of Police Culture and Demographics. *Policing and Society, 18*(1), 35–45.

Skolnick, J. (2011). *Justice Without Trial: Law Enforcement in Democratic Society* (4th ed.). New York: Wiley and Sons.

Smith, D., & Gray, J. (1985). *Police and People in London: The PSI Report.* Aldershot: Gower.

Soeters, J. (2000). Culture in Uniformed Organizations. In N. Ashkanasay, C. Wilderom, & M. Peterson (Eds.), *Handbook of Organizational Culture and Climate* (pp. 465–482). London: Sage.

Steyn, J., & Mkhize, S. (2016). 'Darker Shades of Blue': A Comparison of Three Decades of South African Police Service Culture. *SA Crime Quarterly, 57,* 15–26.

Thompson, M., Ellis, R., & Wildavsky, A. (1990). *Cultural Theory.* Boulder: Westview Press.

van Hulst, M. (2013). Storytelling at the Police Station: The Canteen Culture Revisited. *British Journal of Criminology, 53*(4), 624–642.

Van Maanen, J. (1973). Observations on the Making of Policemen. *Human Organization, 32*(4), 407–418.

Van Maanen, J. (1975). Police Socialization: A Longitudinal Examination of Job Attitudes in an Urban Police Department. *Administrative Science Quarterly, 20*(2), 207–228.

Van Maanen, J. (1978). Kinsmen in Repose: Occupational Perspectives of Patrolmen. In P. Manning & J. Van Maanen (Eds.), *Police: A View from the Street* (pp. 115–127). Santa Monica: Goodyear Publishing Company.

Wacquant, L. (1992). Toward a Social Praxeology: The Structure and Logic of Bourdieu's Sociology. In P. Bourdieu & L. Wacquant (Eds.), *An Invitation to Reflexive Sociology* (pp. 1–47). Cambridge: Polity Press.

Waddington, P. (1999a). Police (Canteen) Culture: An Appreciation. *British Journal of Criminology, 39*(2), 287–309.

Waddington, P. (1999b). *Policing Citizens.* London: UCL Press.

Walklate, S. (2000). Equal Opportunities and the Future of Policing. In F. Leishman, S. Savage, & B. Loveday (Eds.), *Core Issues in Policing* (2nd ed., pp. 232–248). Harlow: Longman Pearson Education.

Walsh, J. (1977). Career Styles and Police Behaviour. In D. Bayley (Ed.), *Police and Society* (pp. 149–175). Beverley Hills: Sage.

Weick, K. (1995). *Sensemaking in Organizations.* Thousand Oaks: Jossey-Bass.

Westera, N., Kebbell, M., Milne, R., & Green, T. (2013). Defining the "Effective Detective". ARC Centre of Excellence in Policing and Security Briefing, 20.

Westley, W. (1970). *Violence and the Police: A Sociological Study of Law, Custom and Morality*. Cambridge, MA: MIT Press.

Westmarland, L. (2005). Police Ethics and Integrity: Breaking the Blue Code of Silence. *Policing and Society, 15*(2), 145–165.

Westmarland, L., & Rowe, M. (2016). Police Ethics and Integrity: Can a New Code Overturn the Blue Code? *Policing and Society*. http://dx.doi.org/10.10 80/10439463.2016.1262365

Whelan, C. (2017). Security Networks and Occupational Culture: Understanding Culture Within and Between Organisations. *Policing and Society, 27*(2), 113–135.

White, S. (1972). A Perspective on Police Professionalization. *Law and Society Review, 7*, 61–85.

Willis, J., & Mastrofski, S. (2017). Understanding the Culture of Craft: Lessons from Two Police Agencies. *Journal of Crime and Justice, 40*(1), 84–100.

Wilson, J. (1968). *Varieties of Police Behaviour*. Cambridge, MA: Harvard University Press.

Young, M. (1991). *An Inside Job*. Oxford: Oxford University Press.

Young, M. (1995). Black Humour: Making Light of Death. *Policing and Society, 5*, 151–167.

# Part II

## Researching Police Socialisation, Identity and Culture

# 7

# The Research: Aims and Methods

Cultural analysis of organisations often begins at the premise that a culture (usually singular) exists and then turns to a consideration of how this culture might be manipulated and changed in the 'interests' of the organisation, whether this might be to improve productivity, to assuage organisational criticism or to smooth over organisational change. The literature on policing cultures, in particular, tends to explore the often static characteristics of those cultures yet neglects any interpretation of their origins. The empirical research, which is to be considered in detail over the next five chapters, aims to take a few steps backwards and consider the influences upon, and changing attitudes of, new police recruits over the course of the first four years of their careers as police constables. It is not enough to acknowledge that a culture exists, nor to be able to describe its characteristics. It is also important to be able to go beyond these descriptions and to understand what shapes and influences those cultural attitudes, values and beliefs about the nature of the job. Paoline (2003) has argued that any future accounts of policing cultures should not rest at providing descriptions of cultural variations within policing services but must instead seek to explain the factors which are relevant in the shaping of those variations. He suggests that longitudinal research may be able to provide this richer and deeper understanding of cultural dynamics,

© The Author(s) 2017
S. Charman, *Police Socialisation, Identity and Culture*,
DOI 10.1007/978-3-319-63070-0_7

particularly during the socialisation stages. This and the following five chapters seek to do just that.

The research project undertaken in this book had two specific aims:

- To assess the presenting and changing attitudes, values and beliefs of the new recruits to the police service in the early stages of their police career.
- To evaluate the key influences upon the formation and development of these attitudes, values and beliefs of new police recruits.

Longitudinal research seeks to do rather more than take a snapshot of a particular group of people or a particular moment in time and instead offers a fuller and deeper explanation of change. It does this through collecting data from a group of people at regular and key intervals over a specified period of time. The very nature of following a group of people over a prolonged period of time brings with it implications with regard to cost, sample size, dropout rates and the inevitable delay in results. However, the richness of the data that can be achieved through this mode of research brings with it substantial rewards. It is particularly effective in providing a deeper analysis of change, particularly attitude change. Longitudinal research studies tend to focus on more quantitative data (Thomson and Holland 2003). Comparisons are then able to be made by an analysis of this data.

However, perhaps more significantly, the subtleties and nuances of a changed identity and changed attitudes, values and beliefs can be assessed through an appreciation of the words, stories and emotions expressed by the sample through the interview process. This is particularly important when attempting to appreciate not only the formation but the development of habitus and its relationship with the field over a period of time. The development of the habitus is being constructed within an ever-changing field and longitudinal research has the potential to capture that. When the longitudinal research can stretch beyond the more routine one- or two-year limits, that case is even stronger. The research upon which this book is based reports the findings and analysis of a sample of new recruits to the police service over the course of the first four years of their policing careers.

Researching an organisation such as the police service brings with it certain complications. Add to this the problematical issues surrounding measuring and researching culture, and with it, beliefs, attitudes and understandings, and some challenging methodological issues begin to be raised. This combination of researching culture and researching the police, individually and collectively, adds to the methodological question. These two issues will be briefly discussed now.

Although there has certainly been a much more constructive relationship between the police service and higher education in more recent years, the police service has historically been highly suspicious of research, and particularly academic research. The understandable scenario of 'little to gain and much to lose' had guided the police in their traditional reluctance to accept outside researchers. This reluctance to accept outside researchers, coupled with some first-hand experience of accepting researchers only to be heavily criticised by them (Smith and Gray 1983), had led to a closed-door policy. Even when access was granted, the low visibility of police work contributed further to the difficulties in researching the police (Reiner 2000). As mentioned, this relationship is a much more constructive one now and certainly would be unlikely to be one of which new recruits would be aware. However, although that relationship may be more constructive, it is not necessarily always an equal one. The College of Policing, which acts as the professional body of the police service, seeks academic partners to collaborate on its research priorities. The opportunity to influence what those research priorities might be is not so apparent. Writing before the College of Policing was considered, Robert Reiner expressed concern about the dangers of following a more policy-focused approach to police research:

> The danger is that the necessarily quicker and more focused assessments of specific problems and attempted solutions may not shed light on the low visibility practices of everyday policing. Our basic knowledge of such basic matters as why people join the force, the extent of the use of discriminatory language, the way day-to-day decisions about the use of powers are made, and other key aspects of cop culture are based on increasingly out-of-date research like the PSI study conducted in the early 1980s. Replication of the classic observational studies of routine police work is badly needed. There are many topics crying out for research of the older kind that sought to understand basic practices without being directed to the immediate solution of practical problems. Ultimately such work can provide a better grounding for policy as well. (2000, p. 226)

The second methodological challenge is of researching culture. "In asking about culture, interviewers are often asking fish to describe the water in which they swim" (Rubin and Rubin 1995, p. 20). Researching culture, cultural change and attitudes is arguably a more complicated process than researching other areas of study. As Henerson, Morris and Fitz-Gibbon have argued, "attempting to demonstrate attitude *change* is probably the most difficult of all evaluation tasks" (1987, p. 11, emphasis in original).

Attitude is not a concrete entity but an abstract construct from which we, as researchers, can only infer meanings. These inferred meanings however should not be any less valued within social science research. Clearly, it is impossible to accurately and precisely measure attitudes, but this is not a search for 'the truth' (Richards 1996, p. 200); it is rather a process of uncovering the perceptions, beliefs and ideologies of those who have control and power over citizen's lives and act as the gatekeepers of the criminal justice system. Richards (1996) goes on to suggest that interviewee reliability might be a concern to those utilising interviewing as their research tool. However, it should also be seen as an advantage. Interviewee *unreliability* and opposing meanings and understandings can reveal as much to the researcher as strictly comparable answers.

Decisions about methodology were affected by a number of factors. The research aimed to focus upon the attitudes, values and beliefs of the new recruits. It did not aim to understand and appreciate their behaviours. As such, it was important to be able to spend time alone with the recruits to understand their aspirations, their fears, their understandings of the policing organisation and their role within it and their acculturation into their new identity. Observations were therefore not considered to be an essential component of this research. Having said that, the amount of time that was spent waiting in and around police stations and listening in to regular radio interruptions meant that some observational research was an unintended consequence of spending time amongst police officers. However, in order to be able to better appreciate the potential scale of change in attitudes of the new recruits, it was deemed necessary to also include a quantitative element to the research. This would enable comparisons between the views and the attitudes expressed by the new recruits at different stages during their early development as police officers and therefore appreciate the movement between one set of opinions and another. Therefore, the research utilised both a qualitative and a quantitative approach in order to maximise the advantages of the longitudinal approach.

The choice was therefore made to concentrate upon the research interview as the primary source of data in which there would be both a qualitative and a quantitative element. Interviews have been alternatively classed as "conversations with a purpose" (Kahn and Cannell 1957, p. 149). A consideration of the literature on this topic reveals an appreciation of the rich, varied and valuable information that can be obtained using this approach:

> I have often favoured this technique for the insights it offers into the culture, organization, and activity of the executives and their firm. (Useem 1995, p. 24)
>
> Warm, vivid contemporary history has almost always been written by authors who have conducted interviews; dull, clinical history is often produced by those who have buried themselves away in libraries and archives. (Seldon 1988, p. 9)
>
> The qualitative research interview is a construction site of knowledge … interviews are particularly suited for studying people's understanding of the meanings in their lived world, describing their experiences and self understanding, and clarifying and elaborating their own perspective on their lived world. (Kvale 1996, pp. 2 & 105)

However, it would be naïve to presume that the interviewee is not assessing and evaluating the interviewer as much as the reverse situation (Van Maanen et al. 1982). Rubin and Rubin have captured the difficulties well:

> You don't have to be a woman to interview women, or a sumo wrestler to interview sumo wrestlers. But if you are going to cross social gaps and go where you are ignorant, you have to recognise and deal with cultural barriers to communication. And you have to accept that how you are seen by the person being interviewed will affect what is said. (1995, p. 39)

The research interview is not a natural setting for a conversation. At the first interview at least, it involved two strangers in a room with a recording device. The interview is not a confessional, and an awareness of how the truth and stories are constructed and how power relations operate within the interview room is an essential component of the research practice (McLeod 2003). I was, after all, relying upon self-reported, rather than observed, behaviours. However, repeated interviews provide the potential for a fuller appreciation of the interviewee, if not the 'truth' of that person (Thomson and Holland 2003). Over the course of four years, it would not be easy to maintain the stance of regularly providing a socially desirable account of their role, their outlook and their identity. The trust and rapport which was built upon at each interview stage, helped by a growing understanding that there was no detrimental impact to them being a part of the research, also played its part. A further advantage was that throughout the entire four-year research process, I, the author of this book, was the sole interviewer. Inevitably therefore, interviewer and interviewees became far more familiar with each other. The stories, the humour and the anecdotes shared (in addition to the occasional tears) revealed in the main an apparently honest account of the officers' views and attitudes to all aspects of the job. This sometimes occurred when the recording device was switched off or when standing in the car park at the end of the interview, but it would be difficult to assume that a façade of socially desirable answers was maintained throughout the four-year research process.

A semi-structured interview was the chosen interview form and falls somewhere in between a structured approach and an unstructured approach. Unstructured interviews take their own course, and although the interviewer will be aware of topics that they wish to cover, the direction is determined by the respondent and each individual interview (Henerson et al. 1987). Conversely, a highly structured approach includes fixed sets of questions that are asked in strict sequence. The advantages of a semi-structured approach are well documented by those who have been involved in researching the police and in researching culture (Henerson et al. 1987; Richards 1996; Reiner 1991; Crewe 1974; Brewer 1993). Standard questioning gives little room for expansion and elaboration by respondents, and can effectively restrict respondents in their answers.

There was both a prospective and a retrospective focus to the interviews, which aimed to build a fuller and more rounded picture of each individual (McLeod 2003).

A further advantage of utilising a semi-structured approach is that interview schedules can be adapted as research continues. It became very clear from the first two interviews with the new recruits, for example, that they quite clearly had a 'pecking order' of who were the most and least influential figures in their development as police officers. The decision to add a quantitative question to this effect came as a direct result of those early interviews. Van Maanen, Dabbs and Faulkner have emphasised the importance of this flexibility:

> [I]f you knew at the outset of a study precisely what it was one wanted to discover and how one should go about such discovery, most qualitative researchers would say "why bother?". (1982, p. 20)

Social research is an adventure through the minds and lives of those being studied, and it is only by embarking on that adventure that a better appreciation of the terrain can be established. Being fully equipped for the adventure is clearly vital, but doggedly remaining on the pre-arranged path when events and circumstances are changing around you is naïve. Research takes place in a living context and not within a vacuum.

The qualitative interviews were framed around the following major themes:

- The role of the police
- How to learn to be a police officer
- The influence of others in learning to be a police officer
- The expectations and realities of being a police officer
- What makes a 'good' police officer
- The major challenges facing policing

Evermord Constabulary (fictional name) is a medium-sized force in the south of England. In conversation with a senior officer from Evermord Constabulary, it became clear that there was an acknowledgement within the police service that police recruits in the early months and years of their policing careers appeared to be quite different in terms of their attitudes towards their role and position as police officers than they were in the first days and weeks of their police training. What influenced those changes appeared to be unclear. As the conversation took hold, it appeared that there was a genuine interest from both sides in trying to analyse those subtle yet significant shifts in attitude over the first four years of their policing career.

Two complete cohorts of new recruits to Evermord Constabulary who began in the autumn and spring of consecutive years were chosen as the sample to study. As the population to be researched was a 'total population' (i.e. *all* members of the two cohorts of new recruits), there could be no attempt to produce a stratified sample which might be able to focus upon areas such as gender and race. The ethnic diversity of the sample was not sufficient enough to warrant any further analysis. Unintentionally, these two cohorts were also one of the first groups of new recruits who all had to pass the Certificate of Knowledge in Policing prior to a formal offer of employment being given. As discussed in Chap. 4, this pre-service qualification began as the Police, Law and Community course in collaboration between the University of Portsmouth and Surrey Police in 2008 and was then extended into a more national framework by the College of Policing.

Following a previous recruitment freeze, these two cohorts were also mostly drawn from a pool of people who already had some previous policing or military experience. This does impact upon the research analysis. The vast majority of the two cohorts had had experience before of working within a policing environment. The analysis of the interviews later revealed that whether serving as a PCSO or as a voluntary Special Constable, this experience had been considered to be important, but had not fully prepared officers for life as a sworn police officer. It had though, as shall be seen later, honed some of the more social and interpersonal skills that these officers later utilised with more regularity than other more combative, available policing tactics. Of the 24 recruits, 14 had served as PCSOs, 6 had been Special Constables and 4 had worked as police staff in, for example, the force enquiry centre, intelligence or training. Five of the recruits had worked in a private sector background before joining the police, 1 had worked as a teacher and 3 had a military background. These numbers do not all commute to 24 (sample size), as some recruits fell into two categories, for example, private sector background and Special Constable. Only 4 out of the sample of 24 new recruits had no previous policing experience, and 3 of these 4 came from a military background. This fact alone makes this research project particularly novel. About 29% of the overall sample were female, which fell broadly in line with the national picture at the time of women joining the police service (Home Office 2014). In terms of educational attainment, 25% of the sample held an undergraduate degree. The recruits were aged between 24 and 44 on joining the police service, but the vast majority of the sample were in the 20s.

In addition to the qualitative-based open questions that formed the bulk of the interview, the research design also utilised a more quantitative element in order to be able to assess with more certainty the nature of the potential changes in views towards a variety of policing issues. These included the role, function and characteristics of a police officer, plus an assessment of their priorities and influences. Recruits were first asked two rank order questions in order to assess their beliefs as to the most important priorities of a police officer and the most important characteristics. Recruits were provided with a choice of five priorities and five characteristics. These were repeated at each of the four interview stages (TIME A, TIME B, TIME C and TIME D). At TIME C (one year into their policing career and having completed most of the formal police training), recruits were also asked to rank order the influences upon their development as a new police officer out of a choice of six options. This was repeated at TIME D (four years after joining the police service). Recruits were then presented with 22 statements about the role of police officers and the job of policing. The statements were designed as a Likert-type scale in order to ascertain the recruits' intensity of feeling towards certain issues and values. The options available were strongly agree, agree, disagree or strongly disagree. A neutral option was not permitted. Significance was assessed using the Friedman test, and any significant results were further analysed using the Wilcoxon signed-rank test and the effect size test.

The first interview (TIME A) with each new recruit took place during their first element of formal policing training at the force's training headquarters. This was known as *Skills Development I*. There were 16 members of the first cohort and 12 members of the second cohort. In the quotes from respondents, which are utilised in subsequent chapters, A–D represent the four interviews with the first cohort and W–Z represent the four interviews with recruits from the second cohort. Table 7.1 outlines the number of respondents and the dropout rate at each of the four research stages. About 92% of those taking part at TIME A were interviewed at TIME B and TIME C, and 71% of those taking part at TIME A were interviewed at TIME D. This compares with 61% in Chan's two-year lon-

**Table 7.1** Numbers of respondents during each research phase

|  | Cohort 1<br>16 officers in total,<br>13 agreed | Cohort 2<br>12 officers in total,<br>11 available at TIME A,<br>all agreed | Additional<br>respondents |
|---|---|---|---|
| Time A | 13 respondents<br>(3 female, 10 male) | 11 respondents<br>(4 female, 7 male) | |
| Time B | 12 respondents<br>(3 female, 9 male)<br>*1 failed<br>interview—<br>deployed twice<br>at the time of<br>interview* | 10 respondents<br>(3 female, 7 male)<br>*1 failed interview—<br>attempted but<br>failed to arrange* | |
| Time C | 12 respondents<br>(3 female, 9 male) | 10 respondents<br>(3 female, 7 male) | Student<br>development<br>recruitment<br>officers—6<br>respondents<br>(3 female, 3 male)<br>Tutors—7<br>respondents<br>(7 male) |
| Time D | 10 respondents<br>(3 female, 7 male)<br>*2 failed<br>interviews—both<br>officers had<br>transferred to<br>other forces* | 7 respondents<br>(2 female, 5 male)<br>*3 failed interviews—one<br>officer had transferred<br>to another force, one<br>officer was dismissed by<br>the force; a further<br>officer was deployed when<br>interview was arranged* | |
| Total | 47 | 38 | 13 |

gitudinal research (2003). Recruits were approximately five weeks into their policing career and undertaking a 13-week initial training course. This was a reduced length of training time from previous cohorts, as some of the knowledge- and legal-based elements of initial police training had already been undertaken via the Certificate of Knowledge in Policing. The research was explained to the recruits by their trainers and they were given the option to take part or not. Recruits were then given time away from their training timetable to read an information sheet and, if interested further, to take part in what was usually a 15- to 20-minute initial interview. The average time of the recorded interview at TIME A was 18.5 minutes.

The second interview (TIME B) took place after approximately six months in service. The new recruits had finished their 13-week initial training course, had been assigned to a shift and a station within the force area, and had completed their ten-week attachment to a tutor constable, known as the 'tutor phase'. This was before the police officers had been granted Independent Patrol Status. All of the interviews took place within the station to which the new recruit had been assigned and during a shift. I had outlined to the officers that the interviews would be likely to take approximately 30 minutes. In reality, the interviews ranged in time from 18 minutes to 54 minutes, with the average time of the recorded interview at TIME B being 30.3 minutes.

The third interview (TIME C) took place after approximately one year in service. The new recruits had all been granted Independent Patrol Status and were back in the force training headquarters for Skills Development II, the intention of which was to provide a better understanding of a number of issues, including mental health and domestic and sexual violence. All the interviews took place within the training headquarters. Being back in training, the officers had less control over their time and each interview followed on from the next. The interviews at TIME C were therefore shorter than the previous interview, ranging from 12 minutes to 40 minutes. The average time of the recorded interview at TIME C was 23.5 minutes.

The fourth and final interview (TIME D) took place after the not-so-new recruits had been in service for approximately four years. The minimum length of service was three years and nine months, and the maximum length of service was four years and three months. These interviews all took place within police stations located around the force area.

All officers taking part had passed their probationary period. Having not seen the officers for three years and, as many of them noted, not often having the opportunity to reflect upon their work in this way, these interviews were longer than the previous interview, ranging from 21 minutes to 54 minutes. The average time of the recorded interview at TIME D was 33.5 minutes.

In addition to the new recruit interviews, an additional 13 interviews were conducted with a small number of tutors ($n$ = 7) and Student Development Recruitment Officers (SDROs) ($n$ = 6). The role of the SDRO is explained in Chap. 8. In the quotes from these respondents, which are utilised in subsequent chapters, 'T' represents a tutor and 'S' represents an SDRO. The average time of the recorded interview with tutors was 40.1 minutes and with SDROs was 31.3 minutes. A thorough analysis of the views, attitudes and beliefs of the new recruits was imperative to a better understanding of the impact of the early career years on their development. However, it was also important to see this development from a different perspective, of the people who are working closely with new recruits on a regular basis. Both tutors and SDROs could comment on the changing nature of new recruits, the difficulties that they believed these new recruits faced and the changes they observed during those early years.

Each of the 98 interviews conducted was recorded using a portable recording device with permission from the interviewee. Assurances were made at the beginning of each and every interview to reassure the interviewees that no part of the data would be used inappropriately and that each interviewee would be assigned with a code which would make it impossible for them to be identified. Neither the force in question has been named, nor the exact date of the start of their policing careers. All officers gave their permission to be recorded. As Reiner (1991) has noted, police officers are perhaps more aware than most of the difficulties of contemporaneous note-taking. Digital recorders are small and relatively unobtrusive. Conversely, there is no way of assessing how obtrusive the notepad might be (Brewer 1993). The recorded interviews were then assigned a code, securely stored and sent away for transcription. In all, there was 2665 recorded minutes of interviews, equating to 44.4 hours. This was in addition to the inevitable conversations that began before the recording device had been switched on and continued once the recording device had been switched off. Notes were taken of these conversations as soon as it was practicable.

The data that was produced by this four-year longitudinal research study was analysed in two directions. First, it was analysed cross-sectionally to identify similarities and differences amongst the key messages expressed across the sample. Second, it was analysed longitudinally within one subject, in order to be able to capture the development of particular values, attitudes or beliefs and how those are expressed over time. By using both quantitative and qualitative data-gathering techniques, it was possible to compare responses across the sample and within the same individual over time. Frequencies and cross-tabulations were also produced to assess the potential differences between male and female respondents. The analysis of qualitative, longitudinal data allows for the forming and shaping of an identity to be identified, rather than a more static account of solitary sentiments. Braun and Clarke's (2006) six phases of thematic analysis played an important role in the analysis of this data. These are data familiarisation, generation of data codes, identification, review and then naming of themes before writing up. The analysis for this research was not wedded to any particular constructionist, contextualist or realist theoretical framework. Nor, however, should it be said that the themes 'emerged' without sufficient acknowledgement being paid to the active role that a researcher plays in any interpretation of data. Immersing oneself in the data through conducting the interviews, checking the transcriptions plus analysis 'by hand', rather than with the aid of a computer package, can all contribute to the depth of understanding of the data. There can be concerns about the integrity of data with the use of computer packages. Whilst these packages certainly aid efficiency, there is the potential for reduced integrity, as they chop the data into small chunks of text, thereby potentially disrupting the developing narrative. Although it has been suggested that there is now no equivalent alternative to the use of computer-assisted data analysis (Richards 2009), there remain critics of its standardised coding and analysis (Brinkmann 2012).

The issue of validity and reliability with regard to research interviews is problematic, as most indicators "do not fit qualitative research" (Rubin and Rubin 1995, p. 85). It is sometimes suggested that 'good research is valid research', and every attempt was made with this research to ensure that the whole process of the research, from design to report, was 'good'. To ensure reliability in positivistic research would entail the ability to replicate the study elsewhere or in a different time period. This is clearly impossible with the semi-structured interview approach that was considering and analysing attitude change within a specific time period. The new recruits' views on policing and those to be policed is also heavily influenced by the social, economic and political issues of the time. These would be different at different time periods and in different parts of the country. Indeed, the changes in how the recruits expressed their frustrations of the job were different as the years passed. This was not only an issue of these recruits becoming more experienced but was also a reflection of changing social and economic times. The formation and development of their habitus was being influenced by the field.

The issue of validity is again complicated in predominantly qualitative research, but it can pertain to the assessment of whether the methodological tools indeed 'measured' what they were supposed to 'measure'. If the question is being asked of whether the methodological choices enabled the 'true story' of the changes in attitudes, values and beliefs of the new recruits to emerge, then the answer must be that we will never know for sure. However, when the situation of "theoretical saturation" emerges (Glaser and Strauss 1967, p. 42), that is, when themes and issues evolve and develop during the research until the stage is reached when new ideas and themes are no longer being raised, then some 'truth' must be emerging. Guest, Bunce and Johnson refer to this stage as being when no new codes are emerging from the research analysis or "thematic exhaustion" (2006, p. 65). The phrase 'theoretical saturation' (or 'conceptual saturation' (Corbin and Strauss 2008)) is commonplace within qualitative research and judged as the measure of adequate sampling. It is however poorly conceptualised (Guest et al. 2006). Decisions on sample size within longitudinal research have to be taken at the outset of the research, and sampling cannot continue until the mystical moment of 'theoretical saturation' is reached. Guest et al. (2006), in their analysis of when this elixir might be reached, have suggested that it occurred after 12 interviews, although they do question how generalisable their findings might be. What they do add though is that three considerations will enhance the likelihood of a smaller sample being sufficient—an element of structure within the interviews, a relatively homogeneous sample and a sample with both shared experiences and potentially shared perceptions and beliefs (Guest et al. 2006). Further research has confirmed these findings (Dahl and Moreau 2007; Miller and Rayner 2012).

Validity can also be enhanced through interview questions that contain questions drawn from the academic literature, through the building of trust and rapport, through the use of interviews of an adequate length and through the use of prompts (Arksey and Knight 1999). All of these techniques were utilised within this research in order to achieve, if not validity and reliability in a positivistic sense, then at the very least, transparency, consistency and communicability.

All attempts were made during the design and implementation of this research to ensure it to be as methodologically sound as possible. Clearly, there were instances of trains being late, of Grade 1 calls coming through and thus necessitating a rearranged interview, of emergency battery changing mid-interview and of respondents being reluctant to talk. However, in the vast majority of cases, the new recruits were only too pleased to discuss their views, their experiences and their ideas about policing, about crime and about the future. The remainder of this book is testament as to whether a correspondingly sufficient *analysis* of this data was achieved.

# References

Arksey, H., & Knight, P. (1999). *Interviewing for Social Scientists*. London: Sage.

Braun, V., & Clarke, V. (2006). Using Thematic Analysis in Psychology. *Qualitative Research in Psychology, 3*(2), 77–101.

Brewer, J. (1993). A Study of Routine Policing in Northern Ireland. In C. Renzetti & R. Lee (Eds.), *Researching Sensitive Topics* (pp. 125–145). London: Sage.

Brinkmann, S. (2012). Qualitative Research Between Craftsmanship and McDonaldization. *Qualitative Studies, 3*(1), 56–68.

Chan, J. (2003). *Fair Cop: Learning the Art of Policing*. Toronto: University of Toronto Press.

Corbin, J., & Strauss, A. (2008). *Basic of Qualitative Research* (3rd ed.). Thousand Oaks: Sage.

Crewe, I. (1974). Introduction: Studying Elites in Britain. In I. Crewe (Ed.), *British Political Sociology Yearbook: Elites in Western Democracy* (pp. 9–54). London: Croom Helm.

Dahl, D., & Moreau, C. (2007). Thinking Inside the Box: Why Consumers Enjoy Constrained Creative Experiences. *Journal of Marketing Research, 44*(3), 357–369.

Glaser, B., & Strauss, A. (1967). *The Discovery of Grounded Theory.* Chicago: Aldine.

Guest, G., Bunce, A., & Johnson, L. (2006). How Many Interviews Are Enough? An Experiment with Data Saturation and Variability. *Field Methods, 18*(1), 59–82.

Henerson, M., Morris, L., & Fitz-Gibbon, C. (1987). *How to Measure Attitudes.* California: Sage.

Home Office. (2014, March 31). *Police Workforce, England and Wales.* Retrieved from https://www.gov.uk/government/publications/police-workforce-england-and-wales-31-march-2014/police-workforce-england-and-wales-31-march-2014

Kahn, R., & Cannell, C. (1957). *The Dynamics of Interviewing.* New York: John Wiley.

Kvale, S. (1996). *Interviews.* California: Sage.

McLeod, J. (2003). Why We Interview Now – Relflexivity and Perspective in a Longitudinal Study. *International Journal of Social Research Methodology, 6*(3), 201–211.

Miller, H., & Rayner, C. (2012). The Form and Function of "Bullying" Behaviors in a Strong Occupational Culture: Bullying in a UK Police Service. *Group and Organization Management, 37*(3), 347–375.

Paoline, E. (2003). Taking Stock: Toward a Richer Understanding of Police Culture. *Journal of Criminal Justice, 31*(3), 199–214.

Reiner, R. (1991). *Chief Constables.* Oxford: Oxford University Press.

Reiner, R. (2000). Police Research. In R. King & E. Wincup (Eds.), *Doing Research on Crime and Justice* (pp. 205–236). Oxford: Oxford University Press.

Richards, D. (1996). Elite Interviewing: Approaches and Pitfalls. *Politics, 16*(3), 199–204.

Richards, L. (2009). *Handling Qualitative Data: A Practical Guide* (2nd ed.). London: Sage.

Rubin, H., & Rubin, I. (1995). *Qualitative Interviewing: The Art of Hearing Data.* California: Sage.

Seldon, A. (1988). *Contemporary History.* Oxford: Blackwell.

Smith, D., & Gray, J. (1983). *Police and People in London IV: The Police in Action*. London: PSI.

Thomson, R., & Holland, J. (2003). Hindsight, Foresight and Insight: The Challenges of Longitudinal Qualitative Research. *International Journal of Social Research Methodology, 6*(3), 233–244.

Useem, M. (1995). Reaching Corporate Executives. In R. Hertz & J. Imber (Eds.), *Studying Elites Using Qualitative Methods* (pp. 18–39). California: Sage.

Van Maanen, J., Dabbs, J., & Faulkner, R. (1982). *Varieties of Qualitative Research*. California: Sage.

# 8

# Quantitative Results: Measuring Attitudes, Measuring Change

The details of the methodological choices for this longitudinal research project are outlined in detail in Chap. 7, along with the biographical details of the sample. As a reminder, 24 new police recruits across two cohorts were interviewed for the first time in the autumn and spring of consecutive years. This was followed by three subsequent interviews in the early years of their police careers. As outlined in Chap. 7, 17 police recruits were interviewed at each of the four stages. Officers were 'lost' from the research due to transferring to other forces, leaving the service or an inability to arrange interviews. As outlined in Chap. 7, interviews were also conducted with seven tutors and six SDROs. The four interviews with new police recruits were conducted at the following times.

| Number of respondents | Timing of interview |
| --- | --- |
| TIME A<br>N = 24 | During the initial training period, within five weeks of joining the police service as a police constable |
| TIME B<br>N = 22 | Six months into the probationary period, whilst attached to a local station, post tutor phase |
| TIME C<br>N = 22 | One year into the probationary period, during the second training school course |

(continued)

© The Author(s) 2017
S. Charman, *Police Socialisation, Identity and Culture*,
DOI 10.1007/978-3-319-63070-0_8

| Number of respondents | Timing of interview | | | |
|---|---|---|---|---|
| TIME D N = 17 | Four years after joining the police service | | | |

| Year 1 | | Year 2 | Year 3 | Year 4 |
|---|---|---|---|---|
| TIME A | TIME B | TIME C | | TIME D |

The main focus of the interviews, as discussed in Chap. 7, was on the format of a semi-structured discussion of the experiences of learning to be and being a new police officer. However, a quantitative element was also a part of the research process. This was done for two specific reasons. First, in order to *measure* and *compare* the opinions of the new recruits across a wide range of issues. In doing this, a clearer sense of the proportionality of opinion could be gauged. Second, in order to be able to assess the potential for a change in those opinions over time. It is therefore the *movement* that may be captured between one set of opinions and another that is of interest. The aim of this research was to better appreciate the changing nature of the new recruits to the police service and one of the ways to achieve this was via an element of quantitative data. This chapter will focus upon the results of that quantitative element. The first section of this chapter will consider the three questions that asked respondents to rank order certain issues relating to policing. These were as follows: what are the most important priorities of a police officer, what are the most important characteristics of a police officer and, finally, who are the people who had influenced their development as officers. The second section of this chapter will then go on to consider a set of statements relating to both policing itself and being a police officer, where respondents were measured upon the extent of their agreement or disagreement.

As discussed in Chap. 7, 29% of the sample were female. Frequencies and cross-tabulations were also produced to assess the potential differences between male and female respondents. No significant differences were found between the responses from women and the responses from men to any of the questions posed. This issue will be returned to in Chap. 12.

# Priorities of a Police Officer

All police recruits were asked to rank order (in terms of importance) the potential priorities of a police officer from a list of five answers. The ranking scheme used was as follows: 1 as most important, and 5 as least important.

Table 8.1 shows that *fighting crime* was consistently rated the *most* important of the five given response options. This was consistent over the four time points, with it slightly increasing in importance over time. This can be seen clearly in Fig. 8.1. As we shall see in the following chapters of this book however, what are seen as the most important priorities of a police officer are not necessarily translated into the actual routine activities of police officers.

**Table 8.1** Mean rank scores[a]—priorities of a police officer at each of the four time points

| Priority—mean rank scores | TIME A | TIME B | TIME C | TIME D |
|---|---|---|---|---|
| Fighting crime | 2.04 (1.12) | 2.00 (1.00) | 1.77 (1.10) | 1.53 (1.00) |
| Enforcing the law | 2.29 (1.30) | 2.57 (1.21) | 2.41 (1.05) | 2.41 (0.94) |
| Public reassurance | 2.67 (1.05) | 2.14 (1.06) | 2.41 (1.10) | 2.94 (1.09) |
| Community engagement | 3.25 (1.03) | 3.57 (0.93) | 3.64 (0.79) | 3.24 (0.97) |
| Education in schools | 4.75 (0.68) | 4.71 (0.78) | 4.77 (0.53) | 4.88 (0.33) |

[a]Lower numbers reflect higher priority; numbers within parentheses reflect standard deviation scores

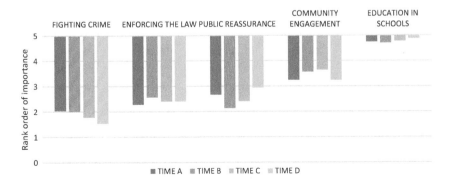

**Fig. 8.1** Most important priorities of a police officer—lower numbers reflect higher priority

*Enforcing the law* was seen to be the *second* most important priority at the first and fourth interviews, with *public reassurance* being seen as the *second* most important priority at the second and third interviews. It is perhaps understandable that *enforcing the law* is considered to be the most important priority for new recruits when they have just completed their pre-join learning, which centres predominantly on legal issues, and during their initial training at training school. *Public reassurance* then takes over as the second most important priority of a police officer when the students are in their first two years as officers. This is an activity which has been encouraged within policing policy (Home Office 2004) and which takes up much of a 'front-line' police officer's time (HMIC 2011). However, after four years within the police service, *enforcing the law* once again takes over from *public reassurance* as the second most important priority of a police officer as the frustration and cynicism associated with these activities begins to develop. This will be explored in more detail within this and the following chapters. *Education in schools* was rated as the *least* important of the five available response options, with no change over time.

## Characteristics of a Police Officer

All police recruits were asked to rank order (in terms of importance) the potential characteristics of a police officer from a list of five answers. The ranking scheme used was as follows: 1 as most important, and 5 as least important.

Table 8.2 shows that *good communication* was consistently rated the *most* important of the five given response options. This was consistent over the four time points and can be seen very clearly in Fig. 8.2. The respondents also discussed the issue at length within the semi-structured interview, which will be discussed in Chaps. 9 and 10. *Empathy/ Understanding* was seen to be the *second* most important characteristic of a police officer and was consistent over the four time points. Whilst *good communication* remained consistently as the most important characteristic, the percentage of respondents choosing *empathy/understanding* did increase from 8.33% in interview A to 17.65% by interview D. *Physical strength* and *suspiciousness* were never chosen as the most important

**Table 8.2** Mean rank scores[a]—important characteristics of a police officer at each of the four time points

| Characteristic—mean rank scores | TIME A | TIME B | TIME C | TIME D |
|---|---|---|---|---|
| Good communication | 1.08 (0.28) | 1.09 (0.29) | 1.09 (0.29) | 1.18 (0.39) |
| Empathy/Understanding | 2.17 (0.56) | 2.00 (0.44) | 2.14 (0.47) | 1.88 (0.49) |
| Authority/Power | 3.13 (0.74) | 3.55 (0.80) | 3.14 (0.83) | 3.47 (0.80) |
| Suspiciousness | 3.96 (0.91) | 3.73 (0.88) | 3.91 (0.81) | 3.76 (0.66) |
| Physical strength | 4.67 (0.48) | 4.64 (0.49) | 4.73 (0.46) | 4.71 (0.59) |

[a]Lower numbers reflect higher priority; numbers within parentheses reflect standard deviation scores

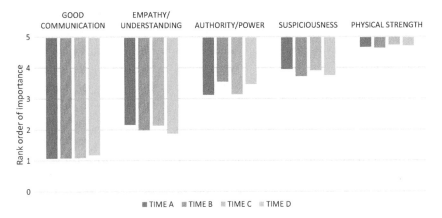

**Fig. 8.2** Most important characteristics of a police officer—lower numbers reflect higher priority

characteristics of a police officer. *Authority/Power* was only chosen as the most important characteristic by one respondent in one interview. *Physical strength* was chosen as the least important characteristic of a police officer by 66.67% in interview A and had increased to 76.47% by interview D. The answers to this particular question, as the qualitative analysis will reveal, reflect not only the type of work that police officers are mostly involved with but also the skills that they are required to call upon on a regular basis. Jobs which require police officers to show physical strength are very rare, and it is argued that better use of the more social and interpersonal skills of policing, for example, empathy and good communication will often negate the necessity for any further action.

# Influences upon a Police Officer According to New Police Recruits

When the new recruits were nearing the end of their probationary period, it became appropriate to ask them who they felt had been the most important influence upon them in terms of their development as a new police recruit. By this stage, they had experienced both the more formal learning and the informal learning that is associated with the early development of police officers. This question was then asked again after they had completed four years' service. Table 8.3 shows that *other police colleagues (e.g. shift)* were rated the *most* important influence and *tutors* were rated the *second* most important influence at TIME C. At TIME D, this had reversed so that *tutors* were rated the *most* important influence and *other police colleagues (e.g. shift)* were rated the *second* most important influence. However, as can be clearly seen in Fig. 8.3, both of these categories scored much more highly than any other category. The 'shift' refers to the group of officers who a new recruit will be assigned to and who work the same working hours and are attached to the same station. A station will typically have five shifts, of which three will work on any one day (e.g. earlies, lates and nights). The pivotal role of the 'shift' (of which the 'tutor' is a part) in the development of the new police recruit is a crucial aspect of this research and will be examined in depth in the qualitative analysis in Chaps. 9 and 10. Whatever formal mechanisms are in place to train and educate the new police recruit, it is apparently in either the less formal ('shift') or the less visible (tutor) aspects of recruit learning where the most significant influence is felt.

**Table 8.3** Mean rank scores[a]—important influences upon a police officer at the last two time points

| Influence—mean rank scores | TIME C | TIME D |
|---|---|---|
| Fellow training school colleagues | 4.70 (0.80) | 4.18 (1.1) |
| Trainers | 2.95 (0.99) | 3.53 (1.1) |
| Tutors | 1.95 (1.1) | 1.53 (0.51) |
| Other police colleagues (e.g. shift) | 1.75 (0.79) | 1.71 (0.77) |
| External influences—family and friends | 4.60 (1.6) | 4.94 (1.1) |
| Student development recruitment officers | 5.05 (0.99) | 5.12 (1.1) |

[a]Lower numbers reflect higher priority; numbers within parentheses reflect standard deviation scores

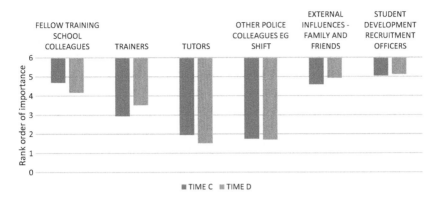

**Fig. 8.3** Most important influences upon a police officer according to new recruits—lower numbers reflect higher priority

Student Development Recruitment Officers (SDROs; now known as Professional Recruitment and Development Officers) were rated as the *least* important of the five available response options, with no change over time. SDROs are involved with the new recruits from the pre-employment assessment centres, through their final interview, their initial training, tutor period and completion of the Diploma in Policing after the two-year probationary period. They meet with mentees regularly throughout the two-year period and are responsible for signing off the new recruits as competent. Their influence however is viewed as the least important of the six options provided. Six SDROs were interviewed as part of this research and the analysis of these interviews will be seen in forthcoming chapters.

# Influences upon a Police Officer According to Tutors

As discussed in Chap. 7, interviews were also conducted with tutors and SDROs to assess their interpretations and understandings of how police officers learn and the impact of their initial learning upon their later attitudes and beliefs about the nature of policing and of their role within it. During these interviews, both tutors and SRDOs were also asked to reflect upon who they felt were the most important influence upon the new recruit in terms of influencing their development. This would inevitably take account of two aspects of their professional life—their experience as recruits themselves and their current role within the training process itself. Table 8.4 shows that tutors rated their own role, that of *tutors*, as the *most* important influence upon new police recruits. Just as the new recruits themselves did, they also rated *other police colleagues (e.g. shift)* as the *second* most important influence. Tutors and new recruits therefore appear to be in close agreement about this issue. As with the new recruits, tutors also rated SDROs as the *least* important influence. Figure 8.4 illustrates these results.

**Table 8.4** Mean rank scores[a]—important influences upon a police officer

| Influence—mean rank scores | |
| --- | --- |
| Training school colleagues | 3.29 (1.3) |
| Trainers | 3.29 (1.1) |
| Tutors | 1.57 (0.54) |
| Other police colleagues (e.g. shift) | 2.00 (0.82) |
| External influences—family and friends | 5.29 (0.76) |
| Student development recruitment officers | 5.57 (0.54) |

[a]Lower numbers reflect higher priority; numbers within parentheses reflect standard deviation scores

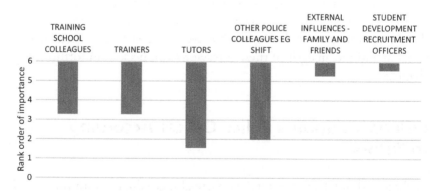

**Fig. 8.4** Most important influences upon a police officer according to tutors—lower numbers reflect higher priority

# Influences upon a Police Officer According to Student Development Recruitment Officers

Table 8.5 shows that SDROs do not view the most important influences upon new recruits in the same way as tutors and new recruits themselves. SDROs rated *tutors, trainers* and *external influences (e.g. family and friends)* as jointly the *most* important influences upon new police recruits. SDROs placed their own role as the *fifth* most important influence, out of six, which does place them in their highest position yet. SDROs rated *training school colleagues* as the *least* important influence, whereas new police recruits placed them fourth out of six. The numbers involved in this part of the research are small and therefore should be treated with caution. It is however perhaps evident that tutors, who spend much time with new recruits both during and after the tutor phase of training, are more in tune with the views and opinions of new recruits than the SDROs, who are not generally involved in the day-to-day policing tasks with the new recruits. Conversely, this could also be interpreted as the new police recruits shaping their attitudes and beliefs to be in line with their tutors and their 'shift'. This aspect of learning will be considered in more depth in Chap. 9. Figure 8.5 illustrates the results of the SDROs' views.

**Table 8.5** Mean rank scores[a]—important influences upon a police officer

| Influence—mean rank scores | |
|---|---|
| Training school colleagues | 4.83 (1.2) |
| Trainers | 2.83 (1.7) |
| Tutors | 2.00 (0.89) |
| Other police colleagues (e.g. shift) | 3.33 (1.8) |
| External influences—family and friends | 3.67 (2.3) |
| Student development recruitment officers | 4.33 (1.0) |

[a]Lower numbers reflect higher priority; numbers within parentheses reflect standard deviation scores

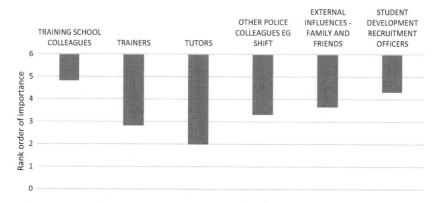

**Fig. 8.5** Most important influences upon a police officer according to student development recruitment officers—lower numbers reflect higher priority

# Doing Policing

The remaining 22 questions were designed as a Likert-type scale in order to ascertain the respondents' intensity of feeling towards certain issues and values surrounding the role of police officers and the job of policing. Respondents were read a statement, which was also presented in written form in front of them. They were asked to indicate how far they agreed or disagreed with the statement by being given a choice of four options: strongly agree, agree, disagree or strongly disagree. A neutral option was not permitted. As the data collected is an ordinal (based on a 1–4) Likert-type scale of strongly agree to strongly disagree, non-parametric versions of Statistical Package for the Social Sciences (SPSS) tests were used, rather than the parametric alternatives, which can only be used when data is normally distributed.

The Friedman test was used on each of the 22 remaining questions to assess the significance or otherwise of the data. This test detects the difference between more than two related samples or repeated measures; for example, this is used to compare the responses received across the four different interview stages. If the results were revealed to be significant, then two further tests were completed. First, the Wilcoxon signed-rank test was completed. This is a non-parametric test that is used to compare two related samples, or repeated measures; for example, if the same variable is measured at two different times, to determine whether there is a significant difference in the variables measured at each stage. The difference is calculated on the ranking of measures, using the mean ranks for each sample (in this case each interview time).

Second, the effect size test was completed. Effect size measures the strength of a phenomenon, for example, relationship/difference. Cohen's (1988) guidance on effect size is used to indicate whether an effect is small (>0.2), medium (>0.5) or large (>0.8). If an effect is smaller than 0.2, whilst it may be statistically significant, it is likely to be trivial. The following equation was used to calculate effect sizes for the Wilcoxon signed-rank test:

$$\text{Effect size} = \frac{Z}{\sqrt{N}}$$

The ordering of the questions was deliberately designed so that the respondents would be less likely to be influenced by an answer to a previous question and be able to temper their thoughts accordingly. For example, the respondents were asked five separate questions in relation to the role of policing but these were spread throughout the 22 questions. A very small number of respondents acknowledged that they were aware of this and asked to go back to see a previous answer before they attempted a question. A contradiction in opinions is as much of interest to the researcher as consistency. However, for the purpose of a clearer analysis, the questions are here loosely grouped into four categories—*cultural characteristics of police officers, the role of policing, the impact of policing* and *how policing should be done.* They are therefore not presented here in the order in which they were presented within the research setting. The results of these 22 questions, which used a Likert-type scale to ascertain the respondents' intensity of feeling towards certain issues and values associated with policing, are as follows.

## Cultural Characteristics of Police Officers

As discussed in Chap. 6, there are a range of characteristics which are regularly cited in the academic literature as being representative of policing cultures. Those most regularly referred to are isolation, solidarity, suspiciousness, secrecy, prejudice, a focus on action and authoritativeness.

These general themes were posed to the respondents in the form of a statement in order to gauge their strength of agreement or disagreement.

Table 8.6 shows that an increasing number of respondents strongly agreed with this statement as the interviews progressed. This rose from 4.2% at interview A to 23.5% of respondents at interview D. The majority of respondents (62.5%) either disagreed or strongly disagreed with this statement when the recruits were in their first few weeks of training. However, by the time the recruits had served for four years in the police service, the majority of respondents (64.7%) either agreed or strongly agreed with the statement. The Friedman test demonstrated that there was no statistically significant change in responses to this statement across the four interview times. New recruits would be unaware in the early stages of their policing careers whether they would feel isolated from their social environment or not. During the four intervening years between interview A and interview D, police officers would have experienced the effects of being a police officer, the public reaction to being a police officer and the associated issues of working a shift pattern. By this stage, it would appear that the majority of police officers were aware that being a police officer did appear to isolate them from their social environment.

Table 8.7 shows that whilst the vast majority of respondents either strongly agreed or agreed with this statement at each of the four interview

Table 8.6 Police officers often feel isolated from their social environment (%)

|  | TIME A | TIME B | TIME C | TIME D |
|---|---|---|---|---|
| Strongly agree | 4.2 | 9.1 | 9.1 | 23.5 |
| Agree | 33.3 | 40.9 | 36.4 | 41.2 |
| Disagree | 54.2 | 36.4 | 50.0 | 35.3 |
| Strongly disagree | 8.3 | 13.6 | 4.5 | – |

Table 8.7 Police officers need to be authoritative (%)

|  | TIME A | TIME B | TIME C | TIME D |
|---|---|---|---|---|
| Strongly agree | 41.7 | 45.5 | 40.9 | 17.6 |
| Agree | 58.3 | 45.5 | 54.5 | 76.5 |
| Disagree | – | 9.1 | 4.5 | 5.9 |
| Strongly disagree | – | – | – | – |

stages, the strength of their agreement did change over time. The percentage of respondents who strongly agreed that police officers need to be authoritative was over 40% at each of the first three interview stages. This dropped substantially to only 17.6% at interview D. However, despite only one respondent in one interview arguing that *authority/ power* was the most important characteristic of a police officer in a previous question, there is still a strong agreement from the respondents that police officers need to be authoritative.

The results of the Friedman test indicated that there is a *statistically significant difference* in the answers given across the final two time points—TIME C (one year into the role of police constable) and TIME D (four years into the role of police constable): $x^2(3, n = 17) = 23.46$, $p < 0.000$. The Wilcoxon analysis revealed a *significant difference* between scores at TIME C and TIME D, $p = 0.002$. The strength of the effect is calculated to be *moderate to large* ($\eta^2 = 0.76$).

Table 8.8 shows that the combined number of respondents who either strongly agreed or agreed with this statement increased at every interview stage. This rose from 70.9% at interview A to 100% at interview D. About 25% of respondents disagreed with the statement at interview A when they were in the first few weeks of their policing careers. At this stage, the new recruits had not experienced working life in a police station as a police constable. The majority of respondents (83%) had experience of working within the policing environment (e.g. as a Special Constable, as a Police Community Support Officer or in a civilian role) but not as a 'front-line' officer. During the intervening four years, all 29.2% of respondents who did not agree that police officers displayed scepticism and cynicism within the context of their work changed their minds and instead agreed or strongly agreed with the statement. This amounted to a

**Table 8.8** Police officers are often sceptical and cynical within the context of their work (%)

|                   | TIME A | TIME B | TIME C | TIME D |
|-------------------|--------|--------|--------|--------|
| Strongly agree    | 29.2   | 27.3   | 27.3   | 58.8   |
| Agree             | 41.7   | 63.6   | 68.2   | 41.2   |
| Disagree          | 25.0   | 9.1    | 4.5    | –      |
| Strongly disagree | 4.2    | –      | –      | –      |

100% rise in the percentage of respondents who strongly agreed that police officers are often sceptical and cynical within the context of their work. Cynicism was a characteristic of police officers that was independently mentioned by the majority of respondents during the qualitative interviews and will be discussed at length in the following two chapters.

The results of the Friedman test indicated that there is a *statistically significant difference* in the answers given across the final two time points—TIME C (one year into the role of police constable) and TIME D (four years into the role of police constable): $x^2(3, n = 17) = 24.54$, $p < 0.000$. The Wilcoxon analysis revealed a *significant difference* between scores at TIME C and TIME D, $p = 0.002$. The strength of the effect is calculated to be *moderate to large* ($\eta^2 = 0.75$).

Table 8.9 shows that the highest percentage of respondents fall under the 'agree' category at all interview stages, and that the figures for the 'strongly agree' are the second highest. This reveals that the majority of respondents agree at all stages. What is interesting about this data is that the overall number of respondents who strongly agree or agree with the statement that 'police officers show high levels of solidarity with each other' is at its highest during the time periods when officers are working in the community rather than in training. The only time when some officers strongly disagreed with the statement was when they were located at their training school (TIME A and TIME C). The percentage of officers who either disagreed or strongly disagreed with the statement when in training was 29.2% (at TIME A) and 27.2% (at TIME C). During the time when officers were working within the community, this was much lower at 9.1% (at TIME B) and 11.8% (at TIME D). The issue of solidarity amongst police officers will be discussed at length in the next two chapters, but was a continuous feature of discussion during the interviews when officers were reflecting on the positive aspects of the job.

**Table 8.9** Police officers show high levels of solidarity with each other (%)

|  | TIME A | TIME B | TIME C | TIME D |
|---|---|---|---|---|
| Strongly agree | 25.0 | 36.4 | 22.7 | 23.5 |
| Agree | 45.8 | 54.5 | 50.0 | 64.7 |
| Disagree | 16.7 | 9.1 | 22.7 | 11.8 |
| Strongly disagree | 12.5 | – | 4.5 | – |

The results of the Friedman test indicated that there is a *statistically significant difference* in the answers given across the final two time points—TIME C (one year into the role of police constable) and TIME D (four years into the role of police constable): $x^2(3, n = 17) = 31.98$, $p < 0.000$. The Wilcoxon analysis revealed a *significant difference* between scores at TIME C and TIME D, $p = 0.000$. The strength of the effect is calculated to be *large* ($\eta^2 = 0.87$).

Respondents were asked as to what extent they felt that the source of this solidarity was working with an 'unsupportive public'. Table 8.10 shows that the views of the respondents remained fairly consistent and split during the course of the interviews. About 41.6% of respondents agreed or strongly agreed with the statement at TIME A, which had increased to 47.1% by TIME D. The small number of respondents in the two categories which required a 'strong' opinion, whether in agreement or disagreement, reflected that the respondents did not feel particularly strongly either way about this question. The clarity of the statement could also be called into question, as some respondents found this a difficult and overly complex statement to disentangle. The intention had been to ascertain the strength of the 'them versus us' argument that is often put forward as a characteristic of policing cultures. The results here however were inconclusive. The Friedman test demonstrated that there was no statistically significant change in responses to this statement across the four interview times.

Table 8.11 shows that at all interview stages, the highest percentage of officers agreed with the statement that 'police officers believe that a suspicious nature is a key ingredient of being a good police officer'. The overall percentage of those agreeing or strongly agreeing with the statement rose at each interview stage. Conversely, the number disagreeing or strongly

**Table 8.10** Strong police solidarity emanates from working with an unsupportive public (%)

|  | TIME A | TIME B | TIME C | TIME D |
|---|---|---|---|---|
| Strongly agree | 8.3 | 13.6 | 9.1 | 11.8 |
| Agree | 33.3 | 27.3 | 27.3 | 35.3 |
| Disagree | 54.2 | 50.0 | 59.1 | 41.2 |
| Strongly disagree | 4.2 | 9.1 | 4.5 | 11.8 |

**Table 8.11** Police officers believe that a suspicious nature is a key ingredient of being a good police officer (%)

|  | TIME A | TIME B | TIME C | TIME D |
|---|---|---|---|---|
| Strongly agree | 8.3 | 9.1 | 9.1 | 11.8 |
| Agree | 62.5 | 68.2 | 72.7 | 82.4 |
| Disagree | 29.2 | 22.7 | 13.6 | 5.9 |
| Strongly disagree | – | – | 4.5 | – |

disagreeing fell at each interview stage, from a high of 29.2% at TIME A to a low of 5.9% at TIME D. The level of agreement therefore increased as they spent longer in the role of a police officer. The assimilation process of becoming a police officer also entails the taking on of the cultural norms and expectations of the job. Being 'suspicious' of people or situations (sometimes referred to as having a 'copper's nose') is unlikely to be an element of an official police training programme. It is much more likely to be found in the informal guidance and advice that comes from officers who have served time in the job. This relates much more to the situated learning that takes place once the officers have left the formal learning environment.

The results of the Friedman test indicated that there is a *statistically significant difference* in the answers given across the final two time points—TIME C (one year into the role of police constable) and TIME D (four years into the role of police constable): $x^2(3, n = 17) = 33.07$, $p < 0.000$. The Wilcoxon analysis revealed a *significant difference* between scores at TIME C and TIME D, $p = 0.001$. The strength of the effect is calculated to be large ($\eta^2 = 0.83$).

Table 8.12 shows that the majority of respondents disagreed with this statement at each time point. However, it is the strength of this disagreement which changes over time. At TIME A, 30.4% of respondents strongly disagreed with the statement that 'officers must observe a code of secrecy amongst themselves to protect fellow officers'. By TIME D, this number had almost doubled to 58.8%, becoming the most common answer. Also by TIME D, no officers agreed or strongly agreed with the statement.

The results appear to indicate a similar story to that of the previous statement about suspiciousness. New recruits, it may be surmised, have

**Table 8.12** Police officers must observe a code of secrecy amongst themselves to protect fellow officers (%)

|                    | TIME A | TIME B | TIME C | TIME D |
|--------------------|--------|--------|--------|--------|
| Strongly agree     | –      | –      | –      | –      |
| Agree              | 17.4   | 9.1    | 4.5    | –      |
| Disagree           | 52.2   | 50.0   | 54.5   | 41.2   |
| Strongly disagree  | 30.4   | 40.9   | 40.9   | 58.8   |

an understanding of what they perceive the world of policing to be about and what skills and qualities may be required, which then changes as they spend more time in the job. Whereas some officers may have believed that a code of secrecy, often referred to as the 'blue code of silence', was potentially an informal requirement of the job, these numbers disappeared as officers became more experienced in their role. The strength of disagreement with the statement also intensified. Chapters 10 and 12 will consider this in more detail, but it is my argument that the realities of a police service with a heavy focus upon professional standards, the routine escalation of complaints and a fear of 'doing the wrong thing' means that the traditional 'blue code of silence' seems to be in the process of being superseded by what I have termed 'the blue code of self-protection'.

The results of the Friedman test indicated that there is a *statistically significant difference* in the answers given across the final two time points—TIME C (one year into the role of police constable) and TIME D (four years into the role of police constable): $x^2(3, n = 17) = 36.38$, $p < 0.000$. The Wilcoxon analysis revealed a *significant difference* between scores at TIME C and TIME D, $p = 0.000$. The strength of the effect is calculated to be *large* ($\eta^2 = 0.90$).

Table 8.13 shows that the majority of respondents strongly disagreed with this statement from the first interview—TIME A—and maintained this position throughout the interviews. A very large percentage strongly disagreed with this statement when compared with responses to other questions. Respondents were more likely to strongly disagree with the statement when they were working within the community (TIME B and TIME D), rather than when they were in training (TIME A and TIME C). This is interesting, as it is sometimes suggested that the formal teaching of 'how things should be done' that emerges during training is

**Table 8.13**  Police officers rarely enforce the law fairly, regardless of gender, ethnicity or class (%)

|                   | TIME A | TIME B | TIME C | TIME D |
|-------------------|--------|--------|--------|--------|
| Strongly agree    | –      | –      | –      | –      |
| Agree             | 4.2    | 4.5    | –      | –      |
| Disagree          | 29.2   | 18.2   | 31.8   | 11.8   |
| Strongly disagree | 66.7   | 77.3   | 68.2   | 88.2   |

replaced by the more informal 'how things are actually done' narrative of shift work. This would appear to show a different story. The question was not designed to assess whether officers displayed discriminatory attitudes towards certain populations, as this is unlikely to be acknowledged, if indeed true, during interviews with a researcher. The question was rather intended to ascertain whether officers were prepared to acknowledge that equality of treatment does not necessarily equate with fairness, that in order to treat people fairly, you may have to treat them differently in order to create an equal playing field. A Likert-type scale such as this is unlikely to be able to catch this more complex understanding of fairness and equality. However, none of the respondents picked up on this aspect of fairness, which may be revealing in two ways. It could be the result of a poorly designed question, but could also potentially reveal from police officers, particularly those recruited within the last ten years, of a fear of saying the wrong thing and a fear of displaying any unacceptable attitudes towards certain groups.

The results of the Friedman test indicated that there is a *statistically significant difference* in the answers given across the final two time points—TIME C (one year into the role of police constable) and TIME D (four years into the role of police constable): $x^2(3, n = 17) = 26.48$, $p < 0.000$. The Wilcoxon analysis revealed a *significant difference* between scores at TIME C and TIME D, $p = 0.001$. The strength of the effect is calculated to be *large* ($\eta^2 = 0.82$).

Table 8.14 shows that no respondents strongly disagreed with this statement, and a decreasing number of respondents disagreed with the statement, except for a very small increase at interview C. What is notable is the large increase in the number of respondents who strongly agreed with this statement, from a low of 18.2% at interview B to a high of

**Table 8.14** Police officers have a desire for action and excitement more than other occupations (%)

|                   | TIME A | TIME B | TIME C | TIME D |
|-------------------|--------|--------|--------|--------|
| Strongly agree    | 25.0   | 18.2   | 22.7   | 47.1   |
| Agree             | 45.8   | 59.1   | 68.2   | 41.2   |
| Disagree          | 29.2   | 22.7   | 9.1    | 11.8   |
| Strongly disagree | –      | –      | –      | –      |

**Table 8.15** Policing is an action-oriented occupation (%)

|                   | TIME A | TIME B | TIME C | TIME D |
|-------------------|--------|--------|--------|--------|
| Strongly agree    | 12.5   | 18.2   | 13.6   | 23.5   |
| Agree             | 79.2   | 72.7   | 72.7   | 58.8   |
| Disagree          | 8.3    | 4.5    | 13.6   | 17.6   |
| Strongly disagree | –      | 4.5    | –      | –      |

47.1% at interview D. The percentage of respondents who either strongly agreed or agreed with the statement rose from 70.8% at interview A to 88.3% at interview D. The Friedman test demonstrated that there was no statistically significant change in responses to this statement across the four interview times. The statement argues that police officers have a *desire* for action, rather than for action reflecting the reality of the work of a police officer. The qualitative interview results will reveal more analysis in this regard, but it is suggested that the increase in those who believe that police officers desire action and excitement more than other occupations could relate to the increasing inactivity that police officers experience as they acclimatise to their new roles.

In relation to the previous question, Table 8.15 considers how far policing actually is an 'action-oriented occupation' in comparison with the *desire* for it to be so. The results from this question show that the majority of respondents agreed with the statement that policing is an 'action-oriented occupation'. The strength of this agreement rose during the interview process, with 12.5% strongly agreeing at TIME A, which rose to 23.5% at TIME D. This is despite the fact that in the qualitative interviews, as will be seen in the following chapters, many officers bemoaned the lack of physical activity involved in the job and were disappointed that much time was spent inside and at a computer. By the time that officers were interviewed at TIME D, they were involved in a variety of roles within the force. A number were on the newly restructured investigations team, which entailed working within a 'call centre' environment, with an occasional diversion to make an arrest. This was described as a very sedentary role. This may be explained by the rise in the number of respondents who disagreed with the statement that 'policing is an action-oriented occupation', from 8.3% at TIME A to 17.6% at TIME D. Those working within the response and patrol teams in local stations however still had the potential to be more active, as the restructuring of the workload of the force meant that the response team did just that, 'respond', and then passed any further work onto the investigations team. The Friedman test demonstrated that there was no statistically significant change in responses to this statement across the four interview times.

## The Role of Policing

The following five questions quite specifically focused upon what the respondents felt was the role of policing. This role was also a key feature of the semi-structured interview questions and is discussed at length in Chap. 10. As stated earlier, very few officers during the completion of these questions noticed that there might be an inconsistency in their answers and returned to check how they had answered earlier questions.

Table 8.16 shows that although the majority of respondents agreed or strongly agreed with the statement 'policing is concerned mainly with upholding the law' throughout the research process, the strength of this agreement did vary considerably. This fell from 79.2% at TIME A to 52.9% at TIME D. At TIME A, the new recruits had all recently com-

**Table 8.16** Policing is concerned mainly with upholding the law (%)

|                   | TIME A | TIME B | TIME C | TIME D |
| ----------------- | ------ | ------ | ------ | ------ |
| Strongly agree    | 4.2    | 22.7   | 13.6   | 23.5   |
| Agree             | 75.0   | 45.5   | 50.0   | 29.4   |
| Disagree          | 16.7   | 22.7   | 36.4   | 41.2   |
| Strongly disagree | 4.2    | 9.1    | –      | 5.9    |

pleted the Certificate of Knowledge in Policing qualification, which focuses heavily upon the legal powers of the police. They were also in the midst of their first training experience with their police force, which focused upon applying the law in everyday policing situations. By the time respondents were at TIME D, they had all served four years within the police force. Respondents were almost split into two halves, with 52.9% being in varying levels of agreement and 47.1% being in varying levels of disagreement that 'policing was concerned mainly with upholding the law'. This would reflect much of the discussion in the qualitative interviews about the reality of the policing role being in contrast to their earlier perceptions. Officers, as will be seen in the following chapters, were surprised by the quantity of non-crime and non-policing issues that they were involved with, particularly around the issues of mental health and missing persons, which it was felt should be dealt with by other agencies. Their role in 'upholding the law' was perhaps a perception of the job, which over time was not realised. The Friedman test demonstrated that there was no statistically significant change in responses to this statement across the four interview times.

Table 8.17 shows that the vast majority of recruits either strongly agreed or agreed that the 'main role of policing is the protection of citizens'. However, there is a change in the strength of agreement of recruits, as the percentage who strongly agreed decreased over time and the percentage who agreed increased over time. The percentage who disagreed is minimal and no respondent strongly disagreed.

The results of the Friedman test indicated that there is a *statistically significant difference* in the answers given across the final two time points— TIME C (one year into the role of police constable) and TIME D (four years into the role of police constable): $x^2(3, n = 17) = 14.39, p < 0.002$. The Wilcoxon analysis revealed a *significant difference* between scores at

**Table 8.17** The main role of policing is the protection of citizens (%)

|                   | TIME A | TIME B | TIME C | TIME D |
|-------------------|--------|--------|--------|--------|
| Strongly agree    | 66.7   | 45.5   | 36.4   | 47.1   |
| Agree             | 29.2   | 54.5   | 54.5   | 47.1   |
| Disagree          | 4.2    | –      | 9.1    | 5.9    |
| Strongly disagree | –      | –      | –      | –      |

**Table 8.18** The primary role of a police officer is to protect society from criminals and deviants (%)

|                   | TIME A | TIME B | TIME C | TIME D |
|-------------------|--------|--------|--------|--------|
| Strongly agree    | 41.7   | 36.4   | 31.8   | 29.4   |
| Agree             | 50.0   | 50.0   | 59.1   | 52.9   |
| Disagree          | 8.3    | 13.6   | 9.1    | 17.6   |
| Strongly disagree | –      | –      | –      | –      |

TIME C and TIME D, $p = 0.005$. The strength of the effect is calculated to be *moderate to large* ($\eta^2 = 0.68$).

Table 8.18 shows that when the percentages of those who agree or strongly agree that 'the primary role of a police officer is to protect society from criminals and deviants' are combined, it is clear that, all interview stages, the majority of respondents agreed with the statement. The number who strongly agreed however fell at each interview stage, from a high of 41.7% at TIME A to a low of 29.4% at TIME D. The percentage of respondents who disagreed with the statement rose from 8.3% at TIME A to 17.6% at TIME D.

In comparison with the previous two questions on this topic, outlined in Tables 8.16 and 8.17, it was found that more respondents considered that the role of the police was concerned with the protection of citizens, rather than with either protecting society from criminals and deviants or upholding the law. Taking TIME D as an example, 52.9% agreed or strongly agreed that 'policing was mainly concerned with upholding the law', 82.3% agreed or strongly agreed that 'the primary role of the police was to protect society from criminals and deviants', whereas 94.2% of respondents at TIME D agreed or strongly agreed that 'the main role of policing is the protection of citizens'. There is only a subtle difference between the last two of these statements and respondents broadly regarded them as similar in their answers. However, one statement specifically mentioned offenders, whereas for the other, the focus was squarely on public protection. The Friedman test demonstrated that there was no statistically significant change in responses to this statement across the four interview times.

Table 8.19 shows that at TIME A, TIME B and TIME C (i.e. during the first year of a police officer's career), the majority of respondents

**Table 8.19** The primary role of a police officer is crime fighting (%)

|  | TIME A | TIME B | TIME C | TIME D |
|---|---|---|---|---|
| Strongly agree | 12.5 | 9.1 | 4.5 | 11.8 |
| Agree | 62.5 | 77.3 | 77.3 | 35.3 |
| Disagree | 25.0 | 13.6 | 18.2 | 47.1 |
| Strongly disagree | – | – | – | 5.9 |

agreed or strongly agreed that 'the primary role of a police officer is crime fighting'. This was at its peak when respondents were first serving as response and patrol officers in force, when 86.4% agreed or strongly agreed. However, that number declined noticeably when officers were interviewed at TIME D (four years into their service). At this point, the majority of officers now disagreed or strongly disagreed with the statement, making a combined total of 53%. The percentage of officers who disagreed that 'the primary role of a police officer is crime fighting' went from a low of 13.6% at TIME B to a high of 47.1% at TIME D. The belief in the notion that 'the primary role of a police officer is crime fighting' was not as apparent as for some other statements on the role of policing. As suggested earlier, the focus on public protection is the strongest amongst these recruits.

The results of the Friedman test indicated that there is a *statistically significant difference* in the answers given across the final two time points—TIME C (one year into the role of police constable) and TIME D (four years into the role of police constable): $x^2(3, n = 17) = 23.02$, $p < 0.000$. The Wilcoxon analysis revealed a significant difference between scores at TIME C and TIME D, $p = 0.001$. The strength of the effect is calculated to be *moderate to large* ($\eta^2 = 0.78$).

Table 8.20 shows that until TIME D, there was a fairly even split between those respondents who agreed or strongly agreed with the statement that 'real police work is about catching criminals' and those respondents who disagreed or strongly disagreed with the statement. At TIME A, it was 52.1% in agreement and 47.8% in disagreement. At TIME B and TIME C, there was a similar pattern of results, with 59.1% and 59%, respectively, in agreement, and 40.9% at both times in disagreement. However, as with many of these statements provided to respondents, it was at the final time point, TIME D, when changes in perceptions

Table 8.20 Real police work is about catching criminals (%)

|  | TIME A | TIME B | TIME C | TIME D |
|---|---|---|---|---|
| Strongly agree | 13.0 | 13.6 | 4.5 | 11.8 |
| Agree | 39.1 | 45.5 | 54.5 | 58.8 |
| Disagree | 47.8 | 36.4 | 40.9 | 29.4 |
| Strongly disagree | – | 4.5 | – | – |

emerged more strongly. At that time, 70.6% were in agreement, whilst 29.4% were in disagreement.

This was the fifth and final statement that was designed to better understand the views and opinions of the new recruits about the nature and role of policing. The belief in the notion that 'real police work is about catching criminals' was not as apparent as for some other statements on the role of policing. A comparison with the other four questions on this topic revealed that more respondents considered that the role of the police was concerned with the protection of citizens, rather than with protecting society from criminals and deviants, upholding the law, fighting crime or catching criminals. Taking TIME D as an example, 47.1% agreed or strongly agreed that 'the primary role of the police is crime fighting', 52.9% agreed or strongly agreed that 'policing was mainly concerned with upholding the law', 70.6% agreed or strongly agreed that 'real police work is about catching criminals', 82.3% agreed or strongly agreed that 'the primary role of the police was to protect society from criminals and deviants', whereas 94.2% of respondents agreed or strongly agreed that 'the main role of policing is the protection of citizens'. The two statements that scored most highly in agreement mentioned the words 'protect' and 'protection'. This does not quite fit with the vision of Theresa May when, in the role of Home Secretary, she decreed that police officers should be "tough, no-nonsense crime-fighters" (May 2011). This alternative focus on public protection relates closely to the qualitative discussions with the respondents on their beliefs and perceptions towards the role of the police, which will be discussed in the following chapters. The Friedman test demonstrated that there was no statistically significant change in responses to this statement across the four interview times.

## The Impact of Policing

The following four questions were concerned more generally with the impact of policing, both on individual officers and on wider society.

Table 8.21 shows that the highest percentage of recruits, at all interview stages, answered that they agreed with the statement that 'policing is the thin blue line between order and chaos'. The percentage of respondents who disagreed or strongly disagreed fell from 20.9% at TIME A to 11.8% at TIME D (although this was even lower at TIME C at 9%). Another noticeable change was seen in the number of respondents who strongly agreed with the statement. This almost doubled from 20.8% at TIME A to 41.2% at TIME D. The most dramatic rise was seen between TIME C (22.7%) and TIME D (41.2%). It would be unusual for those working within public service to deem their job to be of low value and policing is no exception. The literature on policing cultures, as discussed in Chap. 6, has often referred to the 'sense of mission' that police officers display as one of their cultural characteristics (Reiner 2010). The results from this question would suggest that police officers are still imbued with a sense of the important role they are fulfilling in maintaining order in an otherwise potentially chaotic society. This does however contradict one of the familiar narratives within modern policing parlance, which was very evident in the qualitative interviews. This narrative focuses upon the police's ineffectiveness as an organisation, given the current fiscal constraints that they are working within. This will be discussed in more detail in Chap. 11.

The results of the Friedman test indicated that there is a *statistically significant difference* in the answers given across the final two time points—

**Table 8.21** Policing is the thin blue line between order and chaos (%)

|                   | TIME A | TIME B | TIME C | TIME D |
|-------------------|--------|--------|--------|--------|
| Strongly agree    | 20.8   | 18.2   | 22.7   | 41.2   |
| Agree             | 58.3   | 63.6   | 68.2   | 47.1   |
| Disagree          | 16.7   | 9.1    | 4.5    | 5.9    |
| Strongly disagree | 4.2    | 9.1    | 4.5    | 5.9    |

**Table 8.22** The police are very successful in preventing crime (%)

|  | TIME A | TIME B | TIME C | TIME D |
|---|---|---|---|---|
| Strongly agree | 8.3 | 4.5 | 9.1 | – |
| Agree | 66.7 | 63.6 | 63.6 | 41.2 |
| Disagree | 25.0 | 31.8 | 22.7 | 41.2 |
| Strongly disagree | – | – | 4.5 | 17.6 |

TIME C (one year into the role of police constable) and TIME D (four years into the role of police constable): $x^2(3, n = 17) = 29.68, p < 0.000$. The Wilcoxon analysis revealed a *significant difference* between scores at TIME C and TIME D, $p = 0.000$. The strength of the effect is calculated to be *large* ($\eta^2 = 0.84$).

Table 8.22 shows that whilst at TIME A, the majority of respondents agreed or strongly agreed that 'the police are very successful at preventing crime', with a combined total of 75%, this had decreased to 41.2% by TIME D. This indicates that by TIME D (when officers had been serving police officers for four years), the majority of respondents disagreed or strongly disagreed with the statement, with a combined total of 58.8%. This is an important change in direction for the beliefs about what is a police officer's role and what they can achieve within that role. The belief in the police's success at crime prevention was at a stage when officers had not served as police constables. It was however at a stage when 58% of the recruits had already been employed previously as a PCSO. The role of the PCSO is very different from that of the Police Constable and focuses much more on patrolling, communications and prevention of crime. This belief that police constables would be involved in the same work was perhaps a result of that earlier experience as a PCSO. The qualitative interviews revealed further data in this regard, as officers felt that budgetary constraints and low police numbers meant that their capacity to *prevent* was effectively curtailed and they could only *react* to current emergencies. This would account for the increasing disagreement with the statement throughout the time periods. This will be discussed in more detail in the following chapters. The Friedman test demonstrated that there was no statistically significant change in responses to this statement across the four interview times.

**Table 8.23** Policing can have a huge impact on the communities it serves (%)

|                   | TIME A | TIME B | TIME C | TIME D |
|-------------------|--------|--------|--------|--------|
| Strongly agree    | 100.0  | 77.3   | 68.2   | 64.7   |
| Agree             | –      | 22.7   | 31.8   | 29.4   |
| Disagree          | –      | –      | –      | 5.9    |
| Strongly disagree | –      | –      | –      | –      |

Table 8.23 shows that all respondents at TIME A strongly agreed that 'policing can have a huge impact on the communities it serves'. This is the only time and the only question that resulted in all respondents providing the same answer. This answer however is perhaps unsurprising, as it relates to the stated motivations behind wanting to join the police service. One of the reasons highlighted by a large number of respondents was a belief that the job would be focused upon helping people in difficult situations and working with victims of crime. This will be examined in depth in the following chapters, where a discussion of the views of police officers towards 'victims of crime' will be analysed, in addition to a discussion about the impact of their work. During the four years after the new recruits joined the service, the strength of their agreement with the statement changed. Whilst a majority of respondents still strongly agreed at TIME B, TIME C and TIME D, an increasing number of respondents signalled a straightforward agreement, rather than a strong agreement. This agreement was 22.7% at TIME B, rose to 31.8% at TIME C and then decreased slightly to 29.4% at TIME D, with 5.9% disagreeing at this point.

The results of the Friedman test indicated that there is a *statistically significant difference* in the answers given across the final two time points—TIME C (one year into the role of police constable) and TIME D (four years into the role of police constable): $x^2(3, n = 17) = 44.78$, $p < 0.000$. The Wilcoxon analysis revealed a *significant difference* between scores at TIME C and TIME D, $p = 0.000$. The strength of the effect is calculated to be *large* ($\eta^2 = 0.88$).

Table 8.24 shows that the time point at which most officers agreed or strongly agreed that 'policing is a highly stressful occupation' was TIME A, with 95.8% of respondents answering in this way. This is before any of these recruits had served as a police constable within a force. This answer

**Table 8.24** Policing is a highly stressful occupation (%)

|                   | TIME A | TIME B | TIME C | TIME D |
|-------------------|--------|--------|--------|--------|
| Strongly agree    | 45.8   | 50.0   | 40.9   | 35.3   |
| Agree             | 50.0   | 27.3   | 36.4   | 47.1   |
| Disagree          | 4.2    | 22.7   | 18.2   | 11.8   |
| Strongly disagree | –      | –      | 4.5    | 5.9    |

could be attributed to a number of factors, but of potential interest could be the nature of police training and the narratives of policing. The new recruits would have just been through the application and interview process of becoming a police officer, completed and passed their Certificate of Knowledge in Policing, and started upon their policing career at the force training school. This in itself could have been a stressful period for them. Similarly, there was also evidence from the qualitative interviews to suggest that police trainers were strongly emphasising the new and responsible role that police officers would have to undertake and were additionally training them in a wide variety of procedural, technical and competency-based skills in a very short period. There is the potential therefore for this to be a stressful period for new recruits, coupled with the expectations of further stress ahead.

However, in reality, the percentage of officers who went on to strongly agree that 'policing is a highly stressful occupation' declined from 45.8% at TIME A to 35.3% at TIME D. At TIME B, when the officers were working as response and patrol officers for the first time, there was the highest level of disagreement that policing was highly stressful, with 22.7% of officers choosing this answer. By TIME D however, those respondents agreeing or strongly agreeing about the stressful nature of the job were getting closer to TIME A levels at 82.4%.

The results of the Friedman test indicated that there is a *statistically significant difference* in the answers given across the final two time points—TIME C (one year into the role of police constable) and TIME D (four years into the role of police constable): $x^2(3, n = 17) = 9.95$, $p < 0.019$. The Wilcoxon analysis revealed a *significant difference* between scores at TIME C and TIME D, $p = 0.317$. The strength of the effect is calculated to be *small* ($\eta^2 = 0.25$).

**Table 8.25** It is the sole responsibility of the police to solve crime (%)

|                   | TIME A | TIME B | TIME C | TIME D |
|-------------------|--------|--------|--------|--------|
| Strongly agree    | –      | –      | –      | –      |
| Agree             | 12.5   | 9.1    | 13.6   | –      |
| Disagree          | 62.5   | 77.3   | 72.7   | 88.2   |
| Strongly disagree | 25.0   | 13.6   | 13.6   | 11.8   |

## How Policing Should Be Done

The remaining three statements that respondents were asked to indicate their strength of agreement with were concerned with how policing should be done and focused primarily on the role that could be played by the public and other agencies. The police have an interesting relationship with the public, as we shall see in further chapters.

Table 8.25 shows a strong belief in the responsibility of other agencies to be involved in solving crime. Whether respondents took this to mean investigating and prosecuting crime or understood it to be in a broader preventative perspective is not clear. However, results from the qualitative interviews would certainly suggest that officers were increasingly frustrated at being seen to be the last and often only resort when dealing with a miscellany of social problems, which they often felt underqualified to deal with. There will be more discussion on this in the following chapters. Whilst there were patterns of change between respondents choosing to either disagree or strongly disagree with the statement 'it is the sole responsibility of the police to solve crime', a level of disagreement was always the most highly chosen option. Disagreement rose from 62.5% at TIME A to 88.2% at TIME D, whilst strong disagreement fell from 25% at TIME A to 11.8% at TIME D. This decline in strong disagreement may be reflected in the perception from officers that whatever collaborative arrangements are in place between public services, the officers' overriding belief is that they are the 'service of last resort' and often feel abandoned by other services.

The results of the Friedman test indicated that there is a *statistically significant difference* in the answers given across the final two time points—TIME C (one year into the role of police constable) and TIME

**Table 8.26** The police need to involve the community in decision-making to increase their accountability and legitimacy (%)

|                   | TIME A | TIME B | TIME C | TIME D |
|-------------------|--------|--------|--------|--------|
| Strongly agree    | 25.0   | 36.4   | 18.2   | 11.8   |
| Agree             | 66.7   | 54.5   | 63.6   | 64.7   |
| Disagree          | 4.2    | 9.1    | 13.6   | 17.6   |
| Strongly disagree | 4.2    | –      | 4.5    | 5.9    |

D (four years into the role of police constable): $x^2(3, n = 17) = 28.02$, $p < 0.000$. The Wilcoxon analysis revealed a *significant difference* between scores at TIME C and TIME D, $p = 0.001$. The strength of the effect is calculated to be *large* ($\eta^2 = 0.8$).

Table 8.26 shows that the majority of respondents either strongly agree or agree that 'the police need to involve the community in decision-making to increase their accountability and legitimacy'. There is however a reduction in the percentage of respondents who strongly agree with this statement, from 25% at TIME A to 11.8% at TIME D. The percentage of respondents who strongly disagreed with the statement rose from 4.2% at TIME A to 17.6% at TIME D. A growing frustration with the seemingly unrealistic expectations of what the police could achieve within what were seen to be unacceptable budgetary constraints appeared to fuel this greater level of caution about community involvement in influencing the priorities and duties of police officers. This was also coupled with an increasing perception that the public understood very little about the realities of policing, particularly relating to domestic, non-crime incidents. Having said that, the results still demonstrate that a majority of respondents were in agreement with the statement. This will be discussed in greater detail in the following chapters. The Friedman test demonstrated that there was no statistically significant change in responses to this statement across the four interview times.

Table 8.27 shows that the majority of respondents at all time points disagree in varying measure that 'public confidence in policing should be the only measure for policing success'. This ranges from a low point of 70.9% disagreement at TIME A to a high point of 94.1% at TIME D. The impetus for this statement came from the Labour Government's

**Table 8.27** Public confidence in policing should be the only measure of policing success (%)

|                   | TIME A | TIME B | TIME C | TIME D |
|-------------------|--------|--------|--------|--------|
| Strongly agree    | 4.2    | 9.1    | –      | –      |
| Agree             | 25.0   | 9.1    | 18.2   | 5.9    |
| Disagree          | 29.2   | 68.2   | 45.5   | 64.7   |
| Strongly disagree | 41.7   | 13.6   | 36.4   | 29.4   |

decision in 2009 to scrap all existing policing targets and to replace them with one single target: that of improving levels of confidence in policing. The Labour Governments of 1997, 2001 and 2005 were regularly criticised for their more populist criminal justice policies, which, it was argued, were designed to appeal to the tabloid press, rather than to any evidence of effectiveness (Charman and Savage 2008). This target was not well received by the police at the time of the announcement (Edwards 2009), and evidence from this research would suggest that it would not be a popular measure now. By TIME D, only 5.9% agreed with the statement. There is a similarity between these results and the results displayed in Table 8.19. In Table 8.19 which examined the extent to which respondents felt that the public should be involved in decision-making and, again, the overwhelming response was that they should not. "As mentioned when discussing Table 8.19, there was a perception that the public understood very little about the realities and pressures of policing, and consultation should be kept to a minimum.

The results of the Friedman test indicated that there is a *statistically significant difference* in the answers given across two different time points. The first was between TIME B (six months into the role of police constable) and TIME C (one year into the role of police constable): $x^2(3, n = 17) = 14.37, p < 0.002$. The second was between TIME C (one year into the role of police constable) and TIME D (four years into the role of police constable): $x^2(3, n = 17) = 14.37, p < 0.002$. The Wilcoxon analysis revealed a *significant difference* between scores at TIME B and TIME C, $p = 0.035$, and between scores at TIME C and TIME D, $p = 0.071$. The strength of the effect is calculated to be *moderate* ($\eta^2 = 0.51$) between TIME B and TIME C. The strength of the effect is calculated to be *small to moderate* ($\eta^2 = 0.78$) between TIME C and TIME D.

The data analysed for this chapter has provided some important initial understandings of the changing attitudes, values and beliefs of new recruits to the police service. The chapter analysed the priorities of police officers, their influences, the impact of their work, the characteristics that they display and their attitudes to those with whom they work. Inevitably, there have been contradictions in the views that they have expressed. Whilst respondents regularly chose 'fighting crime' as the top priority of a police officer when presented with a list to choose from, this was not reflected in a strong agreement later that this was their primary role. Here, there was a clear emphasis placed by respondents on the role of public protection and the protection of citizens.

Where there was no contradiction was in the decision to choose who had the most influence upon them during their first few years as a new recruit to the service. Overwhelmingly, tutors and police colleagues (in the form of the shift that they work with regularly) were highlighted as the most influential. The more formal delivery of police training, via trainers and SDROs, was not rated highly. Respondents were also asked, in a variety of ways, which characteristics they displayed and which characteristics they felt were important to display within the context of their work. Those scoring highly were authoritarianism, suspiciousness, empathy, good communication, cynicism and solidarity. The notion of the importance of protecting other officers was not adhered to. The more detrimental effects of policing upon the recruits' lives were stress and social isolation.

Respondents believed that the realities of the job meant that there were areas of work, particularly crime prevention, where the police were not successful. It was felt that other agencies should be playing their part in this crime reduction goal. However, there was a more general belief in the important impact of their work, most notably upon the communities that they policed and in maintaining an orderly society. Whilst they had a belief in their community impact and a focus on public protection, these did not extend to a belief that the views of these communities should be taken into account when setting policing priorities, nor should the level of confidence that the public have in them be the marker of policing success. There was a belief that the police were there to provide an important service but not to be instructed by the public as to what that service might be.

This quantitative data reveals that there have been significant changes in the views and opinions of police officers during their first four years as police constables. From a statistical perspective, this change has been significant in 13 of the 22 statements, and in all but the last statement, this change was seen between TIME C (one year into the role of police constable) and TIME D (four years into the role of police constable). These quantitative results have provided some insights into the important priorities of police officers, the influences upon them, and the cultural characteristics they feel they display and that are important to them. The results describe the impact of their work and their attitudes towards the agencies they work alongside and the communities they police. The quantitative analysis describes the situation and paints this important initial sketch of the changing realities of life as a new recruit to the police service. However, in order to be able to appreciate a more complete picture and go beyond these initial ideas, it is important to consider, through lengthy semi-structured qualitative interviews, what underpins those attitudes, values and beliefs, and what might impact upon their potential for change. This will potentially reveal more of the justifications, the rationales and the explanations as to why these changes might be apparent. The remaining chapters of this book will examine that data in depth.

# References

Charman, S., & Savage, S. (2008). Controlling Crime and Disorder: The Labour Legacy. In M. Powell (Ed.), *Modernising the Welfare State: The Blair Legacy* (pp. 105–124). Bristol: Polity Press.

Cohen, J. (1988). *Statistical Power Analysis for the Behavioural Sciences* (2nd ed.). Hillsdale: Lawrence Erlbaum Associates.

Edwards, R. (2009, November 26). British Policing 'Has Lost Its Way in Target Culture'. *Daily Telegraph*. Retrieved from http://www.telegraph.co.uk/news/uknews/law-and-order/6656699/British-policing-has-lost-its-way-in-target-culture.html

HMIC. (2011). *Demanding Times*. London: The Stationery Office.

Home Office. (2004). *Building Communities, Beating Crime: A Better Police Service for the 21st Century (Cm 6360) [Electronic Version]*. London: HMSO.

May, T. (2011). *Speech to the Conservative Party Conference.* Retrieved from http://www.politics.co.uk/comment-analysis/2011/10/04/theresa-may-speech-in-full

Reiner, R. (2010). *The Politics of the Police* (4th ed.). Oxford: Oxford University Press.

# 9

# Qualitative Findings I: Learning to Be a Cop

The quantitative data which was analysed in Chap. 8 revealed significant changes in the views and opinions of police officers during their first four years as a police constable. The limitation of that form of quantitative data is that the underlying reasons behind those shifts in attitudes and beliefs could not be explored in more depth. However, as discussed in Chap. 7, the predominant focus of the interviews with new recruits over a four-year period and a sample of tutors and SDROs was actually on the open-ended conversations with the new recruits. The focus of the questions inevitably shifted as the officers became more experienced in their role, but centred around three broad areas, which I have termed *learning*, *becoming* and *being*. The first of these, *learning*, will be the focus of this chapter.

Whilst discussing their *learning*, the new recruits answered questions about how they could best 'learn' to become a police officer and be a part of the policing organisation. They also considered the role and impact of each of the important players in the training process. Chapters 4 and 5 considered both the formal and informal processes involved in learning to become a police officer. Formally, this involved the recruits completing the IPLDP, which entailed classroom training, a period with a tutor constable and a community placement. Student officers were required to

© The Author(s) 2017
S. Charman, *Police Socialisation, Identity and Culture*,
DOI 10.1007/978-3-319-63070-0_9

complete an electronic Student Officer Learning and Assessment Portfolio (e-SOLAP), which would map their competencies against ten NOS. The "e-So crap", as it has been labelled by officers, has not been warmly embraced and is regarded with hostility by many of those completing it (Constable and Smith 2015, p. 54). More informally, learning to become a part of an organisation involves having the tools (e.g. the equipment, the knowledge, etc.) but also the language and an appreciation of the normative practices of that organisation. The use and application of this language must become almost implicit in order to be assimilated into that organisation (Fielding 1984). Van Maanen (1976) argues that the purpose of socialisation is to provide the new member with the knowledge, the ability and the motivation to be able to perform their role. By doing this, it will ensure the continuity of normative values and practices, and make sense of the organisation to the new incumbent (Cable and Parsons 2001).

# How Police Officers Learn

Respondents were asked a number of questions related to their learning at all stages of the interview process. The first of these asked how they felt someone learns to become a police officer. This question was asked at TIME A, TIME B, TIME C and TIME D. There were no noticeable differences in views between the time periods, so officers did not change their views on how it was to learn the 'art' or 'craft' or 'science' of policing. Their views on how this is and should be done can be categorised into six areas: *learning from doing, learning from watching, learning from mistakes, learning from common sense/instinct, learning from experience* and *learning from adaptation.*

## Learning from Doing

Learning 'on the job' has historically always been valued more highly than any other form of training or education within the police service (Oakley 1994; Bayley and Bittner 1984). This is particularly the view of officers from more junior ranks. The opinions of the recruits interviewed for this research were no different. The most regularly cited answer to the question about how one learns to become a police officer is exemplified by the following responses:

> I think you learn best from being out there and just doing the job. (Y7)
> I can't see any other way you could actually become a good police officer other than doing it. (S3)

The reason that was outlined by the respondents for why this was the most appropriate form of learning was that the classroom-based learning was not able to teach the particularities of each type of incident that the officer might be exposed to. The practical realities of the job meant that it was only possible to "properly learn" (W2) when faced with these real-life incidents:

> On the streets ... it's kind of the same in a sense as driving, you don't actually properly learn to drive until you pass your test and you're out on the road on your own. I think it's the same as policing. You can do all this classroom stuff but unless you can put it into practice out on the streets it's no good. (W2)
> You've got to learn by actually being out there. Not sitting behind a desk ... not just read it in a book or learn the law of it. (X2)
> 20 per cent in a classroom and then the rest of it you just have to learn as you go along I guess ... you can write as many procedures and policies as you want but in the heat of the day, you know, if the situation hits you then you have to deal with it as you do on the day; try and remember policy as best as possible but, yes, you learn from mainly just doing it really. (W10)
> [F]or me it's mainly on the job learning because every time it's different really, every job you get is slightly different ... just being out there doing it. (Y11)

Officers were also of the view that they were 'thrown in' into the role of policing. This view could suggest that they felt underprepared to deal with what they were facing on the streets. The opinions expressed later in this chapter about the nature of police training would perhaps suggest that this is the case. The new recruits' views on being 'thrown in' in this way were mixed, but the majority that expressed this felt that this was a reasonable approach to take. However, it should be noted that three out of the following four statements were from officers who had served four years in the police service, where the effects of time served may have lessened the feelings of anxiety they suffered at the time:

> I was very much thrown in the deep end and although that is a good thing in certain circumstances it meant my tutor would stand back while I was dealing a fight or something. (D3)
>
> You really just learn by doing … getting dumped on your own … you do ten weeks and then my sergeant kicked me out the door on my own, and made me walk for three or four shifts on my own, bricking it, walking around going, argh. (D6)
>
> I've learnt actually if you just throw yourself into things generally you muddle through, and it's the best way of learning. (B8)
>
> [Y]ou're just pretty much thrown into it and you're sent running, so it's just getting out and about and interacting, then learning as you go along. (Z7)

A comprehensive police training programme that results in an officer perceiving that they are 'thrown in' without being fully equipped initially to deal with what they are facing and are merely 'muddling through' is an issue that police training has historically struggled to get to grips with. In the past, student officers have been counted as supernumerary on a shift and were therefore in a better position to observe, before being required to act. However, in recent years, in Evermord Constabulary, and with pressures over police numbers, student officers are counted as part of the regular numbers on a shift and therefore have little option but to assume the policing role immediately.

However, respondents also conveyed their views on the nature of much of the police work they were involved with. In much the same way as a manual worker would gain expertise from repetitively completing tasks, so police officers also felt that the repetitive nature of the jobs that they were regularly attending to contributed to their learning of the nature of the job: "you learn from repetitiveness" (B3), "the repetition of dealing with things" (Y11) and "repeatedly going to sort of similar jobs" (D13).

## Learning from Watching

What was perhaps the most interesting response to the question of how one learns to become a police officer was the overwhelming consistency in answers from recruits about watching and copying from others. This provides some explanation for why, in the quantitative element of the research, the answer to who were the most influential people in the recruits' development as junior officers was both tutors and other police colleagues, that is, their 'shift'. It is through watching and then selecting and copying others' behaviours that police officers are 'taught' not only the descriptive ways of becoming a police officer but also the normative language and practices that are acceptable to other officers and their new policing family. It is here that we can see more clearly how many of the enduring characteristics of policing cultures find their origins in new recruits to the police service. This form of 'hereditary learning' can be seen from the new recruits and from their tutors and SDROs, and exemplifies how cultures are transmitted and sustained within an organisation. Having felt that the more formal elements of police training (as we shall see shortly) have not equipped them to deal with the realities of their policing role, officers can learn through mimicking others' behaviours what it means to both become a police officer and, importantly, be accepted as a police officer. As we shall see in the following chapter, 'fitting in' and conforming with colleagues is an important aspect of the assimilation process. There were a large number of examples of this 'learning from watching' behaviour; those below form a very small selection:

> [A]t the beginning, I was almost a mini her for like ten weeks, and then after her I was still a mini [name] for a long time … I learn a lot from watching other people do things … and then next time I go out and I'm okay. (B10)
>
> Talk to your colleagues, they give you advice and they've been there, they've done that, so it's a case of following what they do really. Obviously, some of them do things correctly, some of them do things slightly short cut way, but ultimately whatever they do you've sort of got to emanate them really. (B7)
>
> [Y]ou mirror what they do … and remember for next time. (B6)

> I watch officers who've got loads of experience and think, right, I'll do that next time. (D13)
>
> I learn better by seeing some of it done, and then copying it. (Y9)

However, although directly 'copying' formed the answer for many respondents, there were almost an equal number of respondents who had a slightly more sophisticated approach to learning what they felt were the skills necessary to become a police officer. This involved the same notions of observation of behaviours but required the student officer to select behaviours and attitudes from different officers in an attempt to almost build and construct their new identity as a functioning police officer. This would undoubtedly be influenced by individual subjective understandings on what makes a 'good' police officer, a topic that will be returned to in the following chapter:

> Seeing how different officers do things. And some people will go, I prefer doing it that way versus that way, what do I want to pick up? He's got communication skills; he might have a nice punch-up every so often, so I'll do it more like him. (D4)
>
> [W]hat I've learnt is that there are so many different styles of policing of, like, individual police officers are so different. My tutor said to me, you know, if you like the way I do something then take that and do that – if you don't then think why you don't and then if somebody else does it differently and you like that then take that from them and become yourself really. (X6)
>
> I personally learn best from working with others and watching how they do things and seeing how different people interact and then you can put your own style on it as well. (Y7)
>
> I have tried to pick here and there what people do and what I don't want to do. (X10)
>
> [E]verybody has their own way of dealing with things and everyone has their own way of speaking to people and what they would do in certain circumstances. I think you take the bits that you like from that and the bits you don't like you don't take and then you, kind of, develop maybe what you would have done before. (Z11)

Tutors themselves appear to be both aware and comfortable with the fact that their student officers are copying their behaviours. Indeed, all seven of the tutors interviewed referred to this aspect of student officers' behaviour. A complex situation therefore arises. First, you have tutors who, in the case of this research, have often not entirely willingly volunteered to become tutors. Second, these tutors have generally dismissed the training for tutors as ineffective, "it was three days and it was three days too long" (T2). Third, these tutors appear to be unaware of the nature and content of the training that takes place with new recruits in training school. Fourth, these tutors then find that they are considered to be the most influential person in the new recruits' early experiences of becoming a police officer. Fifth, their own behaviours and attitudes and even mannerisms are then copied, sometimes almost entirely, by the new recruits. More detail on these issues with the tutors will be considered later in this chapter, but the quotes below illustrate some of the issues referred to above:

> I almost have to keep myself in check sometimes, because I don't want to impart that on the student. And they do, they pick up … they are like a bit of a sponge. But as well as taking the knowledge, they take your mannerisms and they take my attitudes on things … I can give you a prime example. When I need to get quite authoritative and I start shouting – which I don't like doing, but every now and then – I point, which is really aggressive, and it's because my tutor pointed, and it's that. And I caught [student name] doing it … hopefully he's lost it. But it did make me think, oh my … if he's picked that up without even thinking about it because he's watched me do it, because there's no other reason I can think for him to have picked that habit up. He's never done it before, he said he's never done it, he can't even remember doing it. But it became quite a … it was happening more regularly. So I think they definitely pick up their tutors' characteristics. (T1)
>
> I know that I definitely tutor the way I was tutored. (T2)
>
> [H]er mannerisms I've picked up as well. (B10)
>
> [M]onkey see monkey do … I do see it actually in [name], some of my mannerisms and things and the way that I approach thing, the way I deal with them, he's continued, but I think you see something, you mimic it and then eventually he'll work with other people and he'll take the best bits from other people and eventually I think it moulds them into his own individual style. (T4)
>
> [T]hey mirror their tutor. (S1)

## Learning from Mistakes

Chapter 3 discussed the importance of the collective memory to an organisation. Of particular importance here is the 'cultural memory', which is fixed in time and relates to the organisational symbols which, over time, become culturally understood as relating to that organisation. Assmann and Czaplicka (1995, p. 130) refer to this as the "store of knowledge" of an organisation. This might be in the form of historical events, texts, rites and so on—the recollection of past experiences and of past support work to reinforce the shared positions that are adopted by the group. In policing terms, this operates as much with negative past experiences as it does with positive past experiences. Reference to the past contributes to the shared identity of officers but also guides future behaviour in indicating what 'works' and what 'fails' in terms of policing responses. This links closely with the literature on organisational culture. Schein (1985) has argued that culture is transmitted in two different ways, either through 'problem-solving'/'positive reinforcement' or through 'anxiety avoidance'/'trauma'. The former refers to a policy of repeating successful work strategies, the latter to a policy of avoiding unpleasant situations by basing thought and action on previous negative experiences. What is important is the power of organisational memories to cement and bolster organisational identities.

New recruits to the police service interviewed as part of this research regularly cited 'learning from mistakes' as influential in their early development as a police officer:

[U]ltimately, it's just spending the years doing it and making mistakes, and having to go back and correct them afterwards. (C4)

Just literally crack on and get on with it and learn from your mistakes. … Certainly from my experience, literally making mistakes every day, that's how you learn. Hopefully you don't make the mistakes again, but if you do you just keep learning, keep developing. (C7)

I learned by my mistakes, if I'm honest. I learned by doing what I've done wrong. I've learned from that and what I've done right, and keep going and then improve on it. (W4)

[G]oing out there you make that mistake, you learn from it and make sure you don't do it again. (X4)

[Y]ou learn from your mistakes, and you learn from other people's mistakes. (Z4)

[I]f they get it wrong they'll learn. (Y9)

I think you learn more from mistakes as well, learn from bad decisions as opposed to good decisions more because you learn what not to do next time. (Z9)

[Y]ou learn quicker from mistakes than you do from doing things well. (T1)

## Learning from Common Sense/Instinct

It is learning from your own innate common sense or from the common sense of more experienced officers that is most highly valued by new recruits (Karp and Stenmark 2011). Police recruits are taught the value of a common-sense approach during training in order to be able to navigate the contrast of the unusual to the usual occurrences that they should expect to witness (McNulty 1994). It has been argued that discussions concerning the 'craft' of policing, the almost innate understandings of practice, have long been overlooked in favour of more 'scientific' solutions (Bayley and Bittner 1984; Willis and Mastrofski 2017). This craft knowledge is often tacitly understood by the organisation's members but not necessarily recognised. As discussed in Chap. 5 when considering the literature on CoP, the very essence of social interactions with work colleagues or across organisational boundaries is about the subconscious exchange of tacit knowledge, which is therefore unlikely to be recognised by participants or indeed measurable (Lave and Wenger 1991). Tacit knowledge is thought to be utilised far more regularly by those who work in naturalistic settings (such as medical diagnosis or policing), as they consider informal workable solutions or adaptations to formal rules (Eraut 2004).

Recruits, tutors and SDROs did not understandably refer to 'tacit knowledge', but used instead terms such as 'common sense' and 'instinct' in its place to verbalise their beliefs in the innate abilities of police officers to perform their role that belie formal training. There was a widespread belief that policing is not something that can be 'taught' in a formal sense, and that officers either had the natural ability to perform or not:

> [A] reasonable level of intelligence to learn the laws and process and things, but I think common sense and … I hate to use the word, streetwise, but just having a bit about yourself. (C1)
>
> I don't think there's anything that beats real life experience. … You can't learn this job from looking in books. It's not possible. (B8)
>
> I don't think you can really teach public speaking and dealing with a group of unpleasant people. (A11)
>
> I don't think you can tell people how to be a police officer, you either can do it or you can't. You can take your theory side of it but it's actually your humanity and your personality that makes you a police officer. (W1)
>
> [Y]ou've either got it in you or you haven't, the basic morals and right from wrong. It's kind of common sense really. (W7)
>
> I think you have to have natural attributes to become a police officer … there's probably certain key elements that you have to have good people skills for instance, you can't learn those. You have to have a natural ability to a degree I suppose, feel comfortable talking to people and feel comfortable in certain situations. (W8)
>
> [Y]ou have to have kind of a little bit of an instinct for it. (X10)
>
> I think it's all down to life skills, I think. It's the most important thing, common sense and life skills. I don't think you can ever learn to do the job, because you never stop learning … I don't think it's something you can say, you can teach someone to be a policeman or a police officer. It's just something that you just either can do or you can't, I think. It is all about life skills, I think, experience and understanding and compassion and empathy is a lot to do with it, the common sense. (T4)

This conception of how policing is 'learned' by police officers fits very much with Amin and Roberts' (2008) work on CoP which introduced a typology of 'knowing in action'. The first of these groupings was the task-/craft-based groups which value informal knowledge, use stories and language to convey knowledge, and place importance on the preservation of existing knowledge and its transmission to new organisational members. This task-/craft-based group is contrasted with the professional group, where knowledge is acquired through long periods of both education and training. This potentially has implications for the proposed professionalisation of policing through degree education.

## Learning from Experience

However, despite the new officers adhering to the traditional views of policing as a craft which requires innate skills of common sense and instinct, they also adhered to a view that learning was a key feature in the development of police officers and one that was ongoing, perhaps throughout their careers:

> [I]t's just a constant learning curve ... you speak to people that have been here for ten odd years and they say they still learn new stuff most days. (B1)
>
> I honestly don't think you can learn this job in years. I think it would literally take years to get comfortable and know exactly everything. (B8)
>
> [Y]ou learn every day on this job and I learn from my colleagues and my colleagues learn from me. You get used to imparting knowledge and teaching. (D10)
>
> I don't think you ever stop learning. (Y2)
>
> [I]t's one of those jobs where I don't think I'll stop learning until I hand in my badge I don't think. (Y10)

As discussed in Chap. 7, the two cohorts of new recruits who were part of this research project began their period of training with Evermord Constabulary after a recruitment freeze. This meant that the majority of officers were taken from a pool of existing PCSOs and Special Constables who had applied to become police constables. Those who had served either as a PCSO or a Special Constable were very keen to stress that this experience had been of immense value in contributing to their learning to become a police officer. One went as far as to suggest that the introduction of this policy was contributing to a 'new breed' of police officer, one that was more heavily focused upon communication as the most important policing tool. This will be discussed in more detail later in the following chapter. However, this experience was seen to be extremely valuable in the learning process:

> [I]t's almost like an apprenticeship. (W11)
>
> My PCSO time to me has been invaluable. I think I've learned an awful lot just through working with them and experience. (A11)
>
> [B]eing a Special and getting out there and doing it is where you learn the most. (W7)

I'm grateful that I was a PCSO first, I think it's really helped me. (D13)

I think my learning came from when I was a PCSO ... I think it gave me much better people skills because I had no PPE [personal protective equipment]. (Z1)

[I]f I hadn't had any experience in the police before I started as a PC I probably wouldn't have made it through my probation. (D3)

I was a PCSO before ... so that helped as a police officer as well, because I haven't had to take my asp out [Armament Systems and Procedures, usually refers to police baton] or my gas in the four years, which is quite good and it's about talking to people I think. (D9)

[T]o become a police officer, it would probably be beneficial if everybody had to be a PCSO first ... they should make it part of the rank structure. (W6)

I was a PCSO for a while and I still think that's a real, real good way to build your knowledge ... I've had a few comments that there is still a bit too much PCSO in me ... well that wound me up really because I thought for me that's invaluable. (X6)

[W]e're having a lot more ex-PCSOs and ex-specials. They are a lot more clued up, a lot more – they're a bit more, sort of, streetwise. (S2)

## Learning from Adapting

The more formal elements of police training in England and Wales have been discussed in Chap. 4. The approach favoured throughout the history of police training has been a militaristic and behaviourist approach which has focused upon the learner being the passive recipient of knowledge which is imparted from the trainer. The introduction of core competencies and NOS has, despite its stated intentions, only exacerbated this issue. The comments from the new recruits indicate that the passive flow of information from trainer to recruit was very evident during the training school process:

[T]hey teach you the 100% way that we want you to do it and then you go to actually doing the job you get to what the real way of doing it. (A1)

It's not so much learning it, it's applying it ... you might know the definition of something but applying it in a policing role is completely different. (C2)

I mean it's alright knowing all the law, but when you turn up to incidents it's not really about that, it's how to deal with that situation ... you can learn the law on the go to be honest. (B3)

Training will only get you so far before you have to deal with a drunken person and try and take a statement from them. (B4)

The best policemen are people that can talk to people ... How to be a policeman ... it's not in the classroom ... it's all on the street. (A6)

[I]n my mind from [name of training school] it was like, right, one person's been assaulted, the other person's entirely not to blame and they're a victim, they're clearly the offender, they're getting arrested in a textbook way, whereas the reality is they've both been as bad as each other, they both want to make a complaint against each other ... there's two different sides, there's a [name of training school ] side and then there's a practical side and how to do things maybe not properly, but effectively. (Z9)

There are currently very limited opportunities for broader philosophical debates and discussion about the nature of policing and its role. This compliance with standards approach to training reinforces the belief that going through the motions of training is all that is required before the 'real' learning happens on the streets. Indeed, an HMIC report on police training even refers to the two different sites of police learning as the "classroom" and "'real' police work" (HMIC 2002, p. 23). One of the tutors interviewed as part of this research highlighted these issues in relation to the completion of the e-SOLAP assessment for new recruits:

[T]hey get quite tunnel vision on this pack, and after every day they want to fill out this pack and write down what they've done so they can get this magic number up. And it sort of detracts from ... I wonder whether when we're having a debrief, whether any of it's actually going in, or whether they're thinking, well, that's good, because now I'm on 62 per cent. (T1)

A more andragogious approach to learning, favoured mostly with adult learners, would utilise both experience and facilitation in a much less prescriptive manner. This might enable those interpretative skills which the recruits themselves found as lacking in the training school to be explored.

In Chan's (2004) research on new recruits to the police service in Australia, she argued that learning within the policing academy was affected by where and with whom field training took place. The historical tendency to use the skills of experienced police officers in a learning environment contributes to the continued reliance upon prescriptive learning. As mentioned in Chap. 4, Macvean (2010) found in her analysis of police education in a university setting that there were divisions between the academic staff and the retired or seconded police officers. The latter group favoured the 'war stories' approach to teaching and valued 'practical knowledge' more highly than 'academic knowledge'.

Unsurprisingly therefore, the vast majority of the new recruits did not hold positive views on the more formal aspects of police training that took place within the force training school. They appreciated its necessity but were critical of its content. They wanted to know 'how' to do policing and were far less interested (at this stage of their careers anyway) in the social context surrounding policing activities and behaviours. This was especially the case for the second of the more formal training courses which took place after a year in service and after the officers had completed their tutor phase. It is unclear whether these more negative views on the second of these courses related to the recruits' belief in the irrelevance of the content of the training or whether they had been influenced by the views of more experienced officers on their shift. The criticisms relating to the training school activities centred on their difference from 'real-world' policing where there were few 'perfect' victim–offender scenarios and a criticism of "everything led up to the arrest" (B5), whereas this was less the norm in most encounters. An overriding impression from many recruits was that the training "didn't prepare me enough" (B2).

The recruits' view on the pre-join Certificate of Knowledge in Policing was even more negative: "[T]here's nothing I liked about it" (A7). These courses were the knowledge- and legal-based elements of initial police training which became a pre-requisite for joining the police. The cohorts in this research project were the first to have to take the qualification in Evermord Constabulary. There were criticisms relating to its level of difficulty, its focus on knowing a small amount about a vast number of topics and the assessment methods. Recruits found themselves searching for the appropriate answer to insert into the question rather than fully understanding what they were learning. One law graduate commented that, although they themselves understood the law, "if I'd learned it through the pre-join course, I wouldn't know anything about it" (no code to protect anonymity).

As indicated in Chap. 7, 25% of the sample held an undergraduate degree, and a number of those officers expressed more positive reactions to the more formal aspects of police training. These were officers who would have spent more time in a classroom setting, and would be more likely to feel comfortable within that setting. Adult learners in a non-familiar classroom setting often express a lack of confidence through a dismissal of the entire process (Norman and Hyland 2003). Some of the more positive comments are highlighted below:

> You get the theory in your brain, you start putting the theory into some sort of practice, then you get given someone to protect you while you're putting it into real practice in the real world, and then you get let loose. Actually, they couldn't do it any better. (B10)
>
> I always like to know the legislation area around what I'm doing. It gives me that confidence that I'm doing the right thing. (X11)
>
> [I]t helped because I have been to university before, so the style of questioning and the kind of thing that they wanted I think I knew a bit more about that having done a degree and A levels before because it was quite academic. (W9)

This perception of the pre-join courses being 'academic' is however a concern for other officers and tutors. There was a sense that in the police service, following this route, many potential officers would be deterred from considering a career in the police, not necessarily through a lack of ability but through a lack of confidence and a lack of finances in taking on what is perceived to be an academic course. This led to some officers suggesting that there was a danger of "middle-class policing" (A1), and that

> there'll be a complete disengagement with the poor and with the youth, because someone from a middle-class background … again, I'm stereotyping all the way … but someone from possibly, a more affluent, middle class

background, who went to a nice school, isn't going to be able to sit on a bench and chat to a load of kids smoking pot, who probably didn't finish school and they live on a council estate, because they haven't anything in common. (C1)

[I]t could alienate a few people because there's quite a high cost implication on doing the pre-join course and there's a huge time commitment. (A12)

[Y]ou're only going to get a certain person of a recruit, I think you're much better off opening your doors to everybody. (T6)

I think they're losing out on certain candidates ... as long as they've got them core skills which are communication and brain on their shoulders and, you know, interpersonal skills and a bit of professional integrity, they'll be your ideal officers and that. Okay, they may know nothing about the law, but as long as they can learn it as they get in to that bit, that's fine. (T7)

These views of serving police officers amidst plans to make policing an all-graduate profession will have interesting implications on the future socialisation, identity and cultures of police officers.

## The Role of the Tutor

New recruits to the police service in England and Wales, at the time of the research, spend a ten-week period of patrolling under the tutelage of a tutor constable. As discussed in Chap. 4, the role of the tutor is one of the least evaluated aspects of police training. Where organisational enquiries have taken place, they have overwhelmingly found the process to be lacking (HMIC 1999, 2002). This was especially in the area of selection, training and the divergence between the official and the unofficial training content. However, at the same time, evidence from Stradling and Harper (1988) and from the quantitative element of this research found that the tutoring phase was the most highly rated aspect of the training process by police officers themselves. It is important therefore to dissect this relationship more closely.

Seven tutors were interviewed as part of this research, but by the time the new recruits were being interviewed after four years in the police service, over a third of these recruits were now also acting as tutors themselves. The concerns that were raised by the HMIC in both 1999 and 2002 referred to above appear to be still apparent in the case of this research. Tutors (both those who tutored the new recruits and the recruits themselves who subsequently became tutors) and SDROs expressed concerns about the process of recruitment and training. In terms of recruitment, these concerns expressed themselves in the less than 'voluntary' nature of their application to the role:

> I sort of volunteered. (D6)
>
> I've never asked to be a tutor. My sergeant asked me. (T1)
>
> [L]et's see, did I want to be a tutor, or was I told you're going to be a tutor? It was a bit of both ... so I think I volunteered, but was told I was volunteering as well, if you see what I mean. (T2)
>
> I kind of was ... more coerced really, I think, if anything else. (T4)
>
> I think the job chooses tutors wrong, I think there's a lot of people that shouldn't be tutors ... I did volunteer I must admit, I was one of those that did volunteer and that's what I was saying about there's people that don't actually want to do it and I think that's wrong. (T5)

Once tutors had been 'selected' for the role, it would be expected that tutors would be trained. One of the tutors stated that they had never taken a training course to be a tutor. The remainder of the tutors (and the new recruit tutors) partook in training which varied from a three-month course taken by one tutor in 2007, to a week-long residential training course run by the police by other tutors and, more recently, to a week-long non-residential course run by an external company that trained public service workers together in mentoring skills. Whichever training routes the tutors had taken, they all were critical of the process, most especially those most recently trained, as seen here:

> It wasn't very good, really ... It was all very fluffy and very learning styles and what colours people are and stuff like that, nothing practical. Then the last half day is with [name of force], people telling you how to actually do it ... it was a bit airy-fairy really. (Z3)
>
> Dire ... the trainers ... broke everything down to such ridiculous small details. We spent like an hour talking about what colour people are ... you can come across fiery red people who might not get along with the

sunshine yellow person very well … We had two days of learning fiery blues and sunshine yellows and then … the third day, when they actually taught us how to fill-in the forms for our students was the most informative bit. (D10)

I don't think I took a great deal from it really. (T6)

Having already placed tutors first out of a list of six potential influences upon their development as a new police officer on two occasions (TIME C and TIME D), the new recruits were then asked to explain more about their views, opinions and relationship with their tutor. Tutors themselves were also asked the same question. Their views diverged quite noticeably between what the new recruits saw the role of the tutor to be and what the tutor saw their own role to be. New recruits spoke in terms of being shown how to do the job and how to cope with the job. This relates to the 'learning by watching' discussion earlier in this chapter:

[T]hey give you the whole groundwork of how to do things … everything really, just everything. (B3)

[T]hey just teach you all the ropes basically, what to do and what not to do. (B6)

[T]he tutor really is there to literally teach you everything … because he realised I just didn't know anything. (B7)

[R]eally shapes you as an officer, because a lot of the ways she deals with things I now deal with things. (B8)

I sit there and I'd watch her and I'd think okay that makes sense, I should have thought about that and then the next time you go there and you do exactly what you've just watched. (B10)

He's taken me under his wing, shown me the ropes, shown me the area, the main offenders. (X4)

[T]o mould you into the best police officer. (X9)

According to the new recruits therefore, the tutor is there to show them *how* to do the job, mainly by replication in order to understand the role of the police officer. This also entails, according to one respondent, identifying those people whom the police need to be suspicious of. This was one of the previous objectives of the tutor constable attachment which has since been replaced (Stradling and Harper 1988). In contrast, the tutors themselves saw their role as a different one. There were two clear objectives of the role of the tutor according to the majority of tutors: to engender a sense of confidence in their tutees and to ensure that they were safe to practice as a police officer:

> To instil confidence … with this job, a lot of it is confidence … all the hard work and the input's frontloaded during their phase at [name of training school], so they get a lot of information and it's all swilling around in there. The main bit really is giving them that confidence to use it and trust that what they're doing is right. (T1)
>
> [S]o that they are safe and confident. (T2)
>
> I want to make sure that he's safe and first and foremost, he's safe, and he does a good job, and I'm giving him effectively the tools to do it. He's got the knowledge. He just needs the tools to do it. (T4)

There were also other functions that were raised by just less than half of the tutors. These related to 'undoing' the training that took place at training school and being a role model to new recruits, who could learn their core values and replicate them. However, these views are not as widespread as those suggesting confidence and safety to practice. Neither a demonstration of how to do the job of a police officer nor instilling confidence is an official key objective of the tutor phase of the IPLDP. There is, at the time of writing, a list of 18 learning outcomes which tutors must demonstrate competence in, but these tie in very much with the methods associated with 'delivering' knowledge, rather than with the expectations of the role itself (College of Policing 2013).

A significant minority of the new recruits also independently raised the issue of the importance of sharing a good rapport with their tutor and the damaging impact that can occur when there is a poor relationship between tutor and tutee. In fact, one tutor even cited the poor relationship between himself and his tutor as a motivating force in taking on the role of tutor himself—"because it didn't really work for me" (T3). It was clear however that only a very small number of the recruits in this sample felt that their own tutor phase had had a detrimental impact both on their development as a police officer and on their sense of belonging to the organisation. Two recruits cited this poor relationship with their tutors as being an important element in their consideration of leaving the force. One of these officers subsequently transferred to another force. For both of these recruits, the relationship breakdown was felt to have been influenced by the hostile tutoring techniques used. More guidance and support was considered to be more appropriate.

Other officers, although not experiencing a poor relationship directly, offered their views on why a poor relationship would be detrimental to a police officer's development:

> You're very reliant on your tutor, if you get a good tutor, who is very proactive, as I've had … I think [it] rubs off on you, because that's the only experience of policing that you've got, so it's not good if you were to get a less than diligent tutor. (X3)
>
> [T]here are some bad tutors out there … you are almost vulnerable during those 12 weeks because you have no idea what you are doing. So you may pick up bad habits. (X6)

However, the vast majority of the sample of officers had a very positive relationship with their tutors, commonly describing it as "massively important" (B8), although a number of recruits, tutors and SDROs described it as "intense" (B10, T7, S4 and X11) or even "tricky" (B3).

## Advice from Other Colleagues

As discussed in Chap. 6, stories and storytelling are a crucial tool in the transmission of common-sense knowledge and practice, most especially to new recruits (van Hulst 2013). Frewin and Tuffin (1998) in their discursive analysis of policing cultures also point to the importance of language for an understanding of the police role. The police construct realities and then operate according to those realities. The new recruits were all asked what they had learned and what was the most important advice they had been given in the early stages of their policing careers. There was a huge variety of responses to this question. Broadly speaking, I have categorised these into advice on being a police officer in the *public sphere* (occupational advice) and advice on being a police officer *within the policing organisation* (organisational advice).

The advice and learning that recruits valued with regard to coping externally with the nature of the job were mostly related to dealing with the public. For many recruits, the most important aspect of policing that they had learned in their first year of training was how to talk to the public and how to read the public, skills that many believed they had begun to develop in previous jobs as either PCSOs or Special Constables—one of the most regularly cited pieces of advice that recruits had received related to the nature of police work. Recruits were informed that a job that they were directed to was rarely how it may first seem, and to "over-think" (C2; Y6) rather than to "go with your gut" (Y9) was dangerous. The reason for this was that whereas in training scenarios, there was a victim, an offender and an offence which invariably led to an arrest, in reality, the waters were rather less clear:

> Don't even plan what you're going to do before you get there because it always goes completely the other way. (C8)

The issue of 'genuine victims' will be referred to in the following chapter, but the belief that "everybody lies" (C10; X2; Y2) or "you can't believe everybody" (C10) was apparent. The 'trope' for this advice was commonly given as "never take something at face value" (Y2; Y11; C4). 'Tropes' is a term from Shearing and Ericson's (1991) work, which explains ways of understanding connections between things. The police officer is the active learner in creating their own set of sensibilities from which to make sense of their working environment. A longer example of this came from one of the respondents:

> [Y]ou get deployed to robbery jobs, for example, you know what the definition of robbery is, having done [name of training school], but you could get deployed to one, one day and one the next day and they're two … they've both come in as robbery, but one is not, because the way it's been reported and what the person is trying to get out of that and then the other one is. (X3)

It was also important not to expect that following the training scenario of victim, offender, arrest, what would then follow would be a conviction and a punishment. Recruits were warned to lower their expectations in this regard: "[Y]ou're not going to win them all" (C4). This issue will be returned to in Chap. 11, where the major challenges facing policing according to the respondents are addressed. Recruits were also advised on how to deal sensitively with the public when necessary. They were urged to "put yourself in the victim's shoes" (C12), "make sure you talk to everybody properly" (Y3) and "every trace leaves a mark" (Y10). This more 'compassionate' yet often overlooked element of policing cultures will be discussed in Chap. 12.

The advice and learning that recruits valued with regard to coping internally with the policing organisation were mostly related to other officers' perceptions of the new recruit. First, new recruits were advised to be extremely thorough in their paperwork and in their handover information:

> [P]eople remember you for the work you do for handover. Everyone remembers a bad handover. (X4)
>
> [O]fficers on other shifts that I never, ever come across, I never see, will judge me on say my report writing, my paperwork and my quality of my handover, so I might have dealt with a job on scene amazingly, but if my paperwork side of things is shoddy or lacking somewhat then I will be judged on that. (X8)
>
> [M]ake sure you do everything thoroughly, you never know who is going to be looking at what job. (X3)
>
> [T]here are three things that will get you into trouble in this job and they're the three P's, which are property, paperwork and police officers. (C10)

Being thorough in paperwork and handovers was also deemed to be important for the reasons of 'fitting in': "[I]f you don't do it you don't fit" (C6), an issue that will be returned to in the following chapter. Second, (and the most regularly cited advice about coping with the policing organisation), new recruits were advised to 'cover themselves'; in fact, one respondent shared the acronym that had been shared with him by his tutor, the "unofficial CARE principle—Cover Arse Remain Employed" (C5). Another stated:

> Cover yourself ... make sure you follow the correct sort of processes so that things can't come back and bite you on the backside. (Y8)

This relates to a further issue that was apparent amongst the new recruits, which will be discussed in the following chapter, a heightened concern to protect themselves, both from physical danger on the streets and from criticism and opprobrium from within the organisation.

## Nature of Student Officers

Tutors and SDROs were asked to describe the characteristics of new student recruits when they have left training school and arrive in force for their tutor period. They were also asked to reflect upon any potential differences between recruits who they had tutored and mentored in the past and the new recruits who were part of this research, who, for the most part, had all had previous experience of the policing organisation, either as a PCSO or as a Special Constable. With only one exception, from an officer who was vehemently opposed to both the pre-join course requirements and the tendency to recruit from within the organisation, all of the samples were extremely positive about the "invaluable" (S4) role that previous experience was playing in the quality of the new recruits who were emerging from training school. Not only was this seen in the recruits' enhanced ability to understand the basic requirements of policing, but it was also seen in their level of commitment to the organisation:

[T]hey're more dedicated. I don't know whether it was too easy to get into the police before, in terms of like with me, I wanted to be in the police so I put in my application, I did the interviews, did the fitness, and I got in. I had to make no effort other than prepare for an interview and prepare to write my application form. (T1)

[T]here's a world of difference … because they are used to certain aspects of the job, mainly the, sort of, confrontational side. (T2)

[T]he quality that we're getting through at the moment, I think it's excelled our expectations, it really has … one of the sergeants went along to review them, and he said they were far better than he's ever seen before. (S1)

[A] lot more clued up, a lot more streetwise … their knowledge is a lot better. (S2)—a combination of Police, Law and Community (PLC) and experience

It's about finding which tool you need for which job … on the first day opening your tool box and rummaging, and going what do I use? Whereas you know PCSOs and ex-specials they will turn up and think ah okay it's that one for this. It's that sort of analogy I think. (S4)

[T]hey come in, they join a shift, a lot more aware of the police environment, you don't have to start right from the basics. Because they've got that background, the tutors are also finding a difference, so they're easier to tutor. So, when you use police jargon, and also just the culture of the police, and the banter in the station, and the demands of the role. Because they have the pre-join qualification, and most of them are ex PCSOs or Specials, then they tend to get on with it a lot quicker. (S6)

This final quote emphasises that not only did the new recruits with a previous policing background understand more about the requirements of the role, but they also understood about the nature of the organisation and the informal workings of the organisation. As you journey through the layers of an organisation, the characteristics become less conscious, tangible and observable, but are nonetheless key characteristics of the culture. An appreciation of these cultural artefacts is extremely important in the new recruit becoming accepted and validated by existing members and in enhancing the group identity. However, other tutors and SDROs commented upon the potential pitfalls of new recruits already being embedded into the organisation:

[A] lot of their behaviours or attitudes have already been embedded … It's easy to teach someone something new, but it has to go down to the way that they behave or their attitude is quite difficult … I'm never going to change that in ten weeks or eight weeks that I have them. So if they've already been in the police service, be it for a special or be it through PCSO or whatnot, I think that's already embedded their influence of how they're going to behave. (T7)

[M]ore knowledge of the policing world, but they also have a tendency to have picked up bad habits along the way. (S3)

I wouldn't go as far as saying cynical but … people are more familiar with the organisation already and know it's working practices, whereas before people had more goodwill towards the extras in terms of what were the requirements for the job. (S5)

There are a number of advantages of utilising the previous experience of PCSOs and Specials, which will be examined in more detail in Chap. 11. However, if the police service extends the use of this recruitment strategy, this issue will need to be carefully considered. Normative practices, attitudes and behaviours are moulded and shaped at an early stage with new recruits. Fekjær (2014), Fielding (1986) and Tuohy et al. (1993) all found that adjustments within the habitus of police officers changed during the very early stages of socialisation. Therefore, the formal and informal training of PCSOs and Special Constables will need to be carefully analysed to consider whether it is fit for purpose not only for the that particular role but for potential roles that those individuals may fulfil later in their careers.

According to the tutors and SDROs, the most notable characteristics of the new recruits to the police service were enthusiasm and drive. There were only two comments referring to "all the gear and no idea" (T3) and of the recruits being "cocky" (T5), but these came from a tutor who verbally interpreted the question as being about his early days in the force and from a tutor who was opposed to recruitment from the ranks of PCSO. The vast majority of comments referred to a sense of keenness on the part of the new recruits in embarking upon their career: "naïve … keen and they want to get stuck in" (S6), "really keen … a drive for the job" (T1), "they're really excited, I think they're really keen to get out there" (S1) and "enthusiastic … very eager to get involved" (S5). One officer related this enthusiasm to part of the motivation for wanting to be a police officer, which will be examined in the following chapter:

> [K]een, enthusiastic, quite excitable … generally people do want to help other people there is that. It's a bit cheesy if you like, but you know they want to make a difference. (S4)

The new recruits who took part in this research undoubtedly placed the value of the learning that took place within the police station as of significantly more importance, more relevance and more interest than the learning which took place within the training school. The majority of officers felt that learning was best achieved through watching other officers performing the role and then by replicating and sometimes adapting what they had witnessed. This can be very much associated with learning *how* to do the job of a police officer. There was an overwhelming perception that the police station was the site of learning to become a police officer. The same was not felt towards the methods of assessment that are contained within the IPLDP, which are coordinated and managed by the College of Policing and which form the basis of the training school curriculum and the subsequent e-SOLAP portfolio. Rather than this being the opportunity for new student recruits to understand and appreciate the wider social context of the role of policing and of the impact of their work, that is, the *why* as opposed to the *what* or *how*, instead the focus was upon fulfilling learning objectives which focused upon the delivery of knowledge and task completion. As discussed in Chap. 4, whilst training involves the acquisition of specific skills to perform certain tasks, education involves the consideration of more conceptual or theoretical analyses, what Lee and Punch refer to as "social capital" (2006, p. 81). There is a prevailing attitude that 'real' learning takes place within the police station, which is an attitude exhibited by new recruits, by the HMIC and by more experienced officers. The truncated time which new recruits spend in training school, coupled with the renewed focus upon competency-based assessments, ensures that this prevailing attitude will continue to flourish.

# References

Amin, A., & Roberts, J. (2008). Knowing in Action: Beyond Communities of Practice. *Research Policy, 37*, 353–369.

Assmann, J., & Czaplicka, J. (1995). Collective Memory and Cultural Identity. *New German Critique, 65*, 125–133.

Bayley, D., & Bittner, E. (1984). Learning the Skills of Policing. *Law and Contemporary Problems, 47*(4), 35–59.

Cable, D., & Parsons, C. (2001). Socialization Tactics and Person-Organization Fit. *Personnel Psychology, 54*(1), 1–23.

Chan, J. (2004). Using Pierre Bourdieu's Framework for Understanding Police Culture. *Droit et Société, 56–57*, 327–347.

College of Policing. (2013). *Police Sector Standards for the Training of Tutors.* Retrieved from http://www.college.police.uk/What-we-do/Standards/Documents/Tutor_Standard.pdf

Constable, J., & Smith, J. (2015). Initial Police Training and the Development of Police Occupational Culture. In P. Wankhade & D. Weir (Eds.), *Police Services: Leadership and Management Perspectives* (pp. 45–60). New York: Springer International Publishing.

Eraut, M. (2004). Informal Learning in the Workplace. *Studies in Continuing Education, 26*(2), 247–273.

Fekjær, S. (2014). Police Students' Social Background, Attitudes and Career Plans. *Policing: An International Journal of Police Strategies and Management, 37*(3), 467–483.

Fielding, N. (1984). Police Socialization and Police Competence. *The British Journal of Sociology, 35*(4), 568–590.

Fielding, N. (1986). Evaluating the Role of Training in Police Socialization: A British Example. *Journal of Community Psychology, 14*(3), 319–330.

Frewin, K., & Tuffin, K. (1998). Police Status, Conformity and Internal Pressure: A Discursive Analysis of Police Culture. *Discourse and Society, 9*(2), 173–185.

HMIC. (1999). *Police Integrity: Securing and Maintaining Public Confidence.* London: HMIC.

HMIC. (2002). *Training Matters.* London: Home Office.

Karp, S., & Stenmark, H. (2011). Learning to Be a Police Officer. Tradition and Change in the Training and Professional Lives of Police Officers. *Police Practice and Research, 12*(1), 4–15.

Lave, J., & Wenger, E. (1991). *Situated Learning.* Cambridge: Cambridge University Press.

Lee, M., & Punch, M. (2006). *Policing by Degrees.* Groningen: de Hondsrug Pers.

Macvean, A. (2010). *A Clash of Cultures: Policing the Academics.* Chester: University of Chester.

McNulty, E. (1994). Generating Common Sense Knowledge Among Police Officers. *Symbolic Interaction, 17*(3), 281–294.

Norman, M., & Hyland, T. (2003). The Role of Confidence in Lifelong Learning. *Educational Studies, 29*(2–3), 261–272.

Oakley, R. (1994). The Police and Black People: The Training Response. In M. Stephens & S. Becker (Eds.), *Police Force, Police Service; Care and Control in Britain* (pp. 85–106). Basingstoke: Macmillan.

Schein, E. (1985). *Organisational Culture and Leadership: A Dynamic View.* San Francisco: Jossey-Bass.

Shearing, C., & Ericson, R. (1991). Culture as Figurative Action. *British Journal of Sociology, 42*(4), 481–506.

Stradling, S., & Harper, K. (1988). The Tutor Constable Attachment, the Management of Encounters and the Development of Discretionary Judgement. In P. Southgate (Ed.), *New Directions in Police Training* (pp. 199–218). London: HMSO.

Tuohy, A., Wrenall, M., McQueen, R., & Stradling, S. (1993). Effect of Socialization Factors on Decisions to Prosecute: The Organizational Adaptation of Scottish Police Recruits. *Law and Human Behaviour, 17*(2), 167–181.

van Hulst, M. (2013). Storytelling at the Police Station: The Canteen Culture Revisited. *British Journal of Criminology, 53*(4), 624–642.

Van Maanen, J. (1976). Breaking In: Socialization to Work. In R. Dubin (Ed.), *Handbook of Work, Organization and Society* (pp. 67–130). Chicago: Rand McNally College Publishing Company.

Willis, J., & Mastrofski, S. (2017). Understanding the Culture of Craft: Lessons from Two Police Agencies. *Journal of Crime and Justice, 40*(1), 84–100.

# 10

# Qualitative Findings II: Becoming and Being a Cop

The focus of the interview questions with the new recruits over a four-year period and with their tutors and SDROs centred around three broad areas, *learning*, *becoming* and *being*. The first of these, *learning*, was the focus of the previous chapter. The book will now turn to the following two areas, *becoming* and *being*. Whilst discussing their *learning*, the new recruits discussed how they could best 'learn' to become a police officer and be a part of the policing organisation. They also considered the role and impact of each of the important players in the training process. On *becoming* a police officer, the new recruits spoke about the characteristics of a 'good' police officer, their motivations for joining the service and whether, and at what stage, they identified themselves as a police officer. Discussions of *being* a police officer focused upon (although not in these terms) both the external behavioural adaptations to the recruits' new role and their internal adaptations to their sense of 'self' through their potentially altered identities. Further areas of enquiry considered what were the areas of satisfaction and dissatisfaction in their new jobs. Many of these questions were designed to not only provide a fuller picture of the changing behaviours, attitudes and beliefs of new recruits to the police service but also appreciate more about the working cultures of the policing organisation, particularly at the lower ranks. In addition to this being

© The Author(s) 2017
S. Charman, *Police Socialisation, Identity and Culture,*
DOI 10.1007/978-3-319-63070-0_10

surmised through the areas mentioned already, the new recruits were also explicitly asked what they felt were the characteristics of police culture as they understood it. This would provide an interesting analysis of what they felt policing cultures were and are, and what the impact of a heavily value-laden term such as 'police culture' might have had upon them. The question asked of all respondents at each interview stage about what were considered to be the major challenges facing modern policing will be discussed in Chap. 11.

# Becoming a Police Officer

## Motivations and Anticipations of Joining the Police

A consideration of the literature on this subject in Chap. 5 revealed a remarkably consistent story of the motivations behind recruits wanting to join the police service across time and space. Research from North America from the 1970s onwards (Hopper 1977; Van Maanen 1973; Ellis 1991; Foley et al. 2008), from the UK (Fielding 1988) and from Australia (Chan 2003) all found that the most prominent motivations for wanting to join the police service were the action-/outdoors-oriented aspect of the work, the community service principles associated with the work and the job security that accompanied the role. Nearly half a century on from that first research, the findings from this sample of officers in Evermord Constabulary were very similar. However, the timing and political context of these recruits' employment agreements and arrangements meant that one of the factors from this previous research was not replicated—that of job security. This issue was not raised by any of the officers in the sample. This is likely to be connected to a number of factors, including the final report of the Winsor review (2012), which was published shortly before these new recruits began their probationary period. This report considered the pay and conditions of police officers whilst at the same time recommending direct entry to the service, higher entry standards, compulsory severance and a lower starting salary. All of this was against a backdrop of austerity across all UK public services. The officers in this sample of recruits had received a reduction in pay from previous cohorts, and many had been accepted by the force, only for their start date to be delayed on a number of occasions. 'Security' was therefore not a term which was likely to be associated with these first few years in the police service. In a similar vein to Fielding's research in the UK (1988) and the quantitative results from this research (see Chap. 8), which found that recruits did not see 'crime fighting' as their primary role, the new recruits very rarely cited 'crime fighting' as a motivational factor in joining the police service.

The respondents raised three primary reasons for wanting to join the police and raised three areas of the job that they were most looking forward to. The three primary reasons for wanting to join the police service were related to the action-/outdoors-oriented aspect of the work, working within a team and the community service principles associated with the work. The areas which were anticipated the most highly were helping people, the variety and diversity of the role, and the ability to take an incident from start to finish. These areas will now be discussed in more depth.

The most regularly cited of the primary reasons for wanting to join the police service was associated with the more community service principles of the role. The most commonly used phrases in this regard were "to help and protect" (D5) and "to make a difference" (B4). The following quotes illustrate just some of these expressed sentiments and also include a comment from one of the tutors:

> I joined the police to help people and to protect them I guess, and that's the main reason I joined … I'd like to speak to someone and leave knowing that they know that if they want me they can speak to me and I'm there, and we are there and they can speak to us and they can call us. (A12)
>
> I joined to help people, so as long as I'm doing that and I'm getting job satisfaction I'll stay. (B2)
>
> [M]y reasons for joining were genuine. I wanted to help people and do a good job and be a better person. (D2)
>
> [F]or me it's about serving the community, stopping crime or trying to build a safer community, and that's why I joined, I love it, I love working with people so that's why I joined. (W1)

[W]e all have the same morals, I think. And we all want to do good. That's what you joined to do, isn't it, to make a difference. And you'll go to certain jobs and you'll think, oh yes, I hope I've really helped that person; or we did a good thing today. (Z1)

I don't think there is one single police officer that actually joined to catch baddies, it was to help people. That's what I joined the police service for and I can guarantee if you ask every single police officer they'll say the same thing. They want to help people. They want to put something back. (T4)

This factor, 'helping people', was also the second most regularly cited answer to the question of what the new recruits were most looking forward to about becoming a police officer. This was a question which was asked of all of the sampled new recruits on their first interview, which took place within five weeks of their first day at training school. "Making a difference" (A11 and W8) and "to help people" (W3 and W7) were all aspects of the work that they were looking forward to. Some of the recruits held very high expectations about the potential impact that the work of policing could achieve:

[T]o help victims and general members of the public, make their areas and lives nicer. (W3)

[H]elping vulnerable people that need protecting from other people, really, and just getting involved in putting right things that have gone wrong. (W7)

[C]hanging the place that I live in for the better and making it a more bearable environment for people to live in. (W8)

As discussed in Chap. 6, Cochran and Bromley's research in the US found that between 25% and 30% of respondents fell into the category of more community service–oriented police officers, what the authors termed a "*nouveau* police sub-culture" (2003, p. 108), with only about a sixth of respondents fitting the crime-fighting stereotype.

However, previous research in this area has shown that as police officers spend more time in the service, they experience increasing levels of disillusionment with community service principles (Ellis 1991; Chan 2003; Alain and Baril 2005; Alain and Grégoire 2008) and their capacity as police officers to influence crime (Tuohy et al. 1993; Garner 2005;

Chan 2003). The problems with a more intrinsic focus upon the values of the job that relate to community service and helping the public are apparent. The 'reality shock' of the disconnect between the expectations and the desires of the job contrasted with the realities of the job leaves officers frustrated and cynical (Chan 2003; Ellis 1991; Sollund 2008). This will be discussed later in this chapter.

The action-/outdoors-oriented aspect of the work was also referred to by the sample of recruits as a motivational factor behind their decision to join the police service. Sometimes, this was expressed as a frustration that they were not involved in as much 'active' work as they would like, with the realisation that for some of them, particularly those moved reluctantly to the new investigations teams, the work was almost entirely computer based. The 'outdoors' aspect of the job, which was so attractive to the police officers studied in the 1970s and 1980s, is not as significant to the modern-day challenges of policing, with increasing amounts of police time being spent at computers. It is however still a motivation for joining, which has the potential for increasing the amount of frustration as the realities of the job reveal themselves:

> [B]eing out and about and responding to 999 calls with all your kit and your uniform on. I think that's why a lot of people join. (D12)
>     I'm on response and this is what I joined up for and really wanted to do. (D13)
>     I really like TPT [Targeted Patrol Teams] as well, that's why I joined. I'm not an office type person. (Y1)
>     [N]ot many people join the job to sit in a classroom. (Y2)
>     [T]hat's why I joined the police, not to sit in an office. (Z1)

This factor is also related to the most regularly cited answer to the question of what the new recruits were most looking forward to about becoming a police officer. The variety and diversity of the role was cited by the majority of police recruits as being the aspect of the job that they were most looking forward to.

Additionally, there was one further motivation for joining which was cited by a majority of the sample. This related to the camaraderie which came with 'team working'. The reason for this additional factor could be attributed to the experience that a number of recruits already had of the police service in their previous role as a PCSO or Special Constable. This positive experience of team working could have impacted upon their decision to apply for the role of Police Constable:

> I think when you join the police you're almost part of a family ... you do feel like you're part of something when you join the police if that makes sense. (A12)
>
> [I]t's one of those reasons why I joined in the first place, because it's a nice team dynamic. (X1)

The third factor which was raised regularly by the new recruits relating to what they were most looking forward to about becoming a police officer related, in part, to their previous experience as a PCSO or Special Constable. They stated that witnessing or being involved in a job from start to finish, which would involve the initial arrest, investigation and potential conviction of an offender, was an aspect of the job that they were looking forward to. This seemed to particularly be the case because of the potential victim satisfaction that this would involve. The work of the PCSO in particular would mean that none of the stages would be their responsibility. However, following on from these first interviews, and in a move designed to achieve the required budget savings outlined in the Spending Review (HM Treasury 2010), Evermord Constabulary reorganised the structure of the force, requiring all police constables to be in one of four areas—Intelligence, Prevention and Neighbourhoods, Response and Patrol, or Investigation. This desire to deal with a case from beginning to end was no longer a possibility and was a later source of frustration and indeed stress for some officers.

## Feeling Like a Police Officer

At TIME A, TIME B and TIME C, all new recruits in the sample were asked whether they 'feel' like a police officer. No other explanation was given or asked for about what a police officer is expected to feel like or what the question specifically meant. TIME A ($n = 24$) was within the first five weeks of joining the police service, TIME B ($n$ = 22) was at six months and TIME C ($n$ = 22) was one year into their service. The results showed that the majority of recruits did not feel like a police officer at TIME A, but by the time they had been in service for six months at TIME B, this had changed. After one year in service at TIME C, five officers either only sometimes felt like a police officer or did not feel like a police officer at all. Figure 10.1 shows this change over time.

The contributing factors to 'feeling' like a police officer were the uniform and making an arrest, and many who argued that they did not feel like a police officer felt that once they were out of training school and working in their stations, this situation might change. As can be seen from the graph, for many officers, this was the case, but for some, they remained uncertain. The contributing factors to this uncertainty appeared to be a lack of confidence in knowing how to act and a feeling that they were "trying to play the role" (B2) and "a sheep in wolf's clothing" (X1). One officer believed that they would only feel like a police officer "when I feel comfortable in doing what I'm doing" (W1). For those officers who identified uncertainty about this question, this was expressed in terms of a lack of confidence and a fear of doing the wrong thing. This issue of fear will be returned to later in this chapter.

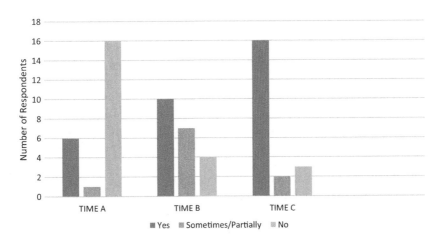

**Fig. 10.1** Do you feel like a police officer?

## 'Good' Police Officers

After serving as police officers for four years, the sample of officers were asked what they considered to be the characteristics of a 'good' police officer. They were not given anything to choose from but were able to speak freely and often provided more than one answer. As such, a wide range of different answers were provided, 17 different characteristics in total. However, of those, where at least a third of officers mentioned the same trait, there were five different characteristics of a 'good' police officer which were mentioned. They were (in order of frequency) good communication skills, empathy, compassion, integrity and good decision-making. These attributes of 'good' police officers are similar to those found by previous research, spanning decades, which focused upon communication skills (Muir 1977; Westera et al. 2013), interpersonal skills and working with the community (Willis and Mastrofski 2016). In utilising the skills of communication, the officers pointed towards the associated benefits of not having to use force:

> The most important is being a good communicator ... as a PCSO I never ever got physical with anybody in three years and I could talk to them, it's the best tool. (W1)
>
> You know those who, when, before they've even gone to a job, their communication skills aren't as good as they could be; they might antagonise people, and you know, it can be a relatively minor incident, but by virtue of the fact that they're going, there will be calls for backup, people are going to be arrested, there's going to be drama. And you get others who can go to a job where you've got a response unit heading towards and it's all done and dusted, and, you know, the person is jumping into the back of the van without handcuffs by the time it's all sorted, because they've got that ability to communicate, to relate to someone, and to sincerely make them think they've got their interests at heart. And it completely changes how you deal with a situation. (D4)
>
> [B]eing able to talk to people. If you can't do that, you're useless. (D6)
>
> [Y]ou probably wouldn't think, oh I need to really know how to talk to people. ... But it is, it's so important. ... I've not been assaulted in the four and a half years I've been in the job. I've been in a few, sort of, rough and tumble sort of scenarios which are unavoidable but I've not actually been

assaulted, punched or anything like that. I think a bit part of that is I can talk to people. (D12)

When you start getting your asp and your gas, it all ends in bother. It's a lot easier if you spend a bit more time trying to calm it all down, explaining what's happening. Because generally you can get situations where there is no outcome but that person needs to be arrested, and so if you spend a bit more time trying to calm them down and do it in a decent manner, you're able to get them into the van or wherever, get them into custody a calm way as opposed to having to use force and then they think they've been hard done by, beaten up by a police officer, they're then not happy in custody, giving custody staff bother, then it all comes to us guys trying to investigate and they're still not calmed down. I just think if you're able to afford an extra half an hour at the start, it's just much easier. (Z6)

These 'softer' policing activities and behaviours, traditionally associated with the more caring and nurturing activities of female police officers but increasingly being regarded as simply 'policing' activities which are not divided upon gender lines, will be discussed in Chap. 12. The quantitative results of this research, discussed in Chap. 8, revealed that where recruits were asked what were the most important characteristics of a police officer, they placed good communication first and physical strength last. When it came to the interview question about what made a 'good' police officer, the officers sometimes went on to explain their reasoning for suggesting communication and comparing this to what might be assumed to be a key attribute of a 'good' police officer—that of physical strength. Below are some examples of this:

[T]hat strength and authority thing is I think a very historic view of the police. (D12)

[Y]ou probably think it's being tough, which does help. It does help but I would rather not get in a fight with someone, to be honest, because I've got to go home and explain why I've got a black eye, so I'd rather not. But I think you've got to be able to speak to people on their level. You've got to be able to speak to the person who's grown up on a council estate, in loads of trouble forever, that does drugs and is a bit of a scumbag. You've got to be able to talk to them on their level, and then you've got to be able to go and speak to someone who lives in a very expensive house. If you can't do that, you can't deal with everyone. (D6)

I probably thought it was more about being physically strong and those sorts of things, whereas it's not. (D13)

In becoming a police officer during the first year of service, police officers are, in principle, acquiring the necessary skills and consciously or unconsciously adapting their 'habitus' in order that they conform with both the organisational demands of the job and, importantly, the cultural demands of the job. This is all part of the process of identity building. As this section has shown, police officers have a clear idea of their motivations for joining the police and what makes a good police officer, and these themes of community service and good communication are closely linked. They are also increasingly identifying themselves as police officers as their time in service extends. With that identification as a police officer, whether it be because of the uniform or the making of an arrest, comes another level of identification—that of being part of the 'policing family'. This identity building takes place within a social context, and as such, it is important to recognise that social identity is not individualistic but concerned with "socially-shared patterns of individual behaviour" (Tajfel 1981, p. 49). The 'habitus' of a police officer is influenced by the social space in which that individual has developed. That social space, as we have seen, is directed by more experienced officers and behaviours are replicated by new recruits. The strength of the recruits' commitment to conformity or their options for rebellion in adapting their 'habitus' will be explored next.

## Being a Police Officer

Van Maanen (1976) discussed the phases of socialisation into the policing environment, or "people processing" (1978a) as he called it, as following three stages—anticipatory socialisation, encounter (or change) and metamorphosis. These were discussed in detail in Chap. 5. This chapter now turns to the latter two of these stages. Through an understanding and analysis of the recruits' changing attitudes to what they consider to be the role of the police and the cultures of the police, we can begin to appreciate the level of conformity, or otherwise, to the prevailing demands of the job, both organisationally and culturally. This section of the chapter will also consider the accounts of the new recruits as they discuss whether their first few years in the job have changed them, and whether the expectations and desires for the job have materialised.

## Role of the Police

Chapter 8 discussed the quantitative results from this research which showed contradictions in what the recruits felt was the role of policing. Whilst when the recruits were provided with a list of priorities, they chose 'fighting crime' as the most important priority of a police officer, this was not reflected in strong agreement later that this was their primary role. Here, there was a clear emphasis placed by respondents on the role of public protection. In the interviews with respondents, all of them were asked at all of the interview stages to discuss what they felt was the role of the police. According to the College of Policing, police constables "maintain law and order, protect members of the public and their property and prevent, detect and investigate crime" (College of Policing n.d.). What was striking about the responses of the new recruits was how much their attitudes changed during the course of the four interviews. The responses given by the recruits to the question of what they felt was the role of the police fell broadly into three categories. First, there were roles associated with crime such as apprehending offenders, making arrests, gathering evidence or reducing crime. Second, there were wider public service sentiments about public protection, visibility and reassurance. Third, there was the more specific role of 'helping' and safeguarding vulnerable people, whether this was due to their status as a victim of crime or their inherent vulnerability owing to their age or mental ill-health.

As can be seen in Fig. 10.2, at TIME A (within five weeks of joining the police service), 35% of the statements made about the role of the police belonged to this first 'crime' category. This increased marginally to 38% at TIME B (six months of service) and fell to 32% at TIME C (one year of service). However, by TIME D (four years into service), this had fallen dramatically to just 9% of the statements made about the role of the police being related to crime. This equated to three separate comments made by only two officers. This reflects, although not so starkly, the results from the quantitative data discussed in Chap. 8, which indicated a drop in those agreeing or strongly agreeing with the statement that 'the primary role of a police officer is crime fighting', which fell from a high of 86.4% at TIME B to 47.1% at TIME D. The following quotes illustrate this change in attitude towards the perceived and actual role of the police:

> 30% crime, 70% social work which is something I didn't really expect. … I thought it'd be a bit more crime fighting. (B1)
>
> We do a lot of customer service, and customer focused work, and a lot of social work, and a lot of mental health assessment. We don't seem to do an awful lot of crime fighting. (C1)
>
> I very rarely deal with crime. (D3)
>
> I can't tell you the last time I went to a crime. (D10)
>
> [C]rime-wise, it's probably the smallest part now, I would say. (D6)

A similar pattern emerges of recruits mentioning the broad public protection and reassurance roles of the police, as can be seen in Fig. 10.2.

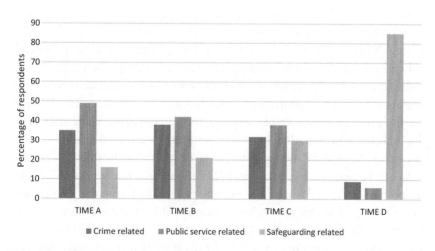

**Fig. 10.2**   What is the role of the police?

This began at 49% at TIME A, fell to 42% at TIME B, fell again to 38% at TIME C and then almost disappeared, with only 6% of the statements made about the role of the police being related to public protection and reassurance. There was also an increasing sense of frustration amongst the recruits regarding community involvement in this aspect of their job:

> I've been in the environment and seen what it used to be like and that's what I wanted to do but it's not like that anymore. It's too fluffy I think. We do what everyone else wants us to do … I bet you can't find anyone of this rank that will say 'ask the community'. Anyone above that will say yes because that's what they need to say. (C6)
>
> All of this rubbish about asking the public is just a front of, we're pretending to involve you … I mean, it's good having some engagement and telling people what you've done but I think it needs to be, this is how we're doing it, this is what we're doing, and then when it works, tell people. If it doesn't work, tell people, rather than asking people what they want us to do, because they'll have us walking around in big hats and hi-vis jackets being completely ineffective, doing anything. (D1)

Finally, there was the more specific role of 'helping' and safeguarding vulnerable people, whether this was due to their status as a victim of crime or their inherent vulnerability owing to their age or mental ill-health. This was rarely raised as a role and function of the police when the new recruits were in training school, where, as can be seen in Fig. 10.2, only 16% of the statements were made related to this area. However, this steadily and then dramatically rose. The figure was 21% at TIME B, 30% at TIME C and then finally 85% at TIME D. Many of the respondents spoke of the amount of their time which was devoted to this area:

> I've learnt a lot about safeguarding, I never really thought about that when I first started. (D9)
>
> The jobs we go to is just ridiculous sometimes. We have to go because they're domestic related and once in a blue moon those jobs go very pear shaped in the long run and so everything is a safeguarding exercise. (D10)
>
> I think it is all about helping people when all is said and done. (B9)
>
> Community oriented, speaking to people, rather than just all action policing. (A9)

This dramatic change from a focus on the role of the police as concerned with crime and the broad principles associated with public protection to a role focused specifically on vulnerability appears to be a reflection of three mutually dependent factors. First, there is the changing role of the police, which not only has become wider and more diverse (Millie 2013), incorporating both the preservation and the production of social order (Reiner 2000), but has also been affected by budgetary cuts elsewhere within the public and care sectors (see Chap. 11). The following quotes indicate an awareness of, and a frustration with, this change:

> There was that vulnerability side and that safeguarding side when I joined that I probably didn't know about when I first started but I think that the job has changed as well and it is geared more now towards safeguarding and vulnerability. I think the nature of crime has changed a lot since I started. It's not just fights in the street. There is a lot more ongoing issues hidden behind closed doors, often like your domestics or the stuff with the child sexual offences. (Z11)
>
> [T]he expectation of what the police should be doing is far greater than it was back many, many years ago. (Z4)
>
> I think quite soon we'll have to make a decision we're either going to deal with crime or just deal with vulnerability, because at the moment we're not particularly doing both. (Z3)

Second, there is the changing realisation from the new recruits of what the role of the police *actually* entails. Many of them initially felt that their role was to "try and make society more cohesive … you try to help people get on with each other" (A2), but the more time they serve, the greater the 'reality shock' as to the limits of their influence, the nature of the more regular activities that they are involved with and the limits of their time.

> What they teach you at [name of training school] is what, you know, what people still believe is the role of a police officer and it's about building files, it's about crime investigation, it's actual victims, you know, and stuff like that. And actually, a large proportion of our work isn't that. It's dealing with people with mental health issues, it's dealing with social issues and all

sorts of stuff. So, actual crime fighting very, very small proportion of our work. (D8)

[W]e don't have time to be proactive. (D9)

The level of disappointment at the perceived gap between the expecta-tions of the job and the realities of the job has the potential, as Chap. 6 discussed, to produce a more cynical, suspicious, alienated officer who displays lower levels of empathy and higher levels of authoritarianism. There is therefore a third explanation as to why the recruits express such a dramatic change in their views on the role of the police and that is influenced by the appearance of cynicism.

Third therefore, there is a strong and growing sense of cynicism in officers which is displayed regularly and knowingly as their length of ser-vice increases. This has the capacity to influence their attitudes both towards their work and towards the public they respond to.

[M]obile social work or mobile marriage guidance counsellor. (C5)

You are a social worker – you're mother, you're father – you're an auntie, you're an uncle. You are Jeremy Kyle, it feels like sometimes. (Z4)

Clearing up people's problems, basically, people who can't live a normal life, is the majority of our work. (D6)

[Y]ou deal with a lot of people's problems where you think, does it really need a police officer here? Should you be wasting police time? And we spend a lot of time … or police time just sorting people's problems out … disputes over property, over relationships … just people moaning about people. (B7)

[I]t's just constant mopping up of people, who literally, cannot run their own lives. (D10)

[G]lorified security guards. (D8)

This issue of cynicism appears to one of the most long-standing and geographically widespread features of policing cultures. It has been found in research which has spanned decades (Reiner 1978, 2010; Crank 1998; De Lint 1998; Scripture 1997; Loftus 2008, 2009), is identified in most corners of the globe (Crank 1998; Chan 2003; Steyn and Mkhize 2016; Sollund 2008) and is exhibited in both verbal behaviour and written blogs (Atherton 2012). The extent to which it is a prevailing feature in this research will be addressed again later in this chapter as the discussion moves to that of policing cultures.

## Policing Cultures

The overriding focus of this book is on the cultures of the police, and of the influences upon the formation and development of these cultural characteristics within the early stages of a police officer's career. The majority of the questions asked of the recruits, whether in the quantitative or the qualitative phases of the research, were designed to elicit more information on this theme. The results of this, which have been discussed thus far, will feed into an overall assessment of the picture of modern policing cultures in Chap. 12. However, the recruits were also explicitly asked the direct question of what they understood by the term 'police culture' and whether they could describe or explain some of its characteristics. This would be interesting to compare with the analysis of the other parts of the research and the extent to which the cultural habitus that the recruits were learning to inhabit was implicit and poorly understood and how much was transparent and observable.

### Solidarity

The theme that was referred to most regularly by the new recruits to describe the organisational culture that they were joining was 'solidarity'. They described being a police officer as being part of a "giant family" (X2) and regularly used the expression that "everyone has each other's backs" (D12). As discussed in Chap. 8, 88.2% of the new recruits at TIME D agreed or strongly agreed with the statement that 'police officers show high levels of solidarity with each other'. As a cultural characteristic of policing, solidarity was first referred to by Skolnick in 1966, and its importance and continued relevance has been highlighted ever since (Muir 1977; Crank 1998; Reiner 2010; Hendriks and van Hulst 2016). Here, the new recruits talk about that solidarity and the reasons for its existence:

Your shift become part of your family. (A4)
[W]e all work together as one big family. (A7)

[I]t's quite a tight group in that you all think on similar lines. Everyone backs each other up where they can. I do believe they do look out for each other, it's not just from the sergeant's level looking down, everyone on your team really does look out for each other. (B7)

[Y]ou're at work when no one else is, at four in the morning. And there's a real, sort of, team camaraderie element to it. (D12)

[Y]ou're always watching your colleague's back. (X7)

[M]y main focus is on my shift because they look after me, they're my backup for anything that I go to … we never stop laughing. We all get on really, really well. (D13)

Knowing that your colleagues have 'got your back' appeared to an important feature of being a police officer and a story that was proudly told. It is easy to dismiss such clichés as being trite and largely meaningless, but they do (just as 'making a difference' earlier in this chapter) provide an easily recognisable shorthand for the acceptable language of the organisational culture. To use clichés can indicate a desire to be inclusive and to offer understandable connections (Abell 2017).

It was Skolnick (1966), when first referring to the issue of solidarity amongst police officers, who noted that it emerged, in part, due to the nature of the policing role, which combined authority, danger and pressure. These were characteristics that were not individually felt only by police officers but were uniquely the only occupation to feel the combination of these characteristics (Skolnick 1966). This solidarity was therefore a response to the public-facing nature of the job. However, although a number of recruits pointed towards this precarious public-facing role as being a factor in the high levels of solidarity between officers, this was not felt to be the only factor. As we shall see in Chap. 11, there is a strong sense of 'us versus them' in policing cultures. The 'them' is not only the public that they are policing, it is also the media that they feel are criticising them and, importantly, it is also the senior police officers who they do not feel are supporting them. So, the solidarity that is apparent (and there are limits to it, as we shall see) is to counteract a range of different pressures that they feel they are experiencing:

[T]here's so much solidarity probably put on here because it's the only people you feel that you get the support from is your other colleagues, nobody else really. … Everybody you are involved with in your job you don't feel supported from so the only people you have that from and they've got your back, I guess, is the people that you work on shift with. (D3)

   [E]veryone has each other's back, quite supportive of colleagues when they're feeling stressed out … I can't think of the right word, but I'd say like constables almost segregate themselves together just to kind of look after each other … just being a constable, even police officers that I don't know, I still kind of look out for them and have their back. (Z7)

So, whilst the recruits generally painted a positive picture of the nature and impact of solidarity within their working environment, this was not necessarily a freely given right on entry to the policing organisation. New recruits are expected to conform with the norms and practices of the group in a process that they themselves regularly describe as 'fitting-in'. Some described the pressure that was felt to do this and others speculated on the potential difficulties had they not been able to successfully assimilate with the group:

   Is there pressure to fit in? Definitely. (C2)

   I think I was so eager to fit in initially, and not everyone wanted to be your mate, and in fact there was an open dislike of the newer people, probationers … you want to be part of the team and you want to get on with everyone, and be appreciated for what you do, and I think that if you don't have that, which you don't when you join, you get blanked. They're experts at that, the police, they ignore you. (D2)

   If you don't fit in with everyone then it's probably really difficult. (D6)

   I'd hate to not feel as if I fitted in. (D13)

   I've always worried what people think of me, but I never try too hard, I don't try and change myself to be accepted, but you just want to be … nobody likes to be disliked … I suppose if you're not accepted then it's a real struggle. (Z6)

**The Limits to Solidarity**

However, we must also begin to question, as Paoline and Terrill (2014) have done, the extent to which this solidarity is absolute and unconditional. In the face of a rapidly changing field, the stability and rigidity of an unmoving habitus must surely be unlikely. Loftus (2008, 2009, 2010) has suggested otherwise and argued that minor changes to the policing habitus should not disguise a more persistent and steadfast organisational culture. However, although this research has found that 'solidarity' is an extremely important element of policing organisational cultures, the recruits were very quick to add that this was not solidarity without limits. 'Having your back' often referred to the support that would be received from colleagues if a fellow officer found themselves in physical danger. This solidarity did not appear to extend, certainly not in the form of active involvement, to other forms of workplace difficulties:

> [W]hen something does go wrong you're pretty much held accountable for your actions. You'd like to think this team thing would count for something then, but it doesn't really, so you're on your own. (B8)
> [I]f you succeeded as a team, you fail as a team – that's what it used to be like. Now it seems that if you succeed as a team, you fail on your own. (W10)
> [I]f something happens to that victim, you don't really have any support from anyone if it goes wrong, it's all like you're totally accountable yourself if something goes wrong. (Z7)

> It's a big club that everybody kind of looks after each other. If I got into a fight right now and I hit my emergency button, I know that – well, I'd hope, should I say – everybody would come running to help me out and they'd look after me and they'd have my back, which is great. Conversely, yeah, we're a big club and we look after each other – if I went into the office over there and said something that was questionable, maybe quite seriously politically incorrect, a racist term or anything like that, then I would be very surprised if pretty much most of the people didn't write a report and say that I was … When you're in the military, I could say anything to anybody and no offence was taken, okay. You can't do that here. I know that when I was in the military, the person either side of me had my back fullstop, end of, no questions asked. (D5)
> I think that's the public's perception that we all, kind of, group together and we're all, you know, we've got each other's back. But actually, this last two years I've realised that a lot of what you go through you go through on your own. (D8)

One recruit, who asked at this point for the recording device to be switched off, recounted a story of feeling let down by colleagues when a complaint was made about him by a member of the public. Body-worn camera footage eventually cleared the officer of all allegations, but he was struck by the lack of solidarity amongst colleagues during this period. He stressed however that in the face of *physical* danger, unstinting loyalty still remained. The 'code of self-protection' amongst new recruits, the propensity to place one's own self-interests before that of the team, appears to be a stronger and more prevailing influence than the unqualified solidarity that has been previously assumed.

It should be noted therefore that this bond of solidarity between officers is not, as is often assumed in the literature, universal across the policing organisation, or even across an individual force or an individual police station:

[M]y team's very different to the team that runs at nights. (D6)

[W]e'll stick together, but it's also I find out within my shift we would all stick together and everyone's really close, but then they'll say bad things about another shift because they do things differently. (Y2)

It's quite bad in between shifts and strands. I think everyone always thinks the shift they're taking over from or the shift they're handing over to isn't very good, won't do a good job. (Z9)

[T]here are differences within different teams it seems. I suppose it's understandable with different teams always feeling they are busy and then seeing others not so busy but, you know, they are doing a different type of work. So, you get shift officers getting wound up with other people, you know, like the beat officers or PCSOs they are not as busy as what we are. So there, kind of, is that barrier in the culture there … a culture within the whole police force? I don't know if there is, but there definitely is a culture within the shift officers. (X6)

The dangers of ascribing cultural characteristics to an entire occupation, with little regard to rank, specialism or location, are evident here. The new recruits spoke regularly about having little or no interaction with any police officer outside of their shift and of the limits to their sense of solidarity. They expressed little surprise at evidence from a previous research project which revealed traffic and firearms officers in another force refusing to share a fridge in a shared rest room.

This characteristic of solidarity reflects a number of issues, particularly, as we shall soon see, the changing nature of the role of the police and the changing nature of police recruits. However, it is also affected by the changing attitudes towards the nature of the policing career. Once seen as an all-encompassing identity change, "it defines who he is. He will always be a cop" (Ahern 1972; cited in Skolnick 2008), the majority of the new recruits were more likely to describe being a police officer as 'a job' and one that they would stay in for as long as it suited them. Tom Winsor's efforts to reframe policing away from the 'job for life' culture appear to have paid off, but with perhaps unintended consequences (2012). The respondents offered their thoughts on this:

> It's a job at the end of the day and if tomorrow it ended, I will go out and find another job. (C8)
> I certainly see it just as a job … my colleagues, my shift, I think most of them literally just come to work because it is work. They do the job, and when the uniform comes off they're just a normal person again. (C7)
> [T]he culture is very much more – certainly on the front line – about getting home in one piece. The front line is so stretched thin at the moment that it is really a case of, I'm going to go in, I'm going to do my time, I'm going to come home safe. (D4)
> [F]amily will still always come first … for me, it's still a job. (C9)
> I'm a police officer at work and then I just leave it all at work. (C10)

Although not widespread, there were a significant minority of officers who discussed leaving the force, mostly due to the stressful nature of the work they were involved with, the frustrations of the job and the feelings of lack of support from more senior colleagues. From those who raised this issue, these comments were typical:

> There are times when I've questioned what I'm doing, whether I want to be a police officer or not. (D5)
> [T]he stuff that I've gone through in the last two years has just been hor-rendous and I just think, you know, God there's so much easier jobs out

there to do … it just takes everything from you … why did I choose this and what else can I do? (D8)

[I]t has just been hell. And so many times I thought, I'm just going to leave because I feel so stressed out by this, what am I getting from it? Nothing. And that comes from the job. (Z1)


# #newbreed

What these differences in the cultural narratives of new recruits to the police service also reveal is a shift in emphasis, one that is moving further away from the law-enforcing crime-fighter and more towards the problem-solving communicator. As Hendriks and van Hulst (2016) have rightly warned, we should not necessarily see the new cultural characteristics replacing the old, but instead they can be viewed as simply adding to the 'sedimentation' of policing practices (2016, p. 13). Within this shift in emphasis, there appears to be a growing divide between those officers with a long record in service and those new to the service. It is here that the phrase "#newbreed" (X7) in Twitter parlance or "different breed" (C8) or "new breed" (Z9) enters the discussion. Although not all used this phrase, a significant number of the new recruits referred to the differences between themselves and more long-serving officers. This difference was seen in two distinct ways. First, there was their different attitudes towards acceptable police behaviour (or their different perceptions of their attitudes and of longer-serving officers' attitudes towards police behaviour). Second, there was the perception of the greater relevance of their policing skills and their style of policing, given the changing nature of the role of the police. In terms of the first of these issues, what is deemed to be acceptable and unacceptable police behaviour, the quotes below are examples of this belief. As a number of the officers expressed these views by way of a story, they are inevitably lengthy quotations:

A colleague I know who was guesting down in [name of city], the sergeant turned out to the van driver and was distinctly disrespectful to the prisoner, and assaulted them to get them in the van. And my colleague said, sorry, that's not right. The prisoner made a complaint, and whereas perhaps previously he would have said, I'm sorry, I was there, but I was dealing with something else, I didn't see it – so I don't think anyone would go to the stage these days of lying for a colleague – he turned round and said, yeah, I saw it; it was not on. (D4)

[The] thugs, they need to go. There were quite a few officers I knew, both in [name of other force] and here, who have, sort of, retired or been pushed. The view these days is very much more, we can't afford to have anyone like that working for the police. And again, the more accountable, the more transparent we are, the more those people stand out. (D6)

[T]hey have this thing at [name of training school], you're told, if you hear something that's not PC, you're supposed to stand there and challenge and you think that will never happen but it does. You go into the workplace and people do because they know they have a responsibility themselves to pick up on things like that … so it does happen … we are a different breed totally, definitely. (C8)

[H]e [member of the public] punched me in the face … we got him in the end, it was fine … but when we came back, we've got a new officer from [name of police force] who said oh, sorry about that mate … in [name of force] we would have given him a right shoeing for that. I said, we don't do that here, that doesn't happen. And he said, really? He said, oh, I had my body worn [body worn video] on, so I couldn't do anything. I said, no, mate, we don't do that. So totally different world. … But they're the type of police officers that give us a bad name. I don't think he would necessarily have done anything, but yeah, if that's how it is over there, no wonder they've got such a bad rep … I've never seen that, ever. Never. And I've done it for seven years in different roles. I have never seen anyone attack anyone. I've seen them put them on the floor for different things, but that's totally different. But I've never seen anyone attack anyone. (Z1)

[I]t might not be as fun because we can't like slap people's heads off a desk and you can't put stuff in their boot and then say they had it on them already and you can't shine a light in people's eyes and get answers out of them, but at the same time, you do a better job and people get … and if you do convict people then you've done it the right way and it's not fudged and it's not unlawful and … yeah, so I imagine it is not as fun as it was but it's more professional now. (X10)

The literature on policing cultures has pointed to a darker side of the characteristic of solidarity which is used not only to support colleagues and to keep them safe but also to protect them from the scrutiny of the law. The 'blue code of silence' has been seen to be an extension of the solidarity between officers (Chan 2003; Goldsmith 1990), with evidence to suggest that the protection of fellow officers from the consequences of illegal brutality or rule-bending is apparent (Westmarland 2005; Westmarland and Rowe 2016). Clearly, this is self-reported behaviours from a small cohort of police officers from one police force, but the indication from this research is that the benefits of the 'blue code of self-protection' are perhaps now outweighing the 'blue code of silence'.

The second difference that many of the new recruits referred to when distinguishing themselves from more longer-serving officers was in relation to their different style of policing, which they perceived to be more suitable to the changing nature of the role of policing. The contrast was drawn between 'old school' officers, with their focus on criminals and arrest rates, and the '#newbreed', whose background in the PCSO and Special Constable role appears to have inculcated a more communicative, more community-focused approach towards policing:

We say #newbreed because we are like a new breed of police officers, but I think we are changing the style of policing because of PCSOs. (X6)

[T]here is a place for strong police officers … but just not all the time. I just think if you're able to speak to people, it just makes the job easier … I've had a few situations and you think, didn't need to get the way that it did, and that was an older officer, they then brought force into that situation, whereas I felt if I had half an hour more, we could have explained the situation a bit better and dealt with it easier. (Z6)

I think the majority of people on shift are more non-old school, and there is almost like a takeover now of, I would suggest, harder working, more motivated officers becoming the majority as opposed to the people that are not … that mentality is creeping out and a new breed is coming in. (Z9)

When I first started, far, far too long ago as a PCSO, the culture in policing was, let's get out there, let's catch the criminals, let's turn them over, let's feel some collars; it was, sort of, quite the cliché – not, sort of, quite the 1980s style of, let's just lock someone up for the hell of it: certainly not – but the idea was, we get out there and we get in criminals' faces. (D4)

[W]e're a totally different breed ... they're still locked in policing when they joined because ... you learn everything, I think, within those first, sort of, four/five years and then I think once you're there that's who you are and that's how you deal with jobs. And it's the same for them but they, you know, they joined, probably some of them before I was even born, and they're still locked into the old-school policing where the social worker element doesn't matter and we're not expected to go and sort people's domestic situations out and everything else. So, you know, I don't necessarily think it's their fault but I think it's just the way; it was a very different policing world when they joined to what it is now. (D8)

[Y]ou're creating an environment where the new recruits are sort of taking on their views and opinions and how they think things should work ... and I guess once we've got so far along we'll stamp some of that out, but it's going to take another ten years probably, at least ... the way they deal with people, the way they look at jobs, they don't have that victim focus or witness thing about them, they just look for the offender and that's it. That to them is the most important thing, whereas we have to think of so many different things now, and public perception is massive. That's the key thing. ... Some of them are very like you see Gene Hunt [fictional, politically incorrect and corrupt TV cop from BBC series *Life on Mars*] from on the television. ... It can't continue ... the way that they were monitored and their standards of professional behaviour are actually different to the ones now, so you can't behave like that. ... They were doing what was okay in their heyday of policing, but now there's so many more boxes to tick, you just have to look at the wider picture much more, not be so offender focused. It was all about catching criminals, never mind about anything else, so long as I get a good job and a good result. (A8)

[T]he old-school police officers ... they've got a very different view on policing. They're still very, kind of, only want to deal with proper criminals and chasing drug dealers and that, you know, the hero hunters. (D8)

A lot of older officers miss the good old days and it's not that they feel the young people are responsible for moving them on. They just know that the way that we're being watched and monitored and accountable it's what's changed it and they miss them. (D10)

There was a widespread belief from the new recruits of this change in habitus as a direct response to both the changing field of policing and the changing nature and experience of the new recruits themselves. Police officers are active cultural agents in the creation and sustainability of their policing cultures. Police officers can then utilise this narrative of #new-breed to guide their action and then navigate the policing terrain.

## Cynicism

However, if we adhere to the notion of the "sedimentation", rather than the replacement, of the cultural characteristics of policing over time (Hendriks and van Hulst 2016), then we should expect to witness some continuity in some of these characteristics. As with solidarity, cynicism has been seen to be a consistent and fairly immutable object in the cultural lexicon of police officers. It is referred to as one of Reiner's key cultural characteristics (2010) and readily acknowledged by Van Maanen (1975), Crank (1998), Fielding (1988), Chan (2003) and Loftus (2008, 2009), amongst many others (see Chap. 6). It was also notably a feature of the discussions with this cohort of new officers—"Never met a more cynical bunch" (C4) and "[I]t is a very cynical profession" (D12) are just two examples.

As discussed in Chap. 8, by TIME D (four years of service), 100% of the police recruits agreed or strongly agreed with the statement that 'police officers are often sceptical and cynical within the context of their work'. More than a quarter of new recruits had disagreed with this statement at TIME A. This would therefore have inevitably included some officers with previous policing experience but at PCSO or Special Constable level. There were a large number of comments about this aspect of policing culture. However, the comments were broadly the same and followed two patterns. First, the officers would refer to the high levels of cynicism amongst themselves and their fellow officers. Second, the officers would then justify this cynicism by attributing it to outside forces which were beyond their control. The two 'causes' of their cynicism which were mentioned were both the responsibility of those outside of the policing organisation—first, the inaction of other parts of the criminal justice system and, second, the nature of the population that police officers are mostly engaging with. These are very typical responses:

We're the most cynical people ever … we just are, I think it's, particularly in the city, the type of people that we deal with all the time … it's mostly because these people that we're dealing with, our main offenders that come up and up and up, that are just leading ridiculous lives that we are constantly trying to fight against. … So you just become more and more, argh, and almost frustrated and cynical about absolutely everything. And I think it's our way of dealing with it in a jokey kind … why we have such a black humour about everything and being cynical goes hand in hand. It's just our way of coping with it. I think it's a coping mechanism more than anything. (D10)

I think it comes from working hard and trying to help victims and not getting the results that you know you should get, and that's because of other external factors. (Z7)

[I]t comes from getting let down by what comes next. You could go out, catch a burglar in the act now, and think that is the best job. I've caught someone breaking into someone's house, brilliant. That's what you joined for, to catch someone there with someone's property on them, brilliant. You come in and then you look at what's happened the next day, already they've been bailed and they're back out on the street. You're like, what is the point? (D6)

There is a cynical side of it because we attend an emergency and arrest somebody and come in the next day and find out they've been released with no further action or something and think, oh, I've just spent hours doing all that work to get a charge on that person and to protect that vulnerable person and they've released them. (D3)

Some of these issues will be discussed in more depth in Chap. 11 when the respondents discussed their views on the challenges to modern policing. However, for now, it is important to at least consider the impact of this cynicism on the cultural identity of police officers. Identity is formed, as was discussed in Chap. 3, through a process of self- or social categorisation. People are motivated towards self-categorisation with the group when they adhere to the values of the group and are given a voice in the group (Bradford et al. 2014). New members to a group will stress and accentuate those behaviours, attitudes and beliefs of theirs which are *perceived* to be fundamental to the essence of the group. Importantly, this includes highlighting the differences between themselves (as members of the in-group) and others (as members of all of the out-groups). The public and the rest of the criminal justice system form part of that out-group, and as such, their behaviours can be highlighted as a source of frustration and therefore cynicism in police officers. However, this negative attitude towards these out-groups can in fact be harnessed to enhance the self-image of the group. It is in this 'constitution of horizons' (Nietzsche 1874/1997) that boundaries can be created and solidarity increased.

## Sources of Changed Identities

Cynicism was not only mentioned as an aspect of policing cultures but also raised as a feature of the new recruits' changing identity as they developed as police officers. All respondents were asked at TIME D whether they felt being a police officer for four years had changed them. Tutors and SDROs were also asked this question regarding their student officers. With the exception of one officer mentioning a growth in confidence and one officer referring to an increase in patience, all of the other responses to this question (if answered directly) were expressed as negative changes. These related to feeling less happy, more stressed, less emotional and more suspicious:

> I'm more suspicious of people … I was a lot happier when I started … I think I'm more stressed, don't have the social life I used to have, don't see my friends and family as much as I used to, I used to always make time for it, whereas now I think I'm just tired and run down … everyone gets a bit desensitised and cynical but I guess it's because you hope that things are going to change and get better and they don't … you feel a bit vulnerable and unsafe. (D3)
>
> [M]y cynicism has come on leaps and bounds. (D5)
>
> I used to be quite an outgoing, sort of, bubbly person. I'm not saying I'm the worst person in the world but I'm certainly not great company … I don't think it's a good change but I, yeah, I definitely think I have changed. (D8)
>
> I'm less emotional about things. I've got a much harder shell about things and I can remove myself from situations and look at them much more independently. (D10)

I wouldn't say I've got horrible but I'd say, yeah, a lot of people have said it's changed me quite a lot. I think it's affected me out of work as well, as in … I don't know, I wouldn't say I'm not as nice as I used to be … I used to be quite sensitive. I'm definitely not like that anymore, I've definitely changed in that sense. It doesn't sound very good, does it, but I'm just being honest … I do get ill quite often. (D13)

[W]hinge more. (Z4)

I'm more cynical, probably less trusting. (Z7)

I think my attitude's changed … I think I am certainly, probably like most police officers, a little bit more suspicious than I would have been before. I don't believe everybody and everything that's said to me anymore whereas perhaps before I did. If somebody gave me a good story I'd probably think that they were telling me the truth, so I think I'm probably a lot more suspicious and maybe even cynical, I don't know … I'm certainly more patient with people and more calm than I was, perhaps. I can get to a situation and if somebody's shouting and swearing at me it doesn't really bother me anymore whereas as a member of the public you'd probably be devastated by that but I just, kind of, see it as part of the job so it doesn't really affect me so, yes, a bit more hardened, I suppose. (Z11)

Becoming a police officer is, in large part, learning to cope with the demands of the role. Notwithstanding the potential for cultural exaggeration and glorification, to which all occupations can be prone, the 'dirty work' of policing (Dick 2005) can be a challenging environment in which to work. Paoline describes the impact of this organisational and occupational policing environment as stress and anxiety (2003). What emerges from this is cynicism towards the public, other parts of the criminal justice system and the policing organisation, and a bond of solidarity between officers. Chan refers to this adaptive response as an "emotional hardening" (2007, p. 147), which is a characteristic clearly exhibited by these cohorts of new officers.

This seemingly more hardened interior of many of the new recruit displays itself to others however as an increase in confidence. When tutors and SDROs were asked how new recruits changed over the period of time that they were responsible for them, the most regularly stated answer was an increase in confidence. The language of the recruits who spoke of being less happy and more stressed does not necessarily equate with higher levels of confidence. However, a discussion of what new officers are exposed to and the mention of "they seem to have grown an old head on young shoulders" (S4) do perhaps provide a more complete picture of what this growth in confidence must entail. However, displaying confidence, whether inwardly felt or not, is also a coping mechanism, and new officers will undoubtedly soon learn that in order to cope both with the occupational and the organisational demands of the job, an appearance of confidence will be an important asset. In terms of the welfare of new officers and of strategies to minimise wastage through resignations, forces however should be mindful of these issues.

In addition to mentioning growing levels of confidence, tutors and SDROs also raised the issue of the growing cynicism and pessimism in the new recruits:

> You also see people being cynical that creeps in quite quickly. … It's the daily grind I suppose with everything you go to. If you go to the same thing day after day after day after day you're head banging against a brick wall half the time unfortunately, that does grind you. (T3)
> I think they're a little bit more pessimistic about the job, they tend to moan a little bit more, everything's like oh god I didn't realise it was going to be like this, I didn't realise it was going to be like that. (T5)
> They sometimes get more cynical quite quickly and frustrated. (S3)

As discussed earlier, this growing cynicism functions not only to cope with the frustrations as the recruits see them, of the nature of the job and the limits of their influence, but also to highlight their adherence to the values of the group, to the perceived behaviours and attitudes that are fundamental to its existence. The outward display of cynicism will announce to the group their commitment to its shared patterns of behaviour. Hacking's 'looping effect', as discussed in Chap. 3, highlights this change in behaviour in order to fit in with common perceptions of what it is to be a member of that group (2011). Indeed, 'fitting in' was a further factor that was raised by both tutors and SDROs as a feature of the changing nature of the new recruits:

[D]rastic change … how to fit into the shift. A shift mentality. I don't mean just a team whoever it is, it's really close knit in the police … you get some integrate faster and some don't. Some don't ever really make it into the team. They don't get accepted into the team so might not be the right sort of person for that team. Or the team might not be right for them. (S2)

[T]rying to please everybody and fit in with everybody else. (S3)

[Y]ou just get more engrained with the culture of policing. (S5)

I think their biggest fear is fitting in with the shift, feeling that they belong to part of the shift. (T4)

## Sources of Enjoyment

Whether 'fitting in' with the shift was a source of anxiety or fulfilled a sense of achievement, it was regularly cited by officers as an aspect of the job that they were most enjoying. All of the new recruits were asked at all stages of the research, with the exception of the first interview, which aspects of the job they were most enjoying. The three elements of the job that provided the most job satisfaction were the variety and diversity of the work they were involved with, the teamwork associated with their colleagues and the ability to help victims of crime. At TIME B (six months service) and TIME C (one year service), the overwhelming majority of the new recruits highlighted variety as a key source of their job satisfaction. However, by TIME D (four years service), no officer mentioned this factor as an element of the job they were enjoying. Conversely, the nature of attending similar incidents with the same, mostly non-crime related problems was highlighted as a source of considerable frustration (see Chap. 11).

This sense of frustration was partially relieved by the sense of teamwork that was apparent in the working relationships between officers. As discussed earlier in this chapter, one of the reasons cited for wanting to join the police service was for the teamwork element, where it was anticipated that the sense of camaraderie would be strong. This research has regularly highlighted the sense of disappointment between the expectations that the new recruits first held about the nature of policing and the subsequent reality of the job. On this aspect of policing, there was little disappointment. Teamwork was regularly cited as an enjoyable aspect of the job:

> [T]he bond you build with your team. (Y10)
>
> [W]orking with the team, that's always good. (B7)
>
> I work with a really good team. Everyone's really nice, really helpful, we have fun, we do the job, and I think it's that I really enjoy being out as part of a team. (C12)
>
> [The] working relationships I have with my team, it's quite good, you can come to work and we work very hard, but we also, sort of, like, pick each other up and have a good laugh, so that's quite good. (Y8)
>
> [Y]ou go back to the station and that's your little cocoon and you sit there and you do your stuff and then you get back in the car and off you go again. So it is like your little base, it's like your little home. I mean, I definitely wouldn't want to live there all the time. But ... it wouldn't be like that if it wasn't for the people that you worked with. (C10)

Research has shown that teamwork not only functions as an enjoyable aspect of the working environment but is also encouraged as an essential working practice by police trainers (Bahn 1984). Research from Obst and Davey (2003) found that the most enjoyable factors associated with police training were all associated with elements of being part of a team, which included camaraderie, bonding, the social life and teamwork being cited as the most important. When asked to rate the factors most likely to be associated with acceptance by fellow officers, new recruits rated being a team player in the top position, whilst being hard-working was down in the seventh position (Ellis 1991).

Working with victims of crime was a further area that was highlighted regularly by the new recruits as a source of satisfaction and enjoyment:

> [D]ealing with victims of crime where you really feel like you've done something positive ... I couldn't see myself doing anything else. (C8)
>
> [T]he biggest thing you get out of it is the job satisfaction; not getting any pat on the back ... it's making a difference in victims' lives even if you don't even get into court ... you've actually made a difference, and they've moved on from their lives. (Z4)

The good work is the people that are genuine, the genuine victims, I would class them as. (D6)

[Y]ou crave a job where there's a genuine victim and you're doing proper policing. (D8)

[G]enuine victims, we always say that it's really nice when you come across a genuine one, which is a bit bad to say really, isn't it? (Y1)

I think probably I like the nice jobs that you go to where you've got a genuine victim ... your genuine victims of crime who are burglary victims and they're mortified and they've ... this is going to sound a bit awful, but they've worked all their lives, they've worked really hard for everything they have and somebody's come in and taken it all from them. And that, dealing with them, really nice people who really want to just have their stuff back, their sentimental stuff, I find that really rewarding that you're actually doing your best for them to get a decent job ... the genuine victims of crime, I like dealing with those jobs. (B3)

[Y]ou want to get results for people ... that genuinely somebody's done something wrong to them and you want justice for them. (B8)

There was a girl when I was working in [name of city], she was getting knocked about left, right and centre by her partner, I mean, seriously, genuine victim, and you want to do everything you can, and those are the kind of people I joined the job to help. (D5)

With the categorisation of the 'genuine victim' must come the reverse of this ideal type, which is considered to be those who have no claim on being a victim, generally because they fluctuate between being offenders and victims. Being a victim of crime at the age of 12 is a very strong indicator of future offending behaviour at the age of 15 (McAra and McVie 2010). This 'victim–offender overlap' has been long acknowledged within the criminological literature (Bottoms and Costello 2010; Jennings et al. 2010), with these victims often being perceived to be 'second-class victims'. As we have been discussing in this chapter, one of the prominent features of policing cultures is the categorisation of people into groups, which generally feature as 'in-groups' and 'out-groups'. This concept of 'othering' has a long history in both sociology and criminology (Taylor et al. 1973; Young 1999; Garland 2001). It does have the potential to bond members of a group, the impact of which can be high levels of solidarity. However, where there are benefits to one group of 'othering', there are always likely to be negative connotations for the excluded. The categorisation that the police are invoking with regard to victims is of 'deserving' and 'undeserving' victims. The following two quotes illustrate the contrast in not only the attitudes towards but also the treatment of the 'undeserving victim':

> We always say with a burglary, for example, that it's not nice for the victim, if you get one where it's a genuine victim, that's a phrase that we hear a lot, a genuine victim, because although they're all victims, the victim might be a drug user or a common thief, and you think, well, I don't really want to give all my time to somebody that I know tomorrow will be committing these offences. Whereas a burglary, as bad as it is for them, it's nice to spend half a day there and a bit more time going through the report and actually giving a bit of time back to people that need it … I like going to burglaries and dealing with genuine victims of crime. (Z9)
>
> Yeah, I think working in the city, I haven't got as much time as maybe other areas, because some of the jobs that we go to we … not give our full attention, but, you know, play it down a little bit and not spend as long there as we possibly could or should … I think there's quite a view on crimes where both parties are, like, bad people, so a lot of drug related and stuff like that, where people are quite cynical … I think they're more inclined to give more attention to people who are genuinely victims of crime, where there's a bad offender, whereas, when it's, like, bad person on bad person, I think people get quite annoyed with that. (X4)

This will be discussed in more detail in Chap. 12 when this issue of categorisation is explored.

This chapter has considered the journey from *becoming* to *being* a police officer. In doing so, it has encountered a huge number of contradictions in the development of the new recruits. On the one hand, we are presented with a compassionate, communicative #newbreed of police officer whose motivation is driven by 'making a difference' and whose solidarity with colleagues does not extend to the dysfunctional. On the other hand, these same officers are sometimes lacking in confidence, feel unsupported by both the public and parts of the policing organisation, and feel a growing sense of cynicism and disillusionment in their approach to their work, which impacts upon their attitudes towards 'deserving' and 'undeserving' victims of crime. These contradictions will be discussed in more depth in Chap. 12. This chapter has also considered what the new recruits felt were the most enjoyable aspects of the job. Inevitably, alongside the enjoyable features of the job of a police officer come the sources of frustration. The following chapter will consider what all of the new recruits, the tutors and the SDROs felt were the major challenges currently facing policing. Just as with their sources of enjoyment, their sources of frustration encompass both the internal organisational aspects of policing and the associated external occupational hazards.

# References

Abell, S. (2017). In Praise of Cliché. *The Times Literary Supplement*. Retrieved from http://www.the-tls.co.uk/articles/public/cliche-terror-attacks/?CMP=Sprkr-_-Editorial-_-TheTLS-_-ArtsandCulture-_-Unspecified-_-Unspecified-_-Unspecified-_-ACCOUNT_TYPE

Alain, M., & Baril, C. (2005). Crime Prevention, Crime Repression, and Policing: Attitudes of Police Recruits Towards Their Role in Crime Control. *International Journal of Comparative and Applied Criminal Justice, 29*(2), 123–148.

Alain, M., & Grégoire, M. (2008). Can Ethics Survive the Shock of the Job? Quebec's Police Recruits Confront Reality. *Policing and Society, 18*(2), 169–189.

Atherton, S. (2012). Cops and Bloggers: Exploring the Presence of Police Culture on the Web. *Internet Journal of Criminology*. Retrieved from https://media.wix.com/ugd/b93dd4_e3fafc746b864462936d254a7c7251c9.pdf

Bahn, C. (1984). Police Socialization in the Eighties: Strains in the Forging of an Occupational Identity. *Journal of Police Science and Administration, 12*(4), 390–394.

Bottoms, A., & Costello, A. (2010). The Phenomenon of Victim-Offender Overlap: A Study of Offences Against Households. In A. Bottoms & J. V. Roberts (Eds.), *Hearing the Victim: Adversarial Justice, Crime Victims and the State* (pp. 104–139). Cullompton: Willan.

Bradford, B., Murphy, K., & Jackson, J. (2014). Officers as Mirrors: Policing, Procedural Justice and the (Re) Production of Social Identity. *British Journal of Criminology, 54*(4), 527–550.

Chan, J. (2003). *Fair Cop: Learning the Art of Policing.* Toronto: University of Toronto Press.

Chan, J. (2007). Police Stress and Occupational Culture. In M. O'Neill & A. Singh (Eds.), *Police Occupational Culture: New Debates and Directions* (pp. 129–151). Oxford: Elsevier JAI.

Cochran, J., & Bromley, M. (2003). The Myth (?) of the Police Sub-culture. *Policing: An International Journal of Police Strategies and Management, 26*(1), 88–117.

College of Policing. (n.d.). *Police Recruitment.* Retrieved from http://recruit. college.police.uk/Pages/home.aspx

Crank, J. (1998). *Understanding Police Culture.* Cincinnati: Anderson Publishing Co.

De Lint, W. (1998). New Managerialism and Canadian Police Training Reform. *Social and Legal Studies, 7*(2), 261–285.

Dick, P. (2005). Dirty Work Designations: How Police Officers Account for Their Use of Coercive Force. *Human Relations, 58*(11), 1363–1390.

Ellis, R. (1991). Perceptions, Attitudes and Beliefs of Police Recruits. *Canadian Police College Journal, 15*(2), 95–117.

Fielding, N. (1988). *Joining Forces: Police Training, Socialization, and Occupational Competence.* London: Routledge.

Foley, P., Guarneri, C., & Kelly, M. (2008). Reasons for Choosing a Police Career: Changes over Two Decades. *International Journal of Police Science and Management, 10*(1), 2–8.

Garland, D. (2001). *The Culture of Control.* Oxford: Oxford University Press.

Garner, R. (2005). Police Attitudes: The Impact of Experience After Training. *Applied Psychology in Criminal Justice, 1*(1), 56–70.

Goldsmith, A. (1990). Taking Police Culture Seriously: Police Discretion and the Limits of Law. *Policing and Society, 1*(2), 91–114.

Hacking, I. (2011). Between Michel Foucault and Erving Goffman: Between Discourse in the Abstract and Face-to-Face Interaction. *Economy and Society, 33*(3), 277–302.

Hendriks, F., & van Hulst, M. (2016). Shifting Repertoires: Understanding Cultural Plurality in Policing. *Innovation: The European Journal of Social Science Research, 29*(2), 161–176.

HM Treasury. (2010). *Spending Review 2010* (Cm 7942) [Electronic Version]. London: HMSO.

Hopper, M. (1977). Becoming a Policeman: Socialization of Cadets in a Police Academy. *Urban Life, 6*(2), 149–170.

Jennings, W., Higgins, G., Tewksbury, R., Gover, A., & Piquero, A. (2010). A Longitudinal Assessment of the Victim-Offender Overlap. *Journal of Interpersonal Violence, 25*(12), 2147–2174.

Loftus, B. (2008). Dominant Culture Interrupted: Recognition, Resentment and the Politics of Change in an English Police Force. *British Journal of Criminology, 48*(6), 756–777.

Loftus, B. (2009). *Police Culture in a Changing World.* Oxford: Oxford University Press.

Loftus, B. (2010). Police Occupational Culture: Classic Themes, Altered Times. *Policing and Society, 20*(1), 1–20.

McAra, L., & McVie, S. (2010). Youth Crime and Justice: Key Messages from the Edinburgh Study of Youth Transitions and Crime. *Criminology and Criminal Justice, 10*(2), 179–209.

Millie, A. (2013). The Policing Task and the Expansion (and Contraction) of British Policing. *Criminology and Criminal Justice, 13*(2), 143–160.

Muir, W. (1977). *Police: Streetcorner Politicians.* Chicago: University of Chicago Press.

Nietzsche, F. (1997). *Untimely Meditations.* In D. Breazeale (Ed.), *Cambridge Texts in the History of Philosophy.* Cambridge: Cambridge University Press. (Original work published 1874).

Obst, P., & Davey, J. (2003). Does the Police Academy Change Your Life? A Longitudinal Study of Changes in Socialising Behaviour of Police Recruits. *International Journal of Police Science and Management, 5*(1), 31–40.

Paoline, E. (2003). Taking Stock: Toward a Richer Understanding of Police Culture. *Journal of Criminal Justice, 31*(3), 199–214.

Paoline, E., & Terrill, W. (2014). *Police Culture: Adapting to the Strains of the Job.* Durham: Carolina Academic Press.

Reiner, R. (1978). *The Blue-Coated Worker.* Cambridge: Cambridge University Press.

Reiner, R. (2000). *The Politics of the Police* (3rd ed.). Oxford: Oxford University Press.

Reiner, R. (2010). *The Politics of the Police* (4th ed.). Oxford: Oxford University Press.

Scripture, A. (1997). The Sources of Police Culture: Demographic or Environmental Variables? *Policing and Society, 7*(3), 163–176.

Skolnick, J. (1966). *Justice Without Trial: Law Enforcement in Democratic Society.* New York: Wiley and Sons.

Skolnick, J. (2008). Enduring Issues of Police Culture and Demographics. *Policing and Society, 18*(1), 35–45.

Sollund, R. (2008). Tough Cop-Soft Cop? The Impact of Motivations and Experiences on Police Officers' Approaches to the Public. *Journal of Scandinavian Studies in Criminology and Crime Prevention, 9*(2), 119–140.

Steyn, J., & Mkhize, S. (2016). 'Darker Shades of Blue': A Comparison of Three Decades of South African Police Service Culture. *SA Crime Quarterly, 57,* 15–26.

Tajfel, H. (1981). *Human Groups and Social Categories.* Cambridge: Cambridge University Press.

Taylor, I., Walton, P., & Young, J. (1973). *The New Criminology.* London: Routledge and Kegan Paul.

Tuohy, A., Wrenall, M., McQueen, R., & Stradling, S. (1993). Effect of Socialization Factors on Decisions to Prosecute: The Organizational Adaptation of Scottish Police Recruits. *Law and Human Behaviour, 17*(2), 167–181.

Van Maanen, J. (1973). Observations on the Making of Policemen. *Human Organization, 32*(4), 407–418.

Van Maanen, J. (1975). Police Socialization: A Longitudinal Examination of Job Attitudes in an Urban Police Department. *Administrative Science Quarterly, 20*(2), 207–228.

Van Maanen, J. (1976). Breaking In: Socialization to Work. In R. Dubin (Ed.), *Handbook of Work, Organization and Society* (pp. 67–130). Chicago: Rand McNally College Publishing Company.

Van Maanen, J. (1978a). People Processing: Strategies of Organizational Socialization. Organizational *Dynamics, Summer,* 19–36.

Westera, N., Kebbell, M., Milne, R., & Green, T. (2013). Defining the "Effective Detective". ARC Centre of Excellence in Policing and Security Briefing, 20.

Westmarland, L. (2005). Police Ethics and Integrity: Breaking the Blue Code of Silence. *Policing and Society, 15*(2), 145–165.

Westmarland, L., & Rowe, M. (2016). Police Ethics and Integrity: Can a New Code Overturn the Blue Code? *Policing and Society.* http://dx.doi.org/10.10 80/10439463.2016.1262365

Willis, J., & Mastrofski, S. (2016). Improving Policing by Integrating Craft and Science: What Can Patrol Officers Teach Us About Good Police Work? *Policing and Society.* Advance publication. Retrieved from http://dx.doi.org/ 10.1080/10439463.2015.1135921

Winsor, T. (2012). *Independent Review of Police Officer and Staff Renumeration and Conditions, Final Report* (Vol. 1). London: The Stationery Office.

Young, J. (1999). *The Exclusive Society.* London: Sage.

# 11

# Qualitative Findings III: Contemporary Policing Challenges

The research data upon which this book is based holds one further area of interest which this chapter seeks to interrogate. One of the areas of questioning in all of the interviews with new police officers was concerned with what they perceived to be the major challenges facing modern policing. It was also a question asked of the other participants in the research project, who acted as tutors or SDROs. These questions were asked in interviews taking place during a time of political, economic and social change. The results of this analysis will therefore seek to achieve two things. First, it will provide a valuable insight into the views of current serving officers (with varying years of experience) as to what they feel are the challenges facing police officers in a rapidly changing policing environment. Second, it will also provide some insight into the changing nature of the priorities of new police officers as they become slowly more integrated within the policing cultures. Their views on the challenges which face police officers are changed not only by their level of experience as officers and by the changing circumstances in which they are policing, but also by their changing attitudes to the role and purpose of the police, which fundamentally alter as they become more culturally embedded within the organisation.

© The Author(s) 2017
S. Charman, *Police Socialisation, Identity and Culture*,
DOI 10.1007/978-3-319-63070-0_11

The question posed to all new recruits at each of the four interview stages and all of the tutors and SDROs was as follows: What they felt were the major challenges facing modern policing? However, this was a different type of question from the rest of the interview, which had, for the new recruits at least, predominantly focused upon them as an individual and on their responses and reactions to their new role within the policing organisation. For some, this was a welcome distraction from the more intimate questions about their own attitudes and beliefs, and enabled them to hold court about the problems as they saw them. Whilst this might be a regular topic of conversation within casual encounters with colleagues, it is a rarer occurrence for new recruits to be asked their opinion on these matters. For others however, more notably in the early interviews, there was more reticence. As shall shortly be seen, the focus of the policing challenges was predominantly placed outside of the organisation itself and at the door of others. As time moved on and as new recruits spent more time working within the policing organisation, the focus of where they saw the major challenges of policing began to subtly shift from outside of the organisation to much more upon the internal workings within the organisation. They also spent much more time expressing their views on this particular question. That is not to say in any way, as shall be seen in this chapter, that the new recruits saw the major challenges to policing as being internal to the organisation, far from it. What it does mean though is that the new recruits, as time went on, were far more prepared to acknowledge that there were challenges within the service, of which they were a part, that needed addressing. This could be accounted for in four ways. First, the new recruits had become more comfortable in expressing their views about the service they were employed by, whether those views were positive or negative. Second, the new recruits, as time went on, were in a better and more informed position to be able to witness for themselves how the organisation might be in a challenging position. Third, there also exists the possibility that the strong organisational cultures of the policing world and the influence of more long-serving colleagues began to make their impact on the new recruits. Fourth, that as the new recruits became more established within the police service, the ambitions they held at the start of their service about public and community service began to diminish in the face of the daily pressures of the job and the daily obstacles in achieving their narrowing aims.

These issues will be analysed in more depth throughout this chapter. It is necessary now to consider in more detail the contemporary policing challenges the new recruits and the tutors and SDROs referred to in the course of the interviews. Interviewees were not given a list of issues to choose from or prompts to assist them. Instead, they were asked for their general views on the challenges to modern policing. The range of issues raised was therefore vast, and the chapter will inevitably focus upon the views that were most commonly expressed by the interviewees. The answers were categorised and the relative frequency of each was assessed. However, despite the array of views and opinions expressed, the issues raised can be broadly considered as belonging to four categories. These are not discrete areas and there is overlap between any of them. Inevitably, the first issue that will be discussed, policing budgets, will have an impact on all of the other three areas. Each feed into one another, but together they provide an emerging picture of what new police officers and a small selection of other officers believe to be the major challenges facing modern policing. The remainder of this chapter will be devoted to a consideration of each of those four areas: financial issues, the public and the media, 'non-policing' issues and, finally, internal and management issues.

# Financial Issues

The challenge to policing that was raised with most frequency at each of the four interview stages with new police recruits was unsurprisingly (given the austerity measures that were being directed towards all public services during the course of these interviews) that of policing budgets. It was independently highlighted by the majority of respondents at each interview stage. Relatedly, the issue of police numbers was the second most mentioned issue by new recruits. It was felt that the reduction in the number of police officers was a challenge to policing. This issue became more prominent throughout the different interview stages. At TIME A, when recruits had only been serving for a matter of weeks, the issue of police numbers came fourth in a list of most frequently mentioned issues.

At TIME B and TIME C, it had moved to the second most mentioned issue, and by TIME D, it was jointly first with policing budgets. It is important to explain the context of this issue of police funding during this period of time.

Most of the funding for each police force in England and Wales is obtained from a central government grant, with the additional monies raised from council tax. Nationally, this council tax revenue makes up almost a quarter of police expenditure, although this varies from force to force (Johnston and Politowski 2016). After a sustained period of investment, the police service in England, Wales and Northern Ireland had seen budgetary cuts of 22% in real terms between 2010 and 2016. This amounted to a £2.2 billion budget reduction (National Audit Office 2015). In terms of workforce reductions, this amounted to a loss of 37,400 staff from March 2010 to March 2015. This was accounted for by a 12% reduction in police officers and a 20% reduction in police staff (Johnston and Politowski 2016). There were widely predicted estimates of 20–25% further cuts expected at the 2015 Autumn Statement and Spending Review from the then Chancellor of the. Exchequer, George Osborne. However, following the coordinated terrorist attacks in Paris in November 2015 resulting in 137 deaths, the Chancellor announced that there would be real-terms protection for police funding and no further cuts (Osborne 2015). Since that announcement however, this claim has been criticised by the Statistics Authority, which has conversely identified a *decrease* in central government grants amounting to £160 million of cuts in 2015–2016 and 2016–2017 (Dilnot 2016). Shortly after the final interviews were completed, the HMIC published one of its annual effectiveness, efficiency and legitimacy reports which highlighted a "deep-red warning flag" over various aspects of policing, including investigation and neighbourhood policing (HMIC 2017a, p. 4). There was concern from the HMIC over decisions being taken, such as not arresting people, that were

> the unintended consequence of changes that forces have made, often in response to the challenge of austerity. (HMIC 2017a, p. 5)

Controversially, the Policing Minister Brandon Lewis denied that the funding cuts were a contributing factor and instead argued that "forces still clearly have more work to do … I expect to see rapid improvements" (Lewis 2017). Overall therefore, the picture of police funding for the new recruits in their first years in the police service had been one of almost continuous cost-saving exercises. According to the new recruits, this impacted upon their ability to do their job in a number of ways.

Respondents referred to the impact of budgetary cuts as "dangerous" (Z9) and "fighting a losing battle" (D3), which was a sentiment widely shared, "[W]e can't afford to do anything where it's getting to almost a ridiculous state" (C5). One recruit with four years within the service suggested that "I think the police service is probably going to hit rock bottom before something really has to get sorted out, and I think it will hit rock bottom" (Z7). This was perceived to have an impact on the recruits' decision-making and an impact on victims.

Officers showed an awareness that victim satisfaction was an important issue for them as a service in a number of ways. Not only did this mean that an incident that they attended might not be reoccurring in the future, adding to existing workloads, but also that a victim with a positive experience of the police response to the incident would be more likely to assist the police then and in the future. The frustration of the police recruits was felt in appreciating victim dissatisfaction, with the lack of police action in some cases, but an inability to counteract this. This also relates to the discussion in Chap. 10 about who was and was not considered to be a 'genuine' victim. It was regularly voiced that less time with those who were considered to be not 'genuine' victims would inevitably mean that the police could engage with what they considered to be 'real police work' with 'real victims'. The following quotes illustrate much of this frustration:

[I]t can be quite frustrating that you turn up to, say, criminal damage, where someone's had something stolen from their car, and you just take a statement, forensics won't come out, and there's no CCTV, no witnesses, and that's basically the end of the job. Here's your crime reference number. Filed. (C1)

I think we've massively lost … this is our bread and butter policing, where we get all our intelligence from. Now, we're not proactive at all, we are just responders. That's wrong. So, we've lost that element of it. I was NPT

[Neighbourhood Patrol Team] for a year and I really loved it, because you could get right in the heart of things. But now you can't because of the budget cuts. (Z1)

I think the amount of time that the victim gets is going to be less ... it's going to be like a domino effect. Victim less happy. More crime is going to happen probably as a result, and not doing enough intel stuff behind the scenes about who's doing what. Be difficult the next few years I think. (Y9)

A potential rise in crime was a key message to come from Police Federation campaigns which aimed to raise public awareness of the police funding cuts and the "dire outcome" (2015) if these issues were not addressed. Whilst the then Prime Minister David Cameron applauded the apparent drop in official crime figures in the years following the first of the funding cuts, the subsequent addition of fraud and cyber-enabled crime to the Crime Survey for England and Wales has reversed this apparent decline (Office for National Statistics 2017).

The new recruits also commented on the apparent lack of both expertise and equipment in dealing with the challenges of modern policing. In terms of expertise, this was most keenly felt in the area of cyber-enabled crime, which, as the research went on, became a more regularly mentioned feature of their concerns:

[W]e're not particularly great with IT and we're not particularly great at cybercrime. (Z11)

The likes of 10 or 15 years ago when I was growing up I remember it was the theft of car stereos, and now you've got, you know, theft of mobile phones, harassment via the internet, there's so many internet-based or technological-based crimes. (W10)

New recruits also spoke regularly about what they felt was inadequate equipment to perform their jobs. Whilst the addition of a personal mobile phone for each officer was welcomed, the perceived poor quality of the phone and the regular interruptions to tasks in order to address the inadequacy of the equipment were a source of frustration. This encompassed many aspects of their equipment, including uniform, phones, personal protective equipment (PPE), computers, cars and even buildings. One officer spoke at length about a potentially fatal incident with a suspect carrying a knife for which he felt inadequately protected against. Some examples of this frustration can be seen here: "Our kit is crap now, our cars are getting worse, our buildings are going" (C6) and from another, "Today we should be out in a vehicle that we don't have" (X3). However, many of the respondents who raised the issue of inadequate equipment due to budgetary cuts also went on to illustrate how this was impacting their decision-making. One officer referred to more senior staff working out the petrol costs of response officers and Criminal Investigation Department (CID), both independently attending a rural burglary, in order to save money. Decisions were also carefully made about whether to arrest or not arrest a suspect:

> You have to be sure you want to arrest someone because there's no custody and it will take at least one officer out of the area. We've got a custody centre just here which is closed because we can't staff it. We try instead to get someone to come in for voluntary arrest ... for example, today we've only got the acting sergeant as area car driver – he's the only area car driver in. (X4)

> At first they wanted us to arrest people. Then it's more they wanted us not to arrest people because investigations were overrun. (D9)

The lack of equipment was noted by a large number, although not a majority, of respondents. However, what was raised as an issue by a majority of respondents to the question of the challenges to modern policing in relation to budgetary constraints was that of police numbers, "a serious lack of numbers" (Y7). Whether or not we subscribe to the notion of police officers as culturally wedded to an imagined past where there were sufficient officers for one on every street corner is irrelevant. Police officers will often engage in stories of a more optimistic past. However, when the new recruits were discussing the difficulties of operating within the current constraints of police numbers, they were utilising both the cultural historiographies of the past and the realities of the present. These new recruits were appointed to the police service when numbers were already declining, although some may have been part of the service as PCSOs and Special Constables. Therefore, their placing of the issue of low police numbers so highly in the list of challenges to modern policing reflects both the difficulties they may face with the current police numbers and the cultural absorption of the stories from more longer-serving officers of the problems they face. This cultural absorption of stories fits well with the research on group emotions which suggests that group members can have strong feelings about an issue they have not been involved with, as feelings are determined by group, rather than personal, histories (Reicher et al. 2010).

A number of officers revealed the potential of this argument by saying, "Someone said we were doing the job of three police officers. I think we are" (Z1), "They've seen it where they had a team of twelve … there's now four of us" (C6) and "They'll have five people to cover a huge area that used to have ten" (A11). This final quote came from an officer with less than a month's experience as a police officer and no time spent within a station in this role. New police recruits may not have appreciated that lower police numbers were the problem behind their inability to perform, but instead might have attributed it to other issues such as rising public dissent or poor policing management. However, they considered neither of these and placed the problem firmly at the door of falling police numbers. This would appear to suggest the influence of police storytelling on the new recruits' narrative of the policing function. Familiar stories were told by the new police recruits of how many officers were on duty on a weekend night in a busy town centre and the detrimental effect that this would have on public confidence if the public knew the actual numbers. These stories were produced with such regularity that it must reflect the preoccupation with this issue amongst the recruits' peers. Here are just a few examples of this much-repeated story:

> [T]he other night we had six officers for [name of city centre] and they all committed within an hour of their shift. It's just really dangerous at the moment. (Z9)

> There's not enough of us. … If people knew how little police officers are policing the cities, let alone the rural beats, unbelievable. It's quite scary to be honest. … There's four of us on tonight covering the whole of [name of city centre]. (C6)

I've sat in [name of station], one of the busiest nicks, and we would brief on a Friday night which was our busiest night, with a sergeant and three police officers, if the public knew that. (A6)

Budget cuts therefore dominated the discussions about what were the challenges of modern policing. This was considered to be something that was imposed from outside the organisation and was a threat to its future.

## The Public and the Media

Learning to be a police officer is as much, if not more, about learning to communicate and interact with the public as it is about understanding police law and procedure. Police officers spend more time with members of the public in the early days of their policing careers than at most other times in their policing careers. It is unsurprising therefore that the public should feature highly in the new recruits' analysis of the challenges to modern policing. The second most regularly mentioned challenge was the public. This was more strongly felt at TIME B and TIME D when the vast majority of respondents were working as response officers. This was also the case for tutors, who worked alongside the new recruits, but not for SDROs, whose more internally focused role resulted in no mention at all of the public.

However, although the public were mentioned with regularity by the respondents, it was not an issue that was expanded upon at length. It was an 'item' on the list of the problems that police officers had to face, but with limited elaboration. The new recruits spoke of the lack of support and respect from the public and the unrealistic expectations the public held. This relates to the 'reality shock' of becoming a police officer, which was discussed in Chap. 6. Previous research found evidence of feelings of increasing alienation from the public (Ellis 1991; Chan 2003; Alain and Baril 2005; Alain and Grégoire 2008). The following quotes illustrate some of these perceptions of the attitudes of the public towards the recruits as police officers: "It's a battle against the public to gain their support and confidence" (D3), "Whatever you do is wrong" (D6), "They just have such a negative outlook on the police" (B10) and "The police are the enemy" (W8).

The majority of new recruits used the same phrase, 'public perceptions' to identify what they considered to be a challenge to modern policing. In a similar vein to the previous discussion about police numbers, it is clearly a well-used phrase, but often without much context provided. An 'unsupportive public' fits well with the cultural narrative of the 'us versus them' account of the police and the public, and has the potential therefore to contribute towards the solidarity of the members of the 'us' against the 'them':

> I do think that the general public are innocent until proven guilty and police officers are guilty until proven innocent. (D9)

> I do kind of feel like the police get the blame for almost everything when it's out of control. (Z7)

As discussed in Chap. 3, differentiating between one group and another (in this case the police and the public), can serve to sustain the group image but also to enhance the individual self-image of the group member. As Tajfel has stated, "We are what we are because *they* are not what we are" (1981, p. 323, original emphasis). However, the views of the new recruits are also influenced by the nature of the work they are involved in. As discussed in Chap. 3, police officers are involved in 'dirty work', which entails regular contact with events and people who are viewed to be undesirable (Dick 2005). As Ashforth and Kreiner (1999) and Dick (2005) also found in their research, rather than face the inherent threat to the occupational identity of 'dirty work', this threat is reversed and the instead attributed to the public. It is the public and their perceived views of the police that becomes the threat. There was surprise expressed by the respondents when research which highlights trust in professions and shows the police as sixth out of a list of 24 professions was mentioned during interviews (Ipsos MORI 2016). This contradicts the accepted cultural narrative of the public's view of the police. When respondents spoke of 'the public' in this way, there was clearly considerable overlap with the media reporting of the police, which, in many interviews, was coupled into the same conversation. The media therefore also require some discussion.

During the four-year research phase of this study, the second coroner's enquiry into the deaths of 96 Liverpool Football Club supporters at Hillsborough in 1989 was held and concluded that the fans were unlawfully killed and played no role in causing the disaster. Match commander Chief Superintendent David Duckenfield was found responsible for manslaughter by gross negligence (Conn 2016). We also witnessed ongoing revelations concerning the 'Plebgate' incident outside Downing Street in 2012, which resulted in claim and counterclaim about what Conservative MP Andrew Mitchell said to a police officer in an altercation at the gates. Subsequently, a Metropolitan Police Service officer was jailed for misconduct over the affair (Halliday 2014). Alongside these events, there were numerous enquiries launched into allegations of historic sex abuse, the report of the Leveson enquiry into press standards that also called into question the relationship between the press and the police (Leveson 2012), the jailing of four police officers over selling information to newspapers (Haria and Turvill 2015) and a major enquiry launched into the controversial activities of undercover police officers (May 2015).

It is undoubtedly in relation to these and other, more local events that many of the respondents articulated their frustration at the supposed negative attitudes from the media towards the police:

[T]hey never show good things in the media to say, look, what this police officer's done. (W5)

It's always easy to pinpoint the police … I suppose they're almost an easy target for the media when things go wrong … so you don't see as many stories in the paper saying, 'This officer's done a great job here'. (W7)

[T]he media is quite detrimental to what the police do. (W9)

[Y]ou might have two or three hundred good stories, but one bad story, and of course it's the bad story that brings the numbers in for the police. (W11)

There was particular frustration from the tutors and SDROs that the events from many years before they joined the service, and in some cases before they were born, had been the focus of more recent criticism of the police:

> I've started seeing in the news about Hillsborough and that's years ago. What the hell has that got to do with me? (T3)

> [W]e go to a job where it's all over the news like Plebgate or Hillsborough at the moment. It's topical, it's corruption, you know, senior police officers are corrupt or it's in the news that a police officer has been arrested for something, and it's not just a police officer from X police, it's a police officer, full stop. So, we're all the same so we all get kind of labelled on the same thing. And it does make our lives difficult. (T4)

> [W]e're being a scapegoat for various different issues, things like the Hillsborough issue, lots of miscarriages of justice in the past that are suddenly our fault, and the majority of the police at the moment were not even in the job when that initially happened. (S5)

> [A] lot of people are influenced by what they read. I'm not saying that's wrong or anything like that, but there seems to be a lot of stuff that's been brought up in the media that's happened a very long time ago ... the reputation of the police has been dragged through the mud quite a lot. (T7)

However, it should be noted that the concerns from new recruits about the media portrayal of their organisation were superseded by other concerns as the research went on. As the relative importance of the media to the respondents fell in terms of challenges to the police, so concerns about the challenges emanating from the internal workings of the organisation became more apparent.

The public and the media have been dealt with together in this section because, in conversation with the new recruits, the recruits either often moved seamlessly between discussing the media and the public, with little differentiation between them, or deliberately placed the public and the media together into one *overall* threat to the police. The attitude of both the public and the media towards the police was seen to be negative. The heightened scrutiny by both, whether it came from the increasing number of camera phones filming incidents or negative press reporting from the media, was unwelcomed and considered to be unwarranted. Conversely, as we saw in Chap. 10, the new recruits had a quite different attitude towards the public they themselves were policing. What we can see here is a case of *differentiated publics*. When 'the public' referred to the mass anonymous British population, reading and being influenced by the media, the perception appeared to be of negativity from them and towards them. However, when the new recruits were referring to *their* public, the local people they policed, most particularly as victims, their attitude was much more positive. The public service ethos of joining the force, the desire to 'help' which so many expressed during their early interviews was still very apparent throughout the interview stages.

## Non-policing Issues

A particular concern of the majority of the new recruits was the amount of already limited resources that were being taken up by incidents that were not felt to be policing matters. This particularly revolved around issues the police felt should be dealt with by other agencies, most notably social services. After budget cuts and the relationship between the police, the public and the media, this was the third most mentioned challenge to modern policing. It was less of a concern during the first interview, when the new recruits were yet to have experienced policing the streets and were still in training. However, as time went on and officers became more experienced and spent more time dealing with the public, these issues became more apparent to them. There were two particular areas of concern from the respondents: missing people and mental illness.

The issue of missing people, particularly teenagers, was raised regularly during the final interview as something that took up large amounts of police time. Officers were aware of the concerns of sexual exploitation that are attached to missing persons and understood the necessity of their actions. However, they also expressed frustration at a system which required the statutory reporting of missing older teenagers, particularly from residential care and often only when late returning back, where there was no evidence of any concerns. The time that was spent dealing with these incidents, at the expense of other work, was regularly highlighted by the new recruits as a challenge to modern policing:

> I very rarely deal with crime, if I'm honest, it's a lot of missing people as well, running around chasing after 11- to 16-year-old girls and boys that don't want to be at home, and their parents have to report them missing at a certain time otherwise it looks bad for them for Social Services so they have to call the police and we have to look for them all night and they didn't want to go home even when we find them. And we have the same people every night usually. (D3)

> I find myself doing a lot of stuff that I wasn't expecting to be doing, like permanently looking for missing teenagers that just can't be bothered to phone home. That's just permanent, I mean, like you wouldn't believe. ... The 17-year-old lad that's already got two kids, and you're thinking, are they really a subject of CSE [Child Sexual Exploitation], but they've gone missing because they've just had enough for an hour or two. (D5)

> We deal with constant missing people who are, I'll be careful how I word it, not always missing. They're reported to us because they're told to report them to us. We go and see a lot of parents who couldn't care less but they report it to us because social services tell them to, and they do it for that reason. We go to a lot of places where people live in supported living, adults who have got lives. Just because they haven't turned up at 11 p m they're reported missing, and we have to keep them as missing until we find them. (D6)

> Well, yesterday I had three MISPERs [missing person] and none of them were real missing people. Two of them I found at the first address that the person reporting them as missing thought they'd be at but weren't able to go to them and get them, and one of them was just to take details of a MISPER but didn't find them, and when you've got a medium or high risk, that's your shift wiped out, more so with the high risk. My colleague today, he hasn't even left the station because the high-risk one he's working on is taking him all day and he's got nothing else that he can do out and about, it's all phone work and Facebook stuff. (Z9)

We're all tied up with high-risk, or medium-risk, missing people who are only missing because they're 16, that's it. They're literally a delinquent 16-year-old who are out at mates every night and the home they're in have to phone them in as missing every night at 11, so we have to then go and take a report, which takes two or three hours, for somebody who's literally just dossing around a mate's house who we don't know, and that happens every single night. (Z3)

Research published by the National Crime Agency would support the view from the new recruits that this type of police work involves considerable time. Data received from 42 English and Welsh police forces indicated that there were 375,694 people reported as missing or absent in 2015–2016, a 23% increase since 2012–2013 (NCA 2017). Although there are variations across the country, this equates to 917 missing or absent people per day per force. There are disproportionately high numbers of 12–17 year olds who are reported as missing or absent, and this age group is not permitted to be graded as low risk, which does not require immediate action. About 59% of the incidents of missing or absent children are repeat cases (NCA 2017).

Much of the early work on policing cultures emanating from the US and the UK, which was analysed in Chap. 6, was actually intended to be more concerned with a sociological analysis of the police officer and police work. What this research revealed was that officers were involved in a multitude of activities, often not related to crime (Banton 1964; Westley 1970). As discussed in Chap. 10, that continues to be the enduring reality of being effectively the only 24-hour multipurpose, emergency, order maintenance service. It is also a source of considerable frustration:

I think what the police force need to do is grow a little bit of a backbone, and actually come out and say, okay, members of the public, what do you think we do? And when the public say, we think you catch criminals, and prevent crime, and stuff like that, we should then say, okay, do you expect your police to be dealing with your mental health people? Do you think your police should be going to neighbour disputes? Do you think the police should be going to deal with fights at schools, and stuff like that? (T2)

[E]veryone expects the police to be all services in one. (X7)

Research from the College of Policing (2015) indicates that non-crime-related incidents account for 83% of all 'command and control' calls that come into police call centres. Additionally, based upon data received from a small number of forces, it is suggested that 'public safety and welfare' incidents now make up the largest category of reported incidents to the police, more than both crime and antisocial behaviour.

However, it was the issue of mental illness that was raised with the most regularity and throughout the four-year research process, referred to by one respondent as a "massive issue" (X11). Estimates from the Independent Commission on Mental Health in Policing suggested that 20% of police time is accounted for by mental illness issues, rising to 40% if the definition is widened to vulnerable people more generally (2013). In his annual review of policing, the HMIC Chief Inspector Tom Winsor referred to the police service being used as the "first resort" for people with mental health problems (HMIC 2017b, p. 8).

The police officers who spoke about this issue were not making reference to offenders or suspects with mental illness but to non-offenders and non-suspects. The problem was perceived to have exacerbated since the financial cuts to other parts of the public sector, most notably social care. Numerous stories were relayed in depth by the respondents about the number of occasions they had been required to provide a service to a member of the public that they felt was not part of their role as a police officer, and perhaps more of concern to them was the fact that it was not a role they felt equipped to deal with. Much of the frustration that was expressed by the respondents was not necessarily that there was a reluctance to get involved (as there was a strong sense from the new recruits that they felt a duty of care towards members of the public), but that there was a sense of fear at being tasked to be involved with an incident that they felt completely ill-equipped to deal with. This fear (as discussed in Chap. 10) revolved around the dual issues of inadequate expertise and 'doing the wrong thing'. Training in mental illness is necessarily limited, as police officers are not medical professionals and, with these respondents, only took place after 12 months in the job. The following quotes from the new recruits are lengthy, but each tells a story that was replicated throughout the sample:

I had a call, there was a guy with severe mental health issues. ... Quick phone call to the crisis team the mental health people that's in the city, 'Oh we've seen him twice this week so we're not seeing him' ... and I actually said to the girl on the phone, 'So what do you want me to do', 'Oh just let him go' and 'Can you talk to him?' I'm like 'Right, yeah, for all the years of mental health training that I've had' ... oh hang on, no I haven't. 'Or maybe give it to a psychiatric nurse or psychiatrist, maybe this is your remit'? 'Oh no, no it's not because he's not in distress'. (B5)

We spent five hours of a shift the other night, with someone with mental health problems, trying to commit suicide. We left them in the care of the hospital, 20 minutes later they let them walk out. And he was suicidal, he said, 'I'm going to kill myself'. So, we left him in the care of the doctors and security ... the hospital detained him under the Mental Capacity Act, so it was their patient. He walked out, rang his partner and said he was going to jump off a bridge ... and then it's back to us ... took him back again, then the hospital said, 'Oh no, we're happy, he's completely fit and well'. So, then we had to section him because he was going to kill himself. ... We sectioned him and he stayed in custody then, until the mental health team saw him in the morning. ... That was five hours plus of shift, two of us out of a shift that had probably four cars out on a Friday night. (B6)

I'll give you an example I can think of ... a female tried to hang herself ... so the police attended with an ambulance and she was taken to hospital for a mental health assessment. Anyway, long story short ... she absconded from the hospital. So, we get called to the hospital to go and try and find her. We find her and she's been mentally assessed by the hospital. ... 'It's not a true attempt on her life', so the ER doctor is saying ... when we find her we say to the hospital, 'Do you want her back then?' They're like, 'No, we don't want her back, we've assessed her and she's fine'. So, it's almost they've phoned it in to make us aware, to cover their arse, basically. We've then graded it as a big high-risk missing person that we need to dedicate two or three police units to. We find her and then the hospital don't want her back. ... You know, that's our purpose, not to let bad things happen to people. Whereas I think, just from speaking to the A&E doctor in charge ... her mind-set was, this hospital's full of hundreds of people dying, if she really wants to do it, she'll do it ... you'd never hear a boss in the police going, 'Do you know what, I appreciate she's been phoned in, just file it. Note it and if we find her, we find her, but actually we're not going to put any resource behind it.' (Z3)

'Failures to act' have been added to wrongful convictions as a significant contributory factor in miscarriage of justice cases (Savage 2007). Whilst 'failure to act' for social services or for the Accident and Emergency department would mean not informing the police of an absconded patient or a missing teenager, this then translates to an 'obligation to act' for the police on all incidents that are passed down the line to them. This 'obligation to act' is governed by the fear of what might happen should inaction follow. There are very limited further options for the police in passing these incidents on to any other agency. In many situations, the 'line' goes no further than the police, which is another well-expressed frustration of officers:

We do everyone else's work. Every other service and agency you can think of, we go there first, give the job to them, then they generally give it back. (B6)

[W]e're doing too much ... we're doing a lot of work that isn't in the police realm. A lot of it gets covered by police who have a duty of care over people, which is fine, and I agree with that. But other agencies have taken advantage of that, and we are the drip tray for all – I would go as far as saying all other services and all other agencies. If they can't do it or it falls in the too difficult box, it lands on our lap. (T1)

We're not stopping and turning people over, we're not stopping cars, we're not doing those sorts of things because we just don't have the time. The reason we don't have the time is because most of our deployments, I would say 65, 70% of our deployments, are either vulnerability or mental health related. That's not to say that many of those deployments aren't absolutely police matters but a lot aren't and a lot is just stuff that falls down the cracks, because I think the organisation is potentially worried that we have another Fiona Pilkington or Baby P or something like that, so we're very worried to make sure that doesn't happen again. Rightly so, but we've almost gone to the further degree. (Z3)

[W]e're the final line. Social services go home at four o'clock, it falls to the police. The mental health team can't be bothered to find an ambulance for somebody, but they want them sectioned, oh it's alright, we'll pitch up, we'll say they're kicking off, the police will come and take them to a secure unit for us. They'll do the transporting. (B4)

This regularly conveyed frustration about the inability of other public services to be able to offer sufficient support outside standard working hours was even expressed in almost identical terms by the civilian Tom Winsor, then Chief Inspector of the HMIC. In a BBC radio interview, and utilising the police 'storylines' expressed above, he said:

It is no good for mental health professionals to ring the police at 4 pm on a Friday saying, 'Here's a list of our most dangerous, or people in greatest jeopardy, let us know how you get on, we'll be back on Monday'. (Winsor 2017)

Although, the majority of the concerns raised by the new recruits about other agencies related to social services, it is not the case that other agencies escaped notice. As discussed in Chap. 8, officers did adhere strongly to the narrative of police officers being the 'thin blue line' between order and chaos, with nearly 90% of respondents agreeing or strongly agreeing with this statement at TIME D. As discussed at the time, police officers still appear to embrace the 'sense of mission' that Reiner identified as an important cultural characteristic (2010). However, that 'sense of mission' is also tempered by a perception that the 'thin blue line' is not being held by any other agency but themselves. There was an unprompted belief from a minority of respondents that other agencies were letting them down:

Since I started the job I feel we're almost responsible for helping for everything, I almost feel like we're ambulance service as well sometimes. I don't know, I feel there's a lot more responsibility placed on the police than I thought there would be before I started. The number of jobs I've been to where ambulance have requested assistance from us and they've not actually turned up themselves. (X7)

CPS won't charge anything unless they know they're going to be able to get a conviction, so a lot of the work they do just gets never actioned or dropped or whatever ... quite frustrating. (A1)

[T]he court system they let us down hugely. (T5)

[T]he criminal justice system doesn't lock people up, or they're on their 158th final warning, and they're just let free, and you just think, is it working? And it's not the barristers and the lawyers and the Judges and the Magistrates that get it in the neck, it's the police. (A5)

These stories and obstructions expressed by the police officers in this research serve a number of purposes. Whilst not underestimating the levels of job frustration it may cause and whilst also appreciating the possible detrimental impact of this work upon other policing functions, these activities and the sharing of stories about these activities perform a strong function in the formation of social identity. As discussed in Chap. 3, the two recognisable stages of social identity formation are categorisation and comparison. In this regard, police officers can effectively enhance their social identity by comparing themselves with other public and social services that have contrasting behaviours and beliefs. By selectively focusing upon the perceived differences between themselves as police officers and 'others' within the public and social services, officers can not only sustain and enhance the group image but also, on a more individual level, contribute to an enhanced self-image. By emphasising the shared meanings and shared behaviours of the group, the differences between members of the group can be minimised whilst at the same time exaggerating the differences with those who are not members of the group (Tajfel 1982).

## Internal and Management Issues

As stated at the outset of this chapter, the respondents were not provided with a list of the potential challenges facing modern policing from which to choose. Inevitably therefore, there were a wide range of issues highlighted by the respondents, which have then been categorised into four areas. The final area is internal and management issues. At TIME A and

TIME B, when officers were still in training or had just completed their tutor phase, the issues raised in this regard were limited and infrequent. However, as time passed and officers spent more time in their role, the range of concerns began to expand. However, although these concerns were numerous, they were in no way seen to be as significant as the areas of budget cuts; the relationship between the police, the media and the public; and the impact of dealing with non-policing issues. At least, that was the case with the new recruits and the group of tutors. The SDROs however had a markedly different set of priorities as to what the challenges to modern policing were. Although all three groups shared the same concerns, for the SDROs, these internal issues took on much greater significance. Unlike the new recruits and the tutors, whose focus was very much external to the organisation and connected to the public they policed and the agencies they collaborated with, the focus of the SDROs was very much on the internal workings of the policing organisation. Given that SDROs were not in a public-facing role, this is hardly surprising. However, it does provide a glimpse into the potential effects of officers spending long periods of time away from the public and immersed within the organisation itself.

The concerns that were raised with most frequency by the respondents were those issues relating to officers' well-being. It was felt by a majority of respondents raising these concerns that the repercussions of both budget cuts to other parts of the public services and, particularly, social care, combined with a drop in police numbers, were a significant contributor to a decrease in levels of police morale and, with it, an increase in levels of police stress. Irrespective of these additional pressures emanating from budgetary constraints, Paoline has argued that the result of both the occupational and the organisational environment that the police officer is required to work within is stress and anxiety (2003). Results from the quantitative part of this research discussed in Chap. 8 highlighted that over 82% of the sample agreed or strongly agreed that 'policing is a highly stressful occupation'. Over a quarter of the respondents indicated that if they could disregard their own financial commitments, they would consider leaving the job:

> [I]t has just been hell. And so many times I thought I'm just going to leave because I feel so stressed out by this … I thought Tesco's would be a better option than coming back into work, being stressed to the eyeballs. (Z1)

[E]verybody's at the point of cracking ... lots of people seem to be coming for a few years now ... and then go to a different job because they can't keep their stress levels down and their mental health and physical health. (D3)

I've spoken to a couple of detectives that have gone off ... with stress and some that are struggling because ... by their nature, a lot of them are quite, sort of, caring and compassionate and they can't physically provide the level of service that they want to provide to the victims because of their workload. (D12)

Other internal and management issues that were raised by the respondents, but not to the same extent as stress, were related to the areas of staffing, management, and pay and conditions. It cannot be argued that these views were widespread throughout the cohort of officers. However, they were mentioned independently by a significant minority of respondents. The publication of the Winsor Review (2012) shortly before the research began was a concern of a small number of respondents, but the broader issue of the pay and conditions of officers (upon which the report was based) was referred to more frequently. One respondent suggested that "this job is not looking as attractive as it was years ago" (W1). The concerns about pay and conditions were linked particularly to the 'uncertainties' around pensions (a perennial concern of police officers) and job tenure.

However, more than their own personal circumstances, a small number of the recruits, tutors and SDROs referred to policing priorities and management decisions being a challenge to policing. This was alluded to in terms of force reorganisation, the regular redeployment of staff and short-term decision-making. As one officer noted, "If you're a specialist on a particular type of aircraft, you're not going to go and put them on trains" (D5). However, it was also felt that more senior management did not provide sufficient levels of support in times of difficulty. The camaraderie amongst officers that was discussed in Chap. 10 was regularly cited as being a necessary requirement in order to cope with not only the potential threats from the public (either as individual potential offenders or as the wider general public) but also the potential threats from senior managers. As one officer said, "It's not just from outside ... it's from senior management as well" (Z7). There were other similar observations:

[T]he lack of support from management, you see it all the time, a blooming stab you in the back culture ... you do a better job if you feel you're getting support. (B2)

If you say things that are right, you kind of get shot down a bit ... by senior management. If you tell them the truth, they don't like hearing it. (Z7)

[W]hen your management does nothing to support you ... it's rubbish ... they would throw you under the bus. (Z1)

This organisational tendency to attribute individual blame, rather than learn organisationally from mistakes, is acknowledged by the College of Policing, which is seeking to change that ethos within policing (Hickey 2016). The presumed lack of support from senior management caused some of the respondents to describe the fearfulness of making the wrong decision, an area discussed in Chap. 10.

As outlined at the beginning of this chapter, the open nature of the question (what were the major challenges facing policing) to the new recruits and the sample of tutors and SDROs inevitably led to a wide array of answers. The focus of all respondents was on policing budgets. Between 2010 and 2015, the level of departmental spending by the UK Government (which includes the administration and delivery of public services) fell by 12.8% (IFS 2015). As we have seen earlier in this chapter, this has had a dramatic impact upon policing and policing services, and has been a preoccupation in the minds of new recruits to the police service. Apart from the more obvious impact in terms of lower police numbers, the new recruits to the police service and the small sample of other officers also considered that the budgetary constraints had had an impact in other more fundamental ways. Officers felt that they were fighting a "losing battle" (D3) to contain the wider social problems of a society characterised by inadequate levels of social care support. There was a level of frustration at financial decisions often dictating action or inaction.

This constrained the officers' abilities to be proactive and to perform their role as they would wish. There is seemingly no doubt that fiscal control of policing budgets would manifest itself in some of the problems highlighted by the new recruits. However, it is the extent to which this is the case which is an interesting question. How far are these frustrations expressed by the new recruits related entirely to the current situation with policing budgets, and how far are these frustrations part of the 'reality shock' felt by a large proportion of new recruits to the service over many years? As discussed in Chap. 5, there is a palpable disconnect between the expectations of the job and the reality of the job. Additionally, there is the absorption of a cultural narrative of decline from other, more experienced officers. This is seen in terms of a preoccupation with police numbers in the past. However, this cultural narrative of decline from more experienced officers is not always appreciated by the new recruits:

> [I]t can be quite demoralising sitting round a table listening to people moan all the time about the police and how … it's not as good as it was and how it's going down the pan … I think it's probably a certain age and breed. I think it's mainly those who maybe are getting near the end of their service or those who have purposely not wanted to do anything else in their career and then they're kind of stuck. (X10)

> [T]hey're all a bit kind of 'oh, it's the same old … oh, it's boring … I wouldn't do this, I wouldn't do that' and I think that's a shame sometimes because when you get the enthusiastic ones who actually do want to do something and do want to learn … it's very much an influential environment … it's very good how they support each other … but, I think, there is a lot of negativity from some senior or longer-serving officers. (W2)

As seen in Chap. 10, their association with themselves as #newbreed is a compelling new narrative.

This chapter has therefore provided an important insight into the views of current serving officers (with varying years of experience) as to what they feel are the challenges facing police officers in a rapidly changing policing environment. Concerns over external perceptions of the organisation, for example, from the media, became less important as concerns over the internal workings of the organisation grew. However, the overriding challenge to the police service throughout the research was inescapably the issue of policing budgets.

This chapter has also provided some insight into the changing nature of the priorities of new police officers as they become slowly more integrated within the policing cultures. As with other aspects of the informal policing cultures discussed in the previous two chapters, the narratives of the policing challenges serve to sustain and enhance the group image through focusing upon the perceived differences between the recruits as 'front-line' police officers and 'others' in the form of the public, the media or police managers. These narratives are influenced both by the changing field of policing which is adjusting to a new financial landscape and by the habitus of the recruits' policing colleagues through the cultural historiographies of the past. Together, the two have an impact upon these narratives and make them although familiar, yet still unique.

# References

Alain, M., & Baril, C. (2005). Crime Prevention, Crime Repression, and Policing: Attitudes of Police Recruits Towards Their Role in Crime Control. *International Journal of Comparative and Applied Criminal Justice, 29*(2), 123–148.

Alain, M., & Grégoire, M. (2008). Can Ethics Survive the Shock of the Job? Quebec's Police Recruits Confront Reality. *Policing and Society, 18*(2), 169–189.

Ashforth, B., & Kreiner, G. (1999). "How Can You Do It?" Dirty Work and the Challenge of Constructing a Positive Identity. *The Academy of Management Review, 24*(3), 413–434.

Banton, M. (1964). *The Policeman in the Community.* London: Tavistock.

Chan, J. (2003). *Fair Cop: Learning the Art of Policing.* Toronto: University of Toronto Press.

College of Policing. (2015). *College of Policing Analysis: Estimating Demand on the Police Service.* Retrieved from http://www.college.police.uk/News/College-news/Documents/Demand%20Report%2023_1_15_noBleed.pdf

Conn, D. (2016, April 26). Hilsborough Inquests Jury Rules 96 Victims Were Unlawfully Killed. *The Guardian.* Retrieved from https://www.theguardian.

com/uk-news/2016/apr/26/hillsborough-inquests-jury-says-96-victims-were-unlawfully-killed

Dick, P. (2005). Dirty Work Designations: How Police Officers Account for Their Use of Coercive Force. *Human Relations, 58*(11), 1363–1390.

Dilnot, A., Sir. (2016). *Police Grant 2016–17 [Letter written March 9, 2016 to Rt Hon Andy Burnham MP]*. Retrieved from https://www.statisticsauthority.gov.uk/wp-content/uploads/2016/03/Letter-from-Sir-Andrew-Dilnot-to-Andy-Burnham-MP-090316.pdf

Ellis, R. (1991). Perceptions, Attitudes and Beliefs of Police Recruits. *Canadian Police College Journal, 15*(2), 95–117.

Halliday, J. (2014). Plebgate Row: PC Keith Wallis Jailed for a Year for Lying About Andrew Mitchell. *The Guardian*. Retrieved from https://www.theguardian.com/uk-news/2014/feb/06/plebgate-keith-wallis-jailed-police-andrew-mitchell

Haria, R., & Turvill, W. (2015). Jailed for More than 20 Years: The Sources Convicted of Selling Stories to Journalists. *Press Gazette*. Retrieved from http://www.pressgazette.co.uk/jailed-more-20-years-sources-convicted-selling-stories-journalists/

Hickey, H. (2016, December 7). Good Officers 'Must Stop Being Hung Out to Dry'. *Police Oracle*. Retrieved from https://www.policeoracle.com/news/children_and_young_people/2016/Dec/06/good-officers--must-stop-being-hung-out-to-dry--says-chief_93631.html

HMIC. (2017a). *PEEL: Police Effectiveness 2016, a National Overview*. Retrieved from https://www.justiceinspectorates.gov.uk/hmic/wp-content/uploads/peel-police-effectiveness-2016.pdf

HMIC. (2017b). *State of Policing: The Annual Assessment of Policing in England and Wales*. Retrieved from https://www.justiceinspectorates.gov.uk/hmic/wp-content/uploads/state-of-policing-2016.pdf

Independent Commission on Mental Health and Policing. (2013). *Independent Commission on Mental Health and Policing Report*. Retrieved from http://www.turning-point.co.uk/media/621030/independent_commission_on_mental_health_and_policing_main_report.pdf

Institute for Fiscal Studies. (2015). *Recent Cuts to Public Spending*. Retrieved from https://www.ifs.org.uk/tools_and_resources/fiscal_facts/public_spending_survey/cuts_to_public_spending

Ipsos MORI. (2016). *Trust in Professions*. Retrieved from https://www.ipsos-mori.com/researchpublications/researcharchive/3685/Politicians-are-still-trusted-less-than-estate-agents-journalists-and-bankers.aspx#gallery[m]/1/

Johnston, N., & Politowski, B. (2016). *Police Funding*. House of Commons Library Briefing Paper 7279.

Leveson, Lord Justice. (2012). *An Inquiry into the Culture, Practices and Ethics of the Press*. Retrieved from https://www.gov.uk/government/publications/leveson-inquiry-report-into-the-culture-practices-and-ethics-of-the-press

Lewis, B. (2017). *Response to HMIC Report*. Retrieved from https://homeofficemedia.blog.gov.uk/2017/03/02/response-to-hmic-report/

May, T. (2015). *Written Statement (HCWS381) Made by The Secretary of State for the Home Department (Mrs Theresa May) on 12 March 2015*. Retrieved from http://www.parliament.uk/documents/commons-vote-office/March%20 2015/12%20March%202015/31.HOME-Undercover-policing.pdf

National Audit Office. (2015). *Financial Stability of Police Forces in England and Wales*. HC 78, London: NAO.

National Crime Agency. (2017). *Missing Persons Data Report 2015/16*. Retrieved from http://www.nationalcrimeagency.gov.uk/publications/783-missing-persons-data-report-2015-16/file

Office for National Statistics. (2017). *Crime in England and Wales: Year Ending Sept 2016*. Retrieved from https://www.ons.gov.uk/peoplepopulationandcommunity/crimeandjustice/bulletins/crimeinenglandandwales/yearendingsept2016

Osborne, G. (2015). *Chancellor George Osborne's Spending Review and Autumn Statement 2015*. Retrieved from https://www.gov.uk/government/speeches/chancellor-george-osbornes-spending-review-and-autumn-statement-2015-speech

Paoline, E. (2003). Taking Stock: Toward a Richer Understanding of Police Culture. *Journal of Criminal Justice, 31*(3), 199–214.

Police Federation. (2015). *Enough Is Enough*. Retrieved from http://www.polfed.org/newsroom/2637.aspx

Reicher, S., Spears, R., & Haslam, S. (2010). The Social Identity Approach in Social Psychology. In M. Wetherell & C. Mohanty (Eds.), *The SAGE Handbook of Identities* (pp. 45–63). London: Sage.

Reiner, R. (2010). *The Politics of the Police* (4th ed.). Oxford: Oxford University Press.

Savage, S. (2007). Putting Wrongs to Right: Campaigns Against Miscarriages of Justice. *Criminology and Criminal Justice, 7*(1), 83–105.

Tajfel, H. (1981). *Human Groups and Social Categories*. Cambridge: Cambridge University Press.

Tajfel, H. (1982). Social Psychology of Intergroup Relations. *Annual Review of Psychology, 33*, 1–39.

Westley, W. (1970). *Violence and the Police: A Sociological Study of Law, Custom and Morality.* Cambridge, MA: MIT Press.

Winsor, T. (2012). *Independent Review of Police Officer and Staff Renumeration and Conditions, Final Report* (Vol. 1). London: The Stationery Office.

Winsor, T. (2017, April 20). *World at One.* London: BBC Radio 4.

# 12

# Conclusion: Reconceptualising Policing Cultures

Tajfel (1981) has been critical of the discipline of social psychology for failing to adequately address the importance of collective behaviour in social life due to a focus on individuals and their interactions. There is a danger that much of the policing cultures literature has been susceptible to the same complaint, a focus upon more individual adaptations to normative practices and attitudes without an appreciation of the social nature of organisational learning and identity formation. Organisational cultures are learned and shared through socialisation with others and through the reinforcement and validation of others. Whilst the individual and their social identity is central to that process, it is how that individual's social identity interacts with group identity and group membership which is important. Group behaviour is not individual behaviour in groups but socially shared patterns of individual behaviour. It is this 'socially shared' aspect of behaviour that is so crucial to very many aspects of policing, not just the cultural characteristics of policing that is the focus of this book, but also the processes by which new recruits start to adopt those characteristics through the socially shared learning environments in which police officers shape their new identities.

© The Author(s) 2017
S. Charman, *Police Socialisation, Identity and Culture*,
DOI 10.1007/978-3-319-63070-0_12

That learning process has been assessed in this book through a consideration of the *development* of the attitudes of new police recruits over a period of four years. The socially shared learning environment which is inhabited by the new recruits influences and affects that sense of self and of identity. The 'self' is not a static entity unaffected by the social environment. As discussed in Chap. 3, Foucault understood the 'self' as emerging through interactions with others (1980). Mead's analysis too was very much outward, rather than inward, focused and understood the 'self' to be an inherently social concept (1934). Whilst the 'I' was conceptualised to be an individual's sense of themselves, it was the 'me' that would respond and react to outside feedback and create a sense of 'self'. It is in the interaction of the 'I' and the 'me' that we can begin to see how identities can be influenced and altered over time, particularly during significant life changes such as the transition into a new organisational group. The research on Evermord Constabulary discussed within this book has indicated that there is significant movement in those attitudes and beliefs in the early years of the recruits' policing careers. 'Snapshot' approaches to organisational cultures which attempt to describe the existing culture are unable to fully appreciate the direction of travel that was required in order to reach that end-state. Through an analysis of the changing nature of the recruits' perceptions concerning the role of policing and how it is learned, the influences upon their development, plus the expectations, realities and challenges facing policing and being a police officer, this research has been able to establish that change is apparent and can indicate the sources of influence upon that change.

It is also important to be mindful of *when* change is at its most apparent amongst new recruits to the police service. When the police recruits were asked to indicate the strength of their agreement or disagreement with a number of statements about the role of police officers and the job of policing, 59% of the answers to those statements saw *significant* change over time. Of that 59%, 92% of that significant change took place between TIME C and TIME D, that is, between the end of the recruits' first year and the end of their fourth year of being a police officer. Attitude change was therefore not immediate and longitudinal research design needs to take account of this. This would reinforce the findings of Chan (2003) and Ellis (1991), who have argued that the impact of training school in inculcating negative dispositions amongst new police recruits has been overstated. An example of this can be seen in the percentage of police officers believing that their organisation can have a considerable impact on communities. This fell from 100% of respondents indicating strong agreement when they were in training school to 64.7% indicating strong agreement after four years in the job.

All of this has implications for police training. If we accept that, first, the 'self' is developed in conjunction with others and, second, social identity is inextricably linked with group identity and, third, behaviour is governed by groups (as the CoP literature would suggest), then it should come as no surprise that the analysis emanating from this research highlights the superior status accorded by the research participants to the role of 'on-the-job' learning that takes place within the policing environment and in conjunction with others. This more *horizontal* approach to learning shares much with the CoP literature and the literature on andragogy (as discussed in Chaps. 4 and 5), which focus upon less directive and more facilitative learning. The police recruits in this research indicated that they learned in six distinct but complimentary ways—*learning from doing, learning from watching, learning from mistakes, learning from common sense, learning from experience* and *learning from adapting*. Those seen to be most influential in the recruits' learning were their tutor constables and their colleagues in the form of their 'shift'. In a period of anxiety and ambiguity in the early stages of a police career, new recruits are seeking out 'reference groups' (Bennett 1984) from whom they can obtain support and guidance. A desire to culturally assimilate with the new group will affect the extent to which they are influenced by those reference groups. Organisational newcomers are much more likely to utilise these reference groups through a strategy of observation rather than enquiry (Morrison 1993). This more observational strategy was a clear strategy of the new police recruits. The focus upon *learning from watching*, particularly via the tutor constable and other shift members, was clearly evident and, again, strengthens the influence of *horizontal* learning within the organisation.

This is not to suggest that the more 'formal' aspects of learning, exemplified by the time spent in police training schools and by the competency-based framework, along with the necessary compliance with NOS, should be abandoned. Instead, any analysis of police training provision needs to

|  | 'FORMAL' LEARNING | 'INFORMAL' LEARNING |
|---|---|---|
| VERTICAL LEARNING | Classroom based learning focusing upon the acquisition of skills and knowledge, passed on from 'expert' to 'novice'. This is exemplified by **police trainers** at force training schools and by the new pre-join qualifications, studied either in a classroom setting or online. | Non-prescriptive direction and advice during early placements within police stations, most notably from **Sergeant** in charge of the shift. |
| HORIZONTAL LEARNING | 'On the job' learning through a process of tutelage or 'shadowing'. The **tutor** period is an aspect of the formal learning process where new recruits spend approximately 10 weeks under the supervision of another constable on shift. Part of the process involves completion of the prescribed tasks on the Police Action Checklist. | Non-prescriptive direction and advice during early placements within police stations. This comes from other constables who are **colleagues** of the same rank as the new recruits although with more experience. There are therefore no line management responsibilities. |

**Fig. 12.1** The square of police learning

appreciate how identities develop, how police officers learn and how important it is to appreciate the 'social' and the 'group' in conjunction with the 'individual'. Any consideration of police training provision should therefore pay heed to what I have termed *the square of police learning*, which incorporates both the style and the direction of learning, and the inherently social process of learning, and attempts to assimilate the major sources of learning for new recruits (Fig. 12.1).

All four sites of learning have an effect on the new police recruit, in predictably different ways and at different times of the process. Whilst some of these elements of learning may be difficult to understand and to monitor, their influence cannot be denied. Additionally, their influence needs to be carefully analysed in order to better harness the positive impact of these relationships but also to guard against its failures. There was a distinct difference in opinions from the new recruits and from the tutors as to the role and function of this aspect of the training process. Neither expressed this in terms of the official role, but the new recruits were under the impression that the role of the tutor was primarily to teach them 'how' to do policing, whilst the tutors themselves saw their role more in terms of instilling confidence and ensuring safety to practice. This situation is compounded by a less-than-voluntary approach to tutor recruitment, poor levels of training, inadequate systems of reward for tutors and inconsistent methods of tutelage.

It is therefore important to consider how to best utilise the experience of police officers and to appreciate how this experience can provide a structure for future learning. Bayley and Bittner (1984) have argued that experience can teach new police officers about goals, about tactical decision-making and about presence, that is, that being an effective police officer is as much about 'being' as it is about 'doing'. In Chap. 9, there was a discussion about what the police recruits from Evermord Constabulary found to be their most valuable advice from others. In each instance, this advice was from someone they worked with in force rather than in training, which was often framed in stories or 'tropes' (Shearing and Ericson, 1991) and would constitute what Sackmann referred to as 'recipe knowledge' (1991). These stories and 'tropes' taught the new recruits about the value of instinct, of suspicion, of lowering their expectations, of sensitivity and of self-protection. Experience of the 'craft' of policing can therefore be utilised within the 'science' of police training. If learning the necessary requirements of cultural assimilation entails a process of interpretation of the meanings attributed to policing from a variety of sources, or 'sensemaking', then it is also important that we pay due attention, as Chan has argued, to the 'sensegivers' (2007a). She refers to these sensegivers in terms of politicians and police leaders, but if we adhere to the potential influences across *the square of police learning*, then we must also acknowledge the important role of those who play a key role in the horizontal learning of new police recruits.

Importantly, all aspects of *the square of police learning* must be acknowledged in any consideration of changes to initial police training. There are clearly significant changes underway in this regard in relation to the Policing Qualifications Framework and the introduction of higher educational requirements for all police officers. The merits or otherwise of this approach are not within the scope of this research, but it should not be presumed that one type of 'learning' takes place within a training setting and another type of 'learning' takes place within the workplace setting. The *square of police learning* is a fluid and dynamic model which emphasises the different types of learning, the different directions in which learning flows, the inherently social process of learning and the impact of organisational cultural characteristics at every stage and every site of this learning process.

Appreciating the impact of organisational cultural characteristics on the learning process is crucial in order to better understand the influences and pressures upon the new recruits to the police service. We also however have to both be very clear about what those organisational cultural characteristics actually are and acknowledge that there is not one but multiple policing fields upon which police officers perform. Chapter 6 considered the long history of worldwide academic enquiry into the nature of policing cultures, which, despite some challenges to its analysis, has also witnessed some steadfast consistencies. Despite what has been suggested in some of the more homogeneously focused police culture literature, it is not possible to discuss police culture in the singular as a compatible set of values, attitudes and beliefs which transcend time, location, role and rank. However, there is value in attempting to describe some of the predominant characteristics of policing cultures amongst the lower ranks of the police service. These characteristics have been derived through an analysis of the data over a period of four years. Police officers do not uniformly display all aspects of these characteristics described. These cultural tools should instead be viewed as being positioned along a continuum, with officers adapting their policing practices according to the context of their position (Campeau 2015). Our social identities do not determine our actions but instead can be understood as a framework of appraisal (Reicher et al. 2010) which is both contextual and situational. During the process of identity formation, police officers engage, as we have discussed, in both categorisation and comparison. They will do this with all groups of which they are a part, whether these be organisational groups, family groups or friendship groups. One's unique identity is then the sum of the social categories which have been adopted. What follows then, with those caveats in mind, are what I would suggest to be both the enduring and the emerging cultural characteristics of policing at the lower ranks—*cynicism, communication, comradeship, code of self-protection, categorisation* and *compassion*.

# Cynicism

As discussed on numerous occasions throughout this book, there is much confusion about the role of the police and the nature of police work. The symbolic imagery of the police in relation to 'crime-fighting defenders of the peace' is difficult to reconcile with the everyday realities of policing in the twenty-first century. This stems from a variety of sources, including the fictional and nonfictional representations of policing, from the perceptions of the public and from pronouncements by governments. How police officers interpret those meanings is part of the sensemaking of policing occupational cultures (Rantatalo 2016). However, this confusion over the role of the police has the potential to create a vacuum in the understandings of new recruits to the police service, which can be filled with other narratives. One of the strongest narratives that fills that space is one which has been highlighted by policing scholars since work began on the nature of policing in the 1960s and that is cynicism.

The new recruits highlighted cynicism as something that they observed in other colleagues and also were aware of it as a growing feature of their own identities. By TIME D, 100% agreed or strongly agreed that police officers were cynical. Initially, almost 30% had disagreed or strongly disagreed. When respondents were asked how they felt they had changed, becoming more cynical was a regular answer. When asked to reveal some of the most useful advice from other colleagues, a version of "everybody lies" (C10, Y2 and Z2) was a common response. Organisational cynicism is functional in that it provides a recognisable language to other group members, provides an exclusive and shared humour, and provides a level of disrespect to those outside the group which cements the group's boundaries. All these functions of cynicism serve to strengthen the group's bonds. In this way, cynicism is closely related to the use of humour, which also serves to contribute positively to group identity. This can be seen through the humour of superiority, the humour of exclusion and the humour of cohesion (Charman 2013).

However, cynicism functions not just to bolster the internal group status but also as an adaptive coping technique. It does this on two different levels. First, cynicism functions as a technique to cope with the nature of the job itself and, second, it functions as a technique to cope with the nature of the disappointment about the job. Each of these will now be dealt with in turn.

First, some scholars have argued that the cultural adaptive techniques of police officers stem from the dangerous and unpredictable nature of the policing task, in which they face a constant threat to their own personal safety. However, any organisational culture will have adaptive strategies whatever be the nature of the 'threat' that they are facing—the threat of redundancies, the threat of unreasonable management, the threat of 'customers', for example. Police officers are coping with potential danger, but probably more relevantly, they are coping with the inaction and inactivity of other public services upon which they often hope to be able to rely and they are coping with what they perceive to be a hostile and unsupportive public and media. It is the group's *perceptions* of the nature of the threat, rather than the *reality* of the threat, which are central because it is the adaptive techniques to that threat which will shape the organisational cultural characteristics and narratives about the nature of the job. As discussed earlier in the book, sensemaking is driven by 'plausibility', rather than by accuracy (Weick 1995). Police officers will frequently find themselves in unpleasant and unpredictable situations, much at odds with the 'hero' status and image that is often presented in television dramas. It is precisely in the incongruity of much of their work that humour and cynicism finds its place. Sociologists have long held that humour is a reaction to the sometimes absurd and paradoxical encounters that people experience (Charman 2013; Critchley 2002; Meyer 1997; Scott 2007). Cynicism therefore functions as a technique to cope with the nature of the job itself.

Second, cynicism functions as a technique to cope with the nature of the disappointment about the job. Research on the motivations for joining the police have changed little since Hopper's work in 1977 which focused upon the variety of tasks involved, the excitement, the outdoors-oriented nature of the job and, importantly, the community service principles of helping others. Both Fielding (1988a) and Chan (2003) in their longitudinal research found that community service principles were strong influences in the decision to join the police. Those community service principles or, as the new recruits termed it, 'making a difference' was the most often cited motivation in this research for wanting to become a police officer. However, this research has also revealed that as time progresses, police officers feel less strongly that policing can have an impact on the communities it serves, which, as was discussed above, fell from 100% indicating strong agreement when they were in training school to 64.7% indicating strong agreement after four years in the job.

There is a palpable disconnect between the expectations of the job and the reality of the job. Participation in both the formal and informal training, plus experience of policing on the streets, resulted, for many officers, in two levels of disappointment. Both these levels (noted by Alain and Grégoire (2008) as endogenous disappointment and exogenous disappointment) can be witnessed in this sample of new recruits. There is, first, a disassociation between the expectations and the realities of the job (endogenous) and, second, the absorption of a cultural narrative of decline from other, more experienced officers (exogenous). Although the cultural narratives of decline from more experienced officers were viewed with a sense of frustration, there was also an acknowledgement that 'fitting in' with the group required participation, rather than challenge. The potential implications of this disappointment are a more cynical police officer. When asked about their changing identities, some officers referred to being less emotional and framed this in mostly negative tones. Chan too found similar results and has suggested that "emotional hardening" (2007b) is an adaptive response to coping with being a police officer.

## Communication

As discussed earlier in this chapter, andragogy refers to the concept of adult education which has a focus upon less directive and more facilitative learning. In addition to the reasons already discussed within this book, there is a further reason why this approach to training and educating police officers is so important. This research has demonstrated that either when provided with a list of attributes to choose from or when officers were asked to discuss the key skills associated with being a 'good' police officer, communication came out on top. It was not simply acknowledged to be the most important skill associated with policing or the most important characteristic of a police officer, but was also regularly highlighted by the new recruits as a feature of their policing style which was most effective. This has been confirmed elsewhere by research from Willis and Mastrofski, which suggested that the interpersonal skills of eloquence, working with the community and a positive attitude were all highlighted as the 'most impressive' characteristics of officers' highest-performing colleagues (2017).

The skills that are deemed to be the most important and the most effective within the recruits' working practices must inevitably relate to the roles that they are performing. Discussions about what the new recruits felt was the role of the police indicated that officers' time is mostly spent in dealing with non-crime-related and traditionally non-policing issues. This is confirmed by evidence from the College of Policing (2015), which indicated that non-crime-related incidents accounted for 83% of all 'command and control' calls that came into police call centres. Additionally, based upon the data received from a small number of forces, it was suggested that 'public safety and welfare' incidents now make up the largest category of reported incidents to the police, more than both crime and antisocial behaviour. Whether this change of focus of the policing role is a source of frustration or of job satisfaction can be left to one side momentarily. What is of importance here is that the evolving changes within the policing role and the changing nature of crime in the twenty-first century mean that the job of policing is also evolving and the approach that police officers must take to their job inevitably also had to change. Adjustments in the 'field' of policing have necessitated adjustments in the 'habitus' in order to be able to more successfully navigate the new policing terrain.

At the initial stages of this research, there was more adherence from the new recruits to the notions of fighting crime, preventing crime and catching criminals. Those narratives about the role of policing changed throughout the course of the research so that, after four years in the job, for example, when asked about the role of the police, 85% of the statements made concerned vulnerability and safeguarding, up from 16% in the first few weeks of the recruits' job. Likewise, statements about the role of the police being crime related fell from 35% at TIME A to 9% at TIME D. These new recruits, as discussed in Chap. 10, were seemingly well aware of the importance of good communication skills and, along with spending more time engaged in communication with the public, highlighted the use of communication as a key explanation for why many of them had not regularly utilised their personal protective equipment. This was also attributed to their previous employment. About 83% of the new recruits had served as a PCSO or Special Constable before joining as a regular police officer. The tutors and SDROs were overwhelmingly positive about the impact of this previous experience. This very community-focused and public engagement role required communication to be the primary tool in their policing practice; indeed, with no personal protective equipment, it was also their first and last resort.

Highlighting one of the most important skills of a police officer as communication was reflected upon by the new recruits, many of whom considered that the focus upon strength and authority was a more historical interpretation of the role of a police officer. The new police recruits attributed communication as the most important characteristic of a police officer and the most important feature of a 'good' police officer. This readiness to attribute communication to this position and the greater appreciation generally of more community service philosophies highlight much of the essence of the #newbreed, which has been discussed in Chap. 10. These officers are less interested in arrest rates and are more communicative and community focused. They are using the narrative of #newbreed to guide their action and navigate the policing terrain. Historically, this may have been categorised as part of the 'softer skills' associated with one aspect of policing, and notably by female police officers. However, we should instead see these characteristics and priorities as a feature of modern policing *per se*, which is divided much more by rank and role than it is along gender lines. Recording no significant differences between male and female respondents in the answers to any of the quantitative questions, plus observing no discernible differences between the qualitative answers from female and male respondents, is testament to this analysis. This also confirms research on firearms teams within the police (Cain 2012) and on integrity within the police (Westmarland and Rowe 2016), which also found no significant differences in attitudes or reported behaviours in terms of gender. As Waddington has suggested, police cultures should be considered less as having their origins in masculinity but rather in policing itself (1999a).

There needs therefore to be a better match between what police officers are learning in their formal learning environment and what they are being required to do in their subsequent role as police officers. The paradox of police training as it is currently formulated is that new recruits are learning in a rigid, inflexible and behaviourist environment but are actually required to understand how to police in a democratic society (Birzer 2003). This involves such complex tasks as neighbourhood disputes, community engagement, the modern threats of terrorism and cyber-enabled crime. A concentration on the more technical aspects of the law and its procedures at the expense of the 'softer' skills of conflict resolution, communication and problem-solving may result in gaps in the required skills of a police officer (Peace 2006). However, this does not account for the other influences upon a police officer's learning as evidenced through *the square of police learning*. It is within these less formal and more horizontal learning environments that those soft skills are more highly valued, and it is here that police officers are learning their importance.

## Comradeship

T.S. Eliot said that "culture may even be described simply as that which makes life worth living" (1948, p. 27). Policing organisational cultures were undoubtedly not the focus of interest for Eliot. However, there was an element of the policing culture that respondents referred to which appeared to make their 'life worth living'. The most positively referred to characteristic, whether explicitly following a direct question in this regard or whether more implicitly through discussions of the nature of the job, was comradeship. This might have been referred to as teamwork, solidarity, camaraderie, 'having your back', bonding or family, but these were all terms used to describe the close bond between colleagues which I have classified as 'comradeship'. This bond was not referred to as stretching beyond the boundaries of the individual shift with which they were serving and therefore was not a term used to describe the 'policing family' as a whole, but it was of enormous importance to the new recruits. This research has four key sources of evidence for this. First, comradeship was cited as a reason for joining the police in the first place, in addition to the action-/outdoors-oriented nature of the job and the community service principles connected with the role. Second, increasing numbers of the new recruits agreed or strongly agreed with the statement that 'police officers have high levels of solidarity with each other', rising from 70.8% to 88.2% after four years. Third, when the new recruits were questioned about the aspects of the job that they were most enjoying, 'teamwork' came out as one of three answers, including job variety and working with victims. And finally, when explicitly asked to describe aspects of policing cultures, the most often cited of these was comradeship.

This is by no means a surprising or novel analysis and was first referred to as one of the 'distinctive cognitive tendencies' of policing by Skolnick (1966), and has continued to feature prominently in cultural analyses of policing. When asked to rate the factors most likely to be associated with acceptance by fellow officers, new recruits rated being a team player in the top position, whilst being hard-working was down in the seventh position (Ellis 1991).

Research has suggested that employees will have an enhanced sense of self and exhibit higher levels of organisational commitment if they perceive the organisation to be supportive of them and their goals, and the socioemotional aspects of social exchange are apparent (Blau 1964; He and Brown 2013; Ashforth and Mael 1989). This is an aspect of the literature on organisational identification or organisational commitment. My research analysed in this book has provided strong evidence of commitment and comradeship amongst the police. New members invest in the group through their support of, and identification with, normative practices and shared values, and, as such, gain the 'social capital' (Bourdieu 1986) which enhances that solidarity.

This is however a much more *horizontal organisational commitment* towards immediate colleagues rather than a more *vertical organisational commitment* towards the wider police organisation. The data analysed for this research provides evidence that this comradeship amongst immediate colleagues is strengthened over time and is a key determinant of the factors related to job satisfaction. In this way, this research both confirms existing work on organisational commitment amongst police officers and significantly extends the analysis from a focus upon vertical organisational commitment to one on horizontal organisational commitment. Unlike most other organisations, as discussed in Chap. 2, vertical organisational commitment amongst police officers decreases as length of service increases. It could be argued that the strength of early socialisation experiences which are cemented over time and include high levels of comradeship place the importance of the 'team' at the forefront of a police officer's organisational experiences. As will be discussed in the section on 'categorisation', these bonds are strengthened and the self-image of the group is enhanced by reference to those who fall outside that boundary, in this case more senior management within the organisation. So, whilst this research would appear to confirm other work in this area, indicating that organisational commitment amongst police officers declines over time, upon dissection of that analysis, it would appear that the distinction between vertical and horizontal organisational commitment would indicate that the latter is strong and indeed strengthens over time. However, there may be repercussions of this. As mentioned above, one of the manifestations of high levels of organisational commitment is an enhanced sense of self. A reduction in organisational commitment over time could have the reverse effect. The perceptions of the recruits as to their changing identities over time, as per the research discussed in Chap. 10, were reported in overwhelmingly negative ways. This could indicate that a low sense of self and, as already has been discussed, growing levels of cynicism might be the price to pay for the high levels of horizontal organisational commitment but shrinking levels of vertical organisational commitment.

It must also be noted that the benefits of comradeship that a new recruit might avail are not entirely freely given. As discussed in Chap. 3, cooperation in groups is driven by either discretionary cooperation (based upon values and attitudes) or mandatory cooperation (based upon sanctions for non-compliance). In this regard, cooperation appears to be driven by a third factor, which I would term *reciprocal cooperation*, which fits somewhere between the two models presented. The very essence of workplace social interactions is about the subconscious exchange of tacit knowledge. These social exchange factors are delicately interwoven into the implicit learning that takes place during the early stages of entry into an organisation. Both the new recruits and the established workforce have something to contribute, and it is in this exchange-based relationship that the development of solidarity can be seen. The established workforce offers solidarity and, with it, the ability to 'watch your back'.

In exchange for that, the new recruits must 'fit in' with the working culture of the organisation, and most especially with 'the shift'. *Reciprocal cooperation* therefore operates for the mutual advantage of the members and creates both shared understandings and shared trust. Whilst the rewards might be very positive and the evidence from the new recruits in this research point to just that conclusion, there is no doubt that to be on the outside of that cultural boundary of acceptance would be a very different scenario. None of the recruits spoke of outright rejection (although interviews were not able to be conducted with the four officers who had left the force), but as discussed in Chap. 10, there was certainly a sense of limitations to that solidarity, which will be discussed in the following section—the code of self-protection.

# Code of Self-protection

The literature on policing cultures has pointed to a darker side of the characteristics of solidarity or 'comradeship', which is not only used to support colleagues and to keep them safe but also to protect them from the scrutiny of the law. The 'blue code of silence' has been seen to be an extension of the solidarity between officers (Chan 2003; Goldsmith 1990), with evidence to suggest that the protection of fellow officers from the consequences of illegal brutality or rule-bending is apparent (Westmarland 2005; Westmarland and Rowe 2016).

Stephenson and Stewart (2001), as discussed in Chap. 3, have outlined a typology of collectivism which moves from trade union collectivism to workplace collectivism and, finally, to the 'social collectivism of everyday life', which is characterised by an extension beyond the workplace and which impacts upon both work life and home life. Evidence from my research would suggest that although historically, policing might have been characterised by the 'social collectivism of everyday life' where more demographically homogeneous officers lived in or close to the station where they policed and socialised routinely with other officers, that situation is changing. The movement appears to be turning more towards workplace collectivism, characterised by mutual support about work or non-work issues but taking place within the physical confines of the working environment. This would also confirm the findings of research in Australia which suggested a decline in the traditional social rituals associated with policing, particularly with regard to socialising through drinking outside the workplace (Brough et al. 2016).

The new police recruits in the research discussed within this book did not refer to the narrative of policing being 'a job for life', and indeed, some spoke of it rather more in terms of a 'job for now', framed in the language of policing being a 'job' rather than a 'lifestyle'. Although an increasing number of the new recruits agreed or strongly agreed with the statement that being a police officer can lead to social isolation, there were still over a third of officers who did not agree with this statement and others who referred to joining the police as having had no impact on their social environment. Paoline and Terrill (2014) have suggested that a decline in social isolation has brought about a change to the bonds of solidarity. Evidence from my research would confirm this. The repercussions are potentially that although comradeship is strong as has been already been discussed, it is not unqualified, and as discussed in Chap. 10, there are limits to solidarity. These limits appear to be especially related to the perceptions of a 'blue code of silence'.

In the first few weeks of the new recruits' careers as police officers, 30.4% of respondents strongly disagreed with the statement that 'officers must observe a code of secrecy amongst themselves to protect fellow officers'. After four years, this number had almost doubled to 58.8% who strongly disagreed with the statement, becoming the most common answer. At the same time, no officers agreed or strongly agreed with the statement. New recruits have an understanding perhaps of what they perceive the world of policing to be about and what skills and qualities may be required. This then changes as they spend more time in the job. Whereas some officers may have believed that a code of secrecy, often referred to as the 'blue code of silence', was potentially an informal requirement of the job, these numbers disappeared as officers became more experienced in their role. The strength of disagreement with the statement also intensified.

There are two opposing explanations for why this might be the case. On the one hand, it could be argued that police officers become more sophisticated in their 'storytelling' to 'outsiders'; that they become more politically aware of the dangers of betraying the more negative aspects of policing cultures. This could be coupled with a growing alignment with other attitudes such as the importance of suspiciousness, the tendency of police officers to 'lay low' and 'not to make waves', and the advice given to the new recruits in terms of 'covering themselves'. This is in addition to the high levels of cynicism that police officers believe are part of the nature of being a police officer.

However, there is an alternative explanation which also needs consideration. The qualitative discussions that took place between the new recruits and the interviewer revealed a far more nuanced account of the intricacies of the notion of a 'blue code of silence' than can be seen through an analysis of the quantitative data outlined above. It is my argument that the changing field and the changing habitus of policing have both impacted in different ways upon this issue. The changing field of policing in relation to accountability means that there is now a heavy focus upon professional standards, the routine escalation of complaints, a fear of 'doing the wrong thing' and a fear of little to no management support when things do go wrong. The changing habitus of police officers (which neither is dictated by the field, nor dictates to the field) is characterised by a lack of tolerance for unacceptable policing behaviours and a belief in integrity, which was mentioned frequently by the new recruits as a feature of a 'good' police officer, after communication, empathy and compassion. This would appear to indicate that the traditional 'blue code of silence' seems to be in the process of being superseded by 'the blue code of self-protection'. According to Waddington (1999a), the prime motivating factor for police officers when undertaking their duties on the street is not the enactment of the more expressive 'backstage' talk but the concern of 'staying out of trouble', or as I have termed it, the 'blue code of self-protection'. The direction of influence therefore could be seen as running from the front stage (street) to the back stage (canteen), rather than the other way around. Chan has argued that the "old 'stand by your mates' framework is no longer sustainable", which has led to some "major behavioural and cultural change" (2007a, p. 343). Myhill and Bradford (2013) have argued for a more fluid understanding of the 'code of silence'. That more fluid understanding can be seen through this suggestion of movement from silence towards self-protection. These are important and interesting changes to the perceptions of the occupational habitus of police officers. It could be argued therefore that there is a subtle shift away from the 'blue code of silence' as a dominant paradigm towards a 'blue code of self-protection'. This has been influenced by a more individualist, risk-averse and publically accountable policing organisation.

## Categorisation

Research on identity formation suggests that self- or social categorisation and comparison are two of the recognisable stages of the process. People are motivated towards self-categorisation with the group when they adhere to the values of the group, are given a voice within the group, support the group's leaders and identify with the role that has been assigned to them (Bradford et al. 2014, p. 529). In order to display commitment to the group, new members will often emphasise those attitudes and behaviours which they perceive to be fundamental to the group identity and will, at the same time, highlight the perceived differences of the attitudes and behaviours of those belonging to the members of 'outsider' groups. Bourdieu (1991) has argued that once a dominant culture is established, all other subcultures are measured by their distance from it.

This distinction or comparison between 'in-groups' and 'out-groups' or the 'us versus them' mentality has a long history in both the criminological literature generally and the policing cultures literature more specifically, as discussed in Chap. 6. Whilst the process of 'othering' or 'ethnocentrism' can clearly work effectively to sustain and to bond the group, it also has the potential to alienate and promote hostility towards those outside of the group's boundaries. In terms of the research in this book, this categorisation could be witnessed at a variety of levels.

There was the potential for anyone outside of the specific station or, more regularly, the specific shift served upon to be part of the 'them'. Verbalising the 'difference' between themselves and 'others' was a key narrative of the recruits in emphasising both the similarities and the comradeship evident within the 'us' grouping. This was seen both externally to the policing organisation and internally. Externally, the new recruits referred to the public, the media, social services and other parts of the criminal justice system as being an occupational challenge. This was seen in terms of the lack of support from others for the maintenance of the 'thin blue line', which the police themselves were engaged with. Internally, the new recruits presented the organisational challenges. Here, there was a sharp divide portrayed between police officers on the 'front line' and more senior police managers, whom they perceived to be 'different' because of their role, their lack of understanding of the issues faced by more junior police officers and their perceived lack of support in difficult circumstances. By categorising and differentiating in this way, the differences within their own in-group can be minimised and the differences within the out-groups can be exaggerated.

'Dirty workers' engage in reframing, recalibrating and refocusing (Ashforth and Kreiner 1999) the more negative and identity-threatening aspects of the job and instead reverse the threat to their occupational identity by attributing that threat outwards instead, to those outside of the network. In doing this, the occupational identity of the group can be enhanced, and any lingering threats to that identity, which might present themselves in the form of role confusion, job dissatisfaction and external criticism, can be reversed and refocused elsewhere.

This tendency towards categorisation is also seen when officers are discussing the public they are policing. With the increasing focus upon safeguarding and vulnerability, as has been evidenced in this book, officers are engaging with victims or potential victims on a regular basis. As was discussed in Chap. 10, these officers sharply delineate between what they see to be 'deserving' and what they see to be 'undeserving' victims—using the label of 'genuine victims' to describe those who fulfil the normative criteria of what it is to be a victim of crime. The characteristics of this ideal-type victim include being vulnerable, often older and female, being 'hard-working' and having no previous association with offending behaviour.

Loftus has argued that cultural change is not inevitable within a changing field of policing. Her belief in this stems from the enduring nature of the police task and the communities which the police direct their attention towards. Couple this with a "contempt towards the poor" being "an integral feature of the culture" (2009, p. 197) and change may not be assured. This categorisation of victims into the deserving and the non-deserving has a long history. The police in the 1970s warned that the Yorkshire Ripper's next victim could be "somebody's daughter", largely ignoring the fact that the seven already murdered women (the majority of whom worked as prostitutes) were 'somebody's daughter' (Kitzinger 2009). The Attorney General declared that the most unfortunate aspect of the murders by the Yorkshire Ripper in the UK in the 1970s was that the "last six attacks were on totally respectable women" (Havers 1981; cited in Kitzinger 2009).

The impact of this 'underpolicing' or 'underprotection' of certain, usually disadvantaged communities has been widely examined (Bowling and Phillips 2003; Rowe 2014) and focuses on the ensuing alienation and discrimination. The legitimacy of the police is not only influenced by the *outcomes* of police actions but crucially lies in the *processes* that lead to those outcomes. A consideration of the social and cultural aspects of legitimacy in policing is therefore just as, if not more, important as a consideration of the more quantifiable measures of policing effectiveness. Adopting an approach towards policing which focuses instead upon procedural justice was outlined in Chap. 2. However, given the expressed attitudes of the new recruits towards what they perceive to be different types of victims with varying degrees of legitimacy, it seems difficult to reconcile how these attitudes would be analogous with the principles of procedural justice, with its focus on dignity, fairness and trust.

## Compassion

Given the reasons provided in the literature as to why individuals choose to join the police service, plus what police officers enjoy about the nature of the job, it should come as no surprise that 'compassion' should be seen as one of the six potential characteristics of police culture at the lower ranks identified in this research. In an article entitled 'Passionate Professionals', Maurice Punch has argued that there is a further story to be told about officers who are "driven by concern and compassion for the victims and their relatives" (2016, p. 27). There is evidence here to begin that story.

Research on the motivations for joining the police have changed little since Hopper's work in 1977 which focused upon the variety of tasks involved, the excitement, the outdoors-oriented nature of the job and, importantly, the community service principles of helping others. Both Fielding (1988a) and Chan (2003), in their longitudinal research, found that community service principles were strong influences in the decision to join the police. This research confirms many of these previous findings and provides more extensive evidence in this regard. First, the new recruits cited community service principles or, as they termed it, 'making a difference' as the key motivator for joining the police service. Second, when asked to choose from a list of the most important characteristics of a police officer, empathy/understanding was second on each occasion (after good communication) and rose in importance during the four-year interview process. Third, when the new recruits were asked what had been the most useful advice they had received from other colleagues, empathy and kindness were regularly stressed. Fourth, when officers were asked what they were most enjoying about the job, 'helping victims of crime' was one of the three most commonly cited answers. Finally, when asked what makes a 'good' police officer, wherein the respondents could answer in any way they chose, empathy, compassion and integrity were featured in the top four responses (again, after good communication).

It could be argued that much of this change derives from a fundamental change to the field of policing, where the focus is much more upon congenial activities such as citizen *protection*, public *reassurance* and *safeguarding*, rather than on more combative activities such as *fighting* crime and *catching* criminals. However, it could also be argued that historically, police officers have always liked to portray the crime-fighting image despite most evidence suggesting that this has only ever constituted a small part of a police officer's role. This is what Manning (2003, p. 16) has referred to as the "drama of control" of the police, where the symbolism of the police is as important as their actions. The narratives of policing then have never quite matched the actions. Perhaps that is where we are seeing the most fundamental change therefore. It is not necessarily in the changing *role* of the police officer, but can instead be found in the changing acceptance of the new *narratives* surrounding the role of the police. Taking the interviews after four years of service as an example and in discussions about the role of the police, the new recruits placed 'protecting citizens' first, then 'protecting society', then 'catching criminals', then 'upholding the law' and then, finally, 'fighting crime'. Policing and police officers, it could be argued, are now more comfortable with their social identity as 'peacekeepers' rather than as 'crime-fighters'. The adherence to crime-fighting has been shed both literally and figuratively. As discussed in Chaps. 2 and 3, research has found that officers who are confident with the sense of their own legitimacy are more likely to utilise the principles of procedural justice in their encounters with the public (Bradford and Quinton 2014). How that legitimacy is established and influenced in the early days of a recruit's career, and through the horizontal, vertical, formal and informal processes of learning found in *the square of police learning*, is therefore of vital importance for the later behaviour of police officers.

## The Geology of Policing Cultures

The research within this book has demonstrated that there are a multitude of models of policing cultures, but far less of a concentration on the sources of cultural formation and development. However, where there are those discussions, they tend to fall between two accounts. On the one hand, there are those who argue that policing cultures and their attitudes, values and beliefs are transmitted from one generation of police officers to another in what could be termed the *cultural inheritance* model of policing cultures. On the other hand, there is a further, less well-discussed analysis of the sources of policing cultures which draws upon Bourdieu's conception of the cultural knowledge (habitus) of an organisation's members as a layering or sedimentation of social history (1986). This analysis stresses the more sedimentary nature of the formation and development of policing cultures, in what could be termed '*cultural sedimentation*'.

The notion of 'cultural inheritance' has held far more prominence in the policing literature over many decades. But is it now time to accommodate the idea of policing cultures as being more influenced by both the field of operation and the habitus of those entering the field? The collective memory is after all influenced by both the 'cultural memory', relating to symbols and cues, and the 'communicative memory', which relates to the immediate present (Assmann and Czaplicka 1995). When policing was more historically perhaps an all-encompassing identity, there may have been more evidence to suggest that the 'desocialisation' prior to 'resocialisation' (or in Goffman's terms, the 'stripping of the self' (1959)) was a rite of passage through which the more homogeneous population of police officers must all pass. However, the more modern recruits to the police service bring with them not just demographic diversity but also a diversity of experiences and cultures. They also adhere much less to the narrative of their identity as a police officer defining who they are. They are therefore as likely to be influenced by their previous pre-police experiences and their future non-police experiences. Hofstede has highlighted that human programming takes place on three levels—the universal (or biological, shared by all), the collective (shared by some) and the unique (2001). Each police officer's unique habitus will have the potential to both sustain and supplement the existing cultural manifestations. The analysis of policing cultures then needs a much more fluid approach, and one that respects the "cultural pluriformity" (Hendriks and van Hulst 2016) of policing practice.

As new or existing cultural characteristics are added to the sedimentation of policing practices, so the existing characteristics are strengthened (e.g. comradeship, cynicism or categorisation), old characteristics appear to become further buried (e.g. the 'blue code of silence' and 'crime-fighting') and new characteristics begin to take shape ('blue code of self-protection', compassion, communication). The weight of the top layers of cultural characteristics will compress and eventually extinguish the bottom layers. This is why it is still apparent that there are a multitude of contradictions in the descriptions of the changing nature of policing cultural characteristics within the lower ranks of the police service. On the one hand, there is evidence of compassion, good communication, 'making a difference', an attachment to the narratives associated with a #newbreed of police officer and a diminishing loyalty to the 'code of silence'. On the other hand, there is also the cultural adherence to the longstanding characteristics of cynicism and categorisation and, in particular, the delineation between the 'deserving' and the 'undeserving' victims. The new characteristics do not replace the old, but, over time, may gradually diminish their prevalence.

All of this however will be affected by the changing nature of the field of policing, which includes both internal changes to the size, demography, role, function and accountability of the organisation and external changes to the society which is to be policed. This brings with it new challenges, new frustrations and, therefore, new adaptive techniques. Those techniques are essential to navigate the new policing terrain. This takes us right back to Skolnick's assessment of the police officer as a 'craftsman', adapting to the environment in which they work (1966, p. 231). Sedimentation is therefore not only a process of the layering of cultural characteristics but also, importantly, in geophysical terms, is influenced by the roughness of the surface over which it moves—in this case, the policing environment.

Change will therefore be slow, incremental and potentially largely unnoticeable, but will nonetheless be occurring—"incomplete revolutions can easily escape notice" (Sklansky 2006, p. 1242). It will take time, as it does in the natural world, to affect the mineral balance of policing cultures. Police officers are active participants who shape the creation and the development of the different elements of policing cultures. Their organisational cultures are learned and shared in an environment that is characterised by socialisation with others and through the validation of others. These complex and often hidden interactions all contribute to the process of learning, becoming and being a police officer.

# References

Alain, M., & Grégoire, M. (2008). Can Ethics Survive the Shock of the Job? Quebec's Police Recruits Confront Reality. *Policing and Society, 18*(2), 169–189.

Ashforth, B., & Kreiner, G. (1999). "How Can You Do It?" Dirty Work and the Challenge of Constructing a Positive Identity. *The Academy of Management Review, 24*(3), 413–434.

Ashforth, B., & Mael, F. (1989). Social Identity Theory and the Organisation. *Academy of Management Review, 14*, 20–39.

Assmann, J., & Czaplicka, J. (1995). Collective Memory and Cultural Identity. *New German Critique, 65*, 125–133.

Bayley, D., & Bittner, E. (1984). Learning the Skills of Policing. *Law and Contemporary Problems, 47*(4), 35–59.

Bennett, R. (1984). Becoming Blue: A Longitudinal Study of Police Recruit Occupational Socialization. *Journal of Police Science and Administration, 12*(1), 47–58.

Birzer, M. (2003). The Theory of Andragogy Applied to Police Training. *Journal of Police Strategies and Management, 26*(1), 29–42.

Blau, P. (1964). *Exchange and Power in Social Life.* New York: John Wiley.

Bourdieu, P. (1986). The Forms of Capital. In J. Richardson (Ed.), *Handbook of Theory and Research for the Sociology of Education* (pp. 241–258). New York: Greenwood.

Bourdieu, P. (1991). *Language and Symbolic Power.* Cambridge: Polity Press.

Bradford, B., & Quinton, P. (2014). Self-Legitimacy, Police Culture and Support for Democratic Policing in an English Constabulary. *British Journal of Criminology, 54*(6), 1023–1046.

Bowling, B., & Phillips, C. (2003). Policing Minority Communities. In T. Newburn (Ed.), *The Handbook of Policing* (pp. 528–555). Cullompton: Willan.

Bradford, B., Murphy, K., & Jackson, J. (2014). Officers as Mirrors: Policing, Procedural Justice and the (Re) Production of Social Identity. *British Journal of Criminology, 54*(4), 527–550.

Brough, P., Chataway, S., & Biggs, A. (2016). 'You Don't Want People Knowing You're a Copper!' A Contemporary Assessment of Police Organisational Culture. *International Journal of Police Science and Management, 18*(1), 28–36.

Cain, D. (2012). *Gender Within a Specialised Police Department: An Examination of the Cultural Dynamics of a Police Firearms Unit, Unpublished Professional Doctorate.* Portsmouth: University of Portsmouth.

Campeau, H. (2015). 'Police Culture' at Work: Making Sense of Police Oversight. *British Journal of Criminology, 55*(4), 669–687.

Chan, J. (2003). *Fair Cop: Learning the Art of Policing.* Toronto: University of Toronto Press.

Chan, J. (2007a). Making Sense of Police Reforms. *Theoretical Criminology, 11*(3), 323–345.

Chan, J. (2007b). Police Stress and Occupational Culture. In M. O'Neill & A. Singh (Eds.), *Police Occupational Culture: New Debates and Directions* (pp. 129–151). Oxford: Elsevier JAI.

Charman, S. (2013). Sharing a Laugh: The Role of Humour in Relationships Between Police Officers and Ambulance Staff. *International Journal of Sociology and Social Policy, 33*(3–4), 152–166.

College of Policing. (2015). *College of Policing Analysis: Estimating Demand on the Police Service.* Retrieved from http://www.college.police.uk/News/College-news/Documents/Demand%20Report%2023_1_15_noBleed.pdf

Critchley, S. (2002). *On Humour.* London: Routledge.

Eliot, T. S. (1948). *Notes Towards the Definition of Culture.* London: Faber and Faber.

Ellis, R. (1991). Perceptions, Attitudes and Beliefs of Police Recruits. *Canadian Police College Journal, 15*(2), 95–117.

Fielding, N. (1988a). *Joining Forces: Police Training, Socialization, and Occupational Competence.* London: Routledge.

Fielding, N. (1988b). Socialisation of Recruits into the Police Role. In P. Southgate (Ed.), *New Directions in Policing Training* (pp. 58–73). London: HMSO.

Foucault, M. (1980). *Power/Knowledge: Selected Interviews and Other Writings.* London: Harvester Wheatsheaf.

Goffman, E. (1959). *The Presentation of Self in Everyday Life.* New York: Doubleday Anchor.

Goldsmith, A. (1990). Taking Police Culture Seriously: Police Discretion and the Limits of Law. *Policing and Society, 1*(2), 91–114.

He, H., & Brown, A. (2013). Organizational Identity and Organizational Identification – A Review of the Literature and Suggestions for Future Research. *Group and Organization Management, 38*(1), 3–35.

Hendriks, F., & van Hulst, M. (2016). Shifting Repertoires: Understanding Cultural Plurality in Policing. *Innovation: The European Journal of Social Science Research, 29*(2), 161–176.

Hofstede, G. (2001). *Culture's Consequences: International Differences in Work-Related Values* (2nd ed.). London: Sage.

Kitzinger, J. (2009). Rape in the Media. In M. Horvath & J. Brown (Eds.), *Rape: Challenging Contemporary Thinking* (pp. 74–98). Cullompton: Willan.

Loftus, B. (2009). *Police Culture in a Changing World.* Oxford: Oxford University Press.

Manning, P. (2003). *Policing Contingencies.* Chicago: University of Chicago Press.

Mead, G. (1934). *Mind, Self and Society.* Chicago: University of Chicago Press.

Meyer, J. (1997). Humor in Member Narratives: Uniting and Dividing at Work. *Western Journal of Communication, 61*(2), 188–208.

Morrison, E. (1993). Newcomer Information Seeking: Exploring Types, Modes, Sources, and Outcomes. *The Academy of Management Journal, 36*(3), 557–589.

Myhill, A., & Bradford, B. (2013). Overcoming Cop Culture: Organizational Justice and Police Officers' Attitudes Toward the Public. *Policing: An International Journal of Police Strategies and Management, 36*(2), 338–356.

Paoline, E., & Terrill, W. (2014). *Police Culture: Adapting to the Strains of the Job.* Durham: Carolina Academic Press.

Peace, R. (2006). Probationer Training for Neighbourhood Policing in England and Wales: Fit for Purpose? *Policing: An International Journal of Police Strategies and Management, 29*(2), 335–346.

Punch, M. (2016). *Passionate Professionals: The Dutch Police Response to the Shooting Down of Malaysian Airlines' MH17 in the Ukraine (2014).* Paper presented at the Third International Conference on Law Enforcement and Public Health. Amsterdam: The Netherlands. Retrieved from http://www.cleph.com.au/files/9914/7803/0755/Punch_Passionate_Professionals_MH17_rev_30_09_mp..pdf

Rantatalo, O. (2016). Media Representations and Police Officers' Identity Work in a Specialised Police Tactical Unit. *Policing and Society, 26*(1), 97–113.

Reicher, S., Spears, R., & Haslam, S. (2010). The Social Identity Approach in Social Psychology. In M. Wetherell & C. Mohanty (Eds.), *The SAGE Handbook of Identities* (pp. 45–63). London: Sage.

Rowe, M. (2014). *Introduction to Policing* (2nd ed.). London: Sage.

Sackmann, S. (1991). *Cultural Knowledge in Organisations.* London: Sage Publications.

Scott, T. (2007). Expression of Humour by Emergency Personnel Involved in Sudden Deathwork. *Mortality, 12*(4), 350–364.

Shearing, C., & Ericson, R. (1991). Culture as Figurative Action. *British Journal of Sociology, 42*(4), 481–506.

Sklansky, D. (2006). Not Your Father's Police Department: Making Sense of the New Demographics of Law Enforcement. *The Journal of Criminal Law and Criminology, 96*(3), 1209–1243.

Skolnick, J. (1966). *Justice Without Trial: Law Enforcement in Democratic Society.* New York: Wiley and Sons.

Stephenson, C., & Stewart, P. (2001). The Whispering Shadow: Collectivism and Individualism at Ikeda-Hoover and Nissan UK. *Sociological Research Online, 6*(3), 1–15.

Tajfel, H. (1981). *Human Groups and Social Categories.* Cambridge: Cambridge University Press.

Waddington, P. (1999a). Police (Canteen) Culture: An Appreciation. *British Journal of Criminology, 39*(2), 287–309.

Waddington, P. (1999b). *Policing Citizens*. London: UCL Press.

Weick, K. (1995). *Sensemaking in Organizations*. Thousand Oaks: Jossey-Bass.

Westmarland, L. (2005). Police Ethics and Integrity: Breaking the Blue Code of Silence. *Policing and Society, 15*(2), 145–165.

Westmarland, L., & Rowe, M. (2016). Police Ethics and Integrity: Can a New Code Overturn the Blue Code? *Policing and Society.* http://dx.doi.org/10.10 80/10439463.2016.1262365

Willis, J., & Mastrofski, S. (2017). Understanding the Culture of Craft: Lessons from Two Police Agencies. *Journal of Crime and Justice, 40*(1), 84–100.

# Appendix 1

## The Research Diaries

Much as I enjoy a good nature documentary, there's something extremely satisfying about the final ten minutes of the modern documentary genre which provides a glimpse into the world behind the camera. Here we discover the huge challenges and sometimes insurmountable obstacles in the way of achieving the ambitious aims of the documentary maker. We discover at these more candid moments on film that the elusive and extremely rare snow tiger only emerges under a waxing moon or when the wind is blowing in a certain direction, and we discover that the particular rainforest bird of interest is not currently interested in performing his courtship ritual for the camera. For it is here that we find out what 'research', in whatever form that might take, actually entails. Of course it is rewarding, exciting and very often rich in potential but at the same time it can be frustrating, messy and arduous.

I am also quite sure that students and new social scientists sometimes feel a sense of trepidation and unease about venturing into the minefield that can be empirical research. Is there an expectation that the research will follow some clearly laid out plan where respondents react as planned,

© The Author(s) 2017
S. Charman, *Police Socialisation, Identity and Culture*,
DOI 10.1007/978-3-319-63070-0

in numbers and on time? Does it assist those new to research to have an array of methodological textbooks which state the different ways in which research can be conducted but spend very little time revealing the realities of social science research? This book has discussed the different types of disappointment associated with occupational socialisation, most particularly endogenous disappointment, which is the disassociation between expectation and reality (Alain and Grégoire 2008). Are we as social scientists as guilty as the policing organisation in preparing new researchers not for what is but for what should or might be?

The purpose of this final section of the book is to reflect on the process itself, not in any way to contribute to any existing literature or to provide a blueprint for the future, as I am not in a position to do either. However, the aim here is just to candidly consider some of the pitfalls, the challenges and the memorable moments of spending four years, on and off, interviewing new police officers. This may have wider resonance with social science researchers more generally; it may not. However, it will hopefully paint a picture of some of the highlights and lowlights of this research project. It will do this through a series of (not to be taken too seriously) dos and don'ts.

## Don't Be Easily Offended

1. Policing tends not to be an appointment-based profession, and the majority of the new recruits during the four-year research project were working as response officers operating out of local stations. Having made appointments with the officers when they were in their stations (TIME B and TIME D), either myself by e-mail or via a liaison working within the police, I would then discover, on arrival, a surprised-looking member of police staff on the front desk or, worse still (see point 8), the locked door of a newly closed police station. My experience with this research was that if an officer was expecting you plus waiting for you, it was an unusual day. More common was the second scenario of an officer not expecting you but being available to see you. Third was the not expecting you, not being at the station, being called on the radio and returning 'shortly'. Finally was the not expecting you

and not able to get back to the station anytime soon. I took three trips to one station at the far end of the force area in an attempt to meet with one officer only to be greeted by that final scenario. This could lead one to become slightly paranoid that as you enter the front door, they depart from the back. Therefore, the key message here is that it is important not to be easily offended. Policing, whilst perhaps not the criminal-catching, car-chasing occupation that some recruits may have hoped it might be, does nonetheless rarely run to a timetable. There were clearly times during the research when officers had no option but to be away from the station during appointment times; that was only to be expected. However, the rarity of officers recalling appointment times was also indicative of not only the nature of the job but also the more action-focused desires of the officers themselves. The constraints associated with diaries and appointments went against some of the more desirable aspects of the job including not only the reactive but the more proactive activities associated with the role. As a note of interest, however, if I was interviewing a female police officer, the chances of the appointment time being remembered were significantly higher.

2. In addition to policing not being an appointment-based profession, I could add that it is also taking some time to come to terms with the job requiring significantly more time spent in front of a computer. Chapter 10 discussed some of the frustrations felt by police officers at the sedentary nature of the job, particularly those who were moved into the investigations teams. Notwithstanding the phenomenal rise in cyber-enabled crime, which is a different issue altogether, the police are also having to adapt to different forms of communication with the public. There have been interesting and significant developments in the use of social media by the police (Crump 2011). However, there is also the routine e-mail communications between the police and the public, either as witnesses or victims. My experience of this research project (coupled with a career delivering part-time degrees to police officers) is that an e-mail can spend some considerable time languishing in an inbox somewhere, before a few reminders later a response may ensue. There is no doubt that the non-essential aspect of my requests would have pushed the communication way down the

priority list, but it also reflects, as mentioned earlier, the desires of many police officers to be in a more action-focused environment, working outside and verbally communicating with others. The "I didn't join for …." statement was often attached to being inside or being computer-based. Therefore, don't expect an immediate reply to an e-mail. Hope for a reply at some point but don't be surprised to receive no reply at all.

3. Chapter 10 considered the characteristic of suspiciousness, which a number of the new recruits mentioned as something that they felt had increased within them during their first four years in service. However, as previously discussed, the vast majority of the new recruits had served as Police Community Support Officer (PCSOs) or Special Constables before joining the force as a constable. Suspiciousness, particularly of 'outsiders' whether they be suspects or not, was apparent from the first stages of this research project. Chapter 4 referred to the historically 'uneasy' relationship between the police service and the higher education sector, and there was certainly a feeling of unease from the new recruits as to the nature of the project. This was exacerbated by a further issue. There were 16 members of the first cohort of officers, of whom 13 agreed to take part. This is a very healthy percentage of over 80%, which most social science researchers would be delighted about. The response rate from the second cohort of new recruits was 100%. The difference was the manner in which the research project was explained. All new recruits had received a one-page explanation of the aims of the research project. However, with the first cohort, one of the police trainers working at the training school where the new recruits were based explained the project to them before they came individually to be interviewed by me in another (very cold – see point 12) outbuilding. All of those who came to be interviewed were under the impression that I was conducting an analysis of the Certificate of Knowledge of Policing pre-join course that they had been the first new recruits to have to complete. Three of the cohort who declined the invitation to take part in the research did so on the basis of their negative experiences of the pre-join course, which they did not wish to discuss. An explanation that this was not the focus of the research was largely unheard. This did mean that the initial stages of the first research interview with the first cohort were

spent 'undoing' their first impressions of the aim of the research and establishing the correct parameters for the content of the interviews. It also meant quickly trying to establish some positive rapport with the new recruits who, although they had agreed to take part, were generally very negative about their pre-join course experiences (see Chap. 9) and were therefore fairly defensive before the interview started. By the time the second cohort had joined the police service, I ensured that I explained the research aims in full myself rather than the task being taken on by someone outside of the research process. Do be careful then in ensuring that your liaison points within an organisation are either well versed in your intentions or leave the explanations to you. An initial 'frosty' start to an interview may be due to some other circumstances than an immediate dislike of yourself as a researcher.

4. When I first started working as a researcher, I transcribed nearly 100 interviews (mostly 60–90 minutes in length) for a research project investigating the growing prominence of the now dissolved Association of Chief Police Officers, which represented the most senior ranks of the police service (Savage et al. 2000). Whilst there is no better way of getting to know your data than by going through this process, it is without doubt a challenging task. Dreaming of keyboards became an occupational hazard. The interviews, however, were clear and easy to decipher, which was a bonus. Interviews with police constables who are working on response do not always equate with such a clear and uninterrupted interview. Not only were there the couple of occasions where interviews were split into various segments due to officers being called elsewhere, there was also the ever-present background noise of the police radio. The now outsourced task of transcribing some of these interviews must not be a straightforward task. So, the now familiar 'eyes into the distance stare' does not (I am confidently maintaining) indicate a lack of interest in the research interview but is often an indication that the police officers are listening to something on the radio. Interestingly this was more likely to occur at the start of the interview with the volume being regularly turned down as the new recruits mostly became more interested and engaged in the topics of discussion. This relates to the final point in the 'don't be easily offended' section.

5. Taking into account the difficulties covered under point 1 in terms of interviewees expecting you, once in a suitable location (more on this in points 11 and 12) with a digital recording device running (more on this too in point 6), I was usually greeted with either a direct or an indirect indication that time was pressing and that the interview would not be able to be too long. Assurances of this nature were provided and, again, no offence taken. A very similar scenario was a regular feature of the senior police officer interviews in the research project mentioned earlier. However, what tended to then ensue was an interview that was much longer than was the original intention of the interviewees. Reiner has acknowledged this when discussing policing research by suggesting that:

> No doubt I was aided by the social researcher's strongest weapon, the delight people take in talking about themselves to an unfailingly rapt audience. (1991, p. 52)

Reiner's point is very valid and his comments which were reflecting upon his interviews with Chief Constables was something that was very recognisable to us in our research which followed (Savage et al. 2000). Senior officers are very used to being asked their opinions on a whole range of issues and are generally only too happy to oblige. However, a similar outcome was evident with the new recruits to the police service, but perhaps for very different reasons. Police officers at the lower ranks of the police service, and most particularly those new to the service, are rarely asked their views and opinions on anything at all. Their position is clearly defined, both formally and informally, and is one of a novice ready to be instructed. Therefore, to be able to spend time with 'an unfailingly rapt audience' that is interested in your views and opinions, not just on the issue of learning to become a police officer but also on the challenges facing modern policing, appeared to be a welcome change. Over the course of four years, there is no doubt that rapport between interviewer and interviewee developed, and these new recruits had an opportunity to comment both on their own personal transition in becoming a police officer (which had for some encompassed varying levels of stress) and also on wider policing and criminal justice issues in which they mostly all had a keen interest. Interviews were therefore in most cases longer than had been antici-pated by both interviewee and interviewer.

## Check and then Double Check

6. Technological advances are mostly the friend of social science research-ers. Small digital recording devices are much less obtrusive and easier to carry than their large recording counterparts of the past. The better quality of these older and larger devices required an electrical socket. During a previous research project, the chief officers who required their staff officers to be called into the office to locate the plug socket revealed much about their individual characters. However, the pocket-sized recording devices today require only batteries. It would be fool-ish, surely, to forget to take spare batteries and then be limping to the end of an interview, red light flashing, warning beeping, without hav-ing had the foresight to have brought some spares. Looking back twenty years, I recalled having experienced a 525-mile round trip to interview a police officer of much historical importance for a previous research project only to find the recording device hadn't worked cor-rectly. One would imagine therefore that checking and rechecking every last detail would have been of particular importance.
7. Whilst checking on equipment, check on location too. Persisting on the phone that you are definitely outside the station when you are actually at a station some miles away is not advisable. This happened to both interviewer and interviewees who were also to be occasionally found in the wrong station, though at the right time.
8. However, all of the checking and preparation in the world can only get you so far when you are greeted with the all too frequent locked doors of the police station. Evermord Constabulary are going through a pro-cess, found in most police forces up and down the country, of either selling off police buildings and moving to larger purpose-built build-ings with no public access or staying within the older buildings but not allowing access to the public. This would not be an issue for this research project except for point 1, meaning that the e-mail asking for

a mobile number to use on the day of the interview was rarely answered. This left you at the mercy of the police station buzzer. The police station buzzer unfortunately does not link you to anybody inside the actual building but instead directs you to the force enquiry centre. In order for the buzzer to be accessible to all, it is usually placed only a short distance from the ground. Trying to relay the details of the person you are trying to contact and the purpose behind your visit through an intercom situated on a road, sometimes a very busy and noisy road, in all weathers, was a difficult, if perhaps comedic, moment of many of the interviews. On a number of occasions, the relaying of the message must have been so unintelligible that an answer was never received. Alternatively, I was told that they would try to contact the officer concerned and again nothing was heard back; presumably even the intercom had a time limit. This led to a couple of different scenarios. Sometimes members of the public would walk past as I waited in hope, and inform me, disgruntledly, that the police station was closed, which was thoughtful but not entirely helpful. On other occasions, I would resort to walking around the building, knocking on windows, a plan that could perhaps be considered foolhardy. It was, however, generally the most successful strategy.

## Be Human

9. Kahn and Cannell have suggested that research interviews can be likened to "conversations with a purpose" (1957, p. 149). However, conversations usually involve a two-way process and generally, for them to be meaningful, there is a requirement that all participants give a little of themselves. In a research interview, particularly cultural analysis of this type, the questions require the respondents to delve into their motivations, experiences, beliefs and indeed their anxieties. For some respondents this was dealt with quite mechanically but for others, particularly those for whom the first few years of their policing careers had not been as smooth and seamless as they would have liked, the stirring up of memories and emotions was a more difficult experience. In one station, my interviews coincided

with a traumatic incident that they had been involved with only the day before, which clearly affected a number of the officers with whom I spoke. The advice then is to be human. What happened when the recording device was switched off was taken as seriously as the more formal interview when the device was switched on. Sometimes, the respondents wanted to talk further. There is comfort sometimes in the listening ear of a stranger who has no working relationship with you and who understands but yet is not involved in your world. Weber discussed the importance of '*verstehen*', of understanding the world of those under the microscope (1922/1978). This can be carefully achieved without 'going native'.

10. Apologies to the transcribers again but the respondents were provided with large amounts of chocolate at TIME C. The new recruits were back in training school and were facing straightforward but long days in the classroom. A bag of chocolate bars was on the table with the recording device. It served as an accompaniment to the completion of the quantitative questions. The chocolate was readily appreciated and I remain convinced that it hovers on the right side of the line of ethical research practices. A number of the respondents mentioned that they had remembered the chocolate (but thankfully not the questions, many of which were repeated) three years after the event. However, be warned that when you subsequently turn up at future interviews without such a bag, you will be remembered for it. Disconcertingly, I was greeted at one station by the sergeant of one of the interviewees with the words, "I've heard about you. We've been expecting chocolate".

## Expect Surprises

11. By surprises, I don't necessarily mean that police officers will regularly suggest interview times before 8 am. They did and that was often the easy bit. What was more difficult was finding a suitable room in a police station or a training school for an interview. Discovering half way through an interview that there was a person behind a screen in another part of the room was a surprise. Being

interrupted in the middle of what was clearly an interview that was being recorded by a member of police staff who came in, prepared a bowl of porridge and sat very nearby in order to eat it also made for an interesting experience.

12. I'm not sure what was most surprising about the interview location of the first of my visits to the new recruits. It may have been that I was housed for two days in a former asylum or it may have been that there was no heating or any access to food or drink. Emergency ration packs (and not forgetting the spare batteries) became a staple part of the planning process. Having said that, being in a stiflingly hot police station in a small interview room with a new recruit with a streaming cold also proved to be one step too far in germ avoidance.

Overall, the research process itself was lengthy, at times difficult to arrange and occasionally frustrating because of the issues raised earlier. But most of all, it was fascinating. Fascinating to gain an insight into the world of new recruits to the police service, to see both their enthusiasm and apprehension in the early stages of the job and to see the changes that ensued over their first four years. Thank you to these new recruits for allowing me that insight. I have threatened to go back and interview them all again after ten years of service ... watch this space.

# References

6, P., Bellamy, C., Raab, C., Warren, A., & Heeney, C. (2006). Institutional Shaping of Interagency Working: Managing Tensions Between Collaborative Working and Client Confidentiality. *Journal of Public Administration Research and Theory, 17*, 405–434.

Abell, S. (2017). In Praise of Cliché. *The Times Literary Supplement.* Retrieved from http://www.the-tls.co.uk/articles/public/cliche-terror-attacks/?CMP= Sprkr-_-Editorial-_-TheTLS-_-ArtsandCulture-_-Unspecified-_-Unspecified-_-Unspecified-_-ACCOUNT_TYPE

Alain, M., & Baril, C. (2005). Crime Prevention, Crime Repression, and Policing: Attitudes of Police Recruits Towards Their Role in Crime Control. *International Journal of Comparative and Applied Criminal Justice, 29*(2), 123–148.

Alain, M., & Grégoire, M. (2008). Can Ethics Survive the Shock of the Job? Quebec's Police Recruits Confront Reality. *Policing and Society, 18*(2), 169–189.

Albert, S., & Whetten, D. A. (1985). Organizational Identity. In L. Cummings & M. Staw (Eds.), *Research in Organizational Behaviour Volume 7* (pp. 263–295). Greenwich: JAI.

Alcott, C. (2012). Reforming the Force: An Examination of the Impact of the Operational Sub-culture on Reform and Modernisation Within the Police Service. *British Journal of Community Justice, 10*(1), 5–14.

© The Author(s) 2017
S. Charman, *Police Socialisation, Identity and Culture,*
DOI 10.1007/978-3-319-63070-0

Alvesson, M. (2002). *Understanding Organizational Culture*. London: Sage.

Alvesson, M. (2013). *Understanding Organizational Culture* (2nd ed.). London: Sage.

Amin, A., & Roberts, J. (2008). Knowing in Action: Beyond Communities of Practice. *Research Policy, 37*, 353–369.

Arksey, H., & Knight, P. (1999). *Interviewing for Social Scientists*. London: Sage.

Ashforth, B., & Kreiner, G. (1999). "How Can You Do It?" Dirty Work and the Challenge of Constructing a Positive Identity. *The Academy of Management Review, 24*(3), 413–434.

Ashforth, B., & Mael, F. (1989). Social Identity Theory and the Organisation. *Academy of Management Review, 14*, 20–39.

Ashforth, B., & Saks, A. (1996). Socialization Tactics: Longitudinal Effects on Newcomer Adjustments. *The Academy of Management Journal, 39*(1), 149–178.

Assmann, J., & Czaplicka, J. (1995). Collective Memory and Cultural Identity. *New German Critique, 65*, 125–133.

Atherton, S. (2012). Cops and Bloggers: Exploring the Presence of Police Culture on the Web. *Internet Journal of Criminology*. Retrieved from https://media.wix.com/ugd/b93dd4_e3fafc746b864462936d254a7c7251c9.pdf

Bahn, C. (1984). Police Socialization in the Eighties: Strains in the Forging of an Occupational Identity. *Journal of Police Science and Administration, 12*(4), 390–394.

Banton, M. (1964). *The Policeman in the Community*. London: Tavistock.

Bardi, A., Buchanan, K., Goodwin, R., Slabu, L., & Robinson, M. (2014). Value Stability and Change During Self-Chosen Life Transitions: Self-Selection Versus Socialization Effects. *Journal of Personality and Social Psychology, 106*(1), 131–147.

Bayley, D., & Bittner, E. (1984). Learning the Skills of Policing. *Law and Contemporary Problems, 47*(4), 35–59.

Beck, K., & Wilson, C. (1997). Police Officers' Views on Cultivating Organizational Commitment: Implications for Police Managers. *Policing: An International Journal of Police Strategies and Management, 20*, 175–195.

Beck, K., & Wilson, C. (2000). Development of Affective Organizational Commitment: A Cross-Sequential Examination of Change with Tenure. *Journal of Vocational Behaviour, 56*, 114–136.

Becker, H. (1963). *Outsiders: Studies in the Sociology of Deviance*. New York: Free Press.

Beetham, D. (1991). *The Legitimation of Power*. London: Macmillan.

Bennett, R. (1984). Becoming Blue: A Longitudinal Study of Police Recruit Occupational Socialization. *Journal of Police Science and Administration, 12*(1), 47–58.

Bergami, M., & Bagozzi, R. (2000). Self-Categorization, Affective Commitment and Group Self-Esteem as Distinct Aspects of Social Identity in the Organization. *British Journal of Social Psychology, 39*, 555–577.

Birzer, M. (2003). The Theory of Andragogy Applied to Police Training. *Journal of Police Strategies and Management, 26*(1), 29–42.

Bittner, E. (1990). *Aspects of Police Work*. Boston: Northeastern University Press.

Blader, S., & Tyler, T. (2009). Testing and Extending the Group Engagement Model: Linkages Between Social Identity Theory, Procedural Justice, Economic Outcomes and Extra Role Behaviour. *Journal of Applied Psychology, 94*(2), 445–464.

Blakemore, B., & Simpson, K. (2010). A Comparison of the Effectiveness of Pre- and Post-employment Modes of Higher Education for Student Police Officers. *The Police Journal, 83*, 29–41.

Blau, P. (1964). *Exchange and Power in Social Life*. New York: John Wiley.

Blears, H. (2004). *Home Affairs Select Committee Proceedings on Police Reform, Q320*. Retrieved from http://www.publications.parliament.uk/pa/cm200304/cmselect/cmhaff/c1038-iv/uc103802.htm

Bond, C., Murphy, K., & Porter, L. (2015). Procedural Justice in Policing: The First Phase of an Australian Longitudinal Study of Officer Attitudes and Intentions. *Crime, Law and Social Change, 64*, 229–245.

Bottoms, A., & Costello, A. (2010). The Phenomenon of Victim-Offender Overlap: A Study of Offences Against Households. In A. Bottoms & J. V. Roberts (Eds.), *Hearing the Victim: Adversarial Justice, Crime Victims and the State* (pp. 104–139). Cullompton: Willan.

Bourdieu, P. (1977). *Outline of a Theory of Practice*. Cambridge: Cambridge University Press.

Bourdieu, P. (1984). *Distinction: A Social Critique of the Judgement of Taste*. London: Routledge.

Bourdieu, P. (1986). The Forms of Capital. In J. Richardson (Ed.), *Handbook of Theory and Research for the Sociology of Education* (pp. 241–258). New York: Greenwood.

Bourdieu, P. (1990). *The Logic of Practice*. Cambridge: Polity Press.

Bourdieu, P. (1991). *Language and Symbolic Power*. Cambridge: Polity Press.

Bower, M. (1966). *The Will to Manage*. London: McGraw-Hill.

Bradford, B. (2014). Policing and Social Identity: Procedural Justice, Inclusion and Co-operation Between Police and Public. *Policing and Society, 24*(1), 22–43.

Bradford, B., & Quinton, P. (2014). Self-Legitimacy, Police Culture and Support for Democratic Policing in an English Constabulary. *British Journal of Criminology, 54*(6), 1023–1046.

Bradford, B., Jackson, J., & Hough, M. (2014). Police Futures and Legitimacy: Redefining 'Good Policing'. In J. Brown (Ed.), *The Future of Policing* (pp. 79–99). London: Routledge.

Bradford, B., Murphy, K., & Jackson, J. (2014). Officers as Mirrors: Policing, Procedural Justice and the (Re) Production of Social Identity. *British Journal of Criminology, 54*(4), 527–550.

Bradford, B., Quinton, P., Myhill, A., & Porter, G. (2014). Why Do 'the Law' Comply? Procedural Justice, Group Identification and Officer Motivation in Police Organizations. *European Journal of Criminology, 11*(1), 110–131.

Braun, V., & Clarke, V. (2006). Using Thematic Analysis in Psychology. *Qualitative Research in Psychology, 3*(2), 77–101.

Brewer, J. (1993). A Study of Routine Policing in Northern Ireland. In C. Renzetti & R. Lee (Eds.), *Researching Sensitive Topics* (pp. 125–145). London: Sage.

Brinkmann, S. (2012). Qualitative Research Between Craftsmanship and McDonaldization. *Qualitative Studies, 3*(1), 56–68.

Britz, M. (1997). The Police Subculture and Occupational Socialization: Exploring Individual and Demographic Characteristics. *American Journal of Criminal Justice, 21*(2), 127–146.

Broderick, J. (1977). *Police in a Time of Change*. Morristown: General Learning Press.

Brodeur, J. P. (1983). High Policing and Low Policing: Remarks About the Policing of Political Activities. *Social Problems, 30*(5), 507–520.

Brogden, M., Jefferson, T., & Walklate, S. (1988). *Introducing Policework*. London: Unwin Hyman.

Brough, P., Chataway, S., & Biggs, A. (2016). 'You Don't Want People Knowing You're a Copper!' A Contemporary Assessment of Police Organisational Culture. *International Journal of Police Science and Management, 18*(1), 28–36.

Brown, M. (1988). *Working the Street: Police Discretion and the Dilemmas of Reform* (2nd ed.). New York: Russell Sage Foundation.

Brown, L., & Willis, A. (1985). Authoritarianism in British Police Recruits: Importation, Socialization or Myth? *Journal of Occupational Psychology, 58*, 97–108.

Burbeck, E., & Furnham, A. (1985). Police Officer Selection: A Critical Review of the Literature. *Journal of Police Science and Administration, 13*(1), 58–69.

Burkhart, B. (1980, February). Conceptual Issues in the Development of Police Selection Procedures. *Professional Psychology*, pp. 121–129.

Butler, A., & Cochrane, R. (1977). An Examination of Some Elements of the Personality of Police Officers and Their Implications. *Journal of Police Science and Administration, 5*(4), 441–450.

Cable, D., & Parsons, C. (2001). Socialization Tactics and Person-Organization Fit. *Personnel Psychology, 54*(1), 1–23.

Cain, M. (1973). *Society and the Policeman's Role.* London: Routledge & Kegan Paul.

Cain, D. (2012). *Gender Within a Specialised Police Department: An Examination of the Cultural Dynamics of a Police Firearms Unit, Unpublished Professional Doctorate.* Portsmouth: University of Portsmouth.

Campbell, M. (2009). Learning in Early-Career Police: Coming into the Workplace. *Asia-Pacific Journal of Cooperative Education, 10*(1), 19–28.

Campeau, H. (2015). 'Police Culture' at Work: Making Sense of Police Oversight. *British Journal of Criminology, 55*(4), 669–687.

Carlson, H., & Sutton, M. (1975). The Effects of Different Police Roles on Attitude and Values. *The Journal of Psychology, 91*, 57–64.

Catlin, D., & Maupin, J. (2004). A Two Cohort Study of the Ethical Orientations of State Police Officers. *Policing: An International Journal of Police Strategies and Management, 27*(3), 289–301.

Chan, J. (1996). Changing Police Culture. *British Journal of Criminology, 36*(1), 109–134.

Chan, J. (1997). *Changing Police Culture.* Cambridge: Cambridge University Press.

Chan, J. (2003). *Fair Cop: Learning the Art of Policing.* Toronto: University of Toronto Press.

Chan, J. (2004). Using Pierre Bourdieu's Framework for Understanding Police Culture. *Droit et Société, 56–57*, 327–347.

Chan, J. (2007a). Making Sense of Police Reforms. *Theoretical Criminology, 11*(3), 323–345.

Chan, J. (2007b). Police Stress and Occupational Culture. In M. O'Neill & A. Singh (Eds.), *Police Occupational Culture: New Debates and Directions* (pp. 129–151). Oxford: Elsevier JAI.

Chappell, A., & Lanza-Kaduce, L. (2010). Police Academy Socialization: Understanding the Lessons Learned in a Paramilitary-Bureaucratic Organization. *Journal of Contemporary Ethnography, 39*(2), 187–214.

Charman, S. (2013). Sharing a Laugh: The Role of Humour in Relationships Between Police Officers and Ambulance Staff. *International Journal of Sociology and Social Policy, 33*(3–4), 152–166.

Charman, S. (2014). Blue Light Communities: Cultural Interoperability and Shared Learning Between Ambulance Staff and Police Officers in Emergency Response. *Policing and Society, 24*(1), 102–119.

Charman, S., & Corcoran, D. (2015). Adjusting the Police Occupational Cultural Landscape: The Case of An Garda Síochána. *Policing and Society, 25*(5), 484–503.

Charman, S., & Savage, S. (2008). Controlling Crime and Disorder: The Labour Legacy. In M. Powell (Ed.), *Modernising the Welfare State: The Blair Legacy* (pp. 105–124). Bristol: Polity Press.

Christensen, W., & Crank, J. (2001). Police Work and Culture in a Nonurban Setting: An Ethnographic Analysis. *Police Quarterly, 4*(1), 69–98.

Christie, G., Petrie, S., & Timmins, P. (1996). The Effect of Police Education, Training and Socialisation on Conservative Attitudes. *The Australian and New Zealand Journal of Criminology, 29*(3), 299–314.

Christopher, S. (2015). The Quantum Leap: Police Recruit Training and the Case for Mandating Higher Education for Pre-entry Schemes. *Policing, 9*(4), 388–404.

Clements, P., & Jones, J. (2009). Police Training and the Impact of Lawrence. In N. Hall, J. Grieve, & S. Savage (Eds.), *Policing and the Legacy of Lawrence* (pp. 193–213). Cullompton: Willan.

Cochran, J., & Bromley, M. (2003). The Myth (?) of the Police Sub-culture. *Policing: An International Journal of Police Strategies and Management, 26*(1), 88–117.

Cockcroft, T. (2015). Golden Ages, Red Herrings and Post Keynesian Policing: Understanding the Role of Police Culture in the Police Professionalism Debate. *Nordisk Politiforskning, 2*(2), 183–196.

Cohen, J. (1988). *Statistical Power Analysis for the Behavioural Sciences* (2nd ed.). Hillsdale: Lawrence Erlbaum Associates.

College of Policing. (2013a). *Police Sector Standards for the Training of Trainers*, Version 2. Retrieved from http://www.college.police.uk/What-we-do/Standards/Pages/Training-Roles.aspx

College of Policing. (2013b). *Police Sector Standards for the Training of Tutors*. Retrieved from http://www.college.police.uk/What-we-do/Standards/Documents/Tutor_Standard.pdf

College of Policing. (2015). *College of Policing Analysis: Estimating Demand on the Police Service*. Retrieved from http://www.college.police.uk/News/College-news/Documents/Demand%20Report%2023_1_15_noBleed.pdf

College of Policing. (2016). *Proposals for Qualifications in Policing.* Retrieved from http://www.college.police.uk/News/College-news/Pages/peqf_consultation.aspx

College of Policing. (n.d.). *Police Recruitment.* Retrieved from http://recruit.college.police.uk/Pages/home.aspx

Collier, P. (2001). Valuing Intellectual Capacity in the Police. *Accounting, Auditing and Accountability Journal, 14*(4), 437–455.

Colman, A., & Gorman, L. (1982). Conservatism, Dogmatism, and Authoritarianism in British Police Officers. *Sociology, 16*(1), 1–11.

Commission for Racial Equality. (2005). *The Police Service in England and Wales.* London: CRE. Retrieved from http://news.bbc.co.uk/1/shared/bsp/hi/pdfs/08_03_05_cre.pdf.

Conn, D. (2016, April 26). Hilsborough Inquests Jury Rules 96 Victims Were Unlawfully Killed. *The Guardian.* Retrieved from https://www.theguardian.com/uk-news/2016/apr/26/hillsborough-inquests-jury-says-96-victims-were-unlawfully-killed

Constable, J., & Smith, J. (2015). Initial Police Training and the Development of Police Occupational Culture. In P. Wankhade & D. Weir (Eds.), *Police Services: Leadership and Management Perspectives* (pp. 45–60). New York: Springer International Publishing.

Conti, N. (2006). Role Call: Preprofessional Socialization into Police Culture. *Policing and Society, 16*(3), 221–242.

Conti, N. (2009). A Visigoth System: Shame, Honour, and Police Socialization. *Journal of Contemporary Ethnography, 38*(3), 409–432.

Conti, N. (2011). Weak Links and Warrior Hearts: A Framework for Judging Self and *Others* in Police Training. *Police Practice and Research, 12*(5), 410–423.

Cooley, C. (1902). *Human Nature and the Social Order.* London: Transaction Publishers.

Cooper, J. (2014). *In Search of Police Legitimacy: Territoriality, Isomorphism and Changes in Policing Practices.* Texas: LFB Scholarly Publishing.

Corbin, J., & Strauss, A. (2008). *Basic of Qualitative Research* (3rd ed.). Thousand Oaks: Sage.

Coser, R. (1959). Some Social Functions of Laughter: A Study of Humor in a Hospital Setting. *Human Relations, 12*, 171–182.

Coser, L. (1974). *Greedy Institutions: Patterns of Undivided Commitment.* New York: Free Press.

Cox, C. (2016). *Police Culture and Socialisation Within a UK University, Unpublished Doctoral Thesis.* Preston: University of Central Lancashire.

Crank, J. (1998). *Understanding Police Culture.* Cincinnati: Anderson Publishing Co.

Crewe, I. (1974). Introduction: Studying Elites in Britain. In I. Crewe (Ed.), *British Political Sociology Yearbook: Elites in Western Democracy* (pp. 9–54). London: Croom Helm.

Critchley, S. (2002). *On Humour*. London: Routledge.

Crump, J. (2011). What Are the Police Doing on Twitter? Social Media, the Police and the Public. *Policy and Internet, 3*(4), Article 7.

Dahl, D., & Moreau, C. (2007). Thinking Inside the Box: Why Consumers Enjoy Constrained Creative Experiences. *Journal of Marketing Research, 44*(3), 357–369.

Davies, A., & Thomas, R. (2003). Talking Cop: Discourses of Change and Policing Identities. *Public Administration, 81*(4), 681–699.

Davies, A., & Thomas, R. (2008). Dixon of Dock Green Got Shot! Policing Identity Work and Organizational Change. *Public Administration, 86*(3), 627–642.

Daymon, C. (2000). Culture Formation in a New Television Station: A Multi-Perspective Analysis. *British Journal of Management, 11*(2), 121–135.

De Lint, W. (1998). New Managerialism and Canadian Police Training Reform. *Social and Legal Studies, 7*(2), 261–285.

Deal, T., & Kennedy, A. (1982). *Corporate Cultures: The Rites and Rituals of Corporate Life*. Reading, MA: Addison-Wesley.

Dick, P. (2005). Dirty Work Designations: How Police Officers Account for Their Use of Coercive Force. *Human Relations, 58*(11), 1363–1390.

Dick, P., & Jankowicz, D. (2001). A Social Constructionist Account of Police Culture and Its Influence on the Representation and Progression of Female Officers: A Repertory Grid Analysis in a UK Police Force. *Policing: An International Journal of Police Strategies and Management, 24*(2), 181–199.

Dilnot, A., Sir. (2016). *Police Grant 2016–17 [Letter written March 9, 2016 to Rt Hon Andy Burnham MP]*. Retrieved from https://www.statisticsauthority.gov.uk/wp-content/uploads/2016/03/Letter-from-Sir-Andrew-Dilnot-to-Andy-Burnham-MP-090316.pdf

Dixon, D. (1997). *Law in Policing*. Oxford: Oxford University Press.

Drummond, D. (1976). *Police Culture*. Beverley Hills: Sage Publications.

Durkheim, E. (1984). *The Division of Labour in Society*. Basingstoke: Macmillan. (Original work published 1893).

Edwards, R. (2009, November 26). British Policing 'Has Lost Its Way in Target Culture'. *Daily Telegraph*. Retrieved from http://www.telegraph.co.uk/news/uknews/law-and-order/6656699/British-policing-has-lost-its-way-in-target-culture.html

Eliot, T. S. (1948). *Notes Towards the Definition of Culture.* London: Faber and Faber.

Elliott, J., Kushner, S., Alexandrou, A., Dwyfor-Davies, J., Wilkinson, S., & Zamorski, B. (2003). *Independent Review of the Learning Requirement for Police Probationer Training in England and Wales.* Bristol/Norwich: University of the West of England/University of East Anglia.

Ellis, R. (1991). Perceptions, Attitudes and Beliefs of Police Recruits. *Canadian Police College Journal, 15*(2), 95–117.

Eraut, M. (2004). Informal Learning in the Workplace. *Studies in Continuing Education, 26*(2), 247–273.

Ericson, R. (1975). *Criminal Reactions: The Labelling Perspective.* Farnborough: Ashgate.

Ericson, R., Baranek, P., & Chan, J. (1987). *Visualizing Deviance: A Study of News Organizations.* Toronto: University of Toronto Press.

Fekjær, S. (2014). Police Students' Social Background, Attitudes and Career Plans. *Policing: An International Journal of Police Strategies and Management, 37*(3), 467–483.

Festinger, L. (1954). A Theory of Social Comparison Processes. *Human Relations, 7*, 117–140.

Fielding, N. (1984). Police Socialization and Police Competence. *The British Journal of Sociology, 35*(4), 568–590.

Fielding, N. (1986). Evaluating the Role of Training in Police Socialization: A British Example. *Journal of Community Psychology, 14*(3), 319–330.

Fielding, N. (1988a). *Joining Forces: Police Training, Socialization, and Occupational Competence.* London: Routledge.

Fielding, N. (1988b). *Joining Forces: Police Training, Socialization, and Occupational Competence.* London: Routledge.

Fielding, N. (1988c). Socialisation of Recruits into the Police Role. In P. Southgate (Ed.), *New Directions in Policing Training* (pp. 58–73). London: HMSO.

Fielding, N. (1989). Police Culture and Police Practice. In M. Weatheritt (Ed.), *Police Research: Some Future Prospects* (pp. 77–87). Aldershot: Gower Publishing Company.

Fielding, N. (1991). *The Police and Social Conflict.* London: Athlone.

Fielding, N. (1994). Cop Canteen Culture. In T. Newburn & E. Stanko (Eds.), *Just Boys Doing Business* (pp. 46–63). London: Routledge.

Fielding, N., & Fielding, J. (1991). Police Attitudes to Crime and Punishment. *British Journal of Criminology, 31*(1), 39–53.

Filstad, C., & Gottschalk, P. (2010). Collectivism Versus Individualism in Police Cultures. *International Journal of Human Resources Development and Management, 10*(2), 117–135.

Flanagan, R. (2008). *Review of Policing: Final Report*. London: HMSO.

Foley, P., Guarneri, C., & Kelly, M. (2008). Reasons for Choosing a Police Career: Changes over Two Decades. *International Journal of Police Science and Management, 10*(1), 2–8.

Ford, R. (2003a). Saying One Thing, Meaning Another: The Role of Parables in Police Training. *Police Quarterly, 6*(1), 84–110.

Ford, S. (Producer). (2003b, October 21). *The Secret Policeman* [Television broadcast]. London: BBC1.

Foster, J. (2003). Police Cultures. In T. Newburn (Ed.), *The Handbook of Policing* (pp. 196–227). Cullompton: Willan.

Foucault, M. (1972). *The Archaeology of Knowledge and the Discourse on Language*. London: Tavistock.

Foucault, M. (1980). *Power/Knowledge: Selected Interviews and Other Writings*. London: Harvester Wheatsheaf.

Fox, S. (2000). Communities of Practice, Foucault and Actor-Network Theory. *Journal of Management Studies, 37*(6), 853–868.

Frewin, K., & Tuffin, K. (1998). Police Status, Conformity and Internal Pressure: A Discursive Analysis of Police Culture. *Discourse and Society, 9*(2), 173–185.

Fuller, A. (2007). Critiquing Theories of Learning and Communities of Practice. In J. Hughes, N. Hewson, & L. Unwin (Eds.), *Communities of Practice: Critical Perspectives* (pp. 17–29). London: Routledge.

Fuller, A., & Unwin, L. (2003). Learning as Apprentices in the Contemporary UK Workplace: Creating and Managing Expansive and Restrictive Participation. *Journal of Education and Work, 16*(4), 407–426.

Gagliardi, P. (1986). The Creation and Change of Organizational Cultures: A Conceptual Framework. *Organization Studies, 7*(2), 117–134.

Ganapathy, N., & Cheong, H. (2016). The "Thinning" Blueline: A Bourdieuian Appreciation of Police Subculture. *International Journal of Comparative and Applied Criminal Justice, 40*(4), 277–294.

Garland, D. (2001). *The Culture of Control*. Oxford: Oxford University Press.

Garner, R. (2005). Police Attitudes: The Impact of Experience After Training. *Applied Psychology in Criminal Justice, 1*(1), 56–70.

Gibbons, F., & Gerrard, M. (1991). Downward Comparison and Coping with Threat. In J. Suls & T. Wills (Eds.), *Social Comparison: Contemporary Theory and Research* (pp. 317–345). Hillslade: Lawrence Erlbaum Associates.

Giddens, A. (1984). *The Constitution of Society: Outline of the Theory of Structuration*. Cambridge: Polity Press.

Glaeser, A. (2000). *Divided in Unity: Identity, Germany and the Berlin Police*. Chicago: University of Chicago Press.

Glaser, B., & Strauss, A. (1967). *The Discovery of Grounded Theory*. Chicago: Aldine.

Glomseth, R., & Gottschalk, P. (2009). Police Personnel Cultures: A Comparative Study of Counter Terrorist and Criminal Investigation Units. *Criminal Justice Studies, 22*(1), 3–15.

Goffman, E. (1959). *The Presentation of Self in Everyday Life*. New York: Doubleday Anchor.

Goldsmith, A. (1990). Taking Police Culture Seriously: Police Discretion and the Limits of Law. *Policing and Society, 1*(2), 91–114.

Gudjonsson, G., & Adlam, K. (1983). Personality Patterns of British Police Officers. *Personality and Individual Differences, 4*(5), 507–512.

Guest, G., Bunce, A., & Johnson, L. (2006). How Many Interviews Are Enough? An Experiment with Data Saturation and Variability. *Field Methods, 18*(1), 59–82.

Haarr, R. (2005). Factors Affecting the Decision of Police Recruits to "Drop Out" of Police Work. *Police Quarterly, 8*(4), 431–453.

Haas, N., van Craen, M., Skogan, W., & Leitas, D. (2015). Explaining Officer Compliance: The Importance of Procedural Justice and Trust Inside a Police Organization. *Criminology and Criminal Justice, 15*(4), 442–463.

Hacking, I. (2011). Between Michel Foucault and Erving Goffman: Between Discourse in the Abstract and Face-to-Face Interaction. *Economy and Society, 33*(3), 277–302.

Hallett, T. (2003). Symbolic Power and Organizational Culture. *Sociological Theory, 21*(2), 128–149.

Halliday, J. (2014). Plebgate Row: PC Keith Wallis Jailed for a Year for Lying About Andrew Mitchell. *The Guardian*. Retrieved from https://www.the-guardian.com/uk-news/2014/feb/06/plebgate-keith-wallis-jailed-police-andrew-mitchell

Hancock, M. (2012, January 7). *Today*. London: BBC Radio 4.

Hannerz, U. (1969). *Soulside: Inquiries into Ghetto Culture and Community*. New York: Columbia University Press.

Haria, R., & Turvill, W. (2015). Jailed for More than 20 Years: The Sources Convicted of Selling Stories to Journalists. *Press Gazette*. Retrieved from http://www.pressgazette.co.uk/jailed-more-20-years-sources-convicted-selling-stories-journalists/

Harkin, D. (2015). Police Legitimacy, Ideology and Qualitative Methods: A Critique of Procedural Justice Theory. *Criminology and Criminal Justice, 15*(5), 594–612.

HASC. (2011). *The New Landscape of Policing*. London: The Stationery Office.

Haslam, S., Jetten, J., Postmes, T., & Haslam, C. (2009). Social Identity, Health and Well-Being: An Emerging Agenda for Applied Psychology. *Applied Psychology, 58*(1), 1–23.

Hazer, J., & Alvares, K. (1981). Police Work Values During Organizational Entry and Assimilation. *Journal of Applied Psychology, 66*(1), 12–18.

He, H., & Brown, A. (2013). Organizational Identity and Organizational Identification – A Review of the Literature and Suggestions for Future Research. *Group and Organization Management, 38*(1), 3–35.

Hendriks, F., & van Hulst, M. (2016). Shifting Repertoires: Understanding Cultural Plurality in Policing. *Innovation: The European Journal of Social Science Research, 29*(2), 161–176.

Henerson, M., Morris, L., & Fitz-Gibbon, C. (1987). *How to Measure Attitudes.* California: Sage.

Hesketh, I., & Williams, E. (2017). A New Canteen Culture: The Potential to Use Social Media as Evidence in Policing. *Policing.* Advance online publication. http://dx.doi.org/10.1093/police/pax025

Heslop, R. (2006). 'Doing a Maslow': Humanistic Education and Diversity in Police Training. *The Police Journal, 79*, 331–341.

Heslop, R. (2011a). Reproducing Police Culture in a British University: Findings from an Exploratory Case Study of Police Foundation Degrees. *Police Practice and Research, 12*(4), 298–312.

Heslop, R. (2011b). Community Engagement and Learning as 'Becoming': Findings from a Study of British Police Recruit Training. *Policing and Society, 21*(3), 327–342.

Hickey, H. (2016, December 7). Good Officers 'Must Stop Being Hung Out to Dry'. *Police Oracle.* Retrieved from https://www.policeoracle.com/news/children_and_young_people/2016/Dec/06/good-officers--must-stop-being-hung-out-to-dry--says-chief_93631.html

HMIC. (1999a). *Managing Learning: A Study of Police Training.* London: HMSO.

HMIC. (1999b). *Police Integrity: Securing and Maintaining Public Confidence.* London: HMIC.

HMIC. (2002). *Training Matters.* London: Home Office.

HMIC. (2011). *Demanding Times.* London: The Stationery Office.

HMIC. (2017a). *PEEL: Police Effectiveness 2016, a National Overview.* Retrieved from https://www.justiceinspectorates.gov.uk/hmic/wp-content/uploads/peel-police-effectiveness-2016.pdf

HMIC. (2017b). *State of Policing: The Annual Assessment of Policing in England and Wales.* Retrieved from https://www.justiceinspectorates.gov.uk/hmic/wp-content/uploads/state-of-policing-2016.pdf

Hobbs, D. (1988). *Doing the Business: Entrepreneurship, Detectives and the Working Class in the East End of London.* Oxford: Clarendon Press.

Hodkinson, P., & Hodkinson, H. (2004). *A Constructive Critique of Communities of Practice: Moving Beyond Lave and Wenger.* Seminar paper presented at 'Integrating Work and Learning – Contemporary Issues' seminar series. Retrieved from http://hdl.voced.edu.au/10707/18014

Hofstede, G. (2001). *Culture's Consequences: International Differences in Work-Related Values* (2nd ed.). London: Sage.

Hofstede, G., Neuijen, B., Daval Ohayv, D., & Sanders, G. (1990). Measuring Organizational Cultures: A Qualitative and Quantitative Study Across Twenty Cases. *Administrative Science Quarterly, 35,* 286–316.

Hogg, M. (2006). Social Identity Theory. In P. J. Burke (Ed.), *Contemporary Social Psychological Theories* (pp. 111–136). California: Stanford University Press.

Hogg, M., & Abrams, D. (1988). *Social Identifications: A Social Psychology of Intergroup Relations and Group Processes.* London: Routledge.

Holdaway, S. (1983). *Inside the British Police: A Force at Work.* Oxford: Basil Blackwell Publisher Ltd.

Holdaway, S. (1989). Discovering Structure: Studies of the Police Occupational Culture. In M. Weatheritt (Ed.), *Police Research: Some Future Prospects* (pp. 55–76). Aldershot: Gower Publishing Company.

Holmes, J., & Marra, M. (2002). Having a Laugh at Work: How Humour Contributes to Workplace Culture. *Journal of Pragmatics, 34,* 1683–1710.

Holmes, J., & Meyerhoff, M. (1999). The Community of Practice: Theories and Methodologies in Language and Gender Research. *Language in Society, 28,* 173–183.

Home Office. (1998). *Review of National Police Training: Draft Report.* London: Home Office.

Home Office. (2004). *Building Communities, Beating Crime: A Better Police Service for the 21st Century (Cm 6360) [Electronic Version].* London: HMSO.

Home Office. (2014, March 31). *Police Workforce, England and Wales.* Retrieved from https://www.gov.uk/government/publications/police-workforce-england-and-wales-31-march-2014/police-workforce-england-and-wales-31-march-2014

Hood, C. (1998). *The Art of the State: Culture, Rhetoric and Public Management.* Oxford: Oxford University Press.

Hopper, M. (1977). Becoming a Policeman: Socialization of Cadets in a Police Academy. *Urban Life, 6*(2), 149–170.

Hughes, E. (1951). Work and the Self. In J. Rohrer & M. Sherif (Eds.), *Social Psychology at the Crossroads* (pp. 313–323). New York: Harper and Brothers.

Hughes, E. (1958). *Men and Their Work*. Glencoe: Free Press.

Hughes, J. (2007). Lost in Translation: Communities of Practice. In J. Hughes, N. Hewson, & L. Unwin (Eds.), *Communities of Practice: Critical Perspectives* (pp. 30–40). London: Routledge.

Independent Commission on Mental Health and Policing. (2013). *Independent Commission on Mental Health and Policing Report*. Retrieved from http://www.turning-point.co.uk/media/621030/independent_commission_on_mental_health_and_policing_main_report.pdf

Institute for Fiscal Studies. (2015). *Recent Cuts to Public Spending*. Retrieved from https://www.ifs.org.uk/tools_and_resources/fiscal_facts/public_spending_survey/cuts_to_public_spending

Ipsos MORI. (2016). *Trust in Professions*. Retrieved from https://www.ipsos-mori.com/researchpublications/researcharchive/3685/Politicians-are-still-trusted-less-than-estate-agents-journalists-and-bankers.aspx#gallery[m]/1/

Jackson, J., & Bradford, B. (2010). Police Legitimacy: A Conceptual Review. *National Policing Improvement Agency Wiki*. Retrieved from http://papers.ssrn.com/sol3/papers.cfm?abstract_id=1684507

Jackson, J., Bradford, B., Hough, M., & Murray, K. (2012). Compliance with the Law and Policing by Consent. In A. Crawford & A. Hucklesby (Eds.), *Legitimacy and Compliance in Criminal Justice* (pp. 29–49). London: Routledge.

Jennings, W., Higgins, G., Tewksbury, R., Gover, A., & Piquero, A. (2010). A Longitudinal Assessment of the Victim-Offender Overlap. *Journal of Interpersonal Violence, 25*(12), 2147–2174.

Johnson, G., & Scholes, K. (1992). *Exploring Corporate Strategy*. Harlow: Pearson Education.

Johnson, G., Scholes, K., & Whittington, R. (2008). *Exploring Corporate Strategy* (8th ed.). Harlow: Pearson Education.

Johnston, N., & Politowski, B. (2016). *Police Funding*. House of Commons Library Briefing Paper 7279.

Jones, G. (1986). Socialization Tactics, Self-Efficacy, and Newcomers' Adjustments to Organizations. *The Academy of Management Journal, 29*(2), 262–279.

Jones, M. (2016). Creating the 'Thinking Police Officer': Exploring Motivations and Professional Impact of Part-Time Higher Education. *Policing, 10*(3), 232–240.

Joyce, D. (1989). Why Do Police Officers Laugh at Death? *The Psychologist, 2*(9), 379–381.

Kahn, R., & Cannell, C. (1957). *The Dynamics of Interviewing*. New York: John Wiley.

Karp, S., & Stenmark, H. (2011). Learning to Be a Police Officer. Tradition and Change in the Training and Professional Lives of Police Officers. *Police Practice and Research, 12*(1), 4–15.

Kerosuo, H., & Engeström, Y. (2003). Boundary Crossing and Learning in Creation of New Work Practice. *Journal of Workplace Learning, 15*(7–8), 345–351.

Kiely, J., & Peek, G. (2002). The Culture of the British Police: Views of Police Officers. *The Services Industries Journal, 22*(1), 167–183.

Kitzinger, J. (2009). Rape in the Media. In M. Horvath & J. Brown (Eds.), *Rape: Challenging Contemporary Thinking* (pp. 74–98). Cullompton: Willan.

Knowles, M. (1990). *The Adult Learner: A Neglected Species* (4th ed.). Houston: Gulf Publishing Company.

Kolb, D. (1984). *Experiential Learning: Experience as the Source of Learning and Development.* Englewood Cliffs: Prentice-Hall.

Kratcoski, P. (2004). Police Education and Training in a Global Society: Guest Editor's Introduction. *Police Practice and Research, 5*(2), 103–105.

Kvale, S. (1996). *Interviews.* California: Sage.

Lave, J., & Wenger, E. (1991). *Situated Learning.* Cambridge: Cambridge University Press.

Lee, M., & Punch, M. (2006). *Policing by Degrees.* Groningen: de Hondsrug Pers.

Levesen, Lord Justice. (2012). *An Inquiry into the Culture, Practices and Ethics of the Press.* Retrieved from https://www.gov.uk/government/publications/leveson-inquiry-report-into-the-culture-practices-and-ethics-of-the-press

Lewis, B. (2017). *Response to HMIC Report.* Retrieved from https://homeoffice-media.blog.gov.uk/2017/03/02/response-to-hmic-report/

Loader, I. (1997). Policing and the Social: Questions of Symbolic Power. *British Journal of Sociology, 48*(1), 1–18.

Loader, I. (1999). Consumer Culture and the Commodifcation of Policing and Security. *Sociology, 33*(2), 373–392.

Loader, I. (2006). Policing, Recognition, and Belonging. *The Annals of the American Academy of Political and Social Science, 605*(May), 202–221.

Loader, I. (2014). Why Do the Police Matter? Beyond the Myth of Crime-Fighting. In J. Brown (Ed.), *The Future of Policing* (pp. 40–51). London: Routledge.

Loftus, B. (2008). Dominant Culture Interrupted: Recognition, Resentment and the Politics of Change in an English Police Force. *British Journal of Criminology, 48*(6), 756–777.

Loftus, B. (2009). *Police Culture in a Changing World.* Oxford: Oxford University Press.

Loftus, B. (2010). Police Occupational Culture: Classic Themes, Altered Times. *Policing and Society, 20*(1), 1–20.

Loftus, B., Goold, B., & MacGiollabhui, S. (2016). From a Visible Spectacle to an Invisible Presence: The Working Culture of Covert Policing. *British Journal of Criminology, 56*(4), 629–645.

Lukes, S. (2005). *Power:Aa Radical View*. London: Palgrave.

Lynn-Meek, V. (1994). Organisational Culture: Origins and Weaknesses. In D. McKevitt & A. Lawton (Eds.), *Public Sector Management* (pp. 265–280). London: Sage Publications.

MacDonald, B., Argent, M., Elliott, J., May, N., Miller, P., Naylor, J., & Norris, N. (1986). *Police Probationer Training: The Final Report of the Stage II Review*. London: HMSO/University of East Anglia.

Macpherson, W. (1999). *The Stephen Lawrence Inquiry Report*. London: HMSO.

Macvean, A. (2010). *A Clash of Cultures: Policing the Academics*. Chester: University of Chester.

Macvean, A., & Cox, C. (2012). Police Education in a University Setting: Emerging Cultures and Attitudes. *Policing, 6*(1), 16–25.

Manning, P. (2003). *Policing Contingencies*. Chicago: University of Chicago Press.

Manning, P. (2010). *Democratic Policing in a Changing World*. Boulder: Paradigm Publishers.

Marenin, O. (1982). Parking Tickets and Class Repression: The Concept of Policing in Critical Theories of Criminal Justice. *Contemporary Crises, 6*(3), 241–266.

Marenin, O. (2004). Police Training for Democracy. *Police Practice and Research, 5*(2), 107–123.

Marique, G., Stinglhamber, F., Desmette, D., Caesens, G., & de Zanet, F. (2013). The Relationship Between Perceived Organizational Support and Affective Commitment: A Social Identity Perspective. *Group and Organization Management, 38*(1), 68–100.

Mastrofski, S., Willis, J., & Snipes, J. (2002). Styles of Patrol in a Community Policing Context. In M. Morash & J. Ford (Eds.), *The Move to Community Policing* (pp. 81–111). Thousand Oaks: Sage.

Mathias, P. (1988). Paving the Way for Philosophy and Practice at Peel Centre. In P. Southgate (Ed.), *New Directions in Police Training* (pp. 100–111). London: HMSO.

Matza, D. (1964). *Delinquency and Drift*. London: Wiley.

May, T. (2011). *Speech to the Conservative Party Conference*. Retrieved from http://www.politics.co.uk/comment-analysis/2011/10/04/theresa-may-speech-in-full

May, T. (2014). HMIC's Inspection of Police Handling of Domestic Violence and Abuse. *Written Statement to Parliament*. Retrieved from https://www.gov.uk/government/speeches/hmics-inspection-of-police-handling-of-domestic-violence-and-abuse

May, T. (2015). *Written Statement (HCWS381) Made by The Secretary of State for the Home Department (Mrs Theresa May) on 12 March 2015*. Retrieved from http://www.parliament.uk/documents/commons-vote-office/March%20 2015/12%20March%202015/31.HOME-Undercover-policing.pdf

McAra, L., & McVie, S. (2010). Youth Crime and Justice: Key Messages from the Edinburgh Study of Youth Transitions and Crime. *Criminology and Criminal Justice, 10*(2), 179–209.

McBarnet, D. (1981). *Conviction: Law, the State and the Construction of Justice*. London: Routledge.

McBride, J., & Martinez-Lucio, M. (2011). Dimensions of Collectivism: Occupation, Community and the Increasing Role of Memory and Personal Dynamics in the Debate. *Work, Employment and Society, 25*(4), 794–805.

McCarthy, D. (2013). Gendering 'Soft' Policing: Multi-Agency Working, Female Cops, and the Fluidities of Police Culture/s. *Policing and Society, 23*(2), 261–278.

McLeod, J. (2003). Why We Interview Now – Relfexivity and Perspective in a Longitudinal Study. *International Journal of Social Research Methodology, 6*(3), 201–211.

McManus, M. (1997, April). Getting Things Right for Policing: Cultural Shift or Elitist Sop? *The Police Journal 70*(2), 99–103.

McNeill, W. (1982). *The Pursuit of Power: Technology, Armed Forces and Society Since AD1000*. Chicago: University of Chicago Press.

McNulty, E. (1994). Generating Common Sense Knowledge Among Police Officers. *Symbolic Interaction, 17*(3), 281–294.

Mead, G. (1934). *Mind, Self and Society*. Chicago: University of Chicago Press.

Mercadillo, R., Alcauter, S., Fernández-Ruiz, J., & Barrios, F. (2015). Police Culture Influences the Brain Function Underlying Compassion: A Gender Study. *Social Neuroscience, 10*(2), 135–152.

Merton, R. (1957). *Social Theory and Social Structure*. New York: Free Press.

Meyer, J. (1997). Humor in Member Narratives: Uniting and Dividing at Work. *Western Journal of Communication, 61*(2), 188–208.

Meyer, J., & Allen, N. (1991). A Three-Component Conceptualization of Organizational Commitment. *Human Resource Management Review, 1,* 61–89.

Miller, H., & Rayner, C. (2012). The Form and Function of "Bullying" Behaviors in a Strong Occupational Culture: Bullying in a UK Police Service. *Group and Organization Management, 37*(3), 347–375.

Millie, A. (2013). The Policing Task and the Expansion (and Contraction) of British Policing. *Criminology and Criminal Justice, 13*(2), 143–160.

Moran, C., & Massam, M. (1997). An Evaluation of Humour in Emergency Work. *The Australasian Journal of Disaster and Trauma Studies, 3,* 1–11.

Morrison, E. (1993). Newcomer Information Seeking: Exploring Types, Modes, Sources, and Outcomes. *The Academy of Management Journal, 36*(3), 557–589.

Moscovici, S. (1972). Society and Theory in Social Psychology. In J. Israel & H. Tajfel (Eds.), *The Context of Social Psychology: A Critical Assessment* (pp. 17–68). London: Academic Press.

Muir, W. (1977). *Police: Streetcorner Politicians.* Chicago: University of Chicago Press.

Mukerji, C., & Schudson, M. (1991). *Rethinking Popular Culture: Contemporary Perspectives in Cultural Studies.* California: California University Press.

Myhill, A., & Bradford, B. (2013). Overcoming Cop Culture: Organizational Justice and Police Officers' Attitudes Toward the Public. *Policing: An International Journal of Police Strategies and Management, 36*(2), 338–356.

National Audit Office. (2015). *Financial Stability of Police Forces in England and Wales.* HC 78, London: NAO.

National Crime Agency. (2017). *Missing Persons Data Report 2015/16.* Retrieved from http://www.nationalcrimeagency.gov.uk/publications/783-missing-persons-data-report-2015-16/file

Neyroud, P. (2011). *Review of Police Leadership and Training.* London: Home Office.

Nickels, E., & Verma, A. (2007). Dimensions of Police Culture: A Study in Canada, India and Japan. *Policing: An International Journal of Police Strategies and Management, 31*(2), 186–209.

Nietzsche, F. (1997). *Untimely Meditations.* In D. Breazeale (Ed.), *Cambridge Texts in the History of Philosophy.* Cambridge: Cambridge University Press. (Original work published 1874).

Norman, M., & Hyland, T. (2003). The Role of Confidence in Lifelong Learning. *Educational Studies, 29*(2–3), 261–272.

O'Neill, M. (2016). Revisiting the Classics: Janet Chan and the Legacy of 'Changing Police Culture'. *Policing and Society, 26*(4), 475–480.

O'Neill, M., & McCarthy, D. (2014). (Re)negotiating Police Culture Through Partnership Working: Trust, Compromise and the 'New' Pragmatism. *Criminology and Criminal Justice, 14*(2), 143–159.

Oakley, R. (1994). The Police and Black People: The Training Response. In M. Stephens & S. Becker (Eds.), *Police Force, Police Service; Care and Control in Britain* (pp. 85–106). Basingstoke: Macmillan.

Oberfield, Z. (2012). Socialization and Self-Selection: How Police Officers Develop Their Views About Using Force. *Administration and Society, 44*(6), 702–730.

Oberweis, T., & Musheno, M. (1999). Policing Identities: Cop Decision Making and the Constitution of Citizens. *Law and Social Inquiry, 24*(4), 897–923.

Obst, P., & Davey, J. (2003). Does the Police Academy Change Your Life? A Longitudinal Study of Changes in Socialising Behaviour of Police Recruits. *International Journal of Police Science and Management, 5*(1), 31–40.

Office for National Statistics. (2017). *Crime in England and Wales: Year Ending Sept 2016.* Retrieved from https://www.ons.gov.uk/peoplepopulationand-community/crimeandjustice/bulletins/crimeinenglandandwales/yearendingsept2016

Osborne, G. (2015). *Chancellor George Osborne's Spending Review and Autumn Statement 2015.* Retrieved from https://www.gov.uk/government/speeches/chancellor-george-osbornes-spending-review-and-autumn-statement-2015-speech

Owers, A. (2012). *Independent Oversight of Police Complaints: The IPCC Eight Years On.* Retrieved from https://www.ipcc.gov.uk/sites/default/files/Documents/speeches/speech_dame_anne_owers_john_harris_memorial_lecture.pdf

Palmiotto, M., Birzer, M., & Unnithan, P. (2000). Training in Community Policing. *Policing: An International Journal of Police Strategies and Management, 23*(1), 8–21.

Paoline, E. (2001). *Rethinking Police Culture: Officers' Occupational Attitudes.* New York: LFB Scholarly Publishing.

Paoline, E. (2003). Taking Stock: Toward a Richer Understanding of Police Culture. *Journal of Criminal Justice, 31*(3), 199–214.

Paoline, E. (2004). Shedding Light on Police Culture: An Examination of Officers' Occupational Attitudes. *Police Quarterly, 7*(2), 205–236.

Paoline, E., & Terrill, W. (2014). *Police Culture: Adapting to the Strains of the Job.* Durham: Carolina Academic Press.

Parsons, T. (1951). *The Social System.* London: Routledge and Kegan Paul.

Peace, R. (2006). Probationer Training for Neighbourhood Policing in England and Wales: Fit for Purpose? *Policing: An International Journal of Police Strategies and Management, 29*(2), 335–346.

Peck, E., Towell, D., & Gulliver, P. (2001). The Meanings of 'Culture' in Health and Social Care: A Case Study of the Combined Trust in Somerset. *Journal of Interprofessional Care, 15*(4), 319–327.

Peters, T., & Waterman, R. (1982). *In Search of Excellence.* New York: Harper and Row.

Peterson, A., & Uhnoo, S. (2012). Trials of Loyalty: Ethnic Minority Police Officers as 'Outsiders' Within a Greedy Institution. *European Journal of Criminology, 9*(4), 354–369.

Police Federation. (2015). *Enough Is Enough.* Retrieved from http://www.polfed. org/newsroom/2637.aspx

Punch, M. (1983). Officers and Men: Occupational Culture, Inter-Rank Antagonism, and the Investigation of Corruption. In M. Punch (Ed.), *Control in the Police Organisation* (pp. 227–250). Cambridge, MA: The MIT Press.

Punch, M. (1985). *Conduct Unbecoming.* London: Tavistock Publications Ltd.

Punch, M. (2016). *Passionate Professionals: The Dutch Police Response to the Shooting Down of Malaysian Airlines' MH17 in the Ukraine (2014).* Paper presented at the Third International Conference on Law Enforcement and Public Health. Amsterdam: The Netherlands. Retrieved from http://www. cleph.com.au/files/9914/7803/0755/Punch_Passionate_Professionals_ MH17_rev_30_09_mp..pdf

Rachal, J. (2002). Andragogy's Detectives: A Critique of the Present and a Proposal for the Future. *Adult Education Quarterly, 52*(3), 210–227.

Rantatalo, O. (2016). Media Representations and Police Officers' Identity Work in a Specialised Police Tactical Unit. *Policing and Society, 26*(1), 97–113.

Reber, A. (1993). *Implicit Learning and Tacit Knowledge: An Essay on the Cognitive Unconscious.* Oxford: Oxford University Press.

Reicher, S., Spears, R., & Haslam, S. (2010). The Social Identity Approach in Social Psychology. In M. Wetherell & C. Mohanty (Eds.), *The SAGE Handbook of Identities* (pp. 45–63). London: Sage.

Reiner, R. (1978). *The Blue-Coated Worker*. Cambridge: Cambridge University Press.

Reiner, R. (1991). *Chief Constables*. Oxford: Oxford University Press.

Reiner, R. (1992). *The Politics of the Police* (2nd ed.). Hemel Hempstead: Harvester Wheatsheaf.

Reiner, R. (2000a). *The Politics of the Police* (3rd ed.). Oxford: Oxford University Press.

Reiner, R. (2000b). Police Research. In R. King & E. Wincup (Eds.), *Doing Research on Crime and Justice* (pp. 205–236). Oxford: Oxford University Press.

Reiner, R. (2010). *The Politics of the Police* (4th ed.). Oxford: Oxford University Press.

Reuss-Ianni, E., & Ianni, F. (1983). Street Cops and Management Cops: The Two Cultures of Policing. In M. Punch (Ed.), *Control in the Police Organisation* (pp. 251–274). Cambridge, MA: The MIT Press.

Rhoades, L., Eisenberger, R., & Armeli, S. (2001). Affective Commitment to the Organization: The Contribution of Perceived Organizational Support. *Journal of Applied Psychology, 86*, 825–836.

Richards, D. (1996). Elite Interviewing: Approaches and Pitfalls. *Politics, 16*(3), 199–204.

Richards, L. (2009). *Handling Qualitative Data: A Practical Guide* (2nd ed.). London: Sage.

Roth, G., & Vivona, B. (2010). Mirth and Murder: Crime Scene Investigation as a Work Context for Examining Humor Applications. *Human Resource Development Review, 9*(4), 314–332.

Rowe, M. (2014). *Introduction to Policing* (2nd ed.). London: Sage.

Rubin, H., & Rubin, I. (1995). *Qualitative Interviewing: The Art of Hearing Data*. California: Sage.

Sackmann, S. (1991). *Cultural Knowledge in Organisations*. London: Sage Publications.

Sackmann, S. (1992). Culture and Subcultures: An Analysis of Organizational Knowledge. *Administrative Science Quarterly, 37*, 140–161.

Sargeant, E. (2015). Policing and Collective Efficacy: The Relative Importance of Police Effectiveness, Procedural Justice and the Obligation to Obey Police. *Policing and Society*. Advance online publication. http://dx.doi.org/10.1080/10439463.2015.1122008

Sato, M. (2003). Police Recruits' Training and the Socialisation Process: From the Network Perspective. *The Police Journal, 76*, 289–303.

Savage, S. (2007a). *Police Reform: Forces for Change*. Oxford: Oxford University Press.

Savage, S. (2007b). Putting Wrongs to Right: Campaigns Against Miscarriages of Justice. *Criminology and Criminal Justice, 7*(1), 83–105.

Savage, S., Charman, S., & Cope, S. (2000). *Policing and the Power of Persuasion*. London: Blackstone Press.

Savery, L., Soutar, G., & Weaver, J. (1991). Organizational Commitment and the West Australian Police Force. *The Police Journal, 64*, 168–177.

Scarman. (1981). *The Brixton Disorders 10–12 April 1981: Report of an Inquiry by the Rt. Hon. The Lord Scarman (Cmnd 8427)*. London: HMSO.

Scerra, N. (2011). Impact of Police Cultural Knowledge on Violent Serial Crime Investigation. *Policing: An International Journal of Police Strategies and Management, 34*(1), 83–96.

Schein, E. (1968). Organisational Socialization and the Profession of Management. *Industrial Management Review, 9*, 1–16.

Schein, E. (1971). Organizational Socialization and the Profession of Management. *Industrial Management Review, 2*, 37–45.

Schein, E. (1984). Coming to a New Awareness of Organizational Culture. *Sloan Management Review, 25*(2), 3.

Schein, E. (1985). *Organisational Culture and Leadership: A Dynamic View*. San Francisco: Jossey-Bass.

Schein, E. (1991). What Is Culture? In P. Frost, L. Noore, M. Louis, C. Lundberg, & J. Martin (Eds.), *Reframing Organizational Culture* (pp. 243–253). London: Sage Publications.

Schneider, B. (1987). The People Make the Place. *Personnel Psychology, 40*(3), 437–453.

Scott, T. (2007). Expression of Humour by Emergency Personnel Involved in Sudden Deathwork. *Mortality, 12*(4), 350–364.

Scripture, A. (1997). The Sources of Police Culture: Demographic or Environmental Variables? *Policing and Society, 7*(3), 163–176.

Seldon, A. (1988). *Contemporary History*. Oxford: Blackwell.

Shammas, V., & Sandberg, S. (2015). Habitus, Capital, and Conflict: Bringing Bourdieusian Field Theory to Criminology. *Criminology and Criminal Justice, 16*(2), 195–213.

Shearing, C., & Ericson, R. (1991). Culture as Figurative Action. *British Journal of Sociology, 42*(4), 481–506.

Shiner, M. (2010). Post Lawrence Policing in England and Wales: Guilt, Innocence and the Defence of Organizational Ego. *British Journal of Criminology, 50*(5), 935–953.

Sillince, J., & Brown, A. (2009). Multiple Organizational Identities and Legitimacy: The Rhetoric of Police Websites. *Human Relations, 62*(12), 1829–1856.

Sklansky, D. (2006). Not Your Father's Police Department: Making Sense of the New Demographics of Law Enforcement. *The Journal of Criminal Law and Criminology, 96*(3), 1209–1243.

Sklansky, D. (2007). Seeing Blue: Police Reform, Occupational Culture, and Cognitive Burn-In. In M. O'Neill, M. Marks, & A. Singh (Eds.), *Police Occupational Culture: New Debates and Directions* (pp. 19–46). Oxford: Elsevier JAI.

Skolnick, J. (1966). *Justice Without Trial: Law Enforcement in Democratic Society.* New York: Wiley and Sons.

Skolnick, J. (2008). Enduring Issues of Police Culture and Demographics. *Policing and Society, 18*(1), 35–45.

Skolnick, J. (2011). *Justice Without Trial: Law Enforcement in Democratic Society* (4th ed.). New York: Wiley and Sons.

Smircich, L. (1983). Concepts of Culture and Organisational Analysis. *Administrative Science Quarterly, 28*, 339–358.

Smith, D., & Gray, J. (1983). *Police and People in London IV: The Police in Action.* London: PSI.

Smith, D., & Gray, J. (1985). *Police and People in London: The PSI Report.* Aldershot: Gower.

Soeters, J. (2000). Culture in Uniformed Organizations. In N. Ashkanasay, C. Wilderom, & M. Peterson (Eds.), *Handbook of Organizational Culture and Climate* (pp. 465–482). London: Sage.

Sollund, R. (2008). Tough Cop-Soft Cop? The Impact of Motivations and Experiences on Police Officers' Approaches to the Public. *Journal of Scandinavian Studies in Criminology and Crime Prevention, 9*(2), 119–140.

Spencer-Oatey, H. (2000). *Culturally Speaking: Managing Rapport Through Talk Across Cultures.* London: Continuum.

Stephenson, C., & Stewart, P. (2001). The Whispering Shadow: Collectivism and Individualism at Ikeda-Hoover and Nissan UK. *Sociological Research Online, 6*(3), 1–15.

Stets, J., & Burke, P. (2000). Identity Theory and Social Identity Theory. *Social Psychology Quarterly, 63*(3), 224–237.

Steyn, J., & Mkhize, S. (2016). 'Darker Shades of Blue': A Comparison of Three Decades of South African Police Service Culture. *SA Crime Quarterly, 57*, 15–26.

Stradling, S., & Harper, K. (1988). The Tutor Constable Attachment, the Management of Encounters and the Development of Discretionary Judgement. In P. Southgate (Ed.), *New Directions in Police Training* (pp. 199–218). London: HMSO.

Stradling, S., Crowe, G., & Tuohy, A. (1993). Changes in Self-Concept During Occupational Socialization of New Recruits to the Police. *Journal of Community and Applied Social Psychology, 3*(2), 131–147.

Sunshine, J., & Tyler, T. (2003). The Role of Procedural Justice and Legitimacy in Shaping Public Support for Policing. *Law and Society Review, 37*(3), 513–548.

Tajfel, H. (1978). Interindividual Behaviour and Intergroup Behaviour. In H. Tajfel (Ed.), *Differentiation Between Social Groups: Studies in the Social Psychology of Intergroup Relations* (pp. 27–60). London: Academic Press.

Tajfel, H. (1981). *Human Groups and Social Categories.* Cambridge: Cambridge University Press.

Tajfel, H. (1982). Social Psychology of Intergroup Relations. *Annual Review of Psychology, 33*, 1–39.

Tajfel, H., & Turner, J. (1986). The Social Identity Theory of Intergroup Behaviour. In W. Austin & S. Worchel (Eds.), *Psychology of Intergroup Relations* (pp. 7–24). Chicago: Nelson Hall.

Taylor, I., Walton, P., & Young, J. (1973). *The New Criminology.* London: Routledge and Kegan Paul.

Terpstra, J. (2016). Occupational Culture of Private Security Officers in the Netherlands: Comparison with Police Officers' Culture. *Policing and Society, 26*(1), 77–96.

Thompson, M., Ellis, R., & Wildavsky, A. (1990). *Cultural Theory.* Boulder: Westview Press.

Thomson, R., & Holland, J. (2010). Hindsight, Foresight and Insight: The Challenges of Longitudinal Qualitative Research. *International Journal of Social Research Methodology, 6*(3), 233–244.

Tönnies, F. (1887). *Gemeinschaft und Gesellschaft.* Leipzig: Fues's Verlag. (Translated, 1957 by Charles Price Loomis as *Community and Society.* East Lansing: Michigan State University Press.)

Travis, A. (1999, February 19). Police Chief: This Can't Go On. *The Guardian.* Retrieved from https://www.theguardian.com/uk/1999/feb/19/lawrence.ukcrime

Trompenaars, F., & Hampden-Turner, C. (1997). *Riding the Waves of Culture: Understanding Cultural Diversity in Business.* London: Nicholas Brearley.

Tuohy, A., Wrenall, M., McQueen, R., & Stradling, S. (1993). Effect of Socialization Factors on Decisions to Prosecute: The Organizational Adaptation of Scottish Police Recruits. *Law and Human Behaviour, 17*(2), 167–181.

Tyler, T. (1990). *Why People Obey the Law.* New Haven: Yale University Press.

Tyler, T., & Blader, S. (2003). The Group Engagement Model: Procedural Justice, Social Identity and Co-operative Behaviour. *Personality and Social Psychology Review, 7*(4), 349–361.

Tyler, T., & Huo, Y. (2002). *Trust in the Law: Encouraging Public Co-operation with the Police and Courts.* New York: Russell-Sage.

Tyler, T., Fagan, J., & Geller, A. (2014). Street Stops and Police Legitimacy: Teachable Moments in Young Urban Men's Legal Socialization. *Journal of Empirical Legal Studies, 11*(4), 751–785.

UKPoliceOnline. (2008). *Thames Valley Community Placement.* Retrieved from http://www.ukpoliceonline.co.uk/index.php?/topic/29094-thames-valley-community-placement/#comment-306626

Useem, M. (1995). Reaching Corporate Executives. In R. Hertz & J. Imber (Eds.), *Studying Elites Using Qualitative Methods* (pp. 18–39). California: Sage.

van Hulst, M. (2013). Storytelling at the Police Station: The Canteen Culture Revisited. *British Journal of Criminology, 53*(4), 624–642.

Van Maanen, J. (1973). Observations on the Making of Policemen. *Human Organization, 32*(4), 407–418.

Van Maanen, J. (1975). Police Socialization: A Longitudinal Examination of Job Attitudes in an Urban Police Department. *Administrative Science Quarterly, 20*(2), 207–228.

Van Maanen, J. (1976). Breaking In: Socialization to Work. In R. Dubin (Ed.), *Handbook of Work, Organization and Society* (pp. 67–130). Chicago: Rand McNally College Publishing Company.

Van Maanen, J. (1978a). People Processing: Strategies of Organizational Socialization. *Organizational Dynamics,* Summer, 19–36.

Van Maanen, J. (1978b). Kinsmen in Repose: Occupational Perspectives of Patrolmen. In P. Manning & J. Van Maanen (Eds.), *Police: A View from the Street* (pp. 115–127). Santa Monica: Goodyear Publishing Company.

Van Maanen, J., & Schein, E. (1979). Toward a Theory of Organizational Socialization. In B. Staw (Ed.), *Research in Organizational Behaviour* (Vol. 1, pp. 209–264). Greenwich: JAI.

Van Maanen, J., Dabbs, J., & Faulkner, R. (1982). *Varieties of Qualitative Research.* California: Sage.

Wacquant, L. (1992). Toward a Social Praxeology: The Structure and Logic of Bourdieu's Sociology. In P. Bourdieu & L. Wacquant (Eds.), *An Invitation to Reflexive Sociology* (pp. 1–47). Cambridge: Polity Press.

Waddington, P. (1999a). Police (Canteen) Culture: An Appreciation. *British Journal of Criminology, 39*(2), 287–309.

Waddington, P. (1999b). *Policing Citizens*. London: UCL Press.

Wagner, J. (1995). Studies of Individualism-Collectivism: Effects on Co-operation in Groups. *The Academy of Management Journal, 38*(1), 152–172.

Walklate, S. (2000). Equal Opportunities and the Future of Policing. In F. Leishman, S. Savage, & B. Loveday (Eds.), *Core Issues in Policing* (2nd ed., pp. 232–248). Harlow: Longman Pearson Education.

Walsh, J. (1977). Career Styles and Police Behaviour. In D. Bayley (Ed.), *Police and Society* (pp. 149–175). Beverley Hills: Sage.

Weber, M. (1977). *Politik Aals Beruf.* Berlin: Duncker and Humblot. (Original work published 1919).

Weber, M. (1978). *Economy and Society*. California: University of California Press. (Original work published 1922).

Weick, K. (1995). *Sensemaking in Organizations*. Thousand Oaks: Jossey-Bass.

Wenger, E. (1998). *Communities of Practice: Learning, Meaning, Identity*. Cambridge: Cambridge University Press.

Westera, N., Kebbell, M., Milne, R., & Green, T. (2013). Defining the "Effective Detective". ARC Centre of Excellence in Policing and Security Briefing, 20.

Westley, W. (1970). *Violence and the Police: A Sociological Study of Law, Custom and Morality*. Cambridge, MA: MIT Press.

Westmarland, L. (2005). Police Ethics and Integrity: Breaking the Blue Code of Silence. *Policing and Society, 15*(2), 145–165.

Westmarland, L., & Rowe, M. (2016). Police Ethics and Integrity: Can a New Code Overturn the Blue Code? *Policing and Society*. http://dx.doi.org/10.10 80/10439463.2016.1262365

Whelan, C. (2017). Security Networks and Occupational Culture: Understanding Culture Within and Between Organisations. *Policing and Society, 27*(2), 113–135.

Whetten, D. A. (2006). Albert and Whetten Revisited, Strengthening the Concept of Organizational Identity. *Journal of Management Inquiry, 15*, 119–234.

White, S. (1972). A Perspective on Police Professionalization. *Law and Society Review, 7*, 61–85.

White, D. (2006). A Conceptual Analysis of the Hidden Curriculum of Police Training in England and Wales. *Policing and Society, 16*(4), 386–404.

White, M., & Escobar, G. (2008). Making Good Cops in the Twenty-First Century: Emerging Issues for the Effective Recruitment, Selection and Training of Police in the United States and Abroad. *International Review of Law Computers and Technology, 22*(1–2), 119–134.

White, D., & Heslop, R. (2012). Educating, Legitimising or Accessorising? Alternative Conceptions of Professional Training in UK Higher Education: A Comparative Study of Teacher, Nurse and Police Officer Educators. *Police Practice and Research, 13*(4), 342–356.

Willis, J., & Mastroski, S. (2016). Improving Policing by Integrating Craft and Science: What Can Patrol Officers Teach Us About Good Police Work? *Policing and Society.* Advance publication. Retrieved from http://dx.doi.org/10.1080/10439463.2015.1135921

Willis, J., & Mastrofski, S. (2017). Understanding the Culture of Craft: Lessons from Two Police Agencies. *Journal of Crime and Justice, 40*(1), 84–100.

Wilson, J. (1968). *Varieties of Police Behaviour.* Cambridge, MA: Harvard University Press.

Wilson, C. (1991). *The Influence of Police Specialisation on Job Satisfaction: A Comparison of General Duties Officers and Detectives, Report No. 109.* Adelaide: National Police Research Unit.

Wilson, C., & Beck, K. (1995). *The Impact of the Redesign of the Job of General Duties Patrol on the Motivation, Job Satisfaction and Organizational Commitment of Patrol Officers, Report No. 109.1.* Adelaide: National Police Research Unit.

Winsor, T. (2012). *Independent Review of Police Officer and Staff Renumeration and Conditions, Final Report* (Vol. 1). London: The Stationery Office.

Winsor, T. (2017, April 20). *World at One.* London: BBC Radio 4.

Wood, D., & Tong, S. (2009). The Future of Initial Police Training. *International Journal of Police Science and Management, 11*(3), 294–305.

Wortley, R., & Homel, R. (1995). Police Prejudice as a Function of Training and Outgroup Contact: A Longitudinal Investigation. *Law and Human Behaviour, 19*(3), 305–317.

Young, M. (1991). *An Inside Job.* Oxford: Oxford University Press.

Young, M. (1995). Black Humour: Making Light of Death. *Policing and Society, 5*, 151–167.

Young, J. (1997). *The Exclusive Society.* London: Sage.

# Index

© The Author(s) 2017
S. Charman, *Police Socialisation, Identity and Culture,*
DOI 10.1007/978-3-319-63070-0

CPI Antony Rowe
Eastbourne, UK
November 27, 2019